Rod Clark

# PREVENTING THE FUTURE
# WHY WAS IRELAND SO POOR FOR SO LONG?

## TOM GARVIN

D0967441

*Gill & Macmillan*

*In memory of John Whyte,*
*who started it*

Published by Gill & Macmillan Ltd
Hume Avenue, Park West, Dublin 12, Ireland
with associated companies throughout the world
www.gillmacmillan.ie

© Tom Garvin 2004
First published 2004
This edition published 2005

ISBN 0 7171 3970 0
Index by Helen Litton 2004; revised by Cover to Cover 2005
Type design: Make Communication
Typesetting and print origination: Carrigboy Typesetting Services, Co. Cork
Printed and bound by Cox and Wyman, Reading, Berks

This book is typeset in Linotype Minion and Neue Helvetica.

The paper used in this book comes from the wood pulp of managed forests. For
every tree felled, at least one tree is planted, thereby renewing natural resources.

A CIP catalogue record for this book is available from the British Library.

5 4 3 2 1

# CONTENTS

# ACKNOWLEDGMENTS

As usual, my intellectual debts are many, and the responsibility for the inevitable errors of judgement or of fact is mine. I would like to thank in particular my old friend and colleague Michael Laffan of University College Dublin's Department of History for encouragement, for his good humour and for his willingness to be a patient sounding board. Conversations with Cyril White initially prompted me to explore this territory. Mary Daly's encyclopaedic knowledge of Irish administrative history has been invaluable. Tim O'Neill discussed Irish rural society with me and opened my eyes to some creative Irish economic thinking of the 1940s that has been almost forgotten. Anthony Keating documented some of the horrors of Irish industrial schools. Peter McDonough of Brooklyn, Michigan, Nevada, Brazilian, Spanish, Portuguese and Jesuit fame supplied many insights and gallantly tried to make this native take rather more account of perspectives beyond *Tonn Chliodhna*. Marie Clarke in UCD's Department of Education has been an unfailing source of information and encouragement. Susannah Riordan has been a source of insight and humour. Pat Clancy put me right on many occasions, as did Niamh Hardiman and Cormac Ó Gráda. John Horgan of Dublin City University gave me the benefit of his unrivalled knowledge of the lives and times of Noel Browne and Sean Lemass. Moore McDowell and John Sheehan tried, with indifferent success, to teach me applied economics. Cathal Guiomar explained to me his dream of the Designer Economy, and how much it differed, sadly, from the real thing. Paul Rouse gave me the facts of life about Irish agriculture. Maurice Manning of UCD's Department of Politics and the Irish Senate has, over many years, recreated the atmosphere of other days in conversation in his inimitable way. Muiris Mac Congail has supplied the relatively rare perspective of a Blueshirt *gaelgeóir*. David Sheehy steered me through some of the thickets of Ireland's ecclesiastical political history. Monsignor Michael Nolan recreated the Dublin of the 1940s. Michael Hopkinson provided an Englishman's view of Ireland from Scotland. Declan Kiberd was his genial and shrewdly helpful self. He also asked the crucial question at an early stage: why did the Celtic Tiger of the 1990s not occur decades earlier? I have attempted to provide the beginnings of an answer. Brigid Laffan forced me to be more alert to the European dimension, as did the little-known private early writings of the late Sean Lemass. I am indebted intellectually also to Bryan Fanning of UCD's Department of Social Policy and to Andreas Hess, Tom Inglis and Stephen Mennell of UCD's Department of Sociology. Muiris MacCarthaigh and Kevin Howard of the Politics Department proofread and commented on an early draft to considerable effect. Conversations over the years with John Coakley, Brian Farrell, Ronan Fanning, David Doyle, Des Fennell, Daniel Seiler, Eileen Connolly, Finbarr Lane, Frank Litton, Eunan O'Halpin, Tony White, William Coventry and Brendan Walsh were very fruitful, often in unexpected ways. Maire Garvin has supported me in innumerable ways, and now knows finally what it was that I was at.

Perhaps my greatest debts are to departed people, in particular Todd Andrews, Des Roche, Tom Barrington, Paddy Burke, Basil Chubb, Paddy Lynch, James Deeny, Robin Dudley Edwards and John Garvin, whose conversations of a generation ago did much to spark the interest of a young fellow in their lives and times. There was a child among them taking notes, possibly inaccurately. My old friend Gus Martin encouraged me to embark on this project, or one a bit like it, just before his untimely death. John Whyte introduced me many years ago to the knotty problem of the relationship between Catholicism and democratic politics. I'm not sure he would quite have agreed with all of my conclusions, but they certainly would have entertained him. Liam de Paor described the political atmosphere of the 1940s with some vividness. Martin Bates and Peter Young of the Irish Army recreated lost worlds. The late Stein Rokkan of the University of Bergen had a huge intellectual influence on me as on countless other European political scientists of the 1970s cohort. He also introduced me to *Weisswurst*.

ACKNOWLEDGMENTS

My debts to other people happily still in the land of the living: Seamus Helferty and Jennifer O'Reilly of the Archives Department, University College Dublin were, as ever, unfailingly obliging. I would also like to thank the staffs of the National Archives of Ireland, the Archive of the Dublin Catholic Archdiocese and the National Library of Ireland. Lastly, I wish to thank my editor and old friend, Fergal Tobin at Gill & Macmillan, whose patience with my occasional AWOLs has been saintly.

T. G.

DUBLIN, APRIL 2004

# PREFACE

This book is concerned with the politics of social and economic development in the Republic of Ireland since the enactment of the Constitution of 1937, which disestablished the Irish Free State. This enactment, together with the declaration of the Republic of Ireland in 1949, legitimated the democratic Irish state created in 1922.[1] The central question addressed is the problematic character of Irish developmental delay after the Second World War: why did Irish economic, social and cultural modernisation not commence until the early 1960s, nearly twenty years after the end of the conflict?

In seeking to explain the relative poverty of Ireland and the delay in the commencement of Irish economic, social and cultural modernisation, this book suggests that deep structural and cultural obstacles lay in the way of any early Irish new departure in the years after 1945. These obstacles were rendered more powerful by the politics of cultural defence initiated in the 1920s and the protectionist economic policies of the 1930s. The Second World War, which isolated neutral Ireland, rendered these obstacles insuperable. The cultural consequences of development and the impact of structural and cultural change on economic transformation after the key cusp dates of 1960 and 1987 are also considered. The argument is informed by the comparative method. Between the date of the enactment of the Constitution and 1959, economic development was sluggish, trade remained stagnant and, despite denials by some writers, cultural activity was under political attack. This cultural war was being waged by linguistic revivalists, Catholic fundamentalists and state censors; writing, painting, theatre, dance and the plastic arts were commonly regarded with indifference, suspicion and even active hostility by the secular and ecclesiastical authorities. This indifference and hostility were also popular in some circles; such activity was commonly regarded as snobbish, pretentious and 'West British'. It was also sometimes associated with immorality and self-indulgence. Censorship of books and film was extremely severe, even savage and commonly philistine.[2]

Alexis de Tocqueville's tyranny of the majority was alive and well in the emergent republican society of independent Ireland. De Valera's own uneasy awareness of this conformism, a conformism that sometimes amounted to outright philistinism, seems to have informed his Institute for Advanced Studies, set up by his government in the late 1930s. His intention was, at least in part, to bypass the generally politically hostile pro-Treaty university system of the time. Mathematics, Cosmic Physics and Celtic Studies were the Institute's principal concerns, reflecting his own impressive if rather unapplied intellectual interests. De Valera's concern with education seems to have been concentrated on these relatively esoteric areas. His interest in general mass education of the kind associated with modern countries was in practice confined to using the elementary educational schools as devices for attempting to change the language generally used in the country from English to Irish. The teaching of English and of science was demoted to make way for a project that was even at that time widely and publicly recognised as being non-educational. The use of education and training as a means of building up human capital appears to have been an idea beyond de Valera and many others of his generation. Economic, intellectual and cultural stagnation went hand in hand; to be a 'culture worker' in such an atmosphere took courage, fortitude and an independence of mind of nearly heroic dimensions.

Emigration, mainly to Great Britain, was, almost proverbially, a way of life and it seemed to many that the entire independence project was a failure. The apparently dismal performance of the Irish independent state belied the high-flown and ambitious rhetoric of the founding fathers and also questioned the formula of independence as the magic cure for Irish underdevelopment. The belief articulated by many eighteenth-century radicals including Theobald Wolfe Tone and Jonathan Swift that the English connection was the source of all of Ireland's many woes seemed to be rebutted by the actual experience of political independence. Rightly or wrongly this real or apparent stagnation is associated with 'the Age of de Valera' and some historians and other commentators have blamed the leader personally for creating a stagnant society. I intend to argue that the causes are far deeper and that cultural, structural and contingent circumstances caused the stagnation that undoubtedly reigned.

# NOTE ON IRISH-LANGUAGE TERMS

A work of this sort is bound to use many terms, as well as occasional long phrases, in the Irish language. To treat them all as foreign-language terms and to use italics consistently would be distracting. I have therefore adopted the contemporary Irish practice of treating some Irish words as being assimilated into Irish English: these are not italicised. Longer phrases and more unusual words have been accented and italicised. I have followed the same policy with French, Latin and German terms, e.g. bourgeois and status quo, but *Weisswurst*.

'You should not be too familiar with, nor too distant from, the clergy.'

—IRISH SAYING, NINETEENTH CENTURY

'In the first place, if there is to be a compulsory liberal education for all up to the age of about eighteen years, there must go with it the abolition of all labour for wealth before that age, and the training for economic life must begin, as it does at present with the professions, at somewhere about that age.'

—MICHAEL TIERNEY, 1919

'... the child himself must be the end in education. It is a curious thing how many times the education of Europe has drifted into error. For two or three centuries people thought that their various religious systems were more important than the child. In the modern world the tendency is to think of the nation; that it is more important than the child ... There is a tendency to subordinate the child to the idea of the nation.'

—SENATOR WILLIAM BUTLER YEATS, 1926

'I doubt if any nation can become prosperous unless it has national faith, and one very important part of national faith is faith in its resources, faith both in the richness of its soil and the richness of its intellect, and I am convinced that as much wealth can come from the intellect of Ireland as will come from the soil and that the one will repay cultivation as much as the other.'

—SENATOR WILLIAM BUTLER YEATS, 1926

'It is true to say that after the two so-called wars [of 1919–23] the newly established Irish Free State enjoyed by far the lowest standard of living in Europe. With widespread unemployment and other social problems, plus a population well versed in lawlessness, things were absolutely "cat".'

—ANDREW S. FORREST, 1990s

'Though I constantly hear it said that the [Catholic] Church is losing its hold on the young people, it will be many years before the effect of this (if it is really happening at all) is felt.'

—ELIZABETH BOWEN, 1940

'No Catholic may enter the Protestant University of Trinity College without the previous permission of the ordinary of the Diocese. Any Catholic who disobeys this law is guilty of mortal sin and while he persists in disobedience is unworthy to receive the sacraments.'

—ARCHBISHOP JOHN CHARLES McQUAID, 1944

'The most serious revelation, however, is that the Roman Catholic Church would seem to be the effective government of this country.'

—*THE IRISH TIMES*, 12 APRIL 1951

'A Department saddled with the herculean task of restoring the language, while acting simultaneously as a major stakeholder between God and Caesar, was in post-independence Ireland more likely to display caution than a sense of adventure.'

—TONY WHITE, 2001

'My own mood, and I find it shared by many of my generation, old Sinn Feiners, is one nearing despair. The dreams we dreamed—and the reality! We are a miserable money-grubbing lot, utterly bereft of ideals. We started with two, both phoney, the Language and the Reintegration of the National Territory. Both collapsed because of their absurdity, leaving us with nothing at all . . .'

—PROFESSOR ROY GEARY TO PROFESSOR JAMES MEENAN,
13 SEPTEMBER 1970

'It must always stand to Mr Lemass's credit that, even if it took him thirty years to grasp the real nature of the economy, he devoted his last decade in public life to repairing the damage he had inflicted as Mr. De Valera's Minister for Industry and Commerce.'

—JOSEPH LEE, *SPECTATOR*, 19 DECEMBER 1970

'[in Ireland] . . . there seemed to be a lack of awareness of the general need for scientific and technical education . . .'

—ORGANISATION FOR ECONOMIC CO-OPERATION AND
DEVELOPMENT, 1966

'. . . Professor Declan Kiberd said the real question should not be why the Celtic Tiger happened, but why its coming took so long.'

—*THE IRISH TIMES*, 13 AUGUST 2002

# INTRODUCTION

## THE STATE OF IRELAND

Between 1913 and 1923, there was a national revolution in Ireland which culminated in the partition of the island into the six-county British province of Northern Ireland (1920) and the 26-county British Dominion styled the Irish Free State (1922). The new state was effectively independent and gradually rid itself of symbols of the old British connection, retitling itself successively Eire/Ireland (1937) and the Republic of Ireland (1949). The new Irish state, which came into existence in international law on 6 December 1922, was apparently greeted with a deep indifference by its own citizens.[1] This seems to have been the case despite the overwhelming vote for independence, or something like independence, that had occurred in December 1918 and which legitimated the subsequent Dáil Eireann's declaration of independence in January 1919. This vote was in part provoked by the executions of the leaders of the 1916 Rising, but probably even more by the London decision to conscript Irish young men in 1918 for the trenches of the World War.

Richard Mulcahy, a prominent IRA leader, claimed later, 'The effect of the general election of December, 1918 was fundamental. A great majority of the people had clearly expressed its will for national independence and Separation from Britain. . . .'[2] A short 'Tan War' or War of Independence followed, and eventually an Anglo-Irish Treaty was signed in December 1921, in which partition was reluctantly accepted by the Irish. Whether the new Irish Free State was authentically sovereign remained a moot point and split the national independence movement, Sinn Féin, into anti-Treaty and pro-Treaty factions. The subsequent short civil war or *Cogadh na gCarad* (war of the friends, relatives) embittered intra-elite relations for forty years and certainly contributed mightily to the stultifying of Irish democratic politics in its first generation of independence. Furthermore, the conflict involved a systematic attempt by a *coupiste* anti-Treaty IRA to wreck the infrastructure of the country and ensure that the Free State remained stillborn. After much killing, this attempt failed. In old age, Mulcahy commented angrily in 1964 on Professor Desmond Williams's strange remark in a Thomas Davis lecture on Irish radio to the effect that the civil war had at least had the good effect of giving Ireland a two-party system. Mulcahy went on to remark acidly, 'Even if a two-party system is desirable a civil war is a very expensive method of achieving it.'[3] The two conflicts had generated a huge debt, which burdened the new state for some years.

In other ways the new state apparently had much going for it. The British had left behind a good physical infrastructure, a well-run and recently overhauled civil service machine and a fair standard of elementary education. Perhaps most importantly, the population possessed a political culture which understood democratic politics if not always possessing a complete understanding of democratic government. Friendly links with the English-speaking world, particularly with the rising superpower in the west, the United States, meant that the Irish had some powerful potential friends and no natural enemies other than those generated by the enmities associated with the divisions within the island of Ireland, divisions which had led to the partition of 1920.[4] Northern Ireland, hived off from the rest of the island in 1920, contained a chronic ethno-religious divide which also existed, but in a milder form, in the Free State. An aloofness between Catholics and Protestants was intensified by an aggressive policy on mixed marriages enforced by the Catholic Church: all children of such marriages had to be reared as Catholics. Within a generation, a large proportion of the Protestant minority in the Free State had been married out of existence. However, the new state treated its minorities well within the confines of an overwhelming and often triumphalist Catholic consensus.

British rule had left behind it some evil legacies: Irish towns had some of the worst slums in Europe; the unresponsive, patronising and often bullying character of British rule had left bad Irish habits, particularly a persistent popular tradition of being 'agin the government'. This *incivisme* was to hobble Irish democracy in many ways in the subsequent decades. However, perhaps the most pervasive legacy of British government in Ireland was the partnership that had developed between the Catholic Church and the British State, giving to the religious organisations the tasks of educating the young, running much of the health system and controlling much of the civic life of the society. This partnership was inherited by the fledgling Irish democracy in 1918–22. In effect, this made the Catholic Church in independent Ireland a powerful and autonomous agency which for many purposes operated like a second government or a state within a state. In the areas of health, education and much of public ideological discourse, the power of the Church was enormous. Above all, the Church attempted to control, some would say enslave, much of the intellectual and emotional life of the entire country.

During the period 1923–38, a complex constitutional evolution occurred, the Free State Constitution of 1922 being replaced by the de Valera Constitution (*Bunreacht na hEireann*) of 1937. An equally complex set of political shifts also occurred, with the original pro-Treaty forces of Michael Collins, William Cosgrave, Kevin O'Higgins and Richard Mulcahy defeating the anti-Treaty forces of Liam Lynch, Frank Aiken and Eamon de Valera militarily in 1922–23. Subsequently, de Valera, having lost the war, won the peace. In a pattern to be repeated often afterward by other republican groups, de Valera led his insurrectionist republicans from militarism to electoral democracy between 1923 and 1932. In 1932 he became President of the Executive Council (prime minister) at the head of his Fianna Fáil party. In the general renaming of constitutional parts that occurred in 1937, de Valera's office was renamed Taoiseach.[5]

The new country was quite successful, both under the pro-Treaty governments of the 1920s and under the partially reconciled anti-Treatyites in the form of Fianna Fáil in the 1930s. Depression in the 1930s and war in the early 1940s made independent Ireland a fairly desirable place to be in the eyes of people in war-torn and depressed Europe. However, Ireland's role in the scheme of things was modest in the changed circumstances of post-1945 Europe and a new world order dominated by the United States and the Soviet Union.

The argument of this book is that Ireland, faced with the conditions and circumstances that pertained in the changed world of 1945, made a series of 'non-decisions' that in the short to medium term were disastrous to the country's development prospects. The reasons for this indecisiveness were both structural and cultural: structures that encouraged the entrenchment of veto groups in key areas of political, economic, cultural and religious life, and cultural mindsets that thought in static and rural ways and in ethical rather than scientific terms. In particular, religious and socio-economic organisations such as trade unions, business, parts of the bureaucracy and the churches defended their turf in ways that effectively preserved a status quo which was increasingly held to be undesirable, unfair and even unendurable by many. It will also be argued that one of the reasons for stasis was a dysfunctional propensity of power-holders to fear other power-holders, thereby exhibiting a lack of self-assurance and moral courage that was quite crippling to the power-holders themselves and to the country as a whole. Powerful people believed that you did not take on other powerful people. An intimidating ecclesiastical apparatus intensified this climate and served as a role model for similar authoritarian behaviour on the part of secular elites.

On top of this, the political split of 1921 seriously demoralised Sinn Féin and led to a much documented but not quite measurable culture of cynicism and disappointment among an emergent and none too self-assured middle class. It is not too much to speak of a collective loss of nerve brought on by the mismanagement of the Treaty issue, by de Valera in particular. To be fair, this mismanagement was partly provoked and exacerbated by the conspiratorial style of the pro-Treatyites on the one hand and the purist and die-hard militarism of the anti-Treatyites on the other.

Quite apart from the 1921 divisions, there was also a clear anti-modernist streak in Irish official and clerical thinking, generating a reluctance to engage seriously with the modern world. Most importantly, the notion of a static and unchanging order that was to be regarded as ideal was quietly accepted, gladly or fatalistically, by much of the population. In the minds of many, modernity was something to be shut out rather than welcomed and coped with.

After all, if one really wanted modernity, one could go next door to England or over the Atlantic to America, where there was plenty of the thing. In turn, these *mentalités* encouraged a cultural pessimism, passivity or even hopelessness. Ireland was to pay dearly for these choices, choices which the country scarcely realised it was making, partly because they consisted not so much of positive decisions as of *non-decisions*, or unspoken decisions, sometimes unconscious ones, not to follow certain policies.[6] The Irish, it sometime seems, were hell-bent on preventing the future while pretending to embrace it.

## PIONEERS

In the late 1950s, an almost panicky decision was finally made to modernise. The two standard pioneering works on the Irish New Departure of the 1950s are Bew and Patterson's path-breaking, if somewhat controversial, *Sean Lemass and the Making of the New Ireland* of 1982 and Brian Girvin's later book, *Between Two Worlds* (1989).[7] Bew and Patterson in particular were indeed brave pioneers, publishing as they did in the early 1980s. The authors used a rather determinedly Marxist class analysis of the policy shift of the 1950s. Their diagnosis was one of a division within the ruling bourgeoisie, between those elements in the business community who were satisfied with the protected home market and those who wished to export and were amenable to permitting foreign, principally American, capital into Ireland and relaxing the protectionist barriers. Interestingly, some Dublin policy-makers of the period complained afterward that they had not been interviewed by the authors; a mechanistic structural Marxism certainly informs the book and gives it a faintly Martian tone in parts. Girvin's later work, published in 1989, built on Bew and Patterson. Girvin's work is more nuanced and pays more attention to the changing relationships between Irish industry and the Irish state, which is seen as having a wider mandate than that of simply reflecting the interests of the bourgeoisie. Girvin suggests that by the late 1950s the perceived interests of the Irish state had begun to increasingly differ from the interests of the owners and managers of the protected industries of the period, mainly because of the economic crisis of the 1950s. In effect, a democratic state was under pressure from far more people than a group of squabbling businessmen, no matter how influential these latter might have been. Sean Lemass, Taoiseach between 1959 and 1966, took advantage of this growing gap to shift what Girvin termed 'the balance of power in Irish society'. Girvin writes:

His administration initiated the most comprehensive attempt at modernisation which had occurred in Ireland. In a broad sense Ireland acquired 'modernity' in this decade, becoming increasingly industrialised, secularised, urbanised and bureaucratised. In retrospect the achievements of the 1960s were partial; more traditional norms quickly reasserted themselves, yet the achievements were real. The crisis of the mid to late 1950s was not simply an economic one, it was also a crisis for traditional Irish society.[8]

Girvin, like Bew and Patterson, emphasises the crucial role of Lemass and a group of like-minded politicians, civil servants, academics, businessmen and trade unionists in breaking away from the isolationism and stasis of the previous decades. John Kurt Jacobsen, in his *Chasing Progress in the Irish Republic* (1994), offers a sophisticated dependency theory analysis of Irish economic and social travails, strongly recommending a statist and developmentalist approach to Irish economic problems. It could be argued that in reality such an approach had had a very determined trial in Ireland and had been found somewhat wanting. More recently Denis O'Hearn has produced a creative *longue durée* discussion of Ireland's three-century entanglement with the world economy, centred first on England and later on the United States.

In this book, I agree with much of what these writers have to say, in particular the very different but complementary diagnoses offered by Girvin and O'Hearn. I also disagree with much, in particular the statist remedies explicitly or tacitly proposed by both Girvin and Jacobsen. I wish to argue, *à la* Girvin, that the crucial long-term change initiated under Lemass was profoundly cultural. The collective imagined project of a successful and modern Irish nation-state was seen as being under increasing threat from traditional policy attitudes assumed in that name. Furthermore, political alliances and vested interests which had grown up under the aegis of de Valeran protectionism had gradually come to be seen as anti-national and obstructive. Ironically, as will become clear, the protectionist apparatus of the 1930s was in large part the brain-child of Sean Lemass, who was Minister for Industry and Commerce for most of the years between 1932 and 1959 and Taoiseach during 1959–66. He was the instigator of not one, but *two* historic reversals of economic policy, one in 1932 and the other in 1959.

In question in the late 1950s was far more than the interests of a ruling bourgeoisie or an aristocracy of labour. What was actually in question was the entire political legitimacy of a democratic state which had, after all, been founded on a revolution and which, like all post-revolutionary states, felt itself vulnerable to the possible challenge of another revolution. The IRA was active, and considerable popular sympathy with its objectives and activities was being expressed by ordinary people and by quite a number of public representatives. Even though they were standing on an abstentionist ticket, four Sinn Féin candidates were elected to the Dáil in 1957. Irish nationalism found that it had to reinvent itself for the umpteenth time and had to do so in a popular and fundamentally democratic way. This process of collective redefinition of the collective self is a process which, although it started in the 1950s, is still going on half a century later.

At that time, even the Catholic Church, that perennial mainstay of Victorian Irish popular nationalism, came to be seen as an obstruction in the eyes of the younger generation and even many of the older people in political office. Many saw the Church as a secret enemy of the republican project, dating back to the time of Fenianism, or even the 1790s. This was the traditional Sinn Féin/IRA viewpoint. However, a new opposition to ecclesiastical power was stirring; this was the new emergent educated middle class, still very small but already becoming restless if not yet openly anti-clerical. The Church continued to have extraordinary political and cultural influence, and could, in many policy areas, effectively veto government policy initiatives. Furthermore, these vetoes were commonly covert and did not impinge on public awareness. The clergy typically used private and secretive channels to get their way; their secrecy of political style with its concomitant non-democratic contempt for public opinion and for public contestation was copied by many laypeople, to the detriment of informed public opinion in Ireland's as yet immature democracy. To be fair, up to at least the year 1960 this clerical power was apparently approved of, or at least acquiesced in, by the vast majority of the population. It was also clear that any significant expansion in the educational system would produce a relatively well-educated and secularised large middle class of a kind that had scarcely existed previously. Furthermore, lay political elites increasingly realised that mass education to a relatively advanced level and of a more applied type was absolutely necessary if the country was to develop economically. The Church was right to fear the expansion of technical and higher education that was projected for the 1960s; it stood to lose its own constituency. Because of the crisis of the mid-1950s, lay political leaders concluded that clerical and other resistance to educational reform and expansion had to be overcome. Eventually, the long-delayed (and much resisted) expansion and modernisation of the educational system in the 1960s inevitably resulted in its secularisation. Equally inevitably, expansion entailed changing its purpose from one of constructing a religious and humanist community to one of producing skilled and productive members of an economy. Much was gained and much was lost in this Irish cultural revolution which occurred between 1960 and 1975. Literacy in the classical languages (Latin and Greek) was replaced by a concern with practical skills and modern languages. History came under siege in favour of subjects such as Economics, Accountancy and Business Organisation. The numbers of students expanded dramatically. Technical education, once the impoverished and disregarded poor relative of the secondary education system, flourished as never before.

The idea of the pious patriot was to be augmented or even replaced by the idea of the useful contributor to the material welfare of the community. An earlier reactionary idealism was defeated by the simple ethical proposition that the nation had the duty to the individual of providing him with the intellectual tools and skills that would enable him (and, increasingly, her) to earn his (or her) living. The idea of citizenship, some would comment, rather got lost between these two poles. The Irish polity has yet to seriously consider the teaching of true citizenship in the way that it is commonly taught in most advanced Western countries. In the 1950–70 period, the Republic slowly and reluctantly learned the lesson of investing in human economic capital; it has not yet, perhaps, really taken on board the idea of investing in citizenship, or in an aspect of what Robert Putnam and his associates commonly refer to as social capital. Even in 2003, the Republic of Ireland had only a rather underdeveloped civic and political education pro- gramme for schools, unlike most advanced democracies. A common complaint at the time, perhaps justified to some extent, was that the changes of the 1960s replaced *sinn féin* (ourselves) with *mé féin* (myself). All of this is not to argue that the Irish polity has lacked good citizens; the story I attempt to tell is in considerable part about the actions of good citizens in key positions in Irish society.[9]

The possible relevance of education to the Irish turnaround of the 1960s is ignored even by Kieran Kennedy and Brendan Dowling in their authoritative early study of the Irish economic shift of 1947–68.[10] The authors readily concede that 'non-economic factors' such as important changes in social, psychological and other forces underlying the economic factors were significant, but there is a certain tendency to shrug an economist's methodological shoulder. Kennedy and Dowling wrote:

> Examples of such changes were the emergence to responsible positions of a new post-Independence generation, placing greater emphasis on solving unemployment and emigration than on ending Partition or restoring the Irish language; the assumption of a greater role in international affairs (as indicated, for example, by the participation of Irish soldiers in the Congo and of Irish diplomats in the United Nations, which Ireland joined in 1955, and Ireland's application to join the EEC in 1961) and the sense of pride and purpose derived therefrom; and the influence of key personalities in dissipating the cynicism, born

of apparent failures, about Ireland's economic prospects and in arousing enthusiasm for economic growth as a prerequisite to the achievement of more fundamental national goals.[11]

Possibly rightly, the authors mainly confine themselves to their own expertise in economics in explaining Irish economic growth between the end of the War and the late 1960s. However, it is hard not to suspect that something rather deeper than an elite decision to reverse the policies of the previous thirty years was going on. I wish to argue that an underground, rather inchoate *popular* rejection of the official policies of the previous thirty years was actually taking place, a rejection that was increasingly being ratified by the children and successors of the revolutionary elite generation itself. Elites had little choice but to embark upon a new departure; the very legitimacy of their ideology, even of the regime itself, was becoming vulnerable in the 1950s.

Admittedly, many of the elites welcomed the change and worked energetically to bring it about. By the 1950s, these men were in their fifties or sixties and they knew that generational succession would shortly curtail their careers and their power. Much incidental evidence suggests that the first generation of Irish political leaders after independence comprised intelligent, energetic and often highly motivated people. Many had been permanently embittered by the events of 1921–23 and suffered from a stubbornness or authoritarianism of personality and social style. They also sometimes had rather strange ideas. Michael Hayes in old age reminisced about what kinds of people they had been in youth. The whole Sinn Féin movement that generated the Irish political elite had been composed of unusual men with strong loyalties to other men rather than to principle and who commonly had a fascination for general ideas or some abstractly conceived general political cause. He also noticed a certain eccentricity: 'all the Sinn Feiners were slightly odd and some of the ASU [Active Service Unit] people were perhaps odder than others.'

There is one other thing that strikes me about the whole [1913–23] business and I feel that it has not got sufficient prominence anywhere and that is, the Sinn Fein movement was a small minority movement and the people who were active in Sinn Fein, and that would include I think the people who were active and leaders in the volunteers, were if you like to call them chosen people, they were very interesting people but they were odd people as they must be in those cases—they were unusual people; they weren't representative of their own class; they weren't ordinary people. For example I was in a company of the volunteers where the captain was a bricklayer, one of the lieutenants was a plumber and the other lieutenant was a carpenter. That might make a particular impression on the reader but the truth is that Eddie Byrne the captain was quite an unusual bricklayer and wound up as a teacher of bricklaying in Bolton Street [technical] schools; Simon Donnelly's father was a master plumber and Simon Donnelly is now a contractor himself, and Mick Malone who was killed in Easter Week [1916] was a well read and very curious fellow, extraordinarily courageous and very dogged and so on. I knew a great many carpenters and I would say Mick Malone was quite an unrepresentative carpenter—I don't know what he was like as a carpenter but he was probably a good carpenter too. All the craftsmen who were in the volunteers were fellows who read—otherwise they wouldn't have come in at all. Joe McGuinness was by no means a typical draper. He was interested in music, song, the volunteers, conversation, everything. They were all quite different. Dev once called them a selection from the left wing of the nation—he said the Dail were a selection from the left wing of the nation.[12]

These leaders inspired powerful loyalties, and this made their political and ideological legacy even harder to jettison in the 1950s. The revolutionary changes of the 1950s and 1960s smelled slightly of parricide, a crime frowned upon despite its undoubted attractions, even in the land of *The Playboy of the Western World*. Like many revolutionaries elsewhere, many of these founding leaders had been excluded from power before 1918, and often had come of a class declared unfit for self-government. This had several psychological effects, one of which was a wish to be seen to succeed, and another of which was an exaggerated view of the capabilities of the state. The almost godlike performance of the mighty British state in governing Ireland before 1914 reinforced the belief that an Irish state could, with goodwill and determination, right most, if not all, Irish wrongs and do so with ease. The Irish state soon displayed a strong propensity to the creation of monopolies. Brendan Walsh commented in 1991 in the course of a review article:

> Tax expenditures are an important feature of our tax system. . . The history of state-sponsored bodies contains several significant examples of confiscation and restriction of property rights: Bord na Mona compulsorily acquired peatland, the ESB closed down private generating plants, CIE prevented people from investing in road transport, the INPC forces us to buy its petrol, Aer Lingus/Aer Rianta force passengers to land at Shannon Airport, and so on. The range of monopoly rights vested in state companies in Ireland is truly remarkable. Furthermore, a type of quasi-confiscation was exercised by the Land Commission, which compulsorily purchased the remnants of the old estates at knock-down prices and transferred the land to small farmers and labourers . . . Finally, the generalized protectionism pursued from 1932 to 1966 was exceptional in its rigour and dictated the consumption patterns of a whole generation. If an index of the state's 'capacity' based on its use of these instruments as well as on the share of GDP it controlled were developed, there is little doubt that Ireland would come out near the top of the international league table (non-socialist division).[13]

In a similar way, non-governmental bodies such as churches, trade unions, professional bodies and other organisations set up monopolies over accreditation systems, schools, demarcation rules, work practices, closing times and price controls, commonly with state connivance. A common rationale for these restrictive practices was to cite the defence of public morality and the curbing of private greed. This tendency toward state-assisted monopoly or rent-seeking in commercial and cultural activities will be looked at in some detail later in the book.

## A LOGIC OF COLLECTIVE ACTION

A useful starting point in examining the causes of stagnation in Irish society is provided by the work of Mancur Olson, the American economist cum political scientist, using his 1982 book, *The Rise and Decline of Nations* and his earlier, seminal *The Logic of Collective Action*.[14] Olson offered a powerful set of explanations for why it is that certain nation-states have experienced sustained periods of economic growth while others, possessing otherwise similar political structure and opportunity, have remained slow growers, have stagnated or have even regressed. Olson confined his main comparative analysis to those nations that comprise the Organisation for Economic Co-operation and Development (OECD), a group of nation-states consisting mainly of the countries of Western Europe, North America, Japan and Australasia. These are countries that are commonly labelled 'First World' and have been historically well developed economically; Olson's comparative politics research strategy had a classic 'most similar systems' design. The explanation for the different economic performances of these countries is of particular interest to a political scientist because Olson, although an economist by initial training, offered an explanation for economic failure and *success* that was rooted in the power structures of the countries involved. Olson in effect argued that in the long run, politics determined economics and that Karl Marx and a cloud of left-wing scribblers were exactly wrong. Olson argued that stable democratic systems, because of their very political tranquillity, tend to develop a culture of elite complacency and lose a sense of the need for urgent change of a wide-ranging kind until a real emergency occurs. Furthermore, such systems develop vested interests with a grip on institutional or cultural power that tend to prevent change, even when such change is agreed to be desirable. Popular governments *pace* the views of political theorists going back to Aristotle, tend to be conservative and elected governments are commonly fairly popular. In this book it will be argued that just such a complacent tranquillity enveloped the Irish polity and that this was intensified by the monolithism of the culture of partitioned Ireland and, in particular, by the intense authoritarianism and appetite for power of a popular Church. Both the cultural monolithism and Church power have weakened considerably since about 1960, and that weakening resulted in part from an elite perception that this intellectual conformism and authoritarianism had failed the country and even endangered its future. This perception was in turn fed by outside pressures and commentators.

Olson's empirical starting point was the pattern of relative rates of economic development of eighteen OECD nation-states between 1950 and 1980. These countries were more or less coterminous with the democratic countries of the West, conventionally seen as the heirs of the European empires. Most of this period was one of historically unprecedented economic growth in the capitalist West. The extraordinary boom of the thirty years from 1943 to 1973 transformed Western societies in an unprecedented way. Among many other things, the boom copperfastened liberal democracy and a governmentally regulated capitalism as the ideological victors in the argument as to whether the future lay with statist socialism or with market capitalism. In effect, the extraordinary success of the Western countries culminated in the massive ideological humiliation of the pseudo-democratic socialist tyrannies of the East. Olson determined that of the eighteen OECD countries, the fastest growth rates were experienced by Japan, Austria, West Germany, Italy and France, in that descending order. The five slowest growers were Ireland, Sweden, New Zealand, the United Kingdom and the United States, in that descending order. Ireland was the fastest of the slowcoaches, but also, fatally, started at the lowest absolute level of economic activity of this slowcoach group; to put it bluntly and sadly, Ireland started the period poor and ended it slightly less poor in gross national product (GNP) per head. In other words, Ireland combined the slow growth rates characteristic of a rich and mature economy with the underdevelopment characteristic of a rather poor country. By way of contrast, the growth rate of Japan was quite phenomenal, being nearly double that of Austria, which was also a little-noticed but impressive success story in the postwar years. Olson's central question was: what is it about the political and social structure of countries that causes or enables growth to occur, or which, on the other hand, tends to stifle growth?

Olson built on a central idea of his own, derived in part from the ideas of the English philosopher David Hume, but elaborated in Olson's earlier book, *The Logic of Collective Action*.[15] Building on an insight of Hume and many other intellectual progenitors of modern rational choice theory, Olson set out to deny the familiar, if often unarticulated, proposition that groups in society which share a common 'objective' interest will inevitably or logically pursue that interest as a harmonious collective entity or alliance. Individuals in collectives do not necessarily pursue their own best interest; there is a lemming effect observable in human society. In particular, in real life there are always 'free riders', individuals who let someone else do the fighting for them: people who see that their own individual contribution to the general common effort and commonwealth is so small that it makes no noticeable difference to the overall outcome. Therefore, it pays to let George do it, and collectives tend to perform suboptimally. It follows, I believe, that the larger the group, the more, proportionately and *ceteris paribus*, the free-rider effect will operate.

This theorem can be applied to large free societies in general, and perhaps to representative democratic processes in particular. In good times, 'letting George do it' is sometimes reflected in electoral truancy (not bothering to vote) and, perhaps more subtly and importantly, in saving on rationality. In effect, this amounts to letting your brain do a bit of free riding: the delegation of one's political mind to a trusted spokesman and the use of 'ideology by proxy'. Charismatic leadership, where an arguably irrational trust is put in one apparently extraordinary person or group of people, is far too conspicuous and common a phenomenon in representative democracies in the post-1918 era not to be related to something like Olsonian processes.[16] Eamon de Valera in Ireland, Charles de Gaulle in France and Franklin Roosevelt in the United States are obvious examples of democratic leaders who were the object of a veneration that was less than totally rational, even if such veneration was possibly deserved, to some extent at least. The election of Hitler with the votes of a large minority of the voting electorate in the Germany of 1932 has often been seen as a classic popular abrogation of rational self-interest and an embracing, in desperation, of an extraordinary mixture of irrationality and utter trust. A revealing Nazi slogan of 1932 was *Wer Rettet für Uns? Nur Hitler* (Who will save us? Only Hitler). To be fair to a despairing German electorate, only one-third of the voters supported the Nazis in the last free election of the Weimar Republic; the real betrayal was that of the conservative and Catholic elites who let Hitler into power. Fear of communism made them rabbits in Hitler's headlights.

Commonly the ideology-by-proxy syndrome is centred in an institution such as a communist party or a religious organisation which is trusted to do the thinking and doing on one's behalf. Again, there is the often demonstrated finding of political scientists that many people in many different political cultures inherit their political loyalties and preferences from their parents. This fact of political life reinforces the claim that the non-rational is an important, perhaps even central, feature of democratic political life. Because of the free-rider effect in particular, large organisations involving thousands or millions of people such as governments, trade unions, churches or professional associations use not only positive incentives such as higher wages, promotions or more generous settlements with employers or fee-payers. These organisations also commonly use negative ones such as compulsory taxation backed by the might of the law and large penalties for evasion. Other devices include 'blacking' of workers who refuse to be unionised, intimidation of dissidents, striking practitioners off the register if they do not toe the line with everyone else or even good old-fashioned boycotting.[17]

These various 'negative incentive' techniques are essentially there to reduce free riding to a minimum. However, and Olson does not make this point, free riding also implies an opposite: what I would like to label high riding, or working too hard, too effectively or in ways that compete 'unfairly' with conventional work practices. In the past, hostility to technical changes such as the use of machinery in agriculture or the rise of motor cars and supermarkets gave rise to Luddism, Captain Swing, Poujadism and other similar attempts to resist the workplace consequences of technical change. A strong streak of Luddism ran through the Irish Land League movement of 1879–81. High riders can be deeply resented, and a spectacular example is provided by the Soviet Union of the 1930s. The regime made a cult out of a worker called Stakhanov, who worked harder and longer than anyone else and did so in the name of the workers of the world. Stakhanov became an official hero and the object of an official cult; the word 'Stakhanovite' entered the language. Naturally the great majority probably secretly hated him as a rate-buster. Such high riding can also be seen in areas of social life conventionally regarded as non-economic and non-productive. In traditional Irish Catholicism, the person who prayed too much and too conspicuously was commonly derided and ridiculed as a 'creeping Jesus'.

In fact, to pursue one's own material, or even spiritual, interest with undue enthusiasm in apparent disregard of the general interests of the collectivity as declared by the leaders of government, of the union movement, of a professional association or of a powerful and popular ecclesiastical organisation such as the Catholic Church can lead to sociological isolation: membership of an out-group. Such very different types of people as class swots, high-rider workers, atheists, scab workers, street traders, whistle-blowers, public saints, ideological non-conformists, innovators who become rich because of their inventiveness, commercialised farmers, adherents of unapproved religions and immigrant ethnic minorities ('they're taking our jobs') can all be seen as high riders from some point of view or other. In academia, a high-performing don can easily be accused by the mediocre of 'neglecting his students'. To pursue one's own material interest while disregarding an alleged collective, communal or general national interest can be declared by the culture to be immoral, anti-national, a betrayal of one's comrades, political 'idiocy' in the classical Greek sense, evidence of a gross lack of 'spirituality', selfishness or thievishness. Such ideological declarations and finger-pointings can suit the private interests as well as the public purposes of elites striving to keep their followers in line. To put a further twist on the argument, one can also become a *professional outsider:* a rebel who achieves popular approval by being against the system in a noisy public way, while being totally dependent upon that same system. In the nature of things, such heroes can only be few; the market for them is limited.

The free-rider syndrome, seen as combined with the logic of liberal individualistic democracy, is also offered by Olson as a way of explaining both the existence of coercive and progressive taxation systems which discriminate formally against the rich *and* the failure of such systems to tax the rich appropriately. It is less in the interest of the rich to 'free ride' *politically* and easier for them to evade or avoid financially because they can wield power directly, acquire foreign domicile or hire expert legal assistance. However, I would argue that it can also work the other way: against the disadvantaged. For example, in the educational system, attempts to make it more egalitarian and more equally accessible to all social classes tend to come up against the greater interest in education of the relatively well-off and their (on average) greater and more effectively organised efforts to exploit the system. The relatively privileged are, again on average, better at high riding. There, it is the poor who, ironically, do something like a self-defeating 'free ride' because the benefits appear less immediate and less probable and also because the system is less exploitable by poorer people who have, again on average, more meagre cultural resources. In this case, free riding occurs for different reasons and with different effects than those suggested by Olson, and the free riding is evidently tragically self-defeating. The irony is that poorer and more vulnerable people are more conservative because they have proportionately more to lose: radicalism is commonly the luxury of the relatively rich.

The declared intellectual ancestor of Olson's system may be Hume, but a tacit informer of it seems to be James Madison, father of the Constitution of the United States and author (as 'Publius') of *Federalist Paper Number Ten*, published in defence of the draft Constitution in 1788. In '*Fed Ten*', Madison passionately argues the desirability of having a large republic rather than a small one. He bluntly asserts that blocking coalitions which are, in effect, hostile to the interests and property rights of either the majority class of citizens or a minority class are far more likely to emerge and get their way in a small republic. In a large republic, political groups are likely to be many, divided and harder to organise, rather than few and easily organised, as in a small republic. In *Fed Ten*, he summarises his argument as follows:

> If a faction consists of less than a majority, relief is supplied by the republican [majoritarian] principle, which enables the majority to defeat its sinister views, by regular vote. It may clog the administration, it may convulse the society; but it will be unable to execute and mask its violence under the forms of the constitution. When a majority is included in a [self-interested] faction, the form of popular government, on the other hand, enables it to sacrifice to its ruling passion or interest, both the public good and the rights of other citizens. . . . The smaller the society, the fewer probably will be the distinct parties and interests composing it; the fewer the distinct parties and interests, the more frequently will a majority be found of the same party; and the smaller the number of individuals composing a majority, the more easily will they concert and execute their plans of oppression. Extend the sphere, and you take in a greater variety of parties and interests; you make it less probable that a majority of the whole will have a common motive to invade the rights of other citizens; or if such a common motive exists, it will be more difficult for all who feel it to discover their own strength, and to act in union with each other.[18]

Olson does not explicitly make the size argument, but whatever the size of the polity, the heart of his theory is the proposition that, in general, because of the nature of things, 'members of small groups have disproportionate organisational power for collective action, and this disproportion diminishes but does not disappear in stable societies.' This is reminiscent of Robert Dahl's famous aphorism to the effect that the making of governmental decisions was not 'a majestic march of great majorities united upon . . . matters of great policy.' Rather, it consists of the 'steady appeasement of relatively small groups'.[19] These propositions govern the behaviour of groups in a Madisonian pluralist political system, that is, an electoral democracy based on the free competition for power of large numbers of small groups. In a small country, that large number can actually amount to a majority of the population passionately fighting against its own common long-term interest under the leadership of a well-organised and trusted minority. D.S.A. Carroll, a well-known Irish industrialist, described Irish economic politics of a later era politely but devastatingly in an essay published in 1984. Writing about the crisis in Irish public finances which followed on the oil shocks of 1973 and 1979, he made a more general diagnosis of the Irish political disease, one that applies *a fortiori* to the 1937–60 period.

The extraordinary thing about this period [1973–83] has been the gap between public policy and government practice. Words and actions have seldom corresponded. Successive governments have proposed policies which they then failed to pursue, have made offers to the electorate which they could not afford, and have responded to factionalist demands of narrow and immediate interest, to the detriment of the broader and long-term interests of the factions themselves, apart altogether from the nation as a whole. Businessmen and business organisations have contributed much to this deterioration in our affairs, because they have demanded from government measures, aid and support which further distort the economic system and which involve still further intervention by the public sector in our economy. In doing so, of course, they have been behaving no differently from all the other interests in Irish society. Trade unions, farmers' organisations, political parties have all become more strident in their clamour for the immediate advancement of their narrow interest. When this kind of development coincides, as it has, with attempts at consensus, as opposed to leadership in national affairs, the result is inevitable. The only consensus possible is one which postpones to a later date fundamental matters of a painful kind. Any consensus reached between factional interests must, in the nature of factions, relate to short-term means rather than long-term ends. Inevitably, expediency dictates that the most powerful faction secures those things which will pacify it now, regardless of subsequent cost.[20]

The nub of the Madisonian argument (as glossed, possibly impertinently, by the present writer) is that the race is to the well organised, the swift, the unscrupulous and the well got. This is the case even in a democracy with frequent, fair and competitive elections, where the rule of law exists and all citizens are more or less genuinely equal in the eyes of that law. Pluralist competition will not cure the free-rider effect where the rational (or irrational) inaction of the poor, the weak, the marginalised and the incompetent benefits, by default, the high-riding strong, rich, clever and determined or the highly organised 'aristocracy of labour'. It also militates against that large constituency of people in every society who simply wish to be left alone. Paradoxically, the expressed will of such a majority, defending its perceived interests, benefits well-organised minorities.

To skip over much of the Olsonian argument, elites in democracies in the medium to long run govern in the interests of the many only in so far as that is actively enforced by the enfranchised many. Furthermore, elites are in part liberated from that obligation by free riding on the part of some citizens in the form of non-participation. This effect is aggravated by the natural tendency of those leaders whom the voters actually do put in power, in the absence of sustained voter and media pressure, to tilt the system in their own favour. A classic example of this is the sustained assault by Labour Party governments in Britain over the past fifty years on grammar schools in England and Wales in the name of comprehensive and allegedly egalitarian schooling. This assault was accompanied by many elites sending their own children to grammar schools or even public schools: caviar for the general, short commons for the ranks. Such tilting can be explained by the Olson effect. Over a long period, this bias permits the development of plutocracies allied with institutional elites in the unions and the bureaucracy based on inherited advantages, whether intellectual or monetary. This inherent bias in favour of elites goes hand in hand with genuine democratic institutions, which moderates, but does not eliminate, privilege.

Large portions of the electorate go along with this situation and even vote for candidates selected from the rich section of society because the voters are, in effect, bought off through mechanisms such as clientelism, social deference and awe of financial power. Alternatively, the unsuccessful vote for the successful in the possibly realistic hope that the success will somehow rub off on them or that someone who has been successful on his own behalf might be equally successful on behalf of the community in general. Other large portions, particularly the poor, though also the able but politically marginalised, are squeezed out in favour of the sheltered sector represented by the state and its allies. The result is a curious alliance between the welfare-dependent and the politically powerful privileged against the innovative, the energetic and the original. In the Irish case, these latter often emigrated, admittedly along with many others, during the depression years and their rather dismal sequel between 1937 and 1960. A perpetual Irish conundrum has been the apparent contrast between the Irish relative lack of economic energy and success at home and the putative success they make of themselves in Britain and the United States. To be minimally fair to independent Ireland, these emigrants were also continuing an old Irish tradition of 'going away' and making their mark somewhere else. Thomas Jefferson, foreseeing such effects in the infant United States, commented that true democracies should have revolutions every thirty years so as to ensure the recycling of institutionalised privilege. Intriguingly, some analysts have claimed to see just such a generational cycle of upheaval and renewal in the actual history of American politics over the past two centuries.[21]

Olson is more interested in economic growth than in institutionalised inequalities, and he derives economic slowdown from elite sclerosis. Business, trade unions, farmers' organisations, government, professional associations and ecclesiastical organisations are often tied together by cross-institutional friendly or secret societies such as the Freemasons or the Knights of Saint Columbanus. These organisations get used to each other and tend to discourage innovation or, at the least, tend to slow up change and discourage new departures. Dominant political parties act similarly as a sociological glue that encourages alliances that are often surprising to the outsider. Elites so organised may develop collective styles of thought that are not truly in the interests of the collectivity, and even become rather self-indulgently detached from reality. Old-fashioned perspectives, badly informed good intentions and simple self-interest entail the less-than-perfect realisation of the national interest. *Lebensraum* was not in Germany's interest in the 1914–45 era; Germany had plenty of space, and the obsession with territory was mainly one derived by cultural processes from old-fashioned elites, thinking as they did in the obsolete perspectives of empire outside the European homeland and also the east-Elbian Junker estates of the pre-1914 era. Similarly, the preservation of empire after 1945 was not in the interest of either Britain or France, but it took fifteen years for the elites in the two countries to accept that proposition. The idea that Ireland's future lay with the revival of the Irish language was an elite conviction after independence in 1922, a conviction essentially derived from Gaelic League ideas. This was never an authentic or widely held popular belief. A quiet scepticism about the possibility or even desirability of linguistic revival accompanied a passive assent to the massive official attempt at revival spearheaded by the schools; if the elites want it, the non-elite needs must follow. Those whose Irish was fluent, whether through ancestral tradition or special schooling, sometimes cashed in that ability in the form of jobs in the public service, academia and electronic journalism. However, the masses continued to speak English and quietly resisted language change in their private lives. Those extremists who wished to kill the English language in Ireland were covertly regarded as daft.

In the following chapters the Irish experience of Olsonian processes in a democratic society is examined in more detail. Chapter 1 argues that popular veto groups, in particular the great agrarian class created by the Land Acts of the late nineteenth century, had much to do with Irish developmental sluggishness, as did veto groups such as the Catholic Church; Irish conservatism contrasted strangely with the rhetoric of the revolution of 1913–23. Chapter 2 discusses the increasing division after the Second World War between the ideological nostalgia of the older political leaders and the emergent urbanising society around them. Gradually, elites reluctantly came to terms with the proposition that a modernising Ireland needed very different policies and even different philosophical points of view. Chapter 3 deals with the final acceptance of economic failure in the 1950s, partly in response to American promptings, and the new departure in economic and social policies that occurred at that time. Chapter 4 deals with the parallel evolution of educational policy from the revolutionary period to the mid-1960s and the reluctance with which ecclesiastical and political elites contemplated the inadequacy of Irish education in preparing young people for the modern world. Chapter 5 looks at the use of government agencies in helping the development of private enterprise in Ireland and the promotion of export drives from 1950 onward. Chapter 6 looks at the cultural and political consequences of the silent revolution of the period 1950–66, consequences which involved the disappearance of an entire social and political order that had grown up after the Great Famine of the 1840s.

# 01 | POLITICS AND DEVELOPMENT IN IRELAND

## LOSE THE WAR, WIN THE PEACE

As discussed in the Introduction, the initially startling observation that the highest rates of economic growth in OECD countries occurred in those nation-states defeated in the Second World War is the main piece of empirical evidence offered by Olson and is the most powerful defence of his general argument.[1]

It could be argued that Ireland had had a revolutionary elite turnover in 1922, and it could also be argued that Sweden has historically done very well economically despite never having had a violent disruption of its civic life in modern times. Sweden grew slowly in the post-war period, but was already prosperous and undamaged by war at the beginning of the period. In other words, Ireland and Sweden seem to be exceptions to the Olsonian rule: Ireland didn't do well enough and Sweden perhaps somewhat too well to 'fit' the Olsonian general model. The Swedes do indeed appear, rather like the Swiss, to have succeeded during the era of the 1940s and 1950s in finding a magical combination of tranquil political life, prosperity and reasonable, if not spectacular, economic growth rates. On the other hand, the Irish, despite having been notionally liberated from British imperialism, didn't do so well.

I would tentatively argue that Irish isolation in a slow-growing British Isles supplies part of the answer, Ireland being trapped in circumstances of having a massive local comparative advantage in 'low-tech' animal and food production. Ireland had the ironic disadvantage of a natural advantage. The Irish, with a further ironic twist, did not see it that way; even Marshall Aid was commonly used for agrarian purposes, admittedly of an urgent nature. On the other hand, Sweden, with its immense resources in high technology and its equally disproportionate natural resources in the form of iron and forestry, could scarcely miss selling to both sides in the 1940s and to the ruined post-war world afterwards. Switzerland, a major world banking centre rivalling London or New York, held all sides' coats, financially speaking. In other words, geography has to do much of the explaining in all three cases; politically and militarily speaking, all three countries were 'islands'. Switzerland can be usefully conceptualised as an island in the sky, Sweden was cut off by the Baltic to the south and Finland to the east, and Ireland was hidden behind Britain and the Atlantic: an island behind an island, in the phrase of Jean Blanchard.

Independent Ireland, however, was also clearly a secession state, taken over as a going concern with effective legal and institutional continuity by a conservative, if democratic, nationalist elite in 1922. The new regime did have considerable institutional continuity with the old regime; civil servants and other officials commonly served their new ex-IRA masters loyally, much as they had done their unionist masters under the British. During the generation before independence, a process by which the government of Ireland was gradually handed over to trusted members of the majority ethnic group had long been taking place. Essentially the British government had tried to change horses in Ireland in the late nineteenth century. Instead of backing the mainly Protestant landlord class and its allies, it attempted to forge an alliance with the leaders of the majority: the Catholic, mainly agrarian population of the island. In many cases, the new Catholic civil servants themselves had actually been rebels against their own employers and been members of Sinn Féin, the IRA or the militant nationalist trade unions. They were therefore, if anything, more loyal to their new masters. Bill Kissane has cogently argued that the new state enjoyed the resources of a highly developed civil society which had been put together by the British state and the Irish churches in the nineteenth century. Legitimacy was lent to the new Free State regime by a popular Catholic Church determined that a Catholic electorate should enjoy that apparent contradiction in terms, a Catholic liberal democracy.

The new elite, its segments being echoed in the party system by Cumann na nGaedheal in the 1920s (later Fine Gael) and the more radically secessionist Fianna Fáil under de Valera in the period after 1932, bears a distant resemblance to secessionist post-imperial elites in Africa and Asia as discussed by American political scientist David Horowitz.[2] Horowitz rather chillingly argues that the educational levels and career opportunities open to elites and potential elites rather than the objective interests of the masses determine whether a region in an imperial state will try to secede and set up shop for itself.[3]

An illustration of the importance of elite ambitions is afforded by Scotland's loyalty to the union with England since the middle of the eighteenth century. As Dr Johnson famously said, the fairest prospect for an eighteenth-century Scotchman was the road to London. Eighteenth-century Scotland was proverbially poor and rather well educated; Scottish universities, dating from medieval times and free of the duopoly imposed on higher education in England and Wales by Oxford and Cambridge, supplied an extraordinarily disproportionate number of engineers, scientists and social philosophers to the joint state of Britain and to the resultant great empire. Because of this favourable career pattern, in effect, an implicit bargain existed between England and Scottish potential elites, and Scottish secessionism was never really on until very recently. Ireland, by way of contrast, was an evidently backward part of the United Kingdom, a part that began to recover from a long-established pattern of semi-endemic famine after 1850. It also began to develop a potential leading class of young men and women who were denied third-level education consonant with their religious preferences by an unholy, or even holy, alliance of British Protestantism and Irish Catholicism until 1908. Furthermore, as Catholics they were discriminated against in employment and promotion, although this was showing some signs of weakening, if not completely fading away, as the twentieth century approached. Dr Johnson, after all, famously advised an Irishman not to have a union with England, 'for we should rob you.'

Thus, representative government in the new Irish nation-state would tend to be used to secure the personal and dynastic interests of a new, ambitious, hungry, nationalist and Catholic local political elite. The population, being rather poor and relatively undereducated, would then tend to 'free ride' to a relatively high degree. Also, in so far as they did participate, such participation would tend to be clientelistic and particularistic; many people might be expected to vote after independence for candidates who were seen to be good local representatives rather than promising national leaders: a parliament of backbenchers. Certainly, the political science literature on Ireland has established that there was a clear tendency for the first generation of ex-revolutionaries in parliament to be gradually replaced by local men.

These new men had no revolutionary glamour, but involved themselves primarily with the day-to-day concerns of their constituency rather than the national interest, and in many cases continuously engaged in a beggar-my-neighbour contest with other local potentates to an extent that sometimes bordered on the surreal. This localist tendency, clearly enforced by the electorate, was reinforced by the workings of the electoral system, proportional representation by means of the single transferable vote (PR-STV). PR-STV handed extraordinary power to the marginal voter, in the sense of the voter just capable of changing his mind because of a personal inducement in the form of a personal promise by an ambitious candidate. The effect was to generate a sometimes pathological personalism and particularism and a disregard of the public interest. The country, being relatively poor and sandwiched between two historical superpowers (nineteenth-century Britain and twentieth-century America), would tend to encourage Exit over Voice, in the terms of Albert Hirschman; if you were discontented, you could protest noisily or leave the country: Voice versus Exit. Naturally, many took Exit; giving out noisily about things gives employment, but not to very many. For most, it merely fills the letters page of *The Irish Times*.

All of this fits much of what we know about the course of Irish politics after independence. Even the Civil War of 1922–23 did not seriously impede the process by which the new leaders—ex-revolutionaries, farmers, professional people, businessmen, journalists, trade unionists and clerics—ensconced themselves in power with the active consent of some and the passive consent, if that is what it can be called, of the many.[4] A helpless anger enveloped some of the effectively disenfranchised many: those whose votes were in vain and whose interests were not addressed, either because they did not suit the interests of elites or because they represented modes of living and ways of earning a living that were obsolescent or declared to be anti-social. Small grocers, booksellers, cinema owners, sweetshop proprietors, long-distance hauliers, women workers, graziers, part-time farmers and bus owners were treated in weirdly similar ways, and were commonly discouraged, or even prevented, by a morally self-righteous government from plying their trades and earning their living. A huge, and sedulously ignored, dispossessed group went into contented or embittered exile, internal or external. Ill treatment, often amounting to criminal abuse, of vulnerable groups such as orphans and the mentally handicapped was hushed up, the Catholic Church in particular assisting in such conspiracies against the public interest. All of this received the quiet assent, or perhaps fatalistic acceptance, of the majority.

The trade unions were fully in co-operation with this quietly repressive and popular regime. It is rarely pointed out, for example, that the trade union movement of William O'Brien and Thomas Foran was clearly hand-in-glove with William Cosgrave, Kevin O'Higgins and other leaders of the early Free State, a regime later to be demonised by left-wing and republican writers. This labour alliance with the pro-Treatyites fit quite comfortably with a pro-business regime and with policies pleasing to the powerful ecclesiastical elites of the time. The trade unions later forged a similar alliance with de Valera's Fianna Fáil. Although there were secular, socialist and communist traditions within the union movement, Catholic trade unionists tended to predominate, much to the baffled rage of Irish anti-clerical communists like Sean

O'Casey or Liam O'Flaherty. The Irish revolution was followed by a very non-revolutionary outcome. This is not to say that it was a failed or betrayed revolution, but rather to put forward the very different argument that the original revolutionaries got more or less the kind of regime they wanted, rather than the regime various commentators have imagined they wanted. Kevin O'Higgins described it with some satisfaction as the most conservative revolution in history. Another aspect of the revolution in Ireland that tends to be glossed over is the exceptionally well-organised and cohesive nature of the new elites. Irish political culture was organisationally adept, and the mass political party could arguably be claimed as an Irish invention. Certainly, Daniel O'Connell's Catholic Association of 1823 was a mass card-carrying and vote-seeking political party with extraordinary levels of regimented popular support. As such, it was unprecedented at that time, and pipped the US Democratic Party at history's winning post by one year as the first true mass-membership political party.

Again, the Catholic Church was an almost proverbially popular and powerful organisation, controlling the educational system, much of the elite culture and, for many, but not all, purposes, the mind of the collectivity. Irish Catholic political culture took its religion from Rome but its politics from a curious and mongrel mixture of Herder, Pearse, Marx, Irish historical memory, English liberalism, American constitutionalism and, in particular, Daniel O'Connell, the often unacknowledged father of Irish democracy. The result was a curiously empty rhetorical democratic radicalism or national populism, behind which abided a deep, unselfconscious and unexamined commitment to liberal democracy and an equally deep and commonly unexamined conservatism.

Secret societies such as the Knights of Saint Columbanus and open recreational associations such as the Gaelic Athletic Association were very well developed, as were cultural organisations such as the Gaelic League. Trade unions and professional associations such as those of the lawyers and the medical profession were highly organised and powerful. A large proportion of professional people were clerics of one kind or another, particularly in the fields of education and health. Also, as the scale of the new system was small, old-school-tie syndromes and nepotism were naturally very common. The new Irish polity, it could be argued, was born mature, rather like the characters in Flann O'Brien's *At Swim-Two-Birds*; Olsonian sclerosis was already set to develop, or could perhaps be said to have been present in the Irish state as institutional foetus. The rise of Fianna Fáil after 1926, built on the ruins of an old IRA eager to escape from the political wilderness, entailed the growth of a highly disciplined, united and popular political party, which took over a going concern in the form of the Free State, a going concern whose surprisingly well-knit character suited de Valera's party well.[5] Alternatively, it could be argued that the Irish state was born between 1850 and 1870, when the Catholic Church was reorganised, the Dublin administration was modernised, political parties were being assembled and the mass of the population became literate and English-speaking; this is an argument which has been associated with the historians Emmet Larkin and David Miller and more recently with political scientist Bill Kissane. The rise of a cheap, popular, mainly nationalist provincial press also occurred during these years, stamp tax on newspapers having been abolished in 1854.

Quite apart from the innate conservatism that characterises large and successful organisations like the Catholic Church or the Irish civil service, it should be remembered that many of the revolutionaries were actually not all that interested in development. On the Griffithian wing, they certainly were quite developmentalist, and Pearse's crazy fantasies of a united Irish-speaking and teetotal Ireland of twenty million, to which Paris would look for cultural guidance, are well known. There is, however, abundant evidence that some of the nationalists embraced what amounts to a Salazarian view; many wished to preside over a moral community with little widespread wealth. In fact, an Irish Catholic admiration for Salazar and the real or imagined merits of Franco and Mussolini was widespread and commonly badly informed. Some also feared that widespread prosperity would sap the national spirit and lead to 'shoneenism' (Anglophile snobbery), or the sort of thing the Soviets, in their brazen way, called 'rootless cosmopolitanism and spiritual emptiness'. It is rarely remembered, partly because republican socialists do not wish it to be remembered, that revolutionary Sinn Féin was heavily financed by the large farmers of central Munster and other fertile areas. Griffithian Sinn Féin had a strong tendency to favour low taxation; among her many other recounted sins, England was accused of overtaxing Ireland in the nineteenth century. Ireland's relative economic stagnation in the period between 1924 and 1960 was certainly mainly a result of overwhelming external facts of life. In particular, the necessity of paying for the IRA's campaign of physical destruction in 1922–23 crippled public finances from the beginning and put the nascent Irish government very much in debt to the banks. This was to be followed after 1929 by the Great Depression. The slump was combined with the beggar-my-neighbour character of international politics and trade in the 1930s and the immediate post-1945 period. Also, very obviously, independent Ireland suffered from the sometimes capricious nature of British economic and trade policy, the overwhelming European and global disaster that was the Second World War and the travails of Ireland's major trading partners of the time. All of this was out of the control of a small, peripheral and puny European state, living through dark times as was the rest of the continent.

However, this stagnation, and the moral and social conservatism that it encouraged and fed, were viewed with a certain fatalism and what amounted to a complacency and even complicity among some of the elites. Certainly, a conservative and even reactionary cast of mind was encouraged by the calamity of the Irish Civil War of 1922–23, which generated a mood of disillusion, fatalism and cynicism which was extraordinarily strong and, perhaps, was intensified by the exaggerated enthusiasm and idealism of the revolutionary period. The general takeover of a large chunk of Irish civic life by the Catholic Church between 1850 and 1940 accentuated the authoritarianism and intellectual conformism of the general culture. It is interesting that it was often sociological 'outsiders' among the elites who were most vocal about the inadequacies of the political and economic system. Among these were people as variegated as Noel Browne, Sean MacBride, various former southern unionists, northern unionist observers and northern Catholics like Sean MacEntee, James Deeny and (marginally) T.K. Whitaker, men who were most vocally alert to the shortcomings of the existing system and looked upon stagnation with most concern: the developmentalists.[6]

Sean Lemass can also be listed among this group of developmentalist 'outsiders' in that he was far younger than the rest of the 'Nineteen Sixteen Men' who formed the backbone of de Valera's cabinet. Unlike his elders, Lemass was not much of a Gaelic Leaguer and, possibly, not much of a religious believer either. On the other hand, his family had Dublin Parnellite political traditions, and a certain anti-clerical and liberal streak often ran through families with such traditions. Like William Cosgrave, whom he greatly admired and looked up to, he was an inner-city Dubliner: a classic 'Dublin Jackeen'. 'Jackeens' were, as are their 'Dub' descendants, notorious for their townie scorn for anything that smacked of the rural, of things 'culchie'. In an odd way, he also resembled his putative political opponent, Michael Collins, more than he resembled his party comrades in his practicality, impatience with purposeless theorising and his private scepticism about cultural politics. Both Lemass and Cosgrave were rather detached from the ruralist sentimentalities that gripped the minds of so many Sinn Féiners.[7] Both mystified more mainline Gaelic Leaguers by their unexpected reactions to ideological argument and apparently 'unprincipled' attitudes toward policy choices.

I hypothesise that it is no coincidence that Ireland's economic upturn occurred half a generation after the general Western economic lift-off in 1960 rather than in 1946; the upturn in Ireland coincided with, and possibly was permitted by, the fading away of the generation of the national revolution. The policies that would have facilitated such an upturn were resisted, and there was also a certain amount of bad luck. In particular, the political sidelining of Lemass that was an unintentional outcome of the Fianna Fáil electoral defeat of 1948 is one example of such misfortune.

However, it took what was seen as the economic disaster of the mid-1950s and the ageing of the Boys of the Old Brigade to force real change; there was a genuine problem of gerontocracy. In the

1950s, the facts of economic life and electoral pressure gradually began to nullify the special interests of older business and ecclesiastical, cultural and labour elites, the people who had essentially carved up the entire country into a set of fiefdoms after 1920 and 1932. The effects of the recommendations of Whitaker and the decisions of Lemass were, of course, vital, but equally so was the weakening of the ageing hands of Eamon de Valera, Thomas Derrig and John Charles McQuaid, whose collective dream of a moral community ('a Christian Civilisation') which was authentic, pious, static and intellectually homogeneous was briefly realised in the 1932–48 period.[8] The erosion of this imposed, sometimes oppressive but oddly popular moral community has continued since 1960 because of the effects of electoral democracy, the mass media, increasing wealth and revolutionary shifts in the international political and economic order.

Irish economic growth was respectable after the retirement of de Valera and has been extraordinary by any standard in the period since 1987. The world-beating explosion of growth in the Republic of Ireland in the 1990s was partly a symptom of how sluggish Irish economic growth had been prior to then, much as the growth in the 1960s was in part a reaction to the stagnation of the previous twenty years. That stagnation had, in turn, been partly caused by government policy as enforced by powerful veto groups who, between them, ensured that only redistribution could occur of what little wealth there was in the country. By focusing on redistribution as the kernel issue, sight was lost of the fact that the country as a whole was poor and, relatively speaking, doomed to grow poorer. Significantly, the dramatic economic growth of the 1990s coincided with the erosion of the power bases of many monopoly groups closely linked to government, including taximen, Aer Lingus, pharmacists and even publicans.

## WEALTH AND POVERTY

Independent Ireland was dominated by a huge, and recently created, farming class, varying in resources from the obsolescent landless labourer at one end of the scale to the great grazier or rancher at the other. There was a new, and large, middle class of over 200,000 farmers with between fifteen and 100 acres, which dominated society and politics because of its massive collective presence in the form of demographic weight, cultural centrality and electoral political clout. Class politics in the Free State were the politics of political competition between different classes of agrarian workers, owners and employers in a context of a propertied community only recently legally ratified by the Land Acts of 1870–1903. Essentially, small-propertied agrarian Ireland was the child of the Famine and of Michael Davitt's Land League in alliance with the Gladstonian Liberals. As late as the mid-1930s, the pressure on the de Valera government to extend land-division programmes from the western and poorer counties to the eastern and southern richer counties was considerable. Fianna Fáil in government backed off from the proposal to break up the great 'ranches' of Leinster and Munster only after 1935, under pressure of fear of wrecking what was left of a commercial farm economy in anticipation of a great new war which many knew was to come shortly. The large commercial farmers survived because de Valera realised that, despite his own sentimental anti-modernism, he could scarcely forego the productive power of what commercialised agriculture the country had in the parlous circumstances of the time. In this case, the veto group (large farmers) was not itself politically powerful; after all, it had suffered political defeat at the hands of de Valera's Fianna Fáil government in the 1930s. Rather, in the prewar situation, this sector was suddenly economically vital and belatedly seen as such by people in power. This economic importance made the sector's enemies stay their hand.

Michael Deegan, a senior expert in the Land Commission, wrote to the Taoiseach in 1943 that land division, as proposed by Fianna Fáil ideology in the period 1926–36, was essentially completed. Further division of agricultural land could now be done only outside the Congested Districts of impoverished western Ireland and would involve handing out twenty-five-acre plots to the landless. 'Experience shows that local approval for land division work can be secured in many cases only by the allocation of some holdings to suitable landless applicants.' Landless men made bad farmers, Deegan argued, for they had 'the grazier spirit'. Furthermore, it was politically a hot potato: '. . . there was local opposition to the settlement of colonies from the Gaeltacht in County Meath and in order to placate the local landless claimants, they (i.e. the Land Commission) distributed among them 4,000 acres for the 600 they gave the migrants.' Much of such divided land got sold off by the recipients to finance a move to English cities. De Valera was in an impossible position and was quietly, if reluctantly, aware that this was the case.

Agrarian issues of this generic kind dominated Irish politics from the time of the Land Acts to the mid-1960s. Policy-makers were naturally profoundly influenced by this huge confederation of agrarian veto groups and their ecclesiastical and democratic allies. Politicians commonly behaved in apparent reaction to pleas for land redistribution by small farmers, landless men and such intellectually unreconstructed worthies as Bishops Cornelius Lucey of Cork and Michael Browne of Galway. In an undated memorandum written circa 1940, Sean MacEntee, Minister for Finance and later Minister for Industry and Commerce, commented in Darwinian style on the backward and parlous character of Irish farming. De Valera's version of village pastoral had its loyal critics inside his own government in MacEntee and McElligott. MacEntee wrote that, in the nineteenth century, Irish agriculture had had a dual structure, an obsolete, essentially hopeless subsistence sector and a go-ahead, modernising sector which showed great promise; the latter seemed capable of ousting the former completely and creating a vibrant, Danish-style modern agricultural industry in Ireland. Irish agriculture in the nineteenth century had

> . . . suffered a number of rude shocks, but had been able to surmount them and adjust itself to changing conditions with a high degree of success. Up to the famine, there were, not one, but two Irish agricultures, of which one—an inherently unstable, subsistence economy developed mainly from the middle of the 18th Cent[ury] and founded on the potato, rack-renting and unlimited breeding—was practically eliminated by the Famine and its sequelae. The other, the specialised market agriculture, seeking always to adapt itself to our peculiar conditions of soil

and climate and the changing competitive conditions of our chief market, grew and developed, though slowly. This development can be shown quite clearly in figures of agricultural activities, and mainly in livestock.[9]

However, he continued, the 'nigger in the woodpile' [sic] was that since 'around 1900' this essentially benign development stopped, and Irish agriculture had stagnated while rival agricultural economies elsewhere 'multiplied many fold, even those like the Danes who enjoy no climatic or soil advantage.' He complained in irritation that for saying such things and blaming no cause 'other than the human' he was 'roundly abused as an upholder of British Imperialism.'[10] The stagnation of Irish agriculture was the root cause of Irish underdevelopment, and measures would have to be taken to overcome it, he argued. Sniping at his own government, MacEntee concluded:

The war of 1914–18 gave us a breathing-space, which we turned to no permanent advantage, either by the use of its exceptional profits to improve technique and stock or by the consolidation of goodwill (the latter, indeed we squandered recklessly, and our only notion of the former was reckless gambling in land). A number of necessary improvements in detail was effected between 1924 and 1932, but they came from above, not from the enterprise of working farmers, as elsewhere, and it could be argued, as special pleading, that in the long run they were injurious for that very reason. On top of all this reluctance to expand came the Economic War, which positively and seriously damaged our agriculture's productive and exporting capacity, and high protectionism, which incidentally obstructed it, especially when applied to forms of agriculture which our farmers had been progressively abandoning. But the devil looks after his own, and, after the termination of the British half of the Economic War in April, 1938 (our half is still going on, in the shape of prohibitive tariffs on British goods), came the present War, again excluding to some extent our competitors, giving us an opportunity of recovering goodwill and of making profits to repair the damages of the Economic War and to tide over such readjustments as the development of a more strongly competitive position might require. I suggested, with details, that present government policy appeared to be opposed to, rather than directed to, the promotion of, such development, and insisted again that exports were necessary not for their own sake but only because people here wanted to consume coal, iron, timber, tin, gold, silver, cocoa, coffee, sugar and thousand[s] of other things, and that such exports depended on either a socialist or capitalist order of competitive efficiency.

But these exports have to be sold in a market in which they have to face the competition of agricultural producers working elsewhere with different techniques and different natural environments, and the conditions of their competition are consequently changing with discovery, invention and organisation. Consequently, the problem of an expanding agricultural economy is one of constant adjustment—breaking out into new lines of production and increasing efficiency in the old . . .

If, as I feared was increasingly the case in this country, the pursuit of this objective was obstructed negatively by passivity on the part of the people on whose enterprise and initiative advance depends or positively by something masquerading as a 'social policy' which is content with some formal secondary objective and ignores the fundamental fact that both general welfare and the power of public authorities are limited by average productivity, then the only visible prospect was one of stagnation, decay, falling standards of living, spreading poverty and, if movement be free, emigration and, if movement be not free, social unrest and émeutes.[11]

MacEntee was essentially violently complaining about what he saw as the stultifying consequences of de Valera's voter-driven wager on the poor and the frugal at the expense of commercial agriculture, an ironic contrast to Patrick Hogan's support for larger farmers in the 1920s and, of course, Stolypin's historically doomed 'wager on the strong' during the last years of the Tsarist regime in pre-Bolshevik Russia. De Valera's wager on the weak majority rather than the strong minority profited him electorally, whatever it may have done to the Irish economy. MacEntee was

thereby suggesting that a native government was basically imi-
tating the British government's pre-1922 policies under the Land
Acts. This ironic imitation of the old imperial regime by a native
government was for similar underlying non-economic reasons:
fear of political unrest and a wish to buy the Irish farmer off. After
all, the Irish farming community was, in effect, the electorate, or
the collective boss of the democratic government of the country.
Irish farmers and their dependants were extremely well organised,
a condition that dated back notoriously to the Parnell period and
even to that of O'Connell.

The British Land Acts had been motivated not by a wish to
produce a vibrant Danish-style commercial export-led agriculture,
but rather by political and distributivist considerations, aiming at
giving as many families as possible a reasonable living, *by the
modest standards of late Victorian times*, on the land. The original
'killing Home Rule with kindness' policy consisted in the British
government's creation of the owner-occupier Irish farmer. British
governments scarcely concerned themselves with the dynamics of
Irish economic development; from their point of view, the Irish
economy was a trivial and rather hopeless part of the British
economy, and Ireland was a suitable case for treatment by massive
subsidy from the ample Imperial Exchequer. In effect, Whitehall
wanted to keep the Paddies happy by throwing land and money at
them, and de Valera found himself doing the same thing on a far
smaller budget. This is the heart of MacEntee's argument; Irish
land ownership was the result of politically motivated British
government priorities, even when these involved economically
irrational policies. The Irish land system owed its structure to
political and social considerations rather than concern about
businesslike efficiency. British concerns focused far more on Irish
political restiveness than on the economic viability of a small, if
fractious, province of the imperial kingdom, a province viewed as
a kind of national larder of the United Kingdom.

Any Irish democratic government that hoped to be re-elected
was bound to continue with this policy of 'kindness'. In fact, it
would be forced to do so by electoral pressures from a well-
organised and mobilised farming political class; after all, it was the

social class of the 'bould tenant farmer' of the universally popular
agrarian ballads which had been organised to fight the Land War
of 1879–81. Furthermore, what was an acceptable standard of
living in 1880 was not going to be such in 1950 or 2000, one could
add. Therefore, the land settlement of the late nineteenth century
had inbuilt structural tendencies toward stagnation, emigration to
a welcoming English-speaking world outside and a very slow,
gradual and reluctant consolidation through land sales into a
commercialised large-farm system. Since land ownership was tied
up with social status and family-enforced inheritance rights, land
was clung to for non-economic reasons, thus making the market
in land 'sticky' and sluggish. Selling to the highest bidder rather
than to a next-of-kin, neighbour or near relative was also frowned
upon by the community, thereby aggravating this tendency toward
stickiness.

Logically, farmers were regarded by bankers as a bad risk; their
only capital was their land, and foreclosure on an indebted
farmer's land was difficult, as the community would be sometimes
quite literally up in arms if the creditors tried to sell it to recoup
their losses. Ireland had a two-century-long tradition of highly
organised and sometimes violent agrarian resistance to clearances,
to rents and, in particular, to buyers from outside the district. As
one witness to the Banking Commission of 1938 put it,

> ... the farmer does not realise that if his neighbour does not pay
> [his debts] and, through his own fault, does not meet his
> liabilities, and his assets are put up for sale and not bought, his
> own credit is being injured.

Land bought after such a forced sale would be 'under a cloud'
and possibly even subject to boycott; in the previous century,
assassination had occasionally been resorted to. Investment in
agriculture in Ireland was problematic in ways that would be seen
as incomprehensible in England, but perfectly understood in rural
France. John B. Keane's well-known play about agrarian land-
hunger, *The Field* (now a film) is, in effect, anthropology as much
as drama; the plot revolves around a small farmer's resistance to

developmental change that threatened his agrarian claim to a neighbour's field. In 1944, as Minister for Industry and Commerce, MacEntee expanded his argument, saying that land policy was driven by political pressures and a wish for social peace rather than by the wish to build a vibrant agricultural economy. He wrote:

> When the original Land Acts were drafted the farmers' position was such that the problem was treated as a social rather than an economic one. At least the economic angle was not emphasised and may be compared in certain aspects with to-day's provision of unemployment assistance: a palliative rather than a remedy; a concern for those immediately affected rather than a proposal for placing agriculture in its true relation to the general economic position.[12]

It was desirable, he argued, that the ownership of farms should be in the main 'confined to persons whose livelihoods depend on their proper use.' He admitted that it was not practicable to exclude from farm ownership people who had other occupations, but it was a situation that should be discouraged, as was multiple ownership of holdings by one owner.[13] MacEntee, because of his Belfast-derived 'outsider' status in cabinet, formed a one-man loyal opposition inside the Fianna Fáil government, although much of his hostile criticism of government policy apparently remained unread by his colleagues. In an undated and apparently unsent missive addressed to the Taoiseach, probably written in 1938, he vented his dissent at length:

> It has been clear to me for some time past that my continuance in office as Minister for Finance is incompatible with the views which you as head of the government and a majority of the Cabinet with you hold in regard to public expenditure. I have not concealed from you or my other colleagues my opinion that we are spending excessively and at a rate which definitely and gravely is injurious to the State and the community. On occasions our differences upon this question have been carried almost to the point of my resignation . . .[14]

He went on to label de Valera 'a spender' who seemed to want to fuel inflation by using public works programmes to employ 200,000 men, describing himself as a consistent opponent of attempts to cure unemployment by public expenditure. The government had distorted the economy by wholesale subsidisation of economic activities, rather than letting entrepreneurial activity find the correct product for the correct market.

> In an effort to cope with this problem of unemployment, we have increased tariffs, we have fostered tillage, we have subsidised dairying and livestock production, we have developed the sugar-making industry, we have raised the price of agricultural commodities, we have restricted the employment of juveniles, we have curtailed female labour, we have shortened the working hours of the employed and given them holidays with pay, we have introduced quota restrictions, *and we have established virtual monopolies* [emphasis added]. We have more regimentation, more regulation, more control everywhere. And more unemployed! We have for one political reason and another increased costs and spent money in every direction and have now to face the inevitable reaction in diminishing production and contracting private expenditure, factors which should operate to their own cure by inducing the government to moderate its demands upon the citizens.[15]

MacEntee had certainly absorbed much of what was termed the 'Finance Attitude' (apparently essentially McElligott's opinions) toward public expenditure.[16] It is difficult not to come to the conclusion that policy-makers, with some exceptions, adhered by and large to a fatalistic and non-developmental view of the Irish economic future. Ireland was going to stay an agricultural country, and the idea of industrialising the economy and making a dash for growth was written off as a fantasy. Ireland, the country of Pearse and Yeats, it might have been remarked, felt it had had enough of fantasies in the early twentieth century. Given the stagnant character of Irish agriculture and the near-impossibility of finding export markets in the years 1929–45, a sceptical view of the prospects for industrialisation was eminently understandable, even responsibly realistic. However, and this is a crucial point, this view persisted during the very changed circumstances of the post-war period. James Dillon, for example, always held that Ireland was, and both would and should remain, an agricultural country and scouted all suggestions of extensive industrialisation, even in the more promising years of the post-war world.[17]

John McGahern, speaking from the point of view of a very poor county, Leitrim, has given us vivid pictures of the society which dominated independent Ireland.

> Between 1915 and 1960, nearly half a million Irish people went to England, and they had hard lives many of them. Most of the people I was at school with went to England, half of my own family went to England, and I think that if that siphoning off of the younger generation hadn't happened then, social change would have happened here far more quickly ... it would have been like an explosion, like the lid blowing off a kettle. In a way, a lot of the Irish problems were avoided through emigration, by getting rid of some of our youngest and best of our people, and that generation who disappeared into England were looked down on by the crowd that stayed, who did very little for the country or anything else ... I'd hate to say I was angry, but the facts are unpleasant, and perhaps they might sound angry because they're unpleasant.[18]

However, some people *did* want to do something, but did not agree on what should, or could, be done. Agriculture versus industry was the usual form the developmentalist argument took, private versus public enterprise being touted by groups on both sides of the Fianna Fáil/Inter-Party fence. Services were always a disproportionately large part of Irish economic activity and, rather oddly, that sector tended to be disregarded by economic planners, with the partial exception of tourism. In the long run, it was this somewhat notional tertiary sector and, within it, the 'high tech' and information technology businesses that were to become the leading sectors in the economy. In effect, Ireland was to skip the classic 'smokestack industry' phase and go directly to tertiary service and quaternary 'infotech' phases: from peasantry to suburbia in two generations. Naturally enough, no one knew this at that time, but it is difficult not to suspect that there was a lingering physiocratic mentality in the minds of policy-makers. Many people felt that economic activity really consisted in making something tangible, 'real', and by means of physical exertion. A man, however intelligent and purposeful, sitting behind a desk writing a report or devising a new technique was not really working, but a man building a wall, however unneeded or ugly that wall might be, was indeed 'really' working. Man must earn his bread by the sweat of his brow; work was doing something that had to be done and something which was generally unpleasant; the idea that work might be enjoyable, creative and fulfilling was subconsciously scouted.

Despite the modernising rhetoric of Local Government and the emergent Health Department, during the war years MacElligott and his colleagues expected to see, and perhaps actually looked forward to, an Ireland which would be more or less as it had been previously: rural, pastoral, static, small-town and Jeffersonian in virtue and religiosity. They imagined the indefinite continuance of a yeoman society, dominated by smallholders. Many agreed with them, but the people who agreed with them most were not the statist developmentalists around Lemass in Fianna Fáil, but the older soldiers of destiny. MacElligott was also sympathised with by many of the people who were to come into office in 1948 in the first Inter-Party government, to be led by Fine Gael. The new government, after all, included the new smallholders' party, Clann na Talmhan, based on the small-farm counties of the west. It must be reiterated that this static prospect was, as McGahern suggests, the accepted one of the conservative, even complacent, majority in a sleepy emigrant society dominated by small farmers. However, the elites were actually divided among themselves, sometimes passionately so.

## A MAN FOR SOME SEASONS, OR THE USES OF NOSTALGIA
Eamon de Valera was, of course, the touchstone of the time. His now proverbial and clichéd radio broadcast of 1943 set forth a vision of a bucolic and virtuous arcadia.

That Ireland, which we dreamed of, would be the home of a people who valued material wealth as the basis of right living, of a people who were satisfied with frugal comfort and devoted their leisure to the things of the spirit—a land whose countryside would be bright with cosy homesteads, whose fields and villages would be joyous with the sounds of industry, with the romping of sturdy children, the contests of athletic youths and the laughter of happy maidens, whose firesides would be forums for the wisdom of serene old age. It would, in a word, be the home of a people living the life that God desires that men should live.[19]

The significant aspect of this speech, broadcast on St Patrick's Day to a mainly Irish-American audience, was that it was not found to be irrelevant or even comic, but was taken with deadly seriousness by many people in positions of power and influence in government, the media, education and religion. More subtly, it was taken literally by young people, who were encouraged to prepare themselves not for the modern world, but for a world that was dying, dead or even imaginary. Presumably de Valera was appealing for political and financial support from Irish-America in anticipation of a general election, much as he was probably appealing for electoral support from his republican wing in offering condolences at the German Legation in Dublin in 1945 on the occasion of Hitler's death. In both cases, an extremely focused short-term purpose informed political and public actions that had extraordinary long-term fallout. Independent Ireland paid for this political opportunism in terms of international credibility in the first case and political respectability in the second.

However, the stabilisation of rural farm society was a long-term, established and passionately defended ideological priority with a large section of the population and with many influential people among the elites, and de Valera had to cope with this, whatever his personal opinions. For example, Jeremiah Newman, a well-known priest who was later to be bishop of Limerick, was at that time an influential academic sociologist who was close to government. As late as 1962, Newman let the ideological cat out of the bag, writing eloquently in favour of the middle-sized farm family, on the interesting and profoundly non-economic grounds that it produced young men who aspired to be priests. Newman pointed out that the ratio of population to priests had gone from 1,376 to one in 1871 to 558 to one in 1961; the Catholic population of Ireland had declined in that near-century by 23 per cent, but, *mirabile dictu*, the number of priests had increased by 87 per cent. The beginning of the Second World War had triggered a further extraordinary jump in this ratio.

Latin, Newman argued, was to be taught to all males in secondary schools so as to prepare them for the priesthood, and apparently not particularly because the language might have some cultural or intellectual value. A rural family atmosphere was more conducive to generating vocations than an urban family environment, according to Newman. Out of 429 students who entered Maynooth seminary between 1956 and 1960, 311 or a massive 72.5 per cent came from 'the open countryside' or from small towns and villages. Government policy should therefore be directed to ensuring that rural farm society be conserved in the interests of the sociological process by which young men were to be transformed into priests. Furthermore, the larger the farm family, the more priests it tended to produce, both in absolute and relative proportions. In Newman's mind, not alone did the economy not exist for society, but society served neither the individual nor the economy, but rather the Deity, or at least His highly organised earthly representatives.[20] Married Irish women were, of course, to be valued for themselves, but to be even more treasured as producers of priests and nuns, an activity at which they were undoubtedly world-beaters. Vocations might have been produced in heaven, as the religious instruction primers claimed, but, to Newman's mind, heaven definitely needed a healthy helping hand from terrestrial sociological and political forces.

The achievement of a parochial, rural, neo-Gaelic and, above all, Catholic arcadia was a goal that absorbed the energies of many Irish educators, clerics, planners and politicians for a generation after independence. It also kept many others busy trying to fend it off and get on with modernising the country, even at the expense of rural and familial values, if necessary. Alternatively, it could be

argued, the politically feeble efforts of modernisers were stifled by
the nostalgic perspectives and sheer sociological dead weight of a
massive, popular and satisfied, if not fatalistic, conservatism derived
from the family farm system, a system stabilised by a steady stream
of emigrants to Britain and America. As Sean O'Faolain put it
bitterly in 1945, the cultural climate in Ireland was conformist and
hostile to free speech because of this sociological circumstance
and because of the ensconcing in power of post-revolutionary
political ideologues, priests and businessmen. The businesspeople
in particular had shifted after 1922; in the 1920s, they had first
supported the Cosgrave government with its low-tax regime, but
they turned to de Valera in the 1930s because he promised them
higher tariff walls. Cumann na nGaedheal was essentially a low-
tariff party, adhering as it did to a policy of free trade with the
United Kingdom, fine tuned by a selective use of low tariffs to
protect a few infant industries. People like J.J. Walsh and Joseph
McGrath, tycoons of the Free State, made their peace very rapidly
with de Valera's protectionist extremism. O'Faolain wrote:

> Between the hard ambitions of these men [the new national
> bourgeoisie] and the simple and pious conservatism of the
> peasant the intellectuals of Ireland were ground to bits—unless
> they came to terms, and the Church quite approved of that
> because churches do not much like intellectuals.[21]

O'Faolain also remarked, significantly and presciently, '. . . on
our present static position, the best one could say for Mr De Valera
would be that his policy may be to give Ireland twenty years of
undisturbed peace in order to stabilise and reconstruct.'[22] The
educational system had been bent by de Valera's government
toward the revival of Irish, wrote O'Faolain angrily, by 'a determined minority of fanatical Gaelic enthusiasts' which had

> for years forced on the whole people, who have, of course, never
> been consulted about the matter, an educational scheme (better
> called a 'schame') of compulsory Irish, led by Mr De Valera himself
> who, with characteristic inconsistency and a characteristic desire

to have his own way (by constitutional means)—whether anybody wants it or not—is convinced, and has even said, that he is
merely implementing the will of the majority. As to how he
knows the majority's will on this subject his heart tells him that.

De Valera had managed to put together what political scientists
would term a blocking coalition, and a very formidable one at
that, by 1945. In particular, he had, in the words of O'Faolain,
managed to 'snaffle' the people who had backed the Treaty forces
in 1922. These had been 'an extraordinary amalgam of hard-
headed idealists (if such a term is possible)', members of the Irish
Republican Brotherhood, businessmen, 'all the former Unionists',
'self-seeking gombeen-men', 'the two Churches almost to a man
and certainly to a bishop', most of the old Irish Party of John
Redmond and quite a few extremist nationalists as well.[23] Dev had
persuaded most of them to make their peace with him by the early
1930s; protectionism and cultural conservatism had a multivariate
appeal in depressed times. The Second World War was a *deus ex
machina*, 'a godsend' to de Valera, O'Faolain argued, as it concealed the essentially irrational nature of Fianna Fáil policies from
the voters and, perhaps, from de Valera himself; self-sufficiency
suddenly made sense because of the extreme and unusual
conditions of wartime. In this he agreed with Sean MacEntee: Dev
had got away with it. In another freak reversal, self-sufficiency
suddenly became a lunatic idea in the new open conditions of the
post-Hitler world of 1945. Again, it took time for the true nature
of this lunacy to dawn on the minds of some people.

O'Faolain, quite brilliantly, put his finger on the centrality of
education for the future, passionately declaring that the existing
system was 'antediluvian'.[24] Against the friendly, uncomprehending and rather mild protests of M.J. MacManus, a Fianna Fáil
supporter and personal friend, he defended the duty of Irish
commentators to beard the government and bear witness that
many of its policies were wrong, and even perverse. Hostility to
books did not go well with an advanced educational system, even
if Ireland had had such an advanced system. He argued quite
strongly that Irish government had, by 1945, seriously lost its way,

to an extent which endangered the future viability of the nation itself. O'Faolain wrote irascibly:

> Surely it is the duty of our writers to keep hammering at such facts as that our children to-day are as hopeless putty in the hands of morons who have imposed on our generation a parody of an educational system beyond all description ignorant, narrow and unrealistic, at which parents growl helplessly, at which the superiors of schools and convents can only wail and wring their hands, but in which the authors thereof obstinately and bearishly persist year after year against the protests of every class and creed?[25]

Certainly, Olsonian processes appear to have governed much of the politics of Irish education at that time. The interests of the churches, the ideological convictions of a generation of politicians conditioned in their youth by the teachings of the Gaelic League, the concerns of a rather small public sector and small business middle class and of the Irish-language lobby seem to have overridden the occasionally incoherent but often clearly expressed wishes of parents for a more practical and financially accessible educational curriculum, and were to continue to do so for another twenty years. Financial security, political orthodoxy and gerontocracy were allied. This political and sociological syndrome is examined in more detail in Chapter 4. However, the roots of this structural stand-off lay partly in cultural problems, particularly in an Irish predilection toward Platonic and moralising styles of argument divorced from the rather grubby everyday realities of Irish life.

## ROOTS: CULTURE AND STRUCTURE

Many observers sensed this deep cultural trouble that afflicted the new country between 1932 and 1960. An acute observer, Desmond FitzGerald, was struck by the contrast between the pedestrian realities of Irish life in the 1930s and the overblown rhetoric of the revolutionaries.[26] He and Frank Hackett, a well-known Irish novelist and journalist, conducted a correspondence on Irish affairs throughout the period 1923–40. Hackett certainly could see the paralysis coming, although he appealed more to personal and cultural explanations than to Olsonian structural conditions, naturally enough. De Valera, Lemass, Aiken and company were seen by him in the 1920s as people who wanted power at virtually any cost. Hackett was fascinated by de Valera, as were so many of his generation. As early as 1928, Hackett commented on the now post-abstentionist leader of Fianna Fáil but still putative President of an imaginary Republic. This latter status was clung to for rather unspiritual financial reasons; the American money could possibly be allocated, in US law, to that imaginary Republic, of which he was evidently and logically the imaginary President.

From the Independent I infer that de Valera is counting on a little rough stuff sooner or later. He is far too slippery, however, to be caught with the naked hand. I do not think that the precise technique of this particular twister has been studied enough by anyone on your side to dispose of him completely ... De Valera is formidable because he is self-deceived. He does not know that he is playing two games at once, having the doctrine of intentions so deeply in his grain. He closes his pub on Sundays, but if a thirsty man enters by the back-door which has been left open for fresh air, how is the lugubrious Eamon to be blamed for the disappearance of two bottles of Guinness and the intrusion of 1s 4d? De Valera's measuring is done with an elastic tape, which is his conscience.[27]

Whatever about the fairness of this assessment, the extraordinary doublethink of the period, its strange atmosphere of 'let's pretend everything is fine', reflected a deep ambivalence at both popular and elite level about the entire nationalist project in Ireland. This ambivalence was symbolised by, and reflected in, de Valera's deep nervousness about the modern secular world in front of him, a world which he sensed, and, perhaps, saw, was probably going to take over eventually, but which he feared in a way that Sean Lemass, for example, did not. Even Lemass had his uneasiness, and admitted it years later, when the die was cast and the decision to modernise was finally taken. At the very least, Lemass, as Todd Andrews put it quite brilliantly, did not confuse modernisation with anglicisation, unlike many of his colleagues. However, creeping commercialisation was going to do the job of transformation slowly or rapidly, despite de Valera's Chinese walls. J.T.N. Jeffries, writing to FitzGerald, commented more forgivingly on de Valera's isolationism in the terrifying days of May 1940: '... poor old Dev came in [in 1932] ... Ireland ... did what he wanted —took the veil, there she was, lonely, perfect and apart.' However, Dev's traditionalism was essentially fake, he wrote, a year later:

> Dev's policy would turn Ireland into a dull, grey, suburban-souled little state, a sort of clerk-state, going to the office every morning and catching the four or the five-thirty home every evening out of the world. Heavens! The old Ireland, persecuted, neglected, sapped, Anglicised Ireland, was a ball of fire. This Ireland is a ball of wool. Through Dev's non-stop Wolfe Tone cinema-show the twenty-six counties drift to their fish and chips, fried over the harp-wood so unaccountably accumulated since the days of Strongbow.[28]

At the end of the nineteenth century, there had already been a sense that all was not well in the cultural matrix between religion and economics in Irish culture. It was eloquently argued by Horace Plunkett and Walter McDonald that Irish Catholics were not very good entrepreneurs and that there was something hostile to moneymaking in the version of Christianity that had won out in Ireland. Plunkett and McDonald were, of course, in good intellectual company, for such was also the thesis of Max Weber's celebrated essay, *The Protestant Ethic and the Spirit of Capitalism* and, with modification, of R.H. Tawney's *Religion and the Rise of Capitalism*.[29]

Weber argued that the rewards of work in this world were regarded by puritan Protestantism as the visible sign of God's approval of the state of the worker's soul; presumably these rewards would be followed by even greater rewards in the next world. Catholicism argued that one's fortune in this world was unconnected with one's fortune in the next; in fact, good fortune in this world might be connected in some unknowable way with bad fortune in the next. Weber, in the *Protestant Ethic*, wrote:

The Puritan wanted to work in a calling; we are forced to do so. For when asceticism was carried out of monastic cells into everyday life, and began to dominate worldly morality, it did its part in building the tremendous cosmos of the modern economic order. This order is now bound to the technical and economic conditions of machine production which today determine the lives of all the individuals who are born into this mechanism, not only those directly concerned with economic acquisition, with irresistible force. Perhaps it will continue to determine them until the last ton of fossilised coal is burnt. In Baxter's view the care for external goods should only lie on the shoulders of the 'saint like a light cloak, which can be thrown aside at any moment.' But fate decreed that the cloak should become an iron cage.[30]

Similarly, Horace Plunkett argued that Catholicism was, at least in Ireland, 'in some of its tendencies non-economic, if not actually anti-economic.'[31] The tendency of Catholicism to shift the focus of life from this world to the next had the effect of checking, he suggested, 'the growth of the qualities of initiative and self-reliance' and particularly had that effect on people who had little education.[32] McDonald made a similar suggestion in 1919.[33] O'Riordan's rebuttal of Plunkett of 1906 pointed to the great achievements of European civilisation when it had been informed by the principles of Catholicism, and pointed to various restrictions on trade that the Irish had had to endure under British or English rule, in particular discrimination against Irish business and commonly against Catholics as well. The debate faded away rather than being resolved one way or another, but the idea that there was a certain disregard for economics inherent in Irish Catholicism lingered on. It is sometimes still offered as an explanation for the slowness of Ireland's economic development. It is perhaps significant that economics became the only developed social science in the emergent, mainly Catholic, new universities in modern Ireland not to have a large Catholic and clerical intellectual input. This relegation of economics to the world of the merely secular is looked at later; effectively, this also meant that economics could become politically important only when Irish political culture had secularised to some extent, clerics had lost some of their intellectual authority and lay intellectuals and academics were taken somewhat more seriously than was traditionally the case.

As argued later, economic and technological change were regarded by many with unease; economic forces were understood far more completely than were the arguably more powerful and important intellectual and technical cultural forces that were allied with them and which conspired to accelerate change. In particular, technological innovation that replaced human labour with machinery was a real threat to the stability of a low-technology social economy: the milking machine, the bicycle, the refrigerator, the radio and the motor car were destabilising influences. Two, perhaps three, of the above depended on rural electrification, which was to start soon after 1945. Rural electrification was a major factor in the liberation of rural women from a life of back-breaking domestic toil. The 'electric' also encouraged reading and radio listening.

In the Dáil in July 1939, de Valera spoke sadly about the flight from the land and expressed a view that economic forces were driving Irish society toward a less desirable future. In an unintentionally comic aside, he solemnly remarked that at one stage he had considered making cheap radio sets available to enliven country living. However, an advisor had gently pointed out to him that radio was one of the devices that exacerbated the discontent of rural people with their lives and enhanced the apparent attractiveness of urban living. Essentially radio was a natural advertisement for the bright lights of the cities. As the American ditty had it, referring to US Army rural doughboys in post-war 1919 Europe, 'How're you going to keep them down on the farm/ Now that they've seen Paree?' De Valera intoned in the Dáil in his inimitable priestly manner:

There is a big flow from villages, small towns and urban areas into the bigger centres. The smaller centres are diminishing. They carried on under a different system in the past. There was not the opening up of the country that has taken place in recent years by

modern methods of transport and other things, which have tended
to bring the people to work and to business in larger centres. There
was a time when you had in a village beside a town or a farm—
and I am thinking of a small village that I knew—two or three
tailors, a couple of boot-makers, and harness-makers. Going back
to an earlier period, I remember that we had mills, stone-dressers,
a blacksmith, and people employed in services which were more
or less ancillary to farming. These people are no longer there, and
the work is done in a different way. That is a tendency for which I
am sorry, but there is no use in hoping that we can put back the
clock. From the purely philosophical point of view, that might
have been a better existence, because when all is said and done
contentment is the thing that matters most. If we are content, we
are happy and we feel we are living a reasonable existence. No
matter what wealth or conditions we have, if we are discontented
we are unhappy. If a person is unhappy he is unhappy. That is all
there is about it. Material things will not help.[34]

## POLITICAL CULTURE AND ECONOMIC DEVELOPMENT

Economics seemed to be, indirectly at least, the science of
immorality and unhappiness in the mind of de Valera and the
minds of many who thought like him on all sides of the Irish
political system. In a fascinating article, Brian Girvin has fleshed
out an argument about the sources of Irish economic stagnation
between 1922 and the 1960s. Girvin focuses on the central
proposition of the nationalists that the union with Britain
necessarily meant poverty and exploitation, whereas independence
necessarily meant prosperity, as long as the leaders of the independent state were patriots. He argues that Irish independence
resulted from cultural and emotional forces which were directly
connected not necessarily to rational calculation, but to political
culture. Furthermore, he argues, much as is argued here, that
culture and *mentalité* combined with Joseph Lee's 'possessor
principle', or rent-seeking by a half-peasant political community,
to hold the country back economically for a generation.[35]
Development was something that was desirable, the ruling
ideology argued, but was something which could be achieved

only by public agencies driven not by a profit motive, but rather by an ethic of community service. The fact that this ideology could serve not only people driven by patriotic zeal but also people driven by rent-seeking motives not unlike those of the heirs of tenant farmers tended to be occluded. State enterprise looked patriotic, private enterprise looked selfish and greedy; an ideological mind-set that justified the crowding out of potential entrepreneurs existed in the minds of many power-holders in Fianna Fáil in particular. In such protected organisations, the zealous and able worker commonly found himself cheek-by-jowl with time-servers, political appointees and manipulative promotion-seekers. The Catholic Church's dislike of commerce and 'unbridled' capitalism echoed a general popular prejudice, encouraged in particular by people who pursued public-enterprise careers, against free trade and, tacitly, in favour of public enterprise. This in turn derived from an economic, or possibly anti-economic, political culture that was fundamentally static and zero-sum in character, non-developmental and even anti-developmental in character.[36] The ultimate in rent-seeking is arranging for the state to provide one with a monopoly licence to sell a commodity or service, and this is precisely what happened under Fianna Fáil governments after 1932 across a vast swathe of the economy. The consumer paid the price in the form of overpricing and low-quality products. The government responded with price controls that probably distorted the market further, increasing inefficiency. This and related themes are examined in later chapters.

Strangely enough, the Irish revival movement both suited the Catholic Church and, in the long run, had within it the seeds of its intellectual sidelining. Richard O'Kennedy, in old age a voluble, entertaining, abusive and intellectually perceptive correspondent of Richard Mulcahy's, commented in 1970 in a private letter, echoing Joyce's protagonist in *A Portrait of the Artist*, but to different ideological purposes, that by teaching Irish to everyone, nineteenth- and early twentieth-century thought in Ireland in the English language was blotted out of the culture. Essentially, this had the effect of letting in the paganism of Yeats, Joyce and AE, as well as the socialism of James Connolly. In other words, by preventing access to modern philosophical, social and scientific thought, the linguistic revival prevented the evolution of an intellectual culture capable of being critical of fascist, communist and romantic-pagan rhetorics. The smothering capabilities of Irish as a revived language were great, its creative capabilities relatively limited. This smothering capacity was itself much valued by obscurantists, many of them clerical. One anonymous, shrewd native speaker of the language had seen this long previously; a west Cork native speaker warned a Gaelic Leaguer intent on learning the language in the first decade of the century to desist from his efforts on the grounds that "twill lave you with a head fit for nothing else.' By allying itself with the patriots, the Catholic Church walked into a cultural and intellectual trap which would profoundly damage it in the long term.[37] This argument is examined in more detail in Chapter 4.

That there was something radically wrong with Irish work culture was not unrecognised by the powers that were. Mancur Olson's model was actually prefigured in the writings of Frank Gallagher, IRA veteran, journalist and director of the Government Information Bureau from 1938 to 1948. He was a propagandist of genius, and the British referred to him rather unkindly during the Second World War as 'Mr De Valera's Dr. Goebbels'. He and Stephen O'Mara, a well-known Limerick businessman and Fianna Fáil backer, corresponded regularly with each other during the war years. O'Mara was an ideological vocationalist and supporter of clerical ideas concerning social organisation. Both were believing Catholics and intellectually exercised about social reform. O'Mara rebuked de Valera, through Gallagher, for having anti-business taxation and social policies (Gallagher passed on all of O'Mara's comments to Dev, and relayed back the Chief's comments as well as his own). Eventually Gallagher replied at length and with some heat to his old friend in April 1940 in a wonderful letter that seems to reveal Fianna Fáil's private view of the situation.

What has curtailed the effectiveness of what the government tried to do—the selfishness of the industrialists and the trade union workers. The industrialists shout all the time against high taxes, and—that pet hobby[horse] of theirs the civil service (being always careful to suggest new schemes so that there will be more civil servants). They shout very loud when they are losing money. Then the government is stale and dead but won't lie down. But when they are making money hand over fist they are as quiet as mice and may admit (though not for publication) that it's not a bad government at all. The trade union workers don't give a damn about the unemployed. They take good care there will be no dilution of labour lest anybody whose mother and father wasn't a plumber might become a plumber and so shake their monopoly. They blather about housing but the wages in the building trade are higher here than in Britain and the output is absurdly less. In all industries it is the same—or nearly all. This beautiful Christian civilisation won't do an honest day's work; just as this beautiful Christian civilisation won't forgo its profits . . . The only people alive in this country is the Government . . .[38]

Like so many others, he saw Ireland as essentially dominated by a rent-seeking culture which encompassed all social classes and creeds, a consequence of which was a collective wish to get the government to do 'everything'. There was too much 'flapdoodle and ballyhoo' and not enough honest thinking about economic and political life. Frank Gallagher had never heard of Mancur Olson.

## DREAMS OF DEVELOPMENT

In 1929–30, a thirty-year-old Fianna Fáil leader, Sean Francis Lemass, IRA veteran, anti-Treaty fighter and inventor of a pragmatic idealist tradition within de Valera's party, wrote a long position paper. He concerned himself with the Irish economic situation on the eve of Fianna Fáil's accession to power and at the beginning of the Great Depression. In this 33-page typescript, he offered a thoroughly thought-out intellectual defence of protectionist policies.

In recent years there has taken place a number of international Conferences of Financiers, Manufacturers, Economists and

Statesmen, who met to consider the general trend of world economic development. From each of these gatherings there have come repeated and emphatic recommendations in favour of the systematic reduction or total abolition of all tariffs and other artificial restrictions on trade. There appears to be a definite movement in influential quarters in support of the idea of an international Economic policy, overriding and replacing the various, and generally conflicting, National policies now in operation. The French Foreign Minister, M. Briand, has by his speeches started men thinking of the possibilities of a United States of Europe, and, as a first step to this end, the feasibility of a European Customs Union is even now being discussed by many practical businessmen. The case put forward by the International Bankers and Industrialists in support of their appeal for change from the present system is very strong. They point to the high level of prosperity now existing in the United States of America, and claim that it is due to the complete absence of trade restrictions and prohibitions in a vast area, with a huge population, which is almost totally self-dependent in the matters of supplies of food and the new materials of industry. They assert that equally prosperous conditions can be produced in Europe, or throughout the whole world, if unlimited freedom of trade is permitted. They argue that the existence of a multitude of Customs barriers has raised the costs of production, depressed the general standard of living, and leads to a wasteful use of the world's capital resources and consequently, to abnormally high rates of interest.

Throughout Europe, where the number of Customs Units has increased from twenty to twenty-seven since the Peace Treaties, Tariffs are in most cases higher to-day than before the war, and show a tendency to increase.[39]

He observed that this syndrome resulted from excessive industrial capacity for peacetime purposes and was yet another consequence of the First World War, and in turn it generated pressures for protectionist policies. Lemass agreed in principle with economic theory's argument in favour of a one-world economy with no tariff barriers, because the total wealth would be greater. Similarly, the Irish Free State would be poorer if each of the twenty-six counties was permitted to have tariff barriers against the other twenty-five: a *reductio ad absurdum* worthy of Myles na gCopaleen. Again, Britain and Ireland as a unit were likely to be richer than the two islands as separate fiscal units, but historically most of the wealth had concentrated in Britain at the expense of Ireland during the period of the union. In the real world, he argued, there are nations that do not want to be crushed by a law of comparative advantage which, in the case of Ireland, extended only to beef and certain other agricultural products.[40] Complete free trade would wipe out the livelihood of half of the population of the Free State. The Cost of Living Index (CLI) was not the only criterion for judging economic policy; in the United States, the CLI was high, but so was the standard of living, he pointed out. The cautious Irish tariff policy of the 1920s had increased employment, and there was no general comparative correlation between standard of living and a low CLI.[41] Irish pastoral agriculture was inefficient and gave little employment relative to productivity, whereas tillage would generate far more employment without necessarily displacing cattle farming; there was no necessary contradiction between the cow and the plough.

However, an industrial 'revival' was needed. For this he bluntly recommended what is nowadays termed Import Substitution Industrialisation (ISI). Ireland had no minerals or other special resources, nor had it 'exceptionally skilful workers in special trades or any of the other considerations which determine the development of particular industries in one country rather than in another.'[42] For a start, the Free State still imported non-tariffed goods in eight general classes: flour and flour products, pigmeat and pigmeat products, paper and cardboard, maize, cement, agricultural implements, wooden boxes and slates. All of these except cement were already made in Ireland to one extent or another. If these were all tariffed, unemployment would be abolished.

The absorption of 50,000 people now idle, into remunerative employment, would result in an increase in the value of the available market and provide scope for further development.

The impetus thus given to the industrial machine, together with the improvement in Agriculture following on the adoption of a more progressive policy would set the Nation marching on the high road to prosperity.[43]

Lemass accepted that there would be problems. Foreigners might move in and take advantage of Irish protection, and legislative steps would have to be taken to ensure that ownership of companies in Ireland would be majority Irish. Again, there was a 'scarcity of skilled workers', and he could not understand why the sensible proposals of a special commission on vocational education had not been immediately implemented. It is now clear that a large part of the reason was clerical opposition to any serious development of vocational education in a form uncontrolled by the churches. The country also needed a central bank of its own, and, in the long run, partition would have to be abolished.[44] He concluded:

In the course of this Paper I have endeavoured to show that the economic policy which, in operation, will prove most beneficial to our people is that which is based on the recognition of our Nationhood and which is primarily designed to protect National interests. The chief of these interests is, and should be, the achievement of economic self-sufficiency, and to that end, the preservation of our population, the improvement of the general standard of living, and the abolition of the twin evils of Emigration and Unemployment. I have endeavoured also to show that the object is attainable, but only by a courageous application of the methods which Economic Nationalism has devised and is now being used throughout Europe. It is widely believed that movements to achieve our political independence of Britain were inspired by sentimental considerations only and had no bearing on material conditions. I know of no man, however, who raised a finger to secure the independence of this country who had not considered the economic advantages which would be gained by people in consequence of it. For generations we have been subject to a system of government which was based on a denial of our Nationality and the economic consequences of that experience should have convinced us that our material welfare is inextricably bound up with the movement for political freedom. We have now secured, in reasonable degree, power to regulate the affairs of part of the country in our own interests and it is amazing that we hesitate to use it. Because of that hesitancy the economic improvement which even opponents of the Treaty expected to follow from the establishment of the Free State government has not materialised. The forces making for the destruction of the Irish Nation are still at work. The need for patriotism did not disappear with the handing over of Dublin Castle. In our efforts to bring prosperity to the country, we will find that the spirit of Irish Nationality—will be our first asset, and our surest guarantee of success.[45]

It was fundamentally this programme that was put into practice by the Fianna Fáil government that swept into power in Depression Ireland in 1932. An inevitable consequence of withdrawal from the world (or, in effect, British) market of the time was the accrual of considerable economic and social power into the hands of political leaders, businessmen, civil servants and the administrators of parastatal companies. A large chunk of the economy became controlled by state monopolies, and market considerations were subordinated to political and 'national' considerations and priorities. Ironically, the experience of the 1930s was actually advantageous from the point of view of surviving the World War of 1939–45. Self-sufficiency had its clear advantages in a world at war. Whether it made economic or developmental sense in any medium- to long-term context was arguable. Certainly Sean Lemass himself saw it as arguable at the time. It is quite clear from the memorandum that he anticipated a free-trade Europe at some point in the future and looked forward to Irish participation in it. What he possibly did not foresee is how long he would have to wait to see this come about.

# 02 | CROSSROADS

## THE NATIONALIST JANUS

In 1945, what had become, at least in iconography, de Valera's independent Ireland had reached a tragic crossroads. The tragedy was that, as a political entity, the country did not clearly realise or fully accept the proposition that there was a decision, or rather a series of decisions, to be taken concerning economic policy, foreign relations, foreign trade and educational policy. Once the divisions over the Treaty of 1921–22 softened with the passage of time, public politics, whatever about elite politics, settled into a mainly agrarian pattern and still revolved around the plough versus the cow, land redistribution and the fantasy of settling as many families as possible on the land. There was certainly a less than full acceptance of the proposition that the future might actually be post-agrarian and urban. Not that some did not understand that an urban and non-farm economy was necessary, but rather that they intensely disliked the cultural and civilisational changes that it would entail. Furthermore, they sometimes did not grasp what modernity entailed, while actually wishing, in some vague way, to modernise; occasionally the attitude was caricatured as wanting a new Ireland with all the traditional values and attitudes; Irish nationalists, like Janus, looked both ways. Ireland's leaders were recently urbanised countrymen, and a dislike of urban mores, combined with what sometimes amounted to an inability to understand cities and city life, was common. The

Ireland they celebrated was rural, racy of the soil, an almost Jeffersonian rural democracy, pious, disciplined and folksy: rather cut off from the great world outside, and a real-life version of *The Quiet Man*.

The Ireland that was actually slowly emerging was citified, outward looking, addicted to Anglo-American popular culture, film, swing, jazz and pulp literature. Some few actually looked to continental Europe for cultural sustenance, commonly in a rather modish way. The motor car and the motorcycle symbolised this gradually emerging mobile, individualistic and commercialised society, a society which had made generations of religiously minded Irish patriots uneasy. This clash between the romantic nostalgias of the revolutionaries and a new urbanism had been satirised as early as 1929 in Denis Johnston's expressionist play, *The Old Lady Says No*. In the play, a deluded actor playing Robert Emmet wanders bewilderedly around the streets of modern Dublin, replete with motor cars, flappers, jazz music, bright lights and cheerful proletarians. He babbles patriotic rhetoric (*Since no man knows my reasons, let no man write my epitaph*, etc.), recites James Clarence Mangan's romantic nationalist poetry noisily (*The Erne shall run red with redundance of blood*, etc.) and gets rebuked for bad language by good but uncomprehending citizens. Many of these good citizens are on their way to Irish-language classes to qualify for civil service and teaching jobs in the new Free State. His Cathleen Ní Houlihan appears as a young queen, as Sarah Curran (Emmet's historical and legendary love) and also as a foul-mouthed old woman selling vegetables in Moore Street. The same theme of comic collision between pseudo-Celtic or nineteenth-century romanticism and modern grubby realities underlies Flann O'Brien's classic *At Swim-Two-Birds* (1939) and Eimar O'Duffy's forgotten satires of the 1920s and early 1930s (*King Goshawk and the Birds, Asses in Clover, The Spacious Adventures of the Man in the Street*). In each case, a hero of yesteryear or of Gaelic tradition encounters the anglicised vulgarities of modern urban Ireland. All three Irish writers confront the past with the present, the rural with the urban and the romantic with the everyday reality to devastating comic effect; in each case again, the effect is deeply subversive of the official ideology. The prototype is, of course, Joyce's *Ulysses*.

Many secretly believed that independent Ireland did not have the capacity to make the kinds of decisions that a new departure entailed, while others believed that no such new departure was desirable. Many policy-makers, for example, expected a rerun of the great depression of the 1930s once the dust had settled on the ruins of Europe: back to an imagined repeat of the remembered stasis of the pre-war world. Some evidently expected a reprise of the boom-and-bust scenario that had followed the First World War. Soviet communism was a well-organised, popular and feared force in France, Italy and Germany, and many expected or feared a communist Europe. Many also expected the United States to return to the isolationist posture it had adopted in 1919–20, leaving a prostrate continent to its own feeble devices. In fact, the United States helped mightily to rebuild a Europe that had been wrecked, defended it against the Soviets and worked enthusiastically for a European union that would be an ally and trade partner. Under the Marshall Plan, billions of US dollars were pumped into Europe, including Ireland, to rebuild the shattered continent. Eastern Europe, under Soviet direction, declined Marshall Aid; having first of all been looted by Berlin and Moscow, these countries were then forced, at Moscow's behest, to refuse American bounty.

Few suspected that the entire post-war Western world was about to enjoy, or undergo, what Brian Barry famously referred to as *La Deuxième Belle Epoque*. This consisted of thirty extraordinary years of a capitalist, free market and social democratic economic expansion, accompanied by massive technological, social and cultural change that was to transform the planet and, some would argue, endanger the balance between man and nature—a balance that was, to some extent, still there even at the end of the Second World War.[1] The French referred to this extraordinary period as *les trentes glorieuses*, a period in which the modern world was established in a way which some writers, most conspicuously among them Francis Fukuyama, have actually claimed constitutes an end to history.

During this thirty-year period, per-head incomes commonly doubled, tripled or quadrupled in many Western countries, atomic power became widely used and space travel went from being a fantasy of children and engineers to being almost a cliché. Mass education of a kind and a scale that were utterly unprecedented was supplied by public and private agencies in the more developed countries, the United States being here an impressive and even revolutionary pioneer. Computers started to become everyday necessities rather than esoteric mysteries, occasionally regarded with superstitious fear by religiously minded people. Birth control and equality for women, rather than being underground or bohemian opinions, became openly victorious causes. Sexual life became less regulated and also less secretive. Religious faith and the custom of deferring to the older generation weakened to an extent unimaginable in 1914, or even 1945.

The idea that economic growth could itself be engineered and might continue indefinitely into the future was seriously entertained and arguably achieved in the form of a managed social capitalism. The old European empires of the Netherlands, Belgium, Britain, France and Portugal disintegrated amid a welter of rhetoric about national liberation commonly followed by the rule of wonderfully corrupt dictatorships in the successor states of empire. The failure of many 'Third World' states because of cultural, structural and demographic forces, the incompetence, aggression and corruption of their governments as well as the often exploitative and interfering activities of both Eastern and Western powers, generated an envy of Western achievement which sometimes developed into a settled hatred. A common form of government in many Third World countries was a form of relabelled fascism, commonly praised by certain Western dissident intellectuals simply because it was noisily anti-Western. In the Muslim world, the hatred of Western secularism and envy of its success eventually spawned a series of radical movements fuelled by undereducated young men under the psychological influence of priestly gurus and populist politicians, rather reminiscent of Ireland half a century earlier. Representative democracy became the form of government to which more and more people paid obeisance, in the form of lip service at least and increasingly frequently in practice.

Mass automobilisation, pioneered in the United States in the 1920s by Henry Ford, occurred in Britain, Germany and France in the 1950s and commenced belatedly in Spain, Ireland and Portugal in the 1960s. Huge motorways, pioneered by Weimar and Nazi Germany in the 1920s and 1930s, covered North America, Britain and Italy in the 1950s and France in the Gaullist years. High-speed train networks covered the sub-continent of Western Europe. Cheap and reliable air transport became commonplace and within the means of relatively poor people. The costs of development and overpopulation, in the form of pollution, extinction of species and desertification of fertile lands, also gradually came to be understood two-thirds of the way through this period. Rachel Carson's classic *Silent Spring* (1963) woke a younger generation up to a new collective fear. Rural France began to die, as did, at a remove of about twenty years, rural Ireland. The suburbanisation of the countryside accelerated. Mass education of a kind and of a scale that were historically unprecedented was supplied by private and public agencies, the United States being a pioneer in this area. Links between government, industry, military authorities and education and research intensified.

Education to a relatively advanced level became a reality for entire populations of younger people in the richer countries, the cultural consequences being profound. New freedoms and new rights were claimed and enforced. Legalised racial segregation in the United States became a taboo and was abolished, although intense racial tensions persisted. In London-ruled Northern Ireland, popular protest against discrimination, inspired by the American black people's civil rights campaign of the 1960s, eventually degenerated into near civil war between a sectarian Protestant regime and the Catholic nationalist minority. In many ways, this new global popular culture was American, as was prophesied back in 1930 by the visionary British science fiction writer Olaf Stapleton in his cult classic, *Last and First Men*. Between 1947 and 1984, a heavily armed military stand-off between the United States and the Soviet Union, the two superpowers of the period, threatened nuclear catastrophe and dominated the imaginations of an entire generation. Mainly because of this perceived possibility of atomic disaster, no general war broke out and a long, uneasy peace prevailed, an indescribable atmosphere of fear prevailing within both the Eastern and Western blocs of nations. In the 1950s and 1960s, the grim police tyrannies of Eastern Europe were a bleak shop window for state socialism, and ordinary people understood, and did not like, what they saw, despite the ranting of fashionable leftist journalists, agitators and academics. In the 1980s, European state socialism in the form of the Soviet Union and its client states was eventually to collapse under its own weight and its intellectual absurdity.

This was the international context in which the Irish stagnation of the 1950s occurred. The Irish were being left behind, increasingly relatively poor and irrelevant. Eventually the Irish were to decide to hitch a ride on this extraordinary post-war boom with all its rewards and costs. However, it took fifteen years after 1945 for them to make this painful decision, or even to figure out both that it had to be made and how to make it. After all, they were encysted in the protectionist and effectively clientelist system which de Valera, Lemass and others had constructed with such energy between 1932 and 1948. It also took what amounted to a generational shift in the political elites, and an almost geological change in the power relationships between political, business, bureaucratic and ecclesiastical leaders, for this particular decision to be made. Moreover, it took the economic and social crisis of the mid-1950s to force through a fundamental rethinking of Irish economic policies and shake up the cosy federation of monopolies that dominated Irish political society. Another factor was the astute perception on the part of many of the Irish elites in Fianna Fáil and parts of Fine Gael that a European union of some sort was coming. This development was presaged by international meetings on trade liberalisation among the developed countries in the early 1950s and the summit meeting in Messina in 1955 of the leaders of France, West Germany, Italy, the Benelux countries, Belgium, the Netherlands and Luxembourg. The British didn't bother to attend, partly because they were still thinking, quite incompetently, in imperial terms; to them, Europe was the two defeated powers: the France of 1940 and the Germany of 1945. Free trade was something to do with the Commonwealth and the Empire, rather than something that was going to bind together mainland Europe, the British Isles and the rest of the developed world. Nasser's nationalisation of the Suez Canal was an action that could be reversed by the use of physical force without recourse to American approval, in the minds of the London government. The humiliation of Suez was shortly to follow in 1956; France, Israel and Britain were taken by the scruff of the neck and sent home from Egypt like small boys found breaking windows by the now hegemonic United States of Dwight D. Eisenhower and John Foster Dulles. The Soviet Union took advantage of the debacle to suppress a rebellion in Hungary with great brutality and treachery.

The idea that the new *rapprochement* between Germany and France, as encouraged by the United States, might represent the future rather than the past was far more immediately acceptable to Ireland than to Britain. On average, the Irish were quicker to wake up to the significance of Europe than were the British. In this they were driven by economic interest, but also by nationalism, the wish to get out of Britain's long shadow and an old, if not always well-informed, fascination with France, Spain and Germany. Catholicism also strengthened its European awareness, containing as it did an almost popular cultural conduit to the European mainland. As the old Irish adage had it, the French were on the Sea; the old myth of there being help across the water from mainland Europe was not quite dead in the land of the *Aisling* jacobite poem and of the *Sean-Bhean Bhocht*. The Irish were also listening to the Americans, working determinedly, as they evidently had been since the mid-1940s, for a friendly, anti-Soviet European Union. The Irish looked from afar, peering hungrily over their huge British neighbour's shoulder at the doings on the European mainland, while dickering inconclusively with the friendly, if slightly absent-minded, Americans; the Irish were waking up.

## SINN FÉIN AMHÁIN, IS MUID FÉIN I GCOMHACHT

The heading on this section means literally 'Ourselves alone, and ourselves in power' in the Irish language. Independent Ireland's isolated little polity had spent half a generation trying to build a little world of its own, possibly in a subconscious way, on the model of nineteenth-century England's Splendid Isolation. The Irish had, the humorists might have said, created a condition of Squalid Isolation, an isolation that was to cost the country dearly in the years after 1945. Ireland's inability to react rapidly to the new circumstances of the post-war world was rooted in political circumstance and intellectual paralysis. The root cause of this situation was a polity in which lay and ecclesiastical elites both prevented others from innovating and also prevented each other from embarking on new departures: a blocked polity. By this time, Irish intellectual life had hit some kind of a nadir; the universities were ingrown, impoverished and persecuted by lobbies or ideological monopolies uninterested in intellectual inquiry but insistent on programmes of moral and cultural rearmament. The Anglo-Irish intellectual tradition lived on, but did not match the brilliance of the generation of Yeats. The state-subsidised Abbey Theatre went into decay and was clearly outshone by its private-enterprise rival, the modernist Gate Theatre. Extremely able men and women existed in academia, the schools, in journalism, medicine, the semi-state bodies and the bureaucracy, often in a condition of internal emigration. Their energies commonly tended to be focused on matters scientific, religious, historical or medieval, and economics and the other social sciences were neglected, commonly resented, despised and little understood. The most popular of the academic projects outside the universities was possibly the impressive cadre of scholars who worked on the analysis of the archives of medieval Celtic civilisation in Ireland. These worked under mainly German inspiration, received considerable public attention and even got into the verses of Myles na gCopaleen. Admiringly, he wrote:

> They rose in their night-shift
> To write for the Zeitschrift,
> Binchy and Bergin and Best.
> They proved they were bosses
> At wrastling with glosses,
> Binchy and Bergin and Best,
> They made good recensions
> Of ancient declensions,
> And careful redactions
> To their three satisfactions,
> Binchy and Bergin and Best.

Other than economics, the social sciences tended to be captured by clerical theorists, commonly appointed by the Archdiocese and engaging in teaching the nostrums of the papal encyclicals rather than developing the subjects of political science, anthropology and sociology. Commonly the talents of academics and other intellectuals were used for practical and everyday purposes rather than for medium- to long-term planning. Many academics were, in effect, part-time. Their poet and parodist was the same many-named national satirist, humorist and civil servant, Myles na gCopaleen/Myles na Gopaleen/Flann O'Brien/Brian Ó Nualláin/Brian O'Nolan. Behind his brilliant and scarifying wit lurked a deep sense of cultural despair and an equally deep commitment to Irish democracy. In many ways, the public service evinced a stronger respect for politics and the social sciences than did academia, but it was forced to do so quietly and 'in house' because of the master to servant relationship that existed between elected politician and career public servant.

The most important ideological monopolies were the Catholic Church and the Irish-language revivalists, sometimes jokingly referred to respectively as the forces of Thomas Aquinas and Fionn Mac Cumhaill. These two highly organised lobbies had numbers and political clout behind them, and each of them was, in its way, dedicated to changing the moral and cultural character of the Irish people, rather than being interested in the material development of society. Each had the ear of many of the

politicians in power and was in control of philosophical and
ideological orthodoxies that isolated, marginalised and stifled
dissent and opposition. Professor James Meenan of University
College Dublin (UCD) has left us, in his private diaries, a vivid
and entertaining set of snapshots of both of these lobbies as
experienced by him during the war years and after. An economist
and a reasonably pious liberal Catholic, Meenan maintained a
robustly independent-minded, if rather privately held, attitude
toward the leaders of his own church. In October 1940, he commented critically, if generally quite favourably, on a speech given
at UCD's annual Red Mass by the Catholic Bishop of Derry:
'Remarkably good if with the usual tilts at science which seem to
be common form. Pity that we don't keep up with the times—or
rather that our Church doesn't . . .'

On another formal occasion, in October 1941, he watched the
new Catholic Archbishop of Dublin, John Charles McQuaid,
appointed in 1940 in part at de Valera's behest, perform with a
similar intellectual arrogance and carelessness. Meenan remarked
uneasily and with considerable perspicacity that '[McQuaid] will
either be a great Archbishop or he will inflict irreparable damage
on the position of the Church in Ireland.'[2] McQuaid was a Holy
Ghost (C.S.Sp.) priest, much influenced by right-wing French
Catholic political thought of the period. He had a significant input
into the social and familial ideological features of the 1937
Constitution. He was made Archbishop of Dublin and Primate of
Ireland with the agreement of the government. Despite McQuaid's
being a friend and intellectual colleague of the Taoiseach, de
Valera and his government were to rapidly realise that they had
caught a tartar in him. He quickly moved to become a kind of
ecclesiastical dictator of the Dublin Archdiocese and dominated
much of its civic as well as its religious life in a quite extraordinary
way. His influence was pervasive, affecting schools, housing
developments, newspaper advertisements, marital relationships,
university life and appointments, schoolteachers' employment and
relationships between Catholics, Protestants and Jews. His word
was law in large sections of the Catholic Church, parts of the civil
service, Dublin Corporation, the university colleges and, of

course, the primary and secondary school systems. Trainee primary teachers were turned out by institutions that often combined brilliant teaching with the ethos of a part-time open prison.

McQuaid was an odd mixture of the progressive, the reactionary, the creative and the authoritarian. He built large sexually segregated schools and gargantuan triumphalist churches. He even tried (unsuccessfully) to prevent young women from emigrating to pagan England by denying them passports; civil servants pointed out, quite reasonably, that such a measure would be illegal under the law of the land, quite apart from any other consideration. Dublin Corporation was forbidden by him to build council houses below a certain size, lest small families and contraception be encouraged by lack of bed space. For several years in the late 1940s, McQuaid ensured that vaginal tampons were forbidden and repeatedly complained to the government about the corset advertisements in the *Irish Independent*. He ensured that education was segregated rigidly by sex and creed, helped to modernise the medical health system, exported illegitimate children, probably illegally, to Catholic homes in the United States and had his spies everywhere. He liked women, enjoyed their company and wished them to be good housewives and cooks, on the model of French women of the time. He used pressure on the government to prevent Doctors Robert Collis and James Deeny from setting up an Irish medical mission to the civilian populations of war-torn Europe in 1944, stating that this was a job for the Red Cross. By this time, he had achieved control of that organisation. His contempt for the civil law was extraordinary. His agents sent him reports on every significant public meeting held in the Archdiocese of Dublin between 1940 and 1972.

He was commonly a very kind man in private, who often rescued people in financial or other personal trouble. For example, he was very fond of, and kind to, his fellow Ulster border man, the poet Patrick Kavanagh, keeping him in victuals and drink during hard times. He also disrupted and even destroyed the careers of people who stepped out of line. During the war years, he ensured that Michael O'Donovan (Frank O'Connor, possibly the best Irish short-story writer of the century) and his girlfriend were deprived of state employment in Irish radio on the grounds that they were creating public scandal by living together. Years later, in 1965, he ensured the dismissal of John McGahern, another well-known top-flight Irish writer, from his job in the teaching profession. In both cases, the obsessively sexual nature of the Archbishop's preoccupations was obvious. In the case of McGahern, the Irish National Teachers' Organisation, of which McGahern was a paid-up member, refused to defend him. A little later, in 1966, McQuaid provoked, possibly unintentionally, the resignation of John Whyte, a distinguished Catholic political scientist, from University College Dublin's Department of Ethics and Politics. This resignation and move to Belfast on Whyte's part in 1966 almost certainly was the unintended result of an extraordinary piece of clerical interference and bullying that rebounded upon McQuaid and on UCD. Whyte was in the midst of writing his standard history of the Catholic Church in independent Ireland, later published in 1969; at McQuaid's apparent instigation, his professor and head of Department attempted to forbid him from continuing with this work. The irony was that the resultant scholarly book, finished in Belfast rather than in Dublin, deeply underestimated clerical power in the Irish state and gave the Catholic Church a rather easy ride. Another irony was that Whyte, as a Catholic historian and political scientist, was apparently rather favoured by McQuaid. However, in 1966 bishops didn't know they needed friends. Whyte was to come back to UCD and was Professor of Ethics and Politics between 1984 and 1990. In a very real sense, McQuaid was the patriarchal and eccentric governor of Dublin Archdiocese, where one-third of the state's population lived; he attempted to run an urban society of a million people as though it were a large feudal community.

In 1944, Meenan's worst fears were realised: McQuaid declared it a mortal sin for any Catholic in his Archdiocese to attend the traditionally Protestant Trinity College Dublin (TCD), thereby herding the sons and daughters of the emergent Catholic upper middle class into UCD. Parenthetically, if one were in a state of mortal sin, one was excommunicate and could not enter heaven—a serious threat in 1944. Presumably he intended to starve TCD or, at least, isolate it politically and culturally by denying it new native

blood in the post-war near future. On 2 February 1944, Meenan
wrote in his diary:

> Consternation in College today. Aubrey Gwynn came in with the
> news that next Sunday's Lenten pastoral will make it a mortal sin
> for parents to send their sons to TCD. This is absolutely appalling
> as an indication of what the man will do before he is finished. The
> TCD aspect is bad enough—it is an example of that kind of
> bigotry we have always accused the North of and have prided
> ourselves that we were free from. But the UCD outlook is far
> worse. Obviously the AB [i.e. Archbishop] wants to make TCD a
> purely Protestant institution—then he will advance on us and
> make us into a Catholic University in which priests must neces-
> sarily rule lay men will be a species of lay brother. This would be
> the most awful disaster imaginable—quite apart from the personal
> angle that no Irish Catholic would ever get a proper university
> education and it would certainly let loose a flood of anti-
> clericalism . . . If this is to be the line of policy all Ireland will be
> anti-clerical in a generation.[3]

Meenan could see that McQuaid's power-seeking and high-
handedness would generate a long-term hostile reaction to the
Catholic Church, an event which duly occurred in the 1960s and
afterwards. He also disliked and feared in particular the clerical
influence on the political attitudes of Catholic undergraduates. In
December 1944, he commented uneasily on the 'dangerous
ignorance and Semi-Fascism' of many UCD students.[4] It should
be reiterated that Meenan was no closet anti-cleric himself, but a
liberal Catholic; for example, he liked and admired the Professor
of Ethics and Politics of the time, Fr Denis O'Keefe. Later in the
decade, he watched with a hostile and wary eye the rise to power
within the UCD power structure of Monsignor John Denis
Horgan, McQuaid's chosen watchdog within the largest college in
the National University of Ireland. In effect, the Archbishop was
attempting to set up a vetting system for future members of the
ruling class in the country, with himself as the director and the
Monsignor as his demiurge. In July 1950, Meenan commented on

the Monsignor's attempt to become a member of the Governing Body of the College: 'if he gets in he will be a damned unpleasant member of the Governing Body.' Horgan won a seat, and Meenan subsequently wrote '. . . Horgan is quite insufferably pleased with himself and I feel that his election will yet cause more trouble to the College than either of the Gaels.'[5]

Horgan became McQuaid's agent in UCD, keeping a watchful eye on the religious lives and intellectual opinions of the professors, lecturers and students, particularly in the moral sciences: philosophy, politics, ethics, sociology, psychology, logic and education. Horgan's inquisitorial style of dealing with people became notorious and persisted as a curious practice right up to the late 1960s. His power then faded, but persisted for some time in the Department of Metaphysics (later styled Department of Philosophy). He is reputed to have submitted regular reports on UCD to McQuaid, and his files in the Archdiocesan archive are sealed until 2009, most others from the period being open. In 1951, Meenan noted about a sermon by the Bishop of Kilmore that its main theme was the necessity of teachers of science, politics and economics to push the Catholic viewpoint more energetically: '. . . just that kind of arrogant ignorance of what people are doing —not that it is really ignorance, rather carelessness, and the arrogance is unintended, which may make it worse—that irritates people.'[6] Meenan resisted attempts to clericalise his Department, thereby ensuring that the possibility of developing a cadre of secular and professional economists in the future would not be closed off by clerical interference.

The other pressure group was the Gaelic League (*Conradh na Gaeilge:* the 'Gaels' of Meenan's diary). Founded in 1893, this cultural organisation was dedicated to the celebration and revival of Irish traditional music, dancing and the re-establishment of the Irish language as the spoken tongue of the population. It was informed by a heavily Victorian version of what Celtic civilisation in Ireland had been all about. For example, the fact that Gaelic society in Ireland and Scotland had such allegedly un-Irish customs as gossipred, fostering, corruption of the blood, blood feud, divorce, relative sexual equality and polygyny tended to be passed over or even repressed. The League had been infiltrated and taken over between 1900 and 1915 by extreme nationalists in the form of the Irish Republican Brotherhood. Like the Gaelic Athletic Association, the League was a major ideological influence on the young men and women who became the elite of the Irish state after 1922. A majority of the leaders of the new polity had been members of the League in pre-independence days and the ideological thinking of the Irish Volunteers (the 'Old IRA') had been heavily coloured by the League as well.

It is clear that the ideology and cult of the League affected these young men and women profoundly. Certainly, the young men of the Irish Republican Army and the young women of Cumann na mBan had their heads stuffed full of neo-Gaelic ideology and idealism, much of it informed as well by a fundamentalist Catholicism that, among other well-known evils, commonly denounced the evidently Protestant or even atheistic idea that the Church and the state should be separated. Few pointed out that the much admired United States had just such a principle as a foundation stone of its constitution. After independence, although the Gaelic League lost much of its dynamism and ideological fervour, it pressed ahead determinedly, the ambivalent sympathies of government behind it, with the Quixotic project of changing the native language of the vast majority of the Irish people from English to Irish. A curious aggression and self-righteousness suffused the Gaelic League, as was the case in many other Irish public organisations of the period. This was, after all, a period which was dominated politically by people who had gone through an experience of revolutionary fervour and *Fronterlebnis*, and who wished for younger people to share in some such similar spiritual or emotional enthusiasm.

The political and cultural isolation of the country during the war years emboldened the League, much as it emboldened integralist Catholicism. In 1943, the League opposed the appointment of W.J. Williams to the Chair of Education in UCD on the grounds that his command of the Irish language was insufficient. In March of the same year, a mass march on UCD's premises in Earlsfort Terrace was organised by Gaelic League activists demonstrating in favour of making the College provide lectures in Irish as well as, or even in place of, English. According to Meenan, the march was broken up by 'hostile students and water hoses.'[7] Professor George O'Brien, Meenan's fellow economist and lifelong friend, regarded the League as 'fascist' at that time, remarking that he believed that de Valera really would like to get rid of all staff members in the College who were unable or unwilling to speak Irish. This was possibly unfair to the Taoiseach, but de Valera certainly put considerable pressure on the College to supply academic lectures in the Irish language, a language little understood by the vast majority of the population.[8] University College Galway had already begun to provide lectures in the language. In the meantime, Irish economic life stagnated under wartime conditions, as was inevitable. Meenan wrote in November 1943, quoting a conversation he had had with his opposite number in Trinity, Joseph Johnston, concerning the parlous state of Irish agriculture, echoing unconsciously the opinions of Sean MacEntee,

... Johnston came in and denounced the Government and agreed with Kennedy on winter-feeding and silage and said farms are growing too small and without even the attention paid to pigs and poultry that could keep small farms in some kind of prosperity. His point however and I agree altogether is that no one and certainly the Government least of all have any conception of increasing output and income. They are all fighting over redistribution of what is already there. There is no attempt to increase the stock. This is only too true—and as good a commentary as any on the complete stagnation of our life. It applies to far more than agriculture.[9]

Meenan's little world of Dublin academia mirrored the slightly larger world of independent Ireland during the decades of the war and post-war era. While the economy stood still, various forces fought for larger slices of a cake which effectively remained the same size, or even got smaller at times: GNP shrank by perhaps 16 per cent during the war years. In effect, Irish politics became zero-sum: anything you gained, I lost. Again, while many individuals worried helplessly about the apparent perversity of economic, social and cultural policies, few seemed determined enough or were in the right political position to do much about it. The Catholic Church monopolised virtually all of Irish primary and secondary education and seemed on course to establish something like a near monopoly of third-level education in the philosophically key intellectual areas of the humanities and social sciences in all third-level colleges other than Trinity College Dublin. The Catholic takeover of huge areas of economic, social and cultural life, whether directly through clerical control or indirectly through secret societies such as the Knights of Columbanus was quite extraordinarily successful. The main effect of all this energy was to inhibit the intellectual development of, and free inquiry in, the social sciences and social philosophy in the period 1940–70.

Using the wisdom of hindsight, it becomes apparent that the war years of 1939–45 were, however, something of a strange interlude in Irish political history. While the rest of Europe was convulsed by the greatest cataclysm that it had seen for centuries, little neutral Eire kept its collective head down and pretended that nothing was happening, or, if it was happening, that it was happening somewhere very far away in a place of which little was known. Ireland felt like a rather down-at-heel sitting room with a large rhinoceros sitting in the corner while everyone pretended it wasn't really there. Censorship of war news was draconian. Tim Pat Coogan described it graphically as *Huis Clos* on a national scale. 'At the end [of the Second World War], many young Irish people had never seen a coloured person or even a continental European.' On the other hand, thousands of Irish men and women worked in British war industries or served loyally in the British armed forces in Britain and all the theatres of war, coming home occasionally to what seemed to be the Land that Time Forgot. The classic joke of the period celebrates the Irish bomber navigator caught in flak over Berlin, muttering to himself 'thank God Dev kept us out of all this.' The Irish playwright Denis Johnston, in his classic memoir *Nine Rivers from Jordan*, described independent Ireland rather entertainingly and fondly as the Fortunate Isle. From time to time, he came home to meet his old friends in the pubs of Dublin, existing in a continuum apart from the real world whose monstrousness he was witnessing as a war correspondent with the allied armies.[10]

Nor was there ever a complete intellectual closedown, despite the draconian moral censorship, the shortage of newsprint and the equally draconian censorship of news; Ireland had some bossy, xenophobic, bigoted and even totalitarian-minded rulers, but they certainly did not have things all their own way. Most famously, perhaps, Sean O'Faolain's liberal and humanist *The Bell* continued to appear throughout the war years, as did the relatively free-thinking Jesuit intellectual magazine, *Studies*; it remained a free country, unusually enough in a Europe of fascism, authoritarian Catholic conservatism and communism. Despite the rhetoric of some and the hypocrisy of other *soi-disant* patriots, independent Ireland remained, tacitly, a protectorate of the British and American liberal and democratic alliance. Civil law, although commonly bent to clerical and neo-Gaelic purposes, remained relatively liberal and usually reasonably respectful of human rights. Furthermore, free debate about the desirability of different relationships between Church and state was never curbed, and the real problem was the classic Tocquevillian one of majority tyranny, but a majority tyranny which itself begrudgingly but authentically accepted the rights of free speech. The haters of free speech were generally small groups of well-organised and not automatically popular people within the Catholic Church, the political parties and other public organisations.

From the point of view of one observer from Northern Ireland, admittedly a fairly privileged one, the south didn't look too bad at all. James Deeny, a young Lurgan Catholic doctor and brilliant epidemiologist, was to become Chief Medical Adviser to the Irish government in 1944. Deeny remembered coming to Dublin from Northern Ireland in 1943 and being struck by the intellectual and psychological liveliness of the city compared to his native Lurgan or even Belfast; from his point of view, Dublin was the capital of the entire island. Admittedly, northern Catholics 'coming south' often felt a natural sense of liberation and release, one that was also sometimes felt by northern Protestants, interestingly enough. Despite everything, independent Ireland had a traditional easygoing character that was attractive, and Dublin was a town of free speech, despite its notorious crocodile-tank intelligentsia, occasionally claustrophobic cultural atmosphere, overweening clerical establishment and official censorship. Deeny was a Catholic, and heavily involved in social action of a kind approved of by the Church; he fell in love with independent Ireland, a country to which he was to contribute so much. Southern sectarianism was a milder beast, even if in some ways a more insidious one, than its northern counterpart. In any case, being a Catholic was not problematic in the south, whereas being a Protestant generally entailed being a member of a small, perhaps somewhat besieged but commonly privileged minority. Deeny wrote a generation later, in words that he repeated many times to this writer with considerable fervour:

> Coming to Dublin was wonderful. For the first time I discovered my country and began the process of getting the repression and bitterness of the North out of my system. Everybody had opinions and expressed them, and to me the atmosphere was heady . . . You were not the recipient of the odd warning to watch what you said and so on . . . I had to realise I was watching a national democracy in place of what I had hitherto experienced, the one-party, long-continuing repressive, fascist-type rule in the North.

A similar portrait of Dublin's intellectual scene comes from a rather unexpected source—a part-time British agent in Ireland, the well-known writer Elizabeth Bowen:

> . . . on the whole, I was struck, in all circles, by the intelligence (if not always the wisdom) and the animation of the talk. The stereotyped, or completely conditioned, mind seemed to me rarer in Dublin than in London . . . officially the Irish R.C. church is opposed to progress, as not good for the people.[11]

At least there was political discussion, and even some intellectual give-and-take, in what were evidently terrible times. Deeny and other senior civil servants and politicians during the war years found themselves improvising desperately from day to day in conditions of extreme shortages and financial penury. Lack of means in the form of money and materials meant that plans, often very ambitious and far-reaching plans at that, could be drawn up in government departments, but nothing much could be done until the war ended. Like the people of Limerick in *Angela's Ashes*, the Irish would have to wait for the death of Hitler.[12] Sulpha drugs (antibiotics), necessary to wipe out the contagious diseases that were widespread, were unavailable and were to remain an American military monopoly until late 1945; tar for the roads was completely unavailable and there was virtually no petrol. Artificial fertilisers were non-existent and the soil of the country was becoming exhausted, a condition that it did not recover from for years after the war.

On the other side of the ledger, so to speak, the country remained physically untouched by war, most people ate adequately and standards of living, though not high, were reasonable for most people. Visitors from Britain commonly came to the country to escape the wartime rationing of foodstuffs that had been, inevitably, imposed on industrial Britain far more severely than on agrarian Ireland; Dublin steak houses did a thriving cross-channel trade. English 'wide boys' and 'spivs' (crooks) used Ireland's formal independence to mastermind shadowy financial schemes, versions of which entered local folklore. In an ironic sense, Ireland's rurality and closeness to a barter economy was the country's saving. Transport was horse-drawn, fertile land was, relative to the small population, quite plentiful and an essentially Victorian economy served the population reasonably well. The war, however, also reinforced Victorian thinking; reversion to a Victorian horse-and-cart economy entailed something of a cultural reversion as well.

Although simply keeping the country going on a shoestring in circumstances of considerable deprivation and even penury was demanding and rather soul destroying, considerable thought was given to what shape the country was to take in an anticipated post-war era. Once it was clear that such a world was not going to be dominated by the Axis powers but rather by the Anglo-Americans and the Soviets, the fear of Germany receded and concern with military matters waned. Was post-war Ireland going to be welfarist, as was proposed for the United Kingdom by Beveridge? If so, was the state, much feared as a Trojan Horse for statism, secularism, socialism and even communism, to dominate such a welfare system? Alternatively, it was envisaged by some that a system should be devised by which vocational bodies such as the medical profession and the churches essentially dominated health-care systems, while the churches and the teachers ran the school systems with mainly passive backing from the governmental Department of Education. In effect, this meant that a confronta-tion of sorts, or series of confrontations, between the Catholic Church and an essentially Catholic but also essentially democratic state might ensue. Again, the debate between rail and road transport began in earnest at this time, a debate that some would argue is still stuck in a debilitating deadlock half a century later. Furthermore, it was at this time that the first notions of expanding the second- and third-level educational systems were expressed seriously, sometimes in a mood of rather pessimistic realism, sometimes in a rather airy-fairy way, but occasionally with considerable creativity and vision.

In a very real sense, the decade of the 1940s witnessed a refound-ing of the polity, a refounding made possible by the death of Treaty politics and the fading energies of the revolutionary generation of political leaders. There was a widespread perception that the issues of 1922 were dead, and the divisions crystallised at that time had become meaningless and sterile. The decision to declare a republic, made by the Inter-Party government in 1948, reflected this awareness and was intended to kill 'Civil War politics' off. The Taoiseach, John A. Costello, actually put it that way: he wished, he said repeatedly, to take the gun out of Irish politics. For independent Ireland, the declaration of the Republic actually worked, completing the process of political legitimisation that had commenced in 1922. The declaration of the Republic of Ireland in 1949 was the end, rather than the beginning, of this process of moving to new issues and controversies.[13] The fact that things ended after 1945 while other things did not really begin was the secret tragedy of independent Ireland; the move to new issues was slow and uneven, more progress being made in some areas than others. There was an exhaustion of ideas, stifling orthodoxies were enthroned in Church and state and new ideas were slow to take root. The Republic ended something just when everything was starting elsewhere in Europe and America; Ireland missed the bus and many opportunities were not grasped, were rejected out of hand or simply not seen. The fact that Ireland had not been touched by war was, in an ironic way, a disadvantage; there was little widespread sense of the urgent need for a new departure in policy. The difficulty was partly one of mentality or political culture and partly structural. Irish democracy was both populist and profound, but also conformist, authoritarian and static. Neither culture nor structures were geared to developmentalism, and forces resistant to change were deeply ensconced in Church, state, the trade unions, business and professional groups, the huge small-farm community of the period and the general population.

The general effect was a condition of social stasis tempered by piecemeal reformism of an occasionally remarkable quality. It was almost as though these odd sparks of brilliance were there to suggest what the country could do if it ever really woke up. For example, under Dr Roy Geary, Ireland enjoyed one of the more advanced central statistics offices in the developed world; again, health care became strikingly modern in the 1950s. Irish weather forecasting services were state of the art. Moreover, the reconstruction by historical science of the medieval Irish world was embarked upon at this time. Independent Ireland had a rather advanced political structure, but it housed an older society, Victorian and, to some extent, even pre-Famine in its cultural and social roots. In the anthropological terms of Clifford Geertz, the new polity constituted a very strong society but a rather weak state whose very legitimacy had been dearly purchased. The price had been not just the physical destruction of the Civil War or the psychological embitterment of a generation of elites, but also the growth of a cultural pessimism that endangered all initiatives designed to modernise the country and lift it out of its under-developed condition.

**FUTURE DREAMS**

On 24 July 1942, the Department of Finance, under the by-line of
Sean T. O'Kelly, wrote to the Department of the Taoiseach
concerning the need to plan for the post-war era. The general line
taken was hostile to the use of state aid to help advance economic
development. O'Kelly wrote '. . . in general, it seems to me that
departments should plan with a view to increasing the prosperity
of the several sections of the community more fully by means of
their own exertions and by cooperation and less by taking the easy
line of having recourse to state aid.' Agriculture was seen as the
prospective motor of economic development, a theme which was
to recur during the following twenty years.[14] A clipping on the file
from *The Irish Times* of 11 November 1942 noted that economic
problems after the war were going to be 'vast', and a major problem
would be immigration of redundant Irish workers from Britain after
the suspension of hostilities. The post-war era was looked forward to
in trepidation rather than with hope, and the idea that the war
might be followed by a great boom simply was not entertained.
The actual turn of events seriously wrong-footed the Republic.
Again, oil was expected to be expensive in the post-war era, understandably enough, and this expectation was used to legitimate the
immediate extensive exploitation of the bogs for fuel. Development
of peat as a fuel was an obsession of Frank Aiken's that was
indulged by Sean Lemass and administered energetically by that
well-known public servant of the period, Todd Andrews.

The Anglo-American takeover of the sources of Middle East oil
was not predicted, and the proposition that cheap Middle Eastern
oil might be more sensibly used than the safe, but wasting, assets
of the Irish bogs was not entertained. Suggestions for post-war
priorities included a merchant navy, afforestation, housing, rural
electrification, quarries and fisheries.[15] A note from the Department
of Local Government and Public Health, dated 14 February 1942,
recommended visionary plans for fast roads around Dublin,
permitting speeds of seventy-five miles per hour, with bypasses for
other major towns.[16]

Lemass, Minister for Supplies and an energetic public propo-
nent of developmentalism in a culture that was less than enthused

by such ideas, was already demonstrating his capacity for mixing extreme pragmatism with a visionary futurism. As early as October 1941, he bemoaned the 'statification' of society that warfare had generated, and as early as December 1944 he called for post-war expansion of technical education. He also reminded his listeners that the post-war recovery was going to be international, not something to be achieved by many independent nations operating in isolation. He certainly grasped very early on that the education of the general population and technical education in particular were the keys to the future. However, many others, some of them in positions of influence, did not. Lemass pointed to Ireland's pre-war total dependence on UK trade, despite the best efforts of twenty years of native government. Presciently he went on to remark '. . . we must make certain that we will partici-pate in the general [international] recovery when it comes, and that is a matter mainly for ourselves.' Two years later, he was already, prophetically as it turned out, poor-mouthing agriculture and claiming that manufacturing was the real future of the Irish economy.

By 1945, Lemass was ensconced in a key position in the Fianna Fáil cabinet. In that year, the Department of Supplies was amal-gamated with the Department of Industry and Commerce under Lemass. *The Irish Times* wrote in wonderment:

How has it come about that his Department—now housed in the State's only new pile of public buildings—has spread its activities over every important branch of the country's economic life and organisation? How is it that services so varied as public transport by rail, sea and air; electricity supplies; employment exchanges and industrial insurance; trades union organisation; price controls; census and statistical records; the disposition and supervision of manufacturing industries; the regulation of import tariff and export bounties; the distribution of children's allowances; tourist development, and the organisation of all productive activities save some which pertain to agriculture, fall to the lot of the Department of Industry and Commerce?[17]

Other departments also made recommendations, as the Department of the Taoiseach had suggested, concerning 'Post War Planning'. The Department of Education responded in Irish in June 1944 to the effect that many new school buildings were needed, but emphasised, in its usual helpless fashion, that the government would have to run everything past the bishops.[18] Industry and Commerce bemoaned the deleterious influence of the war on the building industry.[19] The Department of Local Government and Public Health wrote again in May 1944, reiterating its concern with the inadequacies of the Irish road system: 'long-term planning to secure that the road system will develop according to standards that have been laid down and related to the faster and denser motor-traffic that is expected to appear over the next fifty years. Under this latter head is included the reconstruction of the country's arterial highways.' Bypasses were to be provided for the Dublin satellite towns of Swords, Santry and Stillorgan.[20] These bypasses were eventually built, but only after more than a generation of neglect had gone by.

However, by mid-1948, the new Minister for Local Government, Tim Murphy of the Labour Party, was commenting not on the inadequacy of the road system, but on the decline of the railway system and the undesirable diversion of increasing amounts of traffic to the road system, such as it was. The trade unions in the form of the Transport Union and the railway lobby, together with the housing programme, had clearly defeated the roads lobby.[21] Railways and railwaymen were national and for the working man; motorcars and motorists were quite evidently bourgeois and elitist. The Department of Industry and Commerce seemed to have few new ideas. In October 1945, a memorandum from that department commented:

When the government took up office in 1932 they initiated an industrial policy which had for its object the establishment and development of industries in this country for which it was clear there was adequate scope and an adequate market—a policy designed to establish a better balance between agriculture and manufacturing industry. To this end, protection was afforded by the Government for the purpose of developing existing industries and with a view to establishing new industries, particularly in their early stages, to meet competition from outside the country so as to assist them to surmount those initial difficulties which are inherent in most, if not all, newly established ventures of the kind.

The memorandum continued by noting the early establishment of the Industrial Credit Corporation and the then still extant policy of favouring Irish ownership; implicit was the accompanying policy of discouraging foreign capital. In July 1946, it reported to the Taoiseach: 'The Minister's general objective will be to do everything possible to have trade and commerce restored to normal conditions on the general basis of his policy in the pre-Emergency period of giving protection to native industry so as to secure maximum employment.'[22] These policies had, in effect, survived the depression and the World War and there seemed no real or urgent sense of a need for any drastic change. Policies suitable for a world in depression and a general preparation for war in the 1930s were seen as suitable for the very different world of American commercial hegemony and European free trade which was already being born.

However, the dog that *really* didn't bark was education, blocked as it was by powerful ideological lobbies. In April 1944, *The Irish Times* commented perceptively in a leading article on official attitudes to education, attitudes discussed in more detail in Chapter 4. The Department of Education, the leader noted, was a 'sleeping partner' and seemed to have no sense of the importance of an educated workforce to any future programme of economic development. It was to be another twenty years before this proposition, so vital to development and modernisation, was to be openly accepted by the official mind as a valid point of view. The profound and liberating idea of investment in human capital was pre-eminently a German and American idea in the early twentieth century, and it was an idea that took time to take root in Ireland. *The Irish Times* commented acidly at the time:

Amid an increasing flow of statements from various Ministers upon post-war conditions and policies, the voice of the Minister of

Education seldom is heard. The reason for his silence can be that he is reluctant to make promises which he may be unable to fulfil; or it can simply be that he has nothing to say. So far as we are aware, he has committed himself to one aim only—the revival of the Gaelic language, of which he is one of the warmest advocates . . .[23]

The paper returned to the fray in August 1944, ascribing the alleged decline in educational standards in the country since 1922 to the bending of the system to the project of general language change at the behest of the Gaelic League.[24] The Minister for Education was an old War of Independence veteran, Thomas Derrig, originally a teacher in a Mayo technical school and indeed an ardent advocate of the revival of Irish through the school system. He had been a student leader in University College Galway during the campaign for independence and had lost an eye during the conflict. The official obsession with the language question persisted throughout the 1950s. This was a period in which the spelling system of the language was rather drastically modernised, the Munster dialect was demoted, moves toward standardisation on the Connacht dialect were made and, for the second time in a generation, the alphabet was changed. These changes mightily bemused and annoyed generations of Anglophone schoolchildren. Meanwhile, the Gaeltachts continued to shrink.

A Council of Education, set up in 1950, reported for the first time in 1954. It emphasised the importance of the Irish language and recommended, quite extraordinarily, that the school-leaving age remain at fourteen; in the United Kingdom it had already been raised to fifteen. Significantly, three members refused to sign the report, one of them a Protestant clergyman, one a state psychiatrist and one a well-known agricultural educationalist. Of thirty-one original members, twelve were clerics, five were non-Catholics and at least five were committed exponents of the orthodoxy of language revival.[25] Many of them were clearly close, temperamentally and ideologically, to a rural culture which saw education beyond a certain level as unnecessary. It must be remembered that in parts of rural Ireland, wives commonly were more educated than their farmer or labourer husbands, the better to do the accounts of the household. Comments on the generally low educational levels in the country were common enough. In 1945, Deeny noted that the lack of post-graduate education '... [has] to my mind been responsible for much of the spiritless mediocrity in quality of a proportion of the medical work in Ireland.' It is striking to note that Donal McCartney's apparently standard Thomas Davis lecture on education policy during the period concerns itself, quite extraordinarily, with language revival *tout court* and has nothing whatsoever to say about educational policy as such.[26] In this, it quite accurately reflects the actual state of affairs at that time. The appalling fact was that there was no overall agreed educational policy whatsoever, other than the policy of linguistic revival and intensification of religious conditioning through the school system. After Fianna Fáil's electoral defeat in 1948, Erskine Childers travelled around the country to do a post mortem. Intriguingly, he wrote that Fine Gael voters in particular were voting against Fianna Fáil because of their perceptions of the educational system's utter inadequacy. '[It is] because they fundamentally believe that the educational system is bad. No domestic economy. No "rural science".' The physical condition of the schools was, he reported, 'appalling'. Fianna Fáil supporters were utterly cynical about the language-revival project, regarding it as a racket that gave them employment, he wrote:

> ... apart altogether from whether it is right or wrong to teach Irish intensively, the men brought from the Gaeltacht to become teachers in many cases have neither the personality nor the qualifications for such work. I was amazed at the appearance, the clothes, and the absence of cleanliness among many of our own Fianna Fáil supporters who were teaching and whom I met during the election; I was amazed too at the number who were obviously heavy drinkers.

The rural lack of interest in further education was weaker in Fine Gael because of the relatively middle-class 'bourgeois' character of the party's support base. The general lack of public political concern about education in the 1940s is quite striking, particularly when one considers, for example, Sean Lemass's prescient and public commitment as early as 1924 to the principle of free education. At a by-election in that year, he had committed himself rhetorically to free education. This was visualised as 'including free books and luncheon' and a 'proper system of scholarships', which would allow the child of the poorest parent to get to third-level education 'if sufficiently brilliant', while recouping his parents the opportunity cost of the loss of his services to the family. John Sheehan, an expert on the economics of education, has commented mildly and devastatingly that the massive reforms in education that occurred elsewhere in Europe after 1945 'largely passed Ireland by . . . the period 1945 to 1962 is, by contrast to what happened later, one of stagnation.' The number of scholarships remained tiny, and although secondary school enrolment increased considerably and the universities showed some expansion, these changes owed little to state policy and much to parental demand for further education for their children.[27] Something had happened to education, or rather, nothing much had; the dog, or rather dogs, that didn't bark in the night added up to a pack of very large Irish Catholic clerical and neo-Gaelic wolfhounds, whose collective obstructiveness and obscurantism amounted to a public scandal. Lemass was not in a position to take up the cudgels for education until the very end of his political career in the 1960s, when much was done to considerable effect in an extraordinary, if very belated, burst of reformism.

## LIFE AND DEATH

Health issues were destined to be the source of much political controversy in the post-war years, unlike education, which slept on until the early 1960s. Health was a huge problem; tuberculosis (TB), polio, diphtheria and venereal disease (VD) in the forms both of syphilis and gonorrhoea were common. In the case of VD in particular, ideological and psychological barriers militated against the disease being tackled scientifically. De Valera's government had abolished the weekly prophylactic issue ('rubbers') in the Army in 1932 at the behest of the Catholic Church, thereby causing the venereal disease rate within and without the armed forces to rocket. As Francis Hackett put it, de Valera's government abolished the routine issue of contraceptives in the armed forces while 'ignoring the increase of syphilis which was bound to follow and which did follow.' Perhaps it was just as well that the Irish Army remained small during most of the period. However, the Archbishop of Dublin, John Charles McQuaid, very honourably eventually forced Catholic hospitals in his jurisdiction in the late 1940s to treat diseases that many Catholics tried to pretend did not exist, or alternatively, if they were recognised as existing, were to be regarded as the (very just) wages of sin. Health was an ecclesiastical obsession because of its close connection to matters of sex, reproduction and marriage.

In 1944, a rather revealing turf war erupted between John Dignan, Bishop of Clonfert, and Sean MacEntee, then Minister for Local Government and Public Health. This revolved around the prelate's proposed reorganisation of the health services under an insurance scheme to be administered by a vocational council derived from the National Health Insurance Society. MacEntee and the department argued that this would create an extra government, unelected and not responsible to parliament, effectively with taxing powers and controlled by doctors and ecclesiastics rather than democratically elected politicians. The department wrote, in the body of a sustained analysis of the Dignan proposals, that they would cost more than double the existing system. Essentially the civil servants argued that the good bishop did not know what he was talking about. They emphatically argued that he was advocating a return to an obsolete and long-abolished system.

The [Dignan] Plan is advocated as one of decentralisation, yet it is a plan for centralising in one Board the powers now vested in many local bodies. However, it would not presumably take over their powers in regard to preventive medicine and housing, so that there would be two health systems side by side, one under a Minister and Parliamentary Secretary responsible to the Oireachtas, the other under an 'untrammelled' Board. This would not be co-ordination; it would be disintegration . . . The removal of health administration from out of the political sphere has been advocated by the protagonists of particular schools of social reform in other countries. Our Constitution gives no countenance to such a radical departure from the principles of democratic control . . . The concentration of patronage in the hands of a body not subject to the usual constitutional safeguards would also carry with it obvious dangers. It is not enough to say that only 'the best available' men and women of proved business or administrative capacity above reproach in their actions and motives, public minded, unselfish, whose only interest will be to do the very best for the [Insurance] Society would be on the Boards and Committee.

MacEntee aggressively announced that he would not tolerate proposals emanating from an unnamed subordinate official in his Department which proposed removing an entire area of public activity from democratic control. The proposal died in favour of the establishment of a regular Department of Health. This was the first approximation to a Church versus state clash that the country had seen since 1922, and prefigured the events of 1951. Dignan was not particularly representative of the hierarchy (a 'Fianna Fáil bishop') and was a relatively easy target. MacEntee received letters of congratulation from several people couching their opinions in anti-clerical terms. A wine and brandy agent in Dundalk congratulated MacEntee in characteristically Irish moderately anti-clerical tones:

It is strong action of this kind that can only save our state from being ruled by Clerics. The Church is right when it minds its own calling, but many of the Clergy are becoming too interfering in State and Commercial matters. I may also add that many people I have come in contact with approve of your action in above matter.

However, various local authorities and local trade union bodies, in particular the Irish Women Workers' Union, sympathised with the good bishop.[28]

Meanwhile, under the emergent Department of Health of Conor Ward and James Deeny, an ambitious programme of health service reforms was instituted. Dr Noel Browne, Minister for

Health 1948–51, spearheaded a TB eradication scheme that had been drawn up and initiated by the previous Fianna Fáil government. TB eradication had been a priority of Irish medical science for some time, St Ultan's Hospital in Dublin being the centre of early research. Under the pioneering guidance of two medical scientists, Dorothy Stopford Price and Pearl Dunlevy, in 1937 Dublin city was the first city in Britain or Ireland to introduce the BCG vaccine which prevented TB. Early inspiration for these workers came from the Scandinavian systems of the period.

Noel Browne and John Horgan have, between them, given a vivid portrait of the horrific effects TB had on thousands of Irish families. Horgan's Browne emerges as an agonised and impassioned man. Looming over his whole life was the curse of TB; both of his parents and two of his sisters died of this disease which, two generations later, is almost unknown in Ireland or, if contracted, is normally swiftly cured. To be a member of a 'tubercular family' was almost to be a pariah in some quarters, and families lived in terror of this almost incomprehensible menace. Horgan relates that Browne's oldest sister, Eileen, who had been a pivotal figure in the move to London and who had actually been essentially a 'surrogate mother' to the entire family in the 1930s, fell ill with TB. She had been sent in the first place to a sanatorium in Hazlemere in Sussex and afterwards had been sent on, in pursuit of purer air as was the medical fashion of the period, to a medical facility in Italy. However, by then her disease was far too advanced for the treatments available, and she died tragically in 1937.[29]

Infant mortality was high by modern standards, but not bad by the standards of the time; well over fifty babies died per thousand mothers in 1949, the modern figure (1999) being well under ten, one of the best such figures in the world.[30] To be fair, the 1949 figure was a substantial improvement on the figure at independence, and good by the standards of inter-war Europe. Deaths of mothers in circumstances of childbirth numbered about 100 in 1949 and numbered about one per year, by way of contrast, in 1999, in an admittedly smaller and younger cohort of mothers (about 75 per cent in absolute terms).[31] Of children aged between one and four, 723 died of various diseases in 1949. Again by way of contrast, 64 died in 1998, over one quarter of these deaths being from non-disease and accidental causes (injury and poisoning). In the 1940s, pneumonia and TB were the chief child-killers; nowadays they scarcely feature. Deaths of mothers were far less common in Dublin than elsewhere in the state because of the existence of three good maternity hospitals in the city and an extensive maternity and child-welfare system. During the war years, these death rates actually increased; the death rates for babies approached nearly eighty per thousand at one stage.[32]

Browne, partly goaded by the left wing of the Labour ministers in the cabinet, in particular William Norton, attempted to set up a comprehensive, free medical-care system, an initiative which promptly involved him in a head-to-head clash with the hierarchy, which he lost in 1951. The bishops were evidently in turn prompted by the Irish Medical Association, acting, like nearly everyone else, in defence of its own collective interest. In particular, the idea that public officials should instruct pregnant women on personal and sexual hygiene mobilised the rather evident subconscious or even conscious sexual obsessions of these usually, if occasionally notionally, celibate men. Browne was destroyed politically in the short term, but became a popular hero and martyr as the man who had taken on the doctors and the bishops to give the poor liberation from the scourge of tuberculosis. He was able to build a second political career on this foundation in popular folklore. Very clearly, the long-term loser, fairly or otherwise, was to be the Catholic Church; the decline in clerical Catholic power in independent Ireland can quite clearly be dated from this incident and the Dignan affair of some years earlier, although it took some time for this to become generally obvious.

## AUTHORITARIANISM AND DEMOCRACY: GOVERNMENT AND SOCIETY

The ruling ideology in the country was familial; the family was held to be the natural building block of society, and the state was enjoined by the Constitution of 1937 to foster the traditional patriarchal family. This family structure derived historically from the emergent free-farmer, owner-occupier yeoman democracy that had evolved out of the Land Acts of 1881–1903. Children were practically the personal property of their parents, and social worker supervision of dysfunctional families scarcely existed. By extension and analogy, priests, brothers and nuns *in loco parentis* had similar unchecked and unsupervised powers over the children committed to their charge in day schools, boarding schools, industrial schools (the equivalent of borstal schools) and orphanages. Physical assault and sexual abuse were eminently possible and quite widespread, essentially because there was no lay or civic control over clerical authorities; the latter were commonly regarded as senior to, and superior to, the former. Furthermore, the Church took the view that the long-term interests of the sacred institution overrode the consideration that might otherwise have to be given to the law of the land. Therefore, criminal offences by clerics should, if necessary, be hushed up, covered over and denied if damage to the public image of the Church might result. Essentially, canon law and practice enjoined what amounted to criminal behaviour on priests, nuns and prelates. Until the 1980s, a conspiracy of silence surrounded the whole area of clerics *in loco parentis* with children. Corporal punishment was permitted and was common as a general device to be used (illegally) for the social control of minors. Education was top-down and authoritarian; memory work and grammar were favoured over encouragement of initiative and conversational skills, with the partial exception of the teaching of Irish, where 'advanced' and 'modern' techniques were sometimes used. Many schools, despite being ill equipped and overcrowded, did inculcate a good education within the limits of their resources. Languages and mathematics were favoured over the sciences, not exactly because of an ideological hostility to the sciences, but rather through a curious lack of interest in them, and also because of a lack of resources in the form of laboratory space and equipment. This lack of interest in the sciences is looked at in somewhat more detail in Chapter 4. Paul Blanshard, an American observer, noticed this absence of scientific culture. In his anti-Catholic *The Irish and Catholic Power* of 1954, he remarked cuttingly and with devastating accuracy that the Catholic Church in Ireland had inherited the 'advantages of scientific progress in the British tradition without being compelled to adopt its strategy and tactics to modern concepts.'

Despite the anti-statist ideology of many powerful people in government and in the Catholic Church, a widespread and often opportunistic bossiness characterised much of the culture; powerful people were seen as likely to be capricious, and even vindictive. A widespread social timidity characterised society and the culture of human rights, although extant, was often weak in the face of the authority system. Who you were was commonly held to be more important than what you were. A well-known nineteenth-century Irish proverb advised: 'Do not be too close to, or too distant from, the clergy.' The twentieth century might have added much of the lay leadership of the country to the clergy of the adage.

An apparently trivial but very illustrative example of this authoritarian propensity is afforded by the Shops (Hours Trading) Act of 1938. Essentially the Act was declaredly intended to limit trading hours by small family-run shops trading 'unfairly' against larger, and more unionised, concerns. In a village and small-town society like mid-twentieth-century Ireland, in which small hucksters' shops and corner stores proliferated, this could be extremely important, and certainly was. Incidentally, the original Act prohibited Sunday trading. This particular ban was lifted immediately in 1938 'because of the outcry from traders'.[33] Authoritarianism tempered by populism was shown to be the unofficial Irish political constitution. The prohibition on Sunday trading still exists in theory, but the entire state has been, rather wonderfully, declared to be an exempted area since 1938 in a panic act of government: an Irish solution to an Irish problem. Labour supported the Shops (Hours of Trading) Bill in the Dáil in 1938. Archie Heron, a well-known Labour TD, commented that the greatest obstacle to legislation of this kind was the existence of 'small shops which employ nobody or employ only relatives, and are in competition with the larger shops.'

> ... I would go further and suggest that the smaller shopkeepers themselves would welcome legislation of this kind ... The small shopkeepers, just as much as anyone else, would be glad to close

on Christmas Day, and other public holidays, but the fact is each
of them is afraid of the other. No small shopkeeper can close as
long as another one is open, and the position today is that a lot
of those small shops are staying open all day and night, week in
and week out, all over the country, and in Dublin City as well as
elsewhere. They would all be glad to close if there was legislation
ensuring that when one was closed, all the others are closed.[34]

In effect, the Act encouraged conspiracies in restraint of trade,
using moral and sociological arguments that happened to suit the
larger concerns to some extent and the trade unions in particular.
Interestingly, the unions were far more hostile to the family shops
than were the large employers; the latter appear to have been more
or less indifferent. The Act also encouraged what amounted to
snitching. To take an example almost at random, a complaint was
made in 1949 by one shopkeeper against another nearby directly
to the Department rather than to the Garda Síochána, so that his
name could be kept out of it. The Department thought his stance
was 'reasonable'.[35] Again, in 1948, a Dublin shopkeeper complained
about 'illegal' competition in his north-city neighbourhood, milk
being an exempted 'refreshment'.

Dear Sir,
I wish to draw your attention to shops keeping open on the
[North] Strand till eleven o'clock at night supposed to be selling
milk. It is a wrong law that I have to close at eight and can sell no
groceries after that time and that the shop next to me can keep
open and sell anything she likes even to rashers and selling them at
black market price. Sure that's not fair to others, what is the use of
making a law when it is not carried out right and besides paying a
licence to sell stuff when it can be sold without a licence.[36]

In 1948, an Irish Army veteran named Doolan attempted to open
a 'late night' shop in Cork city, selling groceries, tobacco, fruit and
vegetables, financing this with his discharge gratuity. Doolan argued
that most of his sale potential was during the period between 4.30
and 9.30 p.m. 'Milk and Cake' shops were permitted to stay open

until midnight, but his shop could not; he had to close at 8.00 p.m. 'This allows the former to capture the business to which we are justly entitled.' Doolan admitted that it was illegal to sell after the stated hour, but wrote plaintively: 'While it was illegal for me to sell an orange in my own shop, I could still purchase one in my neighbour's.' He continued, 'Furthermore while it is still illegal for me to sell sweets after 8 p.m., it is quite legal to purchase a half-dozen cakes in another shop . . . is this common sense, is it natural, is it moral?' Doolan explained that most of his trade was with country people whose timetable entailed (naturally) coming into town in the late evening to shop and socialise.

It is very probable that general social control and, in particular, fear of sexual encounters between young people constituted part of the sub-text of official policy. The incomprehension and arrogance of some of the civil servants enforcing the 1938 Act were quite evident. The officer in the department proudly looked back on seven years of regulation of closing time and claimed that the vast majority of shopkeepers, especially small shopkeepers, liked the system; there was a place for everybody, and everybody was in his place. Doolan didn't really know much about his chosen trade, he opined. Rather prissily, he wrote, 'The small shopkeeper has found that the casual late customer has been compelled to become more orderly in his shopping.'[37]

By 1949, a growing unrest was observable among shopkeepers. 'There is a growing volume of protest against the 1947 Order [under the 1938 Act and a Fianna Fáil government] from small shops all over the country.' Rather defensively, the officer appended a remark to the effect that many of the shops involved were 'sweat shops', essentially retreating to an *ad hominem* and logically illegitimate argument in favour of government and Department of Industry and Commerce policy.[38] As late as 1961, the hairdressers of Cork city were making the government enforce closing times so as to ensure that no rate-buster would force them all to work late. This was a general pattern; the state, in effect, enforced the law only where local traders wanted it, or where they actually forced the state to enforce it by political intrigue or agitation. Elsewhere, the law was quite routinely winked at. The Department, now evidently going through an internal palace revolution of some sort, commented rather devastatingly: 'It has been the policy to make [closing time] orders only where there is evidence that the majority of traders affected in the area are in favour of the order and the order is required to bring the minority into line with the wishes of the majority.'[39]

After the 1960s, the Act gradually became a dead letter and the police essentially refused point blank to enforce its provisions, having better things to do in a modernising brave new Ireland of murderers, Provos, ganglands, amateur revolutionaries, rogue motorists, paedophile clerics, international fraudsters, corrupt politicians and civil servants, car bombers and drug smugglers. In 1969, the Department's Research Unit carried out a clever and interesting empirical analysis, evidently informed by training in economics and the other social sciences, of the practical effects of the Act. The Unit concluded, quite devastatingly, that towns in which the local traders succeeded in getting the Act enforced experienced markedly lower growth rates than those which ignored the law; economic development was actively discouraged by the law. Galway and Dundalk were conspicuous victims of the tendency, inherent in the 1938 Act, to strangle trade. In Waterford, the hairdressers were still able to use their collective political weight to prevent late-evening haircutting.[40] It is impossible to estimate, but frightening to contemplate, how much economic growth in the Republic of Ireland was being systematically stifled by a moralistic and anti-economic governmental fixed policy dating from 1938. By the year 1969, the Department was effectively burying the Act, but doing so on the quiet. The Department now proceeded to take the view that, within very wide limits, hours of trading were really no concern of government. Its Research Unit concluded rather wittily:

Arguments frequently used to support control by public authorities of the opening hours of retail establishments—apart from the protection of the employee—include those of avoiding *excess competition in service between retailers—a competition that can increase the costs of distribution* [emphasis in the original]— and the need to protect the small independent owner from the temptation to work excessive hours. Legislation to deal with the first problem is rather cumbersome and in any case the role of public authorities should surely be that of ensuring as far as possible, that innovations and innovators are not thwarted by defenders of the status quo. As to the second argument it is difficult to see why this should apply to retailers and not to farmers, to painters or to university professors.[41]

This Act was one example among many of a huge series of regulatory devices which, with the best or worst of intentions, caused the country to run its economy with the brakes on. Insidiously, this braking activity appeared to be effected with the passive approval of the great majority, as represented by the unions, the governing party, existing businesses adverse to increased competition and to new entrants into the trade, combined with elements in the civil service hostile to trade: a Madisonian collective tyranny incorporating a strong Luddist tendency. Another conspicuous example of this kind of thinking was the prohibition imposed on local lorry owners to engage in goods haulage outside their own home county, a crazy prohibition commonly evaded with the quiet, 'commonsensical' connivance of the police. This ban was there to protect the monopoly of public transport of the nationalised transport company, Córas Iompair Éireann (CIE, or Irish Transport System). A common unkind gibe was that the initials really stood for Crawling In Erin, the 'winged sphere' emblem on its green buses being known fondly as the 'Flying Slug'. Private bus operators were similarly restricted to marginal and local services, and most of the big companies had been forcibly closed down by state action. The real victim was the unorganised market consumer and the taxpayer who had to pay for the service twice over.

## GROWTH AND STAGNATION

Despite all these structural rigidities and irrationalities, in the immediate post-war years some economic growth did occur. Marshall Aid was made available, and a boom of sorts was visible between 1945 and 1949. In part, this was a recovery from the abnormal conditions of wartime, rather than a true developmental boom. The volume of personal spending went up by about a quarter between 1945 and 1950. As Brendan Walsh has commented, 'It was natural that a consumer spree should occur as the purchasing power that had been pent up during the war was released. But growth also occurred in the level of exports, as Irish industry took advantage of the expansion of overseas markets, and tourism benefited from the shortages of food and foreign exchange in Britain.' Pressure to encourage exports also came from the post-war international economy. Raw materials and machinery after 1945 were, in the nature of things, available only for US dollars, and dollars were therefore badly needed. Marshall Aid apart, the only way to get dollars was by exporting. Exporting entailed opening the country to imports in the medium to long term. Padraig Ó Slattara, a civil servant close to Lemass, pointed quite emphatically to this fact of life as the true turning point as far as economic thinking was concerned.[42] The Irish would be given access to foreign markets only if the foreigners were permitted to trade inside the Republic. Exports grew for a few years, but an apparent new dawn was recognised as illusory in 1951 and subsequently. Brendan Walsh wrote:

The 1950s were not very old . . . before the grounds for optimism were swept away. Adverse external developments compounded by inappropriate policy responses quickly halted the economic growth of the immediate post-war years . . . we must bear in mind the importance of the balance of payments in the mind of economic policy-makers both in Ireland and abroad during this period. If domestic demand was allowed to expand too rap-idly . . . resources would be diverted from export markets, imports . . . drawn into the country . . . and the balance of payments deficit would rise to an alarming level . . . The possibility that the payments deficit would set in train deflationary forces, and thus prove largely self-correcting, was not seriously entertained by orthodox opinion in Europe or America at this time.[43]

Brendan Walsh argued that the authorities believed, rightly or wrongly, that the state would have to take corrective action sooner or later by deflating the economy by fiscal action (higher taxes and public-sector cuts) or by taxing imports more heavily.[44] In Chapter 3, we shall see the consequences of this mentality.

However, it is also clear that the Irish government, or at least its Department of Finance, had little regard for, or real comprehension of, the idea that infrastructural development aimed at helping economic activity, financed from the public purse, might be essential if any prospect of long-term growth were to exist. Patrick McGilligan noted in July 1950, 'It cannot be seriously argued that roads rank equal in importance for capital with such things as agricultural and electricity development, housing, public health services, hospitals or schools . . .' *The Leader* had agreed with him in advance; in January 1950, it trumpeted to the effect that local rates (property taxes) were a 'cruel burden on people of the middle-class group'. The Dublin–Bray road was not necessary, the paper averred, and, rather revealingly, suggested that Ireland didn't need 'two-lane' roads. The writer seems not to have known what a road lane was, and possibly, like so many people at that time, did not know how to drive. Many Irish roads were indeed one-lane in effect.

> The spenders of public money must be taught the elementary lessons of economics; they can have the finest two-lane roads [sic] in the world if they wish, but they cannot have new houses and schools for the people at the same time, unless they are determined to impose taxes that endanger the whole economy.[45]

However, McGilligan went on to remark in his private memorandum that the recent termination of the Bray road development project (a four-lane road) was a symptom of a general and apparently deep-seated reluctance to develop motor roads. That particular project was not resumed for forty years afterward, despite the growth in car usage from the early 1950s on and despite the general automobilisation of Irish society that occurred in the 1960s. Small-town shopkeepers, powerful in both of the major parties, successfully prevented the building of bypasses all across the country, for fear of losing 'the passing trade'. One of the few major dual-carriageway projects that was eventually completed by the early 1960s, the so-called 'Naas bypass', in effect was exactly the opposite of a bypass. The dual carriageway actually funnelled all the traffic from Dublin into the main street of the village of Naas, apparently at the behest of the local shopkeepers. In the 1950s, whenever governments were desperate for funds, which was pretty well all the time, the 'Road Fund' was raided, this fund consisting of money derived from motor taxes and theoretically earmarked for road-building. People who paid motor tax were regarded as fat cats and therefore as legitimate targets of the taxman.

Road-building was also massively resisted by a simple and very traditional process of masterly inactivity. Roadworks were seen as outdoor relief for political party workers and local indigents rather than as investment in a modern transport network. Modern road-building techniques were not used because local workers and their political patrons in the political parties naturally preferred more labour-intensive 'bucket of tar' methods. As in many other Western democracies, but to what seems to have been an extreme extent, road construction was regarded as a source of 'nickel-and-dime' patronage in the hands of local political honchos. It was also quite clear to McGilligan that Finance was hostile to road development; it should always be remembered that many of the senior officials lived in Dublin and did not know how to drive a car. Roads, rather than being seen as an essential infrastructural resource for developmental purposes, were actually regarded as a source of outdoor relief. McGilligan wrote:

The present system of road making and maintenance is specially designed to make both operations as expensive as possible, because roadwork in rural Ireland has become indissolubly linked with relief works in the minds of all members of Local Authorities. Consequently the price of a quiet life for the County Engineer is to ensure that a given fraction of every annual appropriation for roads is spent in the residential area of each Councillor and that in its spending the maximum amount is laid out in wages payable to the County Councillor's neighbours. The correct procedure is the exact opposite, and the only way in which this procedure can be forced on the rural community is to abolish the system whereunder each Local

Authority is responsible exclusively for the roads situated within its own administrative area.[46]

Furthermore, he noted, the areas involved were far too small for the effective use of modern equipment. This archaic system stayed in existence, despite the fact that the motor car was coming with a vengeance. There were now (1950), he wrote, 122,000 cars in the state, the pre-war figure being 75,000.[47] McGilligan's pessimism seems to have been rooted in his contemplation, in 1949, of a report on the Republic (a 'Country Study') issued under the European Recovery Program by the Economic Cooperation Administration, Washington, DC, in February of that year. He noted that GNP had fallen to 86 per cent of 1938 levels by 1944, had recovered by 1947 and had risen a little since then. However, half the workforce was still in agriculture, the diet was 'poor', less than 45 per cent of homes had electricity and in 1946 there were only twenty telephones, sixty radios and three cars per 1,000 people. The marriage rate was low, he wrote, and infant mortality was 150 per cent that of the United Kingdom and 200 per cent that of the United States. TB deaths in 1939 were 112 per 100,000, whereas the equivalent UK figure was 63.[48]

The view of a younger man, another northerner, Thomas Kenneth Whitaker, then in his early thirties, echoed McGilligan's gloominess, but with a characteristic mix of Ulster directness and intellectual practicality, again in reaction to the American assessment. Evidently both men welcomed the devastating critique of Irish conditions coming from such a detached source which could not be accused, in time-honoured Irish fashion, of being *parti pris*. Generally speaking, American advice was welcome in Ireland in a way that the advice of British or local experts might not be. Whitaker wrote coldly in a Finance minute:

There is room for conscious discussion of the question whether we can ever hope to make a stable economic entity of the twenty-six counties, or even of the whole of Ireland, while our standards of income, social security and leisure are set by those of a much richer country.

There was a huge labour force surplus, relieved mainly by emigration. 'Trade Union restrictions on entry to trades, and insistence on impossible wage standards—higher in many cases than Britain—is one of the factors that limit the opportunities for employment in Ireland.' Even with full employment, there would always be emigration, given the restrictive character of Irish society. In what was backhandedly a devastating comment on the reigning familial, social and political culture of the time, he wrote clinically and pungently, 'Wanderlust and the desire for emancipation from parental and religious discipline will always lure people abroad.'[49]

Free-rider syndromes, both elitist and populist, conspired to strangle the economy and the culture. One writer of the period, Professor James Hogan of University College Cork (UCC), was convinced that the electoral system was responsible for the weaknesses of the political system; in fact, he was almost obsessed with its allegedly deleterious effects. He believed that PR-STV encouraged 'professionalised and caucus politics' and prevented politicians from taking a long-term view of issues. Whether or not PR aggravated the tendency toward passivity and fragmentation of the policy process, it is certain that the exceptional electoral instability of the 1950s aggravated the general apparent inability of government to frame and implement coherent policy strategies.[50]

It is equally evident from subsequent referendums on the electoral system in 1959 and 1968 that the Irish electorate, profoundly populist and equally profoundly democratic in its collective instincts, had no intention of permitting its politicians to change that electoral system. Even in 1959, when the referendum to abolish PR was twinned with de Valera's campaign to be elected President, the electorate rejected the abolition of PR and elected de Valera by a small margin. Correctly, the voters sensed a Fianna Fáil opportunism, as distinct from an enlightened reformism, behind the proposals. This was even more the case in 1968, the amendments of that year being clearly designed by sea-green republicans Neil Blaney and Kevin Boland to shore up declining electoral strongholds in the west for the soldiers of destiny, rather than to improve the quality of democracy in Ireland. In each of those years, the Irish electorate, profoundly and rightly sceptical of the bona fides of its rulers and, furthermore, rather fond of the extraordinary power the Irish system gave to the ordinary voter, rejected proposals by Fianna Fáil to replace PR-STV with versions of the British First-Past-the-Post system.

Many observers had a very clear understanding of what they considered to be wrong with Fianna Fáil's Ireland. Alfie O'Rahilly, for example, a well-known academic, publicist and, later, ecclesiastic, wrote in 1946:

> The workers and employers are both organised and as a result the trade unionists would get a great deal more pay than undergraduates. As a result of this there was the tendency to displace the middle class and it was all happening by default because these people are pretty well organised and the middle class are not. Hence unless they wake up the middle class will be mopped up and wiped out.[51]

The middle class had not yet quite got into the saddle. As ever, the problem was partly an intellectual one, but mainly a cultural and structural one. An unsigned and very perceptive memorandum emanating from the civil service in 1946, in a review of an academic article in *The Annals of Collective Economy*, portrayed government-driven economies as essentially unproductive and predatory, in a fashion that anticipated the post-Keynesian economic thinking of the era after 1973. The main example used was the Third Reich of the late 1930s, driven to conquest because of its own inherently statist and therefore predatory nature.

> The statement in the last paragraph of the article, to the effect that the present system of planned economy in Russia follows the lines of the German war economy in 1914–1918, and it is now unquestionable that under the system Germany was on the verge of collapse economically when she went to war in 1939 and was only saved temporarily from economic ruin by her easy conquests in the early stages of the war.[52]

Even in the hour of the glorious victory of the Soviet people in the Great Patriotic War of 1941–45, there was little fashionable reverence in the senior echelons of the Department of Finance for state socialism or the glories of Stalin's Workers' Paradise. Little of Todd Andrews's sneaking regard for German and Soviet state-driven developmentalism existed. A cool and occasionally quite humorous intelligence prevailed, and the eventual collapse of an inherently predatory and incompetent Soviet Union was indirectly suggested. Statist developmentalists of the 1960s and 1970s, such as Patrick Lynch of UCD and Eamon Smullen of Sinn Féin the Workers' Party, excoriated as conservative and obscurantist an attitude that was, in fact, derived from a strong and coherent intellectual mind-set.

However, *étatiste* ideas in a moderate 'Keynesian' form tended to get publicity, in part because of the emergence of the Beveridge Report next door in Britain, but also because of the rise of Labour there. In 1945, Arnold Marsh, a well-known commentator of the time and a headmaster in Drogheda, published a study of Irish and comparative economics, entitled *Full Employment in Ireland*, urging an extensive programme of public works involving infrastructure, housing, educational facilities, reafforestation, agricultural improvement and the construction of advance factories to be offered to domestic and foreign entrepreneurs.

## GERONTOCRATS AND REBELS

The Fianna Fáil government was tired in 1947, and the harsh winter of that year did not help. The same men who had stormed into office as Young Turks in 1932 held office and, in the eyes of many people, had become increasingly complacent in office. During the war years, it seemed that many ministers were immune from the privations which other people had to endure. Brian Inglis remembered:

> There was a feeling that Fianna Fail had grown smug; the die-hard republicans, as somebody put it, were settling down to become live-easy politicians, so accustomed to office that they could barely visualise themselves out of it.[53]

Protectionist policies had, in effect, given considerable power to senior ministers of government and to civil servants. Foreign entrepreneurs were sought out, and in some cases 'hot money' from Britain and farther afield sought a resting place in Ireland. Popular perceptions were that shady deals had been done and that the old puritan and austere values of republicanism were being tarnished by low standards in high places. One colourful midlands politician, Oliver J. Flanagan, was particularly voluble in his accusations. Eventually judicial enquiries were set up to investigate apparent asset stripping of a well-known distillery (Locke's of Kilbeggan) by foreign nationals, allegedly with government connivance, and accusations of tax-dodging were made against a junior minister. In both cases there was little substance to the rumours, but the mud did stick. Populist hostility to elites was easy to mobilise in Dublin in particular. Describing Clann na Poblachta's attacks in the 1948 General Election against government self-indulgence, Inglis wrote that such attacks did not make much impact in farming communities. However, they did have an impact in towns and on the policies of the new Inter-Party government of 1948. Inglis continued:

> As for the onslaught [by Clann na Poblachta] on luxury hotels (those bought by the tourist board), luxury aircraft (Constellations bought for the trans-Atlantic run) and luxury cinemas, these things might be evidence of misspending by city slickers, but they did not impinge on the everyday life of the farmers of the west.[54]

This refusal to spend money on infrastructural projects, airlines and education did not really spring mainly from what a later generation would term 'monetarist economics', but rather from populist, short-term economic egalitarianism. The Inter-Party government was later to spend money on welfare, housing and health, so much so that Joseph Brennan, Governor of the Central Bank, felt by the end of 1948 that there was an absence of any real monetary policy on the part of the new government. Effectively, he saw it as being caught between the spenders of Labour and Clann na Poblachta and the low-tax policies of Fine Gael and

Clann na Talmhan. The real villain was the Irish voter. 'Ministers, he [i.e. Brennan] said, were vying with one another in their prom- ises of lavish expenditure by the state,' wrote León Ó Broin.

> There was no attempt to check the inflationary flood and it would be impossible to reduce prices, as desired by the govern- ment, while consumption was being stimulated by large-scale expenditure and government borrowing. Neither could the balance of payments position, which was even worse than pre- viously, be rectified. On St. Patrick's Day 1949 after a military parade through College Green Brennan entertained the Taoiseach and a number of ministers in the Bank, and thought that Costello was ill-mannered in talking all the time with his colleagues 'without troubling to address a remark to me.'[55]

Costello was possibly more worried about the economic theories of the voter than about those of the Governor of the Central Bank. The former had more power. In some ways, Inter-Party economic and social policies were, rather like de Valera's, still intellectually pre-economic. The difference was that Costello was more afraid of the voters than was de Valera, and rightly. The latter watched the Irish voter as a hunter stalks his prey, and understood the voter as perhaps no one else of his generation did.

The tyranny of the majority could be self-defeating. The insistence that transatlantic airliners land at Shannon Airport before flying on to Dublin or elsewhere scarcely mattered in the 1940s, as the aeroplanes of the period could scarcely make it across the Atlantic. However, the 'Shannon Stop', in attenuated form, still exists over half a century later. Arguably, it has been insisted upon not only to counterbalance the country's demographic concentra- tion on Dublin, but also because of the highly organised character of the political parties and interest groups in the Limerick and Shannon region. It could also be argued that Dublin lost whatever chance it ever had of becoming an airline hub because of this veto. In 2002, the chairman of the Dublin Chamber Transport Committee described it as 'an act of national sabotage'. Asserting that the stopover was doomed anyway, he said, 'I don't believe that any Irish government could engage in an act of national sabotage indefinitely and the proper way to react now to the inevitable abolition of the stopover should be to plan for change.'[56] *Plus ça change, plus c'est la même chose.* The watershed of 1948 is looked at in more detail in Chapter 3.

The sense that the country was indeed at some kind of crossroads and unsure of what road to take is well expressed in a contemporary leading article in *The Irish Times* of 10 March 1950. The writer observed that industrial employment in the Republic had risen from 102,000 in 1926 to 200,000 in 1949. But that figure was, by the standards of other countries, 'regrettably low'. In fact, the proportion of industrial workers to other workers was possibly 'the lowest in Europe'. Sixty million pounds' worth of goods were imported in 1949, goods which could easily have been made in Ireland with a potential employment value of 45,000 jobs. The Minister of Industry and Commerce, Daniel Morrissey, had recently commented that if this went on, there would be 'no hope of checking emigration, for agriculture cannot absorb the surplus of seekers after work.' The writer continued, having a sideswipe at the Irish left and *étatistes* of the time:

> The complaint still rises that Irish 'capitalists' are reluctant to sink their money in Irish manufacturing enterprises. We doubt the truth of that complaint, in view of the evident fact that virtually every issue of shares by a new Irish industrial enterprise is over-subscribed to such an extent that hosts of investors who want shares cannot get them until they are quoted at a substantial premium. The fault, assuredly, does not lie with the investing public. It lies, rather, with the lack of opportunity for investment. The fact is that we number very few industrialists who are capable of envisaging new industries, who would put the people's idle money to use. What is wanted, in short, is a class of men of vision and courage, who can think of a product that the public need, and can take the necessary steps to see that they get it.[57]

A certain air of Irish hopelessness, with which development-mentalists had to battle, the struggle often going on inside their own heads, seems to have been pervasive after the boomlet of the late 1940s spluttered to a halt. However, some were trying to read the signpost at the crossroads, and the aspiration to modernity was not snuffed out by the intellectual climate. Even as early as mid-1945, a memorandum from the Department of Industry and Commerce commented that it could nowadays be taken as absolute that 'the threat of insecurity' could no longer be accepted in a 'fatalistic spirit' by the modern world and that no democratic government could ignore this change in public opinion and expectation. In particular, the farming community was going to have to be 'completely rehabilitated'.

> ... in the next five years the Government will have to consider taking far-reaching steps of an educational character to improve agricultural methods, to raise the whole level of personal and domestic hygiene and economy, to encourage self-help and throw off the shackles which still enslave the minds of the people in so many undesirable directions. At the very least 50% of the now very poor could provide a frugal living for themselves given the initiative and the knowledge.[58]

# 03 | AGONISING REAPPRAISAL

## CRITICAL ELECTION

In February 1948, Fianna Fáil lost a general election, partly because of populist resentment of apparent privilege and rumoured corruption. De Valera went into opposition for the first time in sixteen years. The entry into the Dáil of a group of purist republicans under the leadership of Sean MacBride took away some of the party's traditional support and also some of its younger and more radical support base. Fianna Fáil's leaders had grown old and tired in office, the outgoing Taoiseach was nearly blind and the experience of ensuring Ireland's simple survival during the war years had exhausted the government both physically and intellectually. The terrible winter of 1947 had exacerbated the situation. The general rebellion of a democratising Europe against older political causes and forces, a rebellion that had thrown out Churchill in Britain in 1945, affected de Valera somewhat similarly in Ireland three years later. Half a generation had gone by without a change of government, and for the first time since 1932 or 1922, the electorate delivered a result that resembled the phenomenon termed a 'critical election' by American political scientists in the very different context of the US political system. A critical election is one that, in Irish terms, changes the party strengths in the Dáil to such an extent as to divert the political system into desirable or undesirable but certainly different directions. In effect, an Irish critical election was one that had the effect of excluding Fianna

Fáil from power. De Valera's reign, in some superficial ways reminiscent of that of Salazar in Portugal, had ended, as it had begun, in an impeccably democratic manner.

The change of government in 1948 has received considerable and perhaps disproportionate attention and interest from academic and journalistic commentators over the decades; people have long sensed that it was a 'watershed', a new departure, the end of an era, the end of 'Treaty politics', etc. This instinct is probably more correct than incorrect, although one should bear in mind that folk memories of the Irish Civil War informed electoral politics as late as the early 1970s. It could also be argued that the exclusion from power of de Valera's party, easily the most powerful and popular party in the Irish system, throughout much of the 1950s (1948–51 and 1954–57) delayed certain decisions which needed to be taken urgently. These were broad decisions of a systemic kind which, because of electoral instability, were not taken early enough. To be fair, the new Inter-Party government took certain innovative decisions, such as the founding of the Industrial Development Authority, the institution of a separate capital budget and the declaration of the Republic, which arguably needed to be made and which would not have been made as rapidly under a Fianna Fáil government. The election has been generally regarded by historians as a benign event, as it discontinued the apparent monopoly on power of de Valera's party and was seen as so doing by commentators at that time. Whether or not it was good for the Irish economy or for Irish social development is another question, but that it was good for Irish democracy is possibly, even probably, the case.

Certainly the Fianna Fáil monopoly of power was over. In sixteen years, the party had woven a web of connections, influence, multiple monopolies and bureaucratic and ecclesiastical alliances that amounted to a kind of large mutual benefit society for powerful institutions and individuals. The harsh treatment of IRA sympathisers and activists, occasionally amounting to judicial murder, alienated many, as did the government's unbending stance on teachers' pay claims and ensuing strike in 1946. In effect, the defeat of 1948 felt to some like a breath of fresh air. Patrick

Lindsay, a prominent Fine Gael politician and lawyer, remembered a garda in Galway offering him a drink rather than a traffic ticket on the day Fianna Fáil was defeated:

I have however one great memory of that 1948 election, or rather of its aftermath. There was no certainty that an Inter-Party government could be put together or that de Valera could be ousted— indeed most Fianna Fail people refused to contemplate such a thing happening, including I believe de Valera himself. In any event the heavy speculation continued up to the last minute.

I was out of Dublin, frustratingly out of touch on circuit in Galway, on the day the new Dail met. I waited as long as I could in Galway to get the result of the election for Taoiseach, but I had to go to Dunmore for a consultation with a solicitor there, Ambrose Nestor.

I was going down the road to Tuam and I saw papal flags flying out of some houses and I said to myself, 'He's back again' the 'he' in question being de Valera. Then I continued on my journey and I met a fellow on a bicycle with his cap turned backways. He looked to me like a typical Fianna Fail road ganger and he looked vicious and disappointed, and I thought, 'There's still hope.' I drove into Tuam and I saw there the large physique of a man, a civic guard, who was standing on the footpath. I pulled in diagonally and lowered the window.

'Guard, is there any news from Dublin?'

'At ten past five this afternoon, Mr. John Aloysius Costello was elected Taoiseach of this Country.'

I knew by the way he said it that this really meant something to him and I said:

'Guard would you like a drink?'

'We'll have two.'

'Will you wait a minute, until I park this car?'

'Leave it where it is. We have freedom for the first time in sixteen years.'

We had more than one drink that day.

De Valera's allegedly monolithic grip on political power and patronage was finally broken. It was commonly claimed that during the period 1932–48, membership of, or broad sympathy with, Fianna Fáil was required for appointment to the police and many local government agencies. This was despite the Local Appointments Commission and the Civil Service Commission, which were supposed to be non-partisan and meritocratic agencies. It is difficult not to suspect that in a society where everyone knew everyone else, everyone expected corruption and clientelism, and this expectation generated clientelist (and even corrupt) behaviour even when such behaviour was often, but to an unknowable extent, unnecessary.

A consortium of opposition parties came together to form the new government. The Inter-Party government was centred on Fine Gael, formed from the old pro-Treaty group that had founded the state, two Labour parties split in part by the usual European leftist and trade union ideological disagreement over the issue of the Soviet Union plus personal antagonisms, the western small-holders' Clann na Talmhan and a new radical republican party composed of a mixture of ex-IRA and radical liberals, Clann na Poblachta (People of the Republic).[1] Clann na Poblachta was coming in from the extra-constitutional cold, much like de Valera in the 1920s or Provisional Sinn Féin in the late 1990s: republicans at the Canossa of Leinster House. Labour was divided into 'Green' versus 'Red' parties, Fine Gael was fighting in a rather leisurely fashion for its electoral life and Clann na Talmhan was hoping to revive the politics of the Land League of the previous century.

The new government thus reflected both forward-looking and backward-looking social forces. The agrarian, the owner-occupier subsistence farmer, the grazier, the urban worker, the rural labourer, the professional and the bourgeois jostled each other. These strange bedfellows formed an equally strange coalition government, a government that turned out to be both destructive and creative. Men who had ordered and stood over the executions of IRA men in 1922–23 were in the same cabinet with men who had hero-worshipped these martyrs and demonised their killers. Again, men whose economic ideas were classically laissez-faire in character governed the country in tandem with men who were essentially state socialist in ideological persuasion. People in favour of tax cuts bargained, with some success, with others who favoured massive redistribution of resources from the rich to the poor. Convinced, even fundamentalist, Catholics were allied with secularist anti-clericals. When put in the context of post-war Europe, where chastened social democrats, Christian democrats, liberals and conservatives were finding common ground in a world of aggressive communism and recently defeated fascism, the Irish line-up of 1948 appears perhaps less odd than it appeared to the eyes of some (mainly British) commentators. However, Fine Gael, backed by large farmers, much of the middle class and the older bourgeoisie, was to have difficulties making common cause with the egalitarians in the new cabinet.

Inevitably, such a group of people as formed the new Irish government were going to have to be led by someone who had innate diplomatic skills, and a Dublin lawyer, John A. Costello, whose hands were clean of IRA blood but who had an honourable Sinn Féin and pro-Treaty pedigree, became Taoiseach. A normally courteous and affable man, Costello had a somewhat peppery personality. A pious Catholic, he was unapologetically obedient to his bishops whenever they expressed opinions on public policy. He was rather looked down upon by British diplomats, for no good particular reason; the superciliousness of even junior British civil servants to Irish political leaders was virtually proverbial at that time. Costello had the unfortunate, if honest, habit of occasionally blurting out opinions in public in a manner that he possibly regretted afterwards.

He certainly had his hands full as leader of this new government, and it has often been remarked that it was an extraordinary achievement to have held together for three years such a fissiparous coalition of contrasting personalities and ideological positions. At the time, it was commonly predicted that the new government would last scarcely a year, and Dev and company were expected to sweep back shortly. The fact that it lasted for three years has been unkindly paralleled with the Johnsonian crack about the dog walking on two legs.[2] Another gibe of Fianna Fáil supporters was to the effect that it was the 'alliance of a dog with its fleas', Fine Gael being the dog, naturally, and the other parties being the fleas. However, it is also fair to these impolite commentators to admit that this pantomime-horse governmental experiment did all end in tears eventually, in an extraordinary Church versus state clash that echoed down the decades after 1951. The Mother and Child affair of 1951 was a major cultural event which permanently altered many Irish people's previous quiet acceptance of the overweening political claims of the Catholic Church; the Catholic Church was finally seen, quite fatally, as acting on the 'unpopular' side.

## A NEW DEPARTURE?

The new government was faced with an extraordinary range of problems and decisions, as were, of course, democratic and democratising governments all over Western Europe at that time. Diplomatically, the environment was a rapidly changing one. The year 1948 saw the Berlin Air Lift which was a calculated facing-down of Stalin's Soviet Union by the Western allies. In that year an institutionalisation of the East–West confrontation occurred that came to be known as the Cold War. This confrontation was to last for forty years. The period also saw the formation of the permanent Western Alliance known as the North Atlantic Treaty Organisation and the defeat of the communist forces in Greece by a Greek government heavily supported by Britain and the United States. In China, Chiang Kai-Shek's nationalist forces were clearly on the way to defeat by Mao Tse-Tung's communists; Chiang fell in 1949 and, with the remnant of his forces, retreated to Taiwan behind an American shield. Europe was being reconstructed with massive help from the American Marshall Plan, and the first moves toward a pan-European union were taking place in the form of the Iron and Steel Community. A chastened France and an even more chastened West Germany made common cause, partly for fear of a renewed military antagonism, but more immediately for fear of an apparently menacing and victorious Soviet Union.

In Ireland, however, economics seemed paramount, but redistribution of wealth was a very sensitive local political issue, particularly since the two Labour parties in particular were determined to bring in policies which favoured the poor over the rich. Housing for the less well off was a huge problem and it had only been partially solved by Fianna Fáil's massive housing programmes of the 1930s. Historically, housing was a chronic problem in Ireland, and one that the Irish weather made even more urgent; 1947 had seen the coldest winter in living memory. Clann na Talmhan muttered slogans about land redistribution, echoing the old Land League tradition of Davitt and Parnell. Only Clann na Poblachta, with its mixture of liberals, socialists and ex-IRA republicans, was genuinely developmentalist in mentality, even if many of its policies were somewhat impractical.

Educational policy was also beginning to be a sensitive issue. However, education's time had not yet come, vulnerable as it was to the Catholic Church's twin obsessions with its extraordinary and increasing control of the primary and secondary school systems and with the project of mass religious indoctrination. Furthermore, the educational system was still saddled with the equally non-educational linguistic-revival project it had, like Fianna Fáil, Fine Gael and Labour, inherited from the revolutionary period. It is no coincidence that the 1951 clash was sparked by the Catholic Church's galvanic reflex reaction to an innocent proposal by a Catholic doctors' guild that expectant mothers be *educated* about their condition and taught hygiene and elementary preventive medicine. Parenthetically, the original idea was James Deeny's, and was acted upon by John Garvin of the Department of Local Government and Public Health, who inserted a proviso into the 1947 Health Bill providing for such instruction in an innocent little pamphlet for mothers-to-be, to be printed at public expense. The pamphlet was the product of a *Catholic* doctors' society. Health, in the sense of the eradication of disease, and, of course, sanitary and modern housing were more in people's minds than economic development or educational reform and expansion. Education also continued to be thought of primarily as a means of moral conditioning rather than as a means of opening young minds to the world around them, let alone a means of producing young people whose abilities and training might enrich both the country and themselves.

De Valera had, famously or notoriously, thirsted for power when in the political wilderness in the 1920s and, after achieving it in 1932, had revelled in it. In the eyes of some, he seemed to think that he *was* Ireland, and certainly set out to reinvent or, more accurately, relabel the country according to his own beliefs. In a way, this was the secret of his extraordinary charisma: a fantastic, even overweening, self-confidence on the part of the prime minister in an unimportant small nation of less than totally self-assured people. John A. Costello immediately afforded an utter contrast to his famous predecessor. A consortium of the leaders of the various parties approached him after the February election and proposed that he be Taoiseach as a compromise figure; the republicans would not tolerate Richard Mulcahy, whom they saw as the butcher of 1922–23. Again, a Taoiseach from the Labour Party was, at that time, inconceivable in the conservative climate that existed in Catholic Ireland. For parallel reasons, a Taoiseach from the ex-IRA ranks of Clann na Poblachta was similarly statute barred. Sean MacBride of Clann na Poblachta and William Norton of Labour both pressed the office on the reluctant, and well-liked, Dublin lawyer.

Costello later claimed to have been 'appalled' at the idea of taking the office.

'I never wanted to be Taoiseach . . . I think my resolve was shaken mainly by the appeals made to me by O'Higgins at Mulcahy's home.' He told one of his closest advisers that he hadn't even wanted to become a minister or Attorney General. Mulcahy later said that Costello had been asked to leave all that his life meant to him, professionally and personally, 'within 24 hours'. On the Sunday, 15 February, after a game of golf, Costello went to see his friend [and fellow lawyer] Arthur Cox, who told him: 'You have been in politics for thirty years, and you cannot refuse the top post. If you play with fire you must expect to get burned some time.' Costello accepted the nomination as Taoiseach later that day.[3]

This government was inevitably to be led by a Chairman rather than a Chief, to use Brian Farrell's well-known and creative dichotomy.[4] Even cabinet posts and the Taoiseach's eleven Senate seats were divvied up between the parties before Costello became Taoiseach; he had to go along with the wishes of his notional subordinates in cabinet. Significantly, when Noel Browne, as Minister for Health, was asked for his resignation three years later, it was his party leader, Sean MacBride, not the Taoiseach, who asked him for that resignation. However, Costello was in his own way a man of some resource. It was through him and his connections in the Law Library, it has been claimed, that Sean MacBride, son of Maud Gonne MacBride and an ex-chief of staff of the IRA, was, as an emergent lawyer, persuaded to enter constitutional politics. Parenthetically, MacBride himself explained his conversion by reference to the 1937 Constitution which, he said, satisfied his republican sensibilities.[5] Costello's father had known James Larkin, so the new Taoiseach had some understanding of, and respect for, Labour's ideological preoccupations and mentality.[6] James Deeny, commenting years later on Costello's brief sojourn as Minister, wrote: 'When he had decided what he wanted to do, he sent for the Secretary of the Department and . . . gave him his orders. As he was Taoiseach as well as Minister for Health and had a positive determined manner, no one dared say anything.'[7]

Other information confirms this impression of a tough-minded decisiveness behind a (usually) mild-mannered exterior. When John Garvin, as Secretary of the Department of Local Government, was planning to build the new road network in 1948, Costello rang him up and abruptly announced the cancellation of the programme which had been lovingly put together during the war years. 'Garvin, we're building no racetracks for plutocrats in this country.' The scheme had actually commenced, and a pioneering half-mile of dual carriageway was built between Galloping Green and Foxrock on Dublin's south suburban Donnybrook–Bray main road before the entire programme was closed down. Patrick McGilligan commented later that 'the Bray road controversy' suggested to him 'that public opinion favours more economy in roads and expenditure. There is certainly no demand for roads like the continental autobahn, although I am not so sure our County Engineers appreciate this.' It is clear that McElligott and other senior officials in Finance agreed with this view, and may even have formed it. Tough-minded or otherwise, the essentially populist and short-termist nature of Irish democracy shone through; government policy was to be redistributivist rather than developmentalist. Under minister Tim Murphy of the Labour Party, the money was spent on a genuinely impressive programme of housing for the working classes and the poor.[8] The Inter-Party government came in with a ten-point programme for government. These were, according to David McCullagh,

1. Increased agricultural and industrial production.
2. Immediate all-out drive to provide houses for the working and middle classes at reasonable rates. Luxury building to be rigidly controlled.
3. Reduction in the cost of living.
4. Taxation of all unreasonable profit-making.
5. Introduction of a comprehensive social security plan to provide insurance against old age, illness, blindness, widowhood, unemployment, etc.
6. Removal of recent taxes on cigarettes, tobacco, beer and cinema seats.
7. Immediate steps to provide facilities for the treatment of sufferers from tuberculosis.
8. Establishment of a Council of Education.
9. Immediate plans to launch a National Drainage Plan.
10. Modification of means test as at present applied to old age, widows and orphans, and blind pensions.[9]

This programme looks impressive, although removing taxes on alcohol and tobacco seems odd to modern eyes. The thinking of that time, before the connection was drawn with lung cancer and liver failure, was that the 'pint and 'baccy' were the poor man's luxuries and should not be heavily taxed. Years later, a similarly benign but more informed idea was to inspire Charles Haughey's ideas on free electricity and television licences for the elderly. The idea of preventing 'luxury' housing betrays the puritan, egalitarian and zero-sum mentality characteristic of the times. Some would label it less kindly as a fine example of Irish begrudgery. Certainly, many achievements of the new government were admirable.

Tuberculosis, for example, was essentially eliminated by the mid-1950s, and one of the most advanced health services in the world, focusing in particular on wide-ranging if somewhat authoritarian programmes of preventive medicine, was put together by Browne, Deeny and the new Department of Health's technical team. The new government was certainly also building on work previously done under the aegis of Fianna Fáil's James Ryan, Sean MacEntee and Conor Ward. As mentioned, housing was made another priority; health considerations also served to encourage concentration on the housing issue. A Council of Education was indeed also established, a rather curious body consisting of twenty-nine people nominated by the Minister for Education:

> . . . 26 professional educators (including 11 clerics of various denominations) and 3 members who represented rural interests. Some aspects of the council were severely criticised, its urban bias, the exclusion of the trade unions and of parents as parents. This latter exclusion is difficult to reconcile with the minister's statement that 'one of the foremost functions which the council would perform would be to emphasise the rights and responsibilities of parents in the matter of education.'[10]

As argued elsewhere, this Council examined the curricula of the primary and secondary schools and concluded that little real change was needed. Seamus Ó Buachalla, in his comprehensive study of Irish educational policy, published in 1988, commented that the two reports from this particular Council revealed a 'conservative and reactionary value system' which didn't see any real need to change the primary school curriculum. Perhaps most crucially, the Council rejected any need for wider access to free secondary education after age fourteen, despite recommendations to that effect from senior policy-makers and no less a figure than the Archbishop of Dublin, John Charles McQuaid, another Ulsterman. 'This latter demand . . . [The Council of Education] described as being untenable, utopian, socially and pedagogically undesirable and economically impossible.'[11] Ó Buachalla goes on to remark rather violently but also devastatingly:

The Council of Education in its reports revealed a sterility and an irrelevance which may have reflected accurately the views of the educational establishment of the fifties and answered to the innate conservatism of most politicians. As educational blueprints its reports were totally alien to the rising hopes and expectations of a younger generation which saw clearly the immense potential of the educational system for economic and social development, a generation that was slowly realising that historically in education, all the children of the nation had not been equally cherished.[12]

Ó Buachalla commented that 'continuity was indeed the most striking characteristic of policy over the thirty five years from independence, continuity in the emphasis placed on process aspects and continuity in the avoidance of structural changes.'[13] Notoriously, Richard Mulcahy was to frankly acknowledge his own servitor role as Minister for Education in 1950: 'he perceived his own role as Minister to be a minimal one, "a kind of dungarees man", who could be expected to "take the knock out of the pipes and . . . link up everything."'[14] The new Council of Education would, Mulcahy announced, 'emphasise the rights and responsibilities of parents in the matter of education' and would 'make clear the field of authority that belonged to the Church' and 'whatever the functions of the state was [sic], it had no power to interfere either with the rights of parents or with the authority of the church.'[15]

Ó Buachalla noted that the Department actively resisted any real attempt to build up contacts between European educational systems in the years after the war; schemes for reform and their subsequent implementation 'should not in any way be in conflict with Catholic educational principles.'[16] Throughout the 1950s, a remarkably defensive and even reactionary stance was maintained by the Department of Education. This was quite clearly designed to defend the interests of a still aggressive Catholic hierarchy and a neo-Gaelic linguistic lobby which was powerful inside the teaching profession and which still had the attention of the ageing revolutionaries in the political elite. It was not until the 1960s that a revolution in education policy was forced through by a Fianna Fáil government. Within the narrow confines of the political realities of the period, Sean Moylan of Fianna Fáil, minister between 1951 and 1954, pushed through some enlightened reforms, including a 'free' half-day per week which was intended to permit teachers to step outside the rigid framework of the curriculum. Moylan favoured technical education and the building of new vocational schools, areas that were to be vital in developed form to the economic progress of the post-1970 era, but did not get very far in promoting them; he died suddenly in 1957. Ó Buachalla sums up:

> The quarter century from 1932 to 1957, encompassing the economically lean years of World War Two and the potentially expansionist years of the postwar period, witnessed no dramatic policy changes in the system. The declining social radicalism of Fianna Fail and the aggressive education policy pursued by the Catholic church resulted in a common cautious response from all the parties and the four ministers. Deirg, de Valera and Moylan, no less than Mulcahy, all accepted the church-dominated status quo and if Mulcahy's rhetoric was inherently more fulsome than theirs, the Fianna Fail ministers were equally committed to avoiding church–state conflict on education.[17]

The comparative literature on economic development emphasises the importance of a literate, highly educated and skilled population; such a population is held to be central to any prospect of real developmental progress. Many spectacular developmental achievements in many countries have been clearly linked to prior expansion of the educational system. The reigning aphorism seems to be change the educational system so as to achieve wider and more equal ranges of opportunity, particularly in the spheres of literacy, practical skills, languages and mathematics, and wait twenty years. Such an expansion was, by and large, successfully resisted by the educational and clerical authorities for over twenty years after 1945. This resistance was buttressed by an unfortunate synergy of blocking coalitions: the language lobby, the Catholic Church, middle-class concern with 'middle class' (meaning, in effect, grammar school) education and farmers' sometimes hostile attitudes toward further education. Arguably, the economic expansion of the 1960s would have been far more spectacular and far less reversible had decisions been taken in the late 1940s to raise the general educational level of the entire population; a very important *non-decision* was taken after the war. As it was, an immediate dearth of qualified personnel became visible in the mid-1960s in an economy that was suddenly and unexpectedly hungry for trained labour, and education and training were belatedly recognised by the political leaders as crucial. Employers were desperate for workers who could handle calculations, assess production routines, argue policy both orally and on paper, manage other workers and generally live in the modern world. It can be argued that, by banking on agriculture, accepting the proposition that education was really about producing priests and patriots and neglecting the idea of investing heavily in human capital, Irish governments had actually been engaging in shadow-boxing rather than engaging in serious development policies. The delayed character of Irish economic development can be traced directly to the limited, inegalitarian, non-technical and ideologised educational system that was enforced on the polity by the lobbies of the period.

Back in 1948, Dillon was to turn out to be a successful minister for agriculture, reversing many of the Fianna Fáil policies of the previous fifteen years. In particular, he reversed the previous government's insistence on growing wheat on an increasingly exhausted soil, a policy originally aimed at ensuring Irish self-sufficiency and weakening the country's dependence on the cattle trade with Britain. This had also been a policy that electorally enhanced Fianna Fáil's position in the Irish political system, as it rallied the smaller, mixed or 'arable' farmers to the party against the cattle farmers who, directly or indirectly, counted on the British export trade. Dillon also reclaimed about 2.5 million acres of land and tried to revive the British market for Irish produce. However, he stuck to his agrarian guns; the Republic of Ireland was a farmers' republic and would always be so. Furthermore, he loved it that way and wished it no other way, an opinion he expressed noisily and entertainingly in his eloquent Churchillian style. Meanwhile, Labour's Tim Murphy and Michael Keyes built houses for the workers in the towns, building almost literally on the formidable achievement of de Valera's housing programme of the 1930s.

However, despite, or possibly because of, the sometimes heroic redistributive efforts of many government ministers and officials, the economy stagnated throughout the decade of the 1950s. This stagnation contrasted glaringly with the spectacular recovery of Europe that characterised the period. Irish economic stagnation went hand in hand with electoral instability and ageing political elites. It also accompanied a political paralysis in the face of the lobbies headed by the Catholic Church, the farmers, the unions, noisy cultural ideologues and professional bodies such as the Irish Medical Association, a lobby whose power had been highlighted by the Mother and Child crisis. The clash between the Minister for Health, Dr Noel Browne, and the bishops was technically resolved in favour of the bishops, but did profound long-term damage to the Catholic Church's standing with the new emerging Catholic middle class in Irish society. On the other hand, throughout the 1950s, fear of clerical ire seems to have permanently weakened the determination of many older political leaders to forge ahead with creative policies in sensitive areas such as health, education and social welfare. Behind the political paralysis apparently generated by the Church lurked other equally obstructive lobbies and the local, highly conservative electorates throughout the country. It could be argued, however, that the 1948 election caused the disintegration of any collective ideological or collective political purpose among the ageing elites without supplying any real generational alternative. The new Young Turks did not arrive until the 1960s, and their arrival was to be resisted and greatly resented by many of the older men.

## INVIDIOUS COMPARISONS
Concern about Ireland's economic sluggishness mounted in the late 1940s and continued to be voiced throughout the 1950s. Significantly, comparative perspectives were used from the start, particularly comparisons with that Other Ireland, always openly

denounced, sometimes covertly respected: Northern Ireland. A northern Unionist leader, Edmond Warnock, certainly ruffled a few feathers in November 1947 when he rather grandly announced publicly on a visit to Dublin that the gross national product per head of the North was probably 30 per cent higher than that of the south. Certainly, one emergent constitutional republican, Sean MacBride, in opposition at the time, put down an angry parliamentary question to the Fianna Fáil government about this claim. Hugh Shearman of the relatively liberal *Belfast Telegraph* wrote acidly in December 1947 that the real reason taxes were lower in the south was that there were so few rich people there to tax in the first place. This was probably a barbed reference to the allegedly parlous condition of the remnants of the old Anglo-Irish establishment after the depredations of the Land Acts and the consequences of independence. Maurice Moynihan, secretary to the government, warned Costello in November 1948 that it might not be wise for the government to get involved in a public debate about the relative wealth of the two parts of Ireland. Moynihan wrote:

There are, I think, two dangers in pursuing the public discussion of the comparative economic and social conditions here and in the Six Counties. One is that in certain matters, such as prices, wages of agricultural workers, derating and social services, we may not come too well out of the comparison; and the second, arising out of this, is that an encouragement may be given to demands for improvements here which, from the Exchequer point of view, we could not afford.[18]

By and large, wage rates were higher in the south than in the North in the first years after the war; in the horrible phrase of the time, the Irish had actually had rather a good war. Also, TB eradication had made more progress in the south, long before Noel Browne took up the tiller at the Department of Health. In late 1947, the Department proudly reported to the Taoiseach that there were 3,000 'TB beds in the south as compared with 600 in Northern Ireland.' However, it was evident to all that British post-war plans, involving massive investment in health care, education and public-sector employment, were going to change things dramatically in Northern Ireland. Whitaker's warning of 1949 echoed a widespread concern about the general viability of the entire independence project. 1948 does indeed seem to have been a true historical and cultural watershed. One acute academic observer, Desmond Williams, writing in 1953, spotted this shift:

> One of the most striking features of Irish politics in recent years has been the frequency with which politicians employ economic phraseology. Englishmen would not regard this as something strange; they have been used to it for many years. In Ireland, however, it is probably only since 1948 that ordinary people have appeared to take an interest in economic debate. This is indeed a universal phenomenon; but for a very long time the language of popular appeal in Irish politics was not an economic one. People in pubs and at fairs were more concerned with questions arising out of history and political science ... The declaration of the republic in 1948-49, however, finished a long chapter in modern Irish politics ... Since that date, the politicians have adopted 'economics'; they affect an understanding of economic terminology, and are courting the affections and interests of professional economists.[19]

The idea that government investment should be redistributivist rather than developmentalist reflected an essentially static view of Irish society, a view that was deeply ingrained in Irish political culture, derived as it was from an economic founding in the form of the distributivist and arguably anti-developmentalist Land Acts of 1870-1903. By deciding to 'kill home rule with kindness', the British were also killing self-reliance, the root meaning of the words *sinn féin*. If I gained, you lost, and if you gained, I lost. This political culture resembled the amoral familism so well described by Edward Banfield in his classic *The Moral Basis of a Backward Society*, as existing in mid-1950s southern Italy. In such a zero-sum culture, it followed that wealth could be achieved only at the expense of others, and the economy was essentially seen as a system by which a few predators, residing, presumably, in 'luxury housing', lived off the efforts of the rest. It seems that it was only in 1948 that public rumblings about this approach to Irish economics began to occur, coinciding with the gradual sloughing off of the memory of British Ireland and the slowly dawning realisation that Ireland was on its own and its government was not almighty. Liam de Paor, who lived through this period as a young man, insistently claimed to this writer that the declaration of the Republic in 1949 actually did settle certain ideological vexed questions and permitted economic issues to take up the centre of the political arena almost for the first time.

The developmentalist idea of an expanding cake being distributed unevenly and even unfairly, of 'a rising tide raising all boats', as Lemass famously put it later, even if the boats ranged in size from a dinghy to a *Titanic*, had not really caught on. The Inter-Party government axed the transatlantic airline project, for which the Irish had been given complete set-down rights in several US cities. A privilege was thrown away with open eyes by an Irish government oblivious to, or sceptical of, the future of post-war aviation and obsessed with tax cuts and redistribution. The five Lockheed Constellations bought by the outgoing Fianna Fáil government were sold off at a profit to the British long-distance aviation company, British Overseas Airways Corporation (BOAC). The transatlantic air service had been a pet idea of Lemass's and was first put forward in cabinet to sceptical colleagues in 1943. It was strongly argued by Lemass in 1946 that Ireland had better get into the Atlantic market quickly, or other airlines would crowd her out. The Inter-Party government was divided; External Affairs, under MacBride, was supportive on the possibly irrelevant grounds of prestige, Finance was doubtful and Fine Gael's Daniel Morrissey, in Industry and Commerce, was against. This was despite Morrissey's clear commitment to developmentalism and industrialisation. The arguments against were cost, the urgency of finance for social purposes such as housing and health services and the evidently privileged character of air travel and air travellers; the last was considered to be an argument from social equity. Why should the general population finance the luxury travel arrangements of privileged people? In a fascinating letter to *The Irish Times* a generation later, Turlough

Lynch wrote that blaming MacBride and Costello for the cancellation of the transatlantic service was misguided. In fact, they had been forced to do so by the populism of the Labour Party. Apparently Labour resented luxury aeroplanes.

Aer Linte [Eireann] was due to start a transatlantic service on St. Patrick's Day, 1948. Offices had been opened in New York and Boston. Five Constellation aircraft were purchased. Crews, including cabin staff, were trained and proving flights completed.

The planes were used by Aer Lingus for a short time on the Dublin–London run and I travelled in them. They were the most advanced and comfortable passenger planes in use at that time.

After the 1948 elections the Labour Party refused to join the coalition government until the proposed transatlantic service was cancelled. The reason: 'Only rich people flew in aeroplanes.' The five Constellations were later sold. I should remember, as I was the first of the 200 staff of Aer Linte/Aer Lingus made redundant. As a section head I got £120.

The BOAC sale was manna from heaven from the British point of view. American companies wanted to block the British on the North Atlantic until they had their own lines up and running, and Constellations were the only suitable machines available; British-made airliners were short haul, many of them merely conversions of bomber types from the Second World War. The British did not have enough dollars to buy the thirty American-built transatlantic planes they needed (BOAC had five Constellations). The Irish took sterling and the BOAC long-haul fleet was doubled overnight, with the help of the Irish. The *Irish Press* commented acidly on 19 May 1948:

At the first hint of the abandonment of the Irish transatlantic project, early last March, the BBC announced that the Aerlinte [Eireann] Constellations would be sold to BOAC for sterling. Although this looked like a gift from the gods for British aviation, commentators in that country regarded the possibility [of an Irish sale] as a remote one. Now it appears that the BBC was right.

The Americans promptly upped the ante on hearing of the sale, American Airways announcing an immediate expansion of its Atlantic services. Fitters at Collinstown (Dublin Airport) strongly objected to being instructed to paint out the Irish tricolours on the tailfins of the aeroplanes and replace them with Union Jacks as required by the contract. Frank Gallagher, Fianna Fáil journalist extraordinaire, wrote angrily afterwards:

> The first step [taken by the Inter-Party government] was to close down the transatlantic air services which in the next few years would have provided those dollar credits which Ireland no less than other nations so desperately needed. The Constellations, bought for a service, which would not only have been economically invaluable, but would have greatly enhanced Ireland's prestige, were sold out of the country . . .

The idea of air travel as a prospective mass industry was still non-existent in the minds of many Irish policy-makers. Dollars were at that time vital to international trade in that they were the trading currency of the only undamaged major world economy, an economy which disposed of about half of total industrial productivity in a war-torn world. According to Todd Andrews, Lemass was 'bitterly disappointed' at the decision to axe the transatlantic service. A plaintive letter from J.J. O'Leary, an aircraft buff of the time, to McGilligan rightly prophesied a huge future for civil aviation in Ireland despite this political tragedy: 'call me a visionary if you like, but I have been in Civil Aviation from the beginning . . .'[20]

He was right, but Irish transatlantic aviation did not resume until 1958. The aviation lobby, given the logic of Irish politics, was too weak in 1948 to compete against the dead weight of Irish public opinion and its electoral reflection in the form of populist politicians. The same was true of the proponents of road-building and of those who advocated a modern telephone system. In the eyes of the Irish democracy and its servants, transatlantic airliners, telephones and motor cars were all the toys of the rich rather than the essential instruments of economic and social advance: the machineries of the future were upper class and therefore to be distrusted. These things were already the machineries of the present in the United States of 1948. In fact, despite pressure from the Americans, the Irish had instituted the compulsory stop at Shannon for foreign airliners on the Atlantic in 1946; arguably, this decision in the long run destroyed any possibility of the emergence of Dublin as a major European hub. However, no one was thinking in those terms at that time. The increased electoral competitiveness of the post-war period ensured that popular and populist views were enforced on political decision-makers looking fearfully over their shoulders. They were looking carefully and probably sympathetically at a hungry electorate that was, in turn, thinking, as people of modest means must, of next week or next month rather than of ten years ahead. As a joke of the period put it, recycling the Irish bulls of the famous Irish eighteenth-century parliamentarian, Sir Boyle Roche, 'Posterity be damned! What did posterity ever do for us?' Those who longed for a return to pre-war simplicities had their opinions reinforced by the electorate.

The Inter-Party government was replaced in 1951 by a shaky Fianna Fáil government, which made its peace with the hierarchy over the health policy issue, de Valera being even more prompt than Costello to accept the bishops' objections. However, de Valera was negotiating from a more powerful position as leader of a united and disciplined one-party government. Fianna Fáil was replaced again in 1954 by a second Inter-Party government. This government, however, consisted of fewer parties. Clann na Poblachta was down to three deputies and the two Labour parties had merged. Fine Gael had strengthened considerably, absorbing much of Clann na Talmhan's electoral support. Costello became Taoiseach in a four-party coalition government. MacBride went to the backbenches and, much to the irritation of some, turned himself into a self-appointed analyst of the country's economic performance and a noisy advocate of state intervention and investment. He was also an advocate of a newfangled thing called 'planning.' However, by now everybody was getting into the game of complaining about the Irish economy. The Minister for Finance was muttering, as were the senior civil servants, the academic economists and the unemployed. A deputy to represent the unemployed, Jack Murphy, was elected to the Dáil in 1957. Murphy was a building worker and had been interned for IRA activities during the Second World War. He was backed by well-known radical activist Peadar O'Donnell and was denounced, quite accurately, by Archbishop McQuaid as 'communist-inspired'. The 1957 election also saw the victories of four anti-regime and abstentionist Sinn Féin/IRA candidates. Also, and possibly more importantly, speaking with their feet rather than with their mouths, the crowds of emigrants were commenting on the situation, many of them now relatively well-got middle-class people who saw no future in Ireland for their children as distinct from themselves.

Meanwhile, the economy languished. Surplus, and often very unskilled, labour was sucked out of the country to participate in the relatively prosperous economy of England. Half-educated young Irishmen built Britain's roads in the ranks of McAlpine's Fusiliers, while half-educated young women worked as chambermaids and nurses. In Western counties in particular, the grim joke was that the prospect for a young landless man was 'the collar or the dollar', that is, join the Catholic clergy in Ireland or emigrate to the United States. John McGahern has provided us with a stark portrait of schooling in County Leitrim in the 1950s, the teacher bluntly warning his pupils to get good Leaving Certificate examination results: 'High marks or the boat [to England].' A huge Irish proletariat accumulated in Britain, building roads and infrastructure for the new Britain rather than for a new Ireland.

MacBride continued to sound a much-needed alarm during the economic collapse of 1956, still reluctantly supporting the second Inter-Party government from the backbenches despite the recrudescence of IRA activity in Northern Ireland. By then, the Republic's growth rate was clearly the slowest of the Western European countries. In November 1956, MacBride presented to government an alarming set of figures taken from an Organisation for European Economic Co-operation report. Between 1953 and 1955, the fastest-growing of the OECD countries had been Austria, temporarily partitioned between West and East, and temporarily shorn of some eastern territories. Impoverished Greece, recovering from Axis invasion and Allied reconquest, followed by a serious civil war, was making a respectable showing, and Ireland was among the slowest, prefiguring the pattern discerned in retrospect a generation later by Mancur Olson. West Germany was in the middle of Ludwig Erhard's *Wirtschaftswunder*, or economic miracle, and resembled a huge building site as the bombed cities were rebuilt. The fact that war-ruined countries were doing so well actually appeared scandalous to the Irish, who had apparently got away more or less scot-free. In fact, Ireland was badly damaged by the war, but in invisible ways. Isolation and self-sufficiency ensured that the country was psychologically ill prepared for the post-war world, and isolation, or even semi-pariah status, also reinforced reactionary, anti-modern and anti-intellectual tendencies that had been there earlier. The spectacle of wrecked countries doing well seemed to suggest that the Irish had no excuse; this in turn led to more defeatism on the part of some. After all, Japan was already rising like a phoenix from its nuclear ashes and was enjoying, or at least experiencing, one of the greatest economic booms ever seen in human history. In hindsight, it is startling to see France as a relatively slow-growth economy, but at that time the French boom was about to start and the country was still recovering from the war and two generations of pathological national division. France was hag-ridden by an impossible constitutional system and riven by political cleavages that, rather like Ireland's, were irrelevant to contemporary concerns. Furthermore, as a great power in decline, France had been saddled with a series of imperial wars in Indochina and Algeria, tragic and brutal conflicts which it could well have done without.

MacBride showed an understanding of general comparative survey analysis and of economic trend analysis that was ahead of its time in Ireland, with the honourable exception of a small coterie of experienced and clever public servants and social statisticians. As a trusted radical among leftists and a respected jurist and quondam senior minister, his views commanded reluctant cross-party respect.[21] His analyses were derivative, naturally enough; they were culled from the publications of international organisations, but they were also to prefigure other people's work arriving at similar conclusions in the late 1950s. MacBride thought that state action was the key, that developmentalism should become a central spirit of Irish government, and in this at least he resembled the Sean Lemass of that time. The opposing ideas that state extravagance would distort and eventually wreck the market economy and that state enterprise was the key to economic progress clashed with each other, and the latter was to win a temporary victory. The idea that private enterprise could often, and perhaps normally, outperform public enterprise ran up against another set of vested interests: the combined phalanx of the Fianna Fáil party, the trade unions and the state servants employed in these often inefficient and sometimes unnecessary semi-state bodies. To be fair, Irish *étatisme* derived from a clearly understood view of pre-war international reality; if everyone else was protectionist, one had very little choice but to go for protectionism and state enterprise oneself. After all, this had been the argument of Lemass two decades earlier. An Irish pattern by which the state tried at the same time to do things which it was naturally equipped to do and things which it was arguably ill equipped to do, to the detriment of both, had grown up over the years since 1932. In fact, an ideology which glorified the 'semi-state bodies' grew up, rationalising their existence and indeed proliferation by reference to the dearth of private investment in the country. Public transport, shipping, air travel, steel production, peat-bog development, tomato growing, broad-casting and power generation were all partly or wholly controlled by these parastatal entities. However, the fact that the future was going to be dominated by free trade threatened local interests, and the public sector was primary among those interests. There was great unease about what was often seen as the threat of foreign competition rather than appreciation of the opportunities offered by a trading world outside the Republic's little domain. Many felt deep down that Irish products and Irish invention would never be able to compete with the great technical prowess and economic muscle of the established industrial countries.

Table 1 reproduces MacBride's findings. Something was certainly rotten in the state of Ireland, and the apparently cold and objective evidence of the statistics seemed to confirm this proposition. Most galling of all was the fact that the United Kingdom, already far richer than its old possession on the other side of the Irish Sea, was actually getting even richer in the 1950s. Even impoverished and semi-literate Portugal appeared to be doing rather better. Ireland was certainly lagging badly in the post-war race to economic prosperity, and *étatiste* planners, often of leftist and nationalist inclination, had little doubt as to the solution: more state enterprise and more state intervention in the economy. Capitalism, the left announced, had failed and state-driven modernisation was the hope of the future. Spectacular Soviet successes in war, economic development and space travel were touted in favour of the statist route to the modern world. Few made the point that wartime destruction and political upheaval had, ironically, their good points from the perspective of developmentalism. McElligott presumably demurred quietly from this apparent consensus, as did Lemass, Whitaker and others.

**Table 1 The View From MacBride: Volume of Indices of National Product at Market Prices, 1952–55**

Base 1952 = 100
Countries listed in order of increase since 1952

| Country | 1953 | 1955 |
|---|---|---|
| Austria | 103 | 130 |
| Greece | 118 | 128 |
| West Germany | 108 | 127 |
| Italy | 107 | 119 |
| Netherlands | 108 | 116 |
| Sweden | 104 | 115 |
| France | 102 | 114 |
| United Kingdom | 104 | 112 |
| Portugal | 106 | 112 |
| Norway | 102 | 111 |
| Belgium | 104 | 109 |
| Denmark | 105 | 109 |
| Ireland | 102 | 106 |
| Mean | 105 | 117 |

MacBride wrote, '. . . the amazing recovery which was made by western European nations since the war is attributable mainly to careful, systematic and scientific planning.'[22] US aid had been a help, but not the central factor, he asserted. Ireland should therefore have a Central Economic Planning Office, staffed by economists. MacBride had come up with the right information and only a partially correct answer. The same post-war fascination with 'scientific planning' was evident and had become a mantra that informed much of Irish economic debate for two decades. MacBride went on to document Ireland's poor economic performance; the numbers of those working in agriculture were falling and the non-agricultural sector was virtually static. He acknowledged that there had been substantial social progress in the form of housing and hospitals, but 'By modern standards we have barely kept abreast of modern developments; in some aspects, such as education and schools, we are well in arrear.'[23] There were no 'lively young economists' around, he complained. He asserted that the country could easily sustain nine million people rather than the actual paltry three million, echoing, in a modest way, a particularly extravagant vision of Patrick Pearse's, half a century earlier. In a classic disappointed revolutionary's plaint, he wrote:

> Our people are disillusioned and bewildered at the lack of progress made in terms of unemployment and production since 1922, but they would be quite prepared to make heavy sacrifices and to work hard on the basis of a plan in which they have confidence and which holds out a definite prospect of really remedying the position.[24]

The crisis of the mid-1950s certainly shook up an apparently pathologically *immobiliste* political system. A flood of emigration, an increasing sense of being 'left behind', increasing support for Sinn Féin, popular sympathy with the resurgent IRA and a general electoral volatility alarmed even the most complacent and stasis-minded of political and social leaders. In 1956, at the height of the crisis, the IRA launched Operation Harvest, a series of badly planned pinprick attacks, mainly launched from the Republic, on

Northern Ireland police and military installations. The IRA campaign collapsed through lack of support for it among Northern Irish nationalists and the determined resistance of the unionist community to what was regarded as an impertinent and vicious attack. Eventually the Second Inter-Party government fell, MacBride withdrawing his party's support because Costello had, in the tradition of W.T. Cosgrave and Eamon de Valera, authorised the interning of IRA activists without trial.[25] By the middle of the decade, emigration had become a torrent and something like panic gripped some powerful figures. In January 1957, Costello spoke of the worrying condition of the economy and of the rise in unemployment. To avoid a Fianna Fáil vote-of-no-confidence motion, Costello dissolved the Dáil and polling day was set for 7 March. De Valera swept in once again in the classic tradition of early Fianna Fáil and formed what was to be his last government. The return of the old gang, with its resultant political stability and relative coherence, was witnessed with relief by many civil servants and businessmen.

On 19 March 1957, in what looks very much like a cleverly co-ordinated move, Charles Carter, Professor of Economics at Queen's University Belfast, gave a public lecture to the Irish Association in Dublin. Significantly, it was immediately circulated on 1 April to members of the government. It was soon reprinted as part of a symposium in *Studies*, a well-known and influential semi-academic journal.[26] Parliamentarians in the Dáil later reacted to it eloquently. Carter estimated that by now the income per head of the Republic was about 55 per cent that of the United Kingdom; the eastern province of Leinster, containing Dublin, was rather higher, at 65 per cent, but the rest of the country was perhaps at a figure of 45 per cent. Furthermore, the Republic was clearly falling further behind.

... it is falling behind, not only in income, but in the technical progress which creates the promise of further income. Though endowed with the great national advantages of closeness to wealthy markets, of the absence of substantial defence expenditure, of large external assets, the Republic achieves her slow progress only by a prodigal dissipation of external assets, occasionally restrained by emergency measures.[27]

Over the years, Irish governments had 'created an immense and tangled jungle of schemes for the encouragement of industry and agriculture, for the relief of unemployment and the improvement of social facilities.' However, these exceeded the capacity of the state to finance them despite high taxation levels. Because of emigration, every year there were fewer native customers for Irish goods. The reunification of Ireland was becoming ever more unlikely and ever more a fantasy. In an evidently calculated outburst of informed common sense, he asserted, 'It seems to me important that economists should say that the coexistence of unemployment and high migration with undeveloped resources is a nonsense, and a nonsense which can very well be put right.'[28] Significantly, he had no sense of despair, but rather a sense of an irrationality that could rather easily be righted. To put it slightly more idiomatically, Carter evidently regarded Irish economic policies as idiotic. He commented further on the general amateurism of Irish business management and also on the technical backwardness of Irish industry, sheltering as it was behind tariffs and presiding over a captive local market since the early 1930s. Working time was wasted because there were no materials, no market research, bad costing, bad layout of plant, absence of work study and a general atmosphere of amateurism, inefficiency and incompetence.[29] There was a low use of fertiliser in farming, and a general absence of trained technical staff who could appreciate new technical knowledge.[30] In an oblique way, the chronic and often bizarre deficiencies of the Irish educational system were also being pointed to.

The effective discouragement of, or even outright exclusion of, foreign capital and companies was largely to blame for this situation of government-wrought mediocrity maintained by vested interests seeking a quiet life in the local market, it was argued. However, Carter wrote, subsidiaries of foreign companies, accustomed to operating in a wider world, did have technical knowledge of the kind the Irish would have to acquire to survive in the new world of free trade that was looming on the horizon. It would be worth enticing them with large tax concessions to come in, partly to create employment, but also to act as role models for native industry. Carter continued:

Unfortunately the execution of such a policy runs against a whole lot of favourite illusions. One is that a locally owned business is better than a foreign one: the opposite is the truth, for advanced technical knowledge flows readily from a great firm to its subsidiaries, and a plant paid for by foreign capital is a great deal better than one which has to be paid for from the scanty savings of the Republic. Another illusion is that there is a virtue in small business; so there is, for certain purposes, and given intelligent management, but it is quite clear that in many branches of industry (and those among the most rapidly progressive) large firms have immense advantages. They can support massive research and development programmes which benefit their subsidiaries; they can buy the best in skill and technical knowledge and good management and diffuse its benefits throughout their empire; they can raise money more easily and on better terms; they can be more adventurous because they can spread their risks. The spread of good practices is much more difficult in industries, such as farming and building, which are necessarily organised in small units.[31]

The second illusion, he argued, was the belief that, somehow or other, small was good. Here, Carter was taking on republican petit-bourgeois hostility to 'Big Business' and the old Sinn Féin and de Valeran idea that the imagined fearsome social and moral consequences of big industry could be bypassed by having many small factories scattered around the country to enrich and reinforce an essentially farm-based economy and society. Griffith and his allies had argued half a century earlier that Ireland needed to bypass what later came to be termed smokestack industry in favour of small, local and even home manufacture. This oddly nostalgic vision of the future had become an Irish political dogma of sorts. Carter, on the other hand, was telling the Irish that small often entailed amateurism. He was further suggesting that small also, to put it bluntly, commonly involved being second rate. A third illusion was that foreign investment 'links you to the foreigner; in this case, to England.'[32] He suspected that this idea owed more to emotion than to reason. Other foreign observers, whose reports were collated for government, echoed some of these comments.[33] These ideas were now taken seriously in a way that would not have been possible ten years earlier. Evidently, this was the case because of the collapse of the protectionist system relative to the rest of Western Europe and the intellectual and psychological bankruptcy of the de Valeran system.

Those complacent about Ireland's stasis and who even wished to preserve and protect it were being gradually defeated, and clearly leaders were increasingly in favour of something which a later generation would term 'modernisation'. Modernity had previously been conceived as traditional social relations augmented by modern gadgets like the telephone or the aircraft; the idea that it entailed a complete transformation of social and power relationships was not completely grasped; in some cases, that proposition *was* comprehended and its consequences feared. The trouble was that not many had a clear idea as to what 'modernity' really was or what it entailed; a clear fear of the cultural and moral consequences of 'modernisation' existed, as did an inability to grasp the utility of modern technical apparatus. A Finance memorandum to government in the wake of the Whitaker 'Grey Book' of 1958 contained the following revealing, even extraordinary, exchange between civil servants:

> The proposed encouragement of the extension of telephone services will mean the diversion of capital to something that is mainly a convenience. Comment: The distinction between the use of the telephone for convenience and for improving efficiency is not a firm one, and in a modern economy an efficient telephone network is an essential basis for progress.

The significant point to be made about this exchange is that this 'advanced' comment actually needed to be made and reiterated over the following decades. Circa 1960 the Republic had 53 telephones per 1,000 population; the equivalent figure for the

United States was 411, for the United Kingdom 148 and Sweden 353. Interestingly, high-flying but culturally unique Japan had only 59 telephones per 1,000 population.[34] In the 1960s, the Republic continued to equip itself with discarded, bargain-basement British telephonic equipment, much of it pre-war, in the strange but ingrained belief that telephones, like modern roads or air travel, were not really essential; they were 'luxuries' to be enjoyed by rich people only.

Electronic communication remained an increasingly moribund government monopoly, the local manned exchange system a source of endless satirical comment and parody. Local post officials were able to eavesdrop on their neighbours' conversations, and even interrupt them with uninvited commentary, in a way that added to both the charm and the irritation, often amounting to despair, of living in Ireland. Because of the state monopoly, telephones were scarce and there was a huge pent-up demand for them; house prices reflected, in part, whether the house came with a telephone installed; powerful politicians 'fixed' telephones for their allies and clients. As ever, scarcity of a resource had its political advantages. Those without political clout quite commonly had to wait years for a telephone; telephones were, like so many other things, subject to Irish monopolistic practices. The fact that the Secretary of the Department of Posts and Telegraphs was a well-known and distinguished contemporary historian who out-produced many career academics as a writer may not be an irrelevant consideration. In fairness, similar situations existed in some other European countries, notably in traditionally statist France.

However, Ireland was an extreme case; the Republic of Ireland did not get a modern telephone service until the late 1980s, thirty years after that exchange of views between civil servants. The Department of Posts and Telegraphs essentially had to be dismembered to bring about that breakthrough, a breakthrough achieved at immense expense. In the 1990s, Arthur C. Clarke's prophecy of 1946 came true; satellite technology and the arrival of the mobile phone were to finally transcend the issue. It could even be argued that it might have been as well to await the mobile phone and abolish the obsolescent public telephone system.

Something of the kind bids fair to happen in Ireland in the early twenty-first century; in parts of the United States, public telephones virtually disappeared in the early years of the new millennium. However, the US had had a modern terrestrial telephone system since the 1920s.

## ANOTHER NEW DEPARTURE?

As early as 1954, Sean MacEntee, in one of his many periodic, meditative and unpublished essays on Irish public policy, wrote that he supported the mooted abolition of de Valera's Control of Manufactures Acts, a keystone of Fianna Fáil's anti-foreign capital and protectionist stance since 1932. These Acts provided for majority Irish capital holding in Irish companies and were aimed at eliminating British control of Irish industry. Parenthetically, one indirect but immediate result of the Acts was the relocation of Arthur Guinness's famous brewing company from Dublin to London and the opening of Park Lane brewery in London. Dublin's famous brewery ceased to be the major world exporter of stout that it had been. MacEntee, always the one-man awkward squad amongst the ranks of the Soldiers of Destiny, was privately questioning the New Testament of 1932. Back in 1927, de Valera had put forward his own economic philosophy in an interview with the liberal *Manchester Guardian*. The paper's correspondent had asked him about his much-touted doctrine of self-sufficiency, preventing imports, discouraging foreign capital and using import substitute industrialisation were he ever to come to power. The journalist queried, '... suppose your expert advisers tell you that by insisting on the use of our own resources you can indeed support a larger population, but only at a lower standard of living, would you [as prime minister] face that?' De Valera had replied:

> You say 'lower' when you ought to say a less costly standard of living. I think it quite possible that a less costly standard of living is desirable, and that it would prove, in fact, to be a higher standard of living. I am not satisfied that the standard of living and the mode of living in Western Europe is a right or proper one ...[35]

This strange anti-economic economics informed much of Fianna Fáil's thinking for a long time. In the case of modernisers like Lemass, statism was a pragmatic response to an unfriendly international economic and political climate. Lemass evidently disagreed completely with his leader's economic theories. However, resistance to modernisation and the sense of the abandonment of the cultural, agrarian and economic ideals of old Sinn Féin were passionately entertained by many Fianna Fáil partisans from the mid-1940s on. Modernisers and traditionalists defended the same protectionist policies, but for very different reasons. Joseph Kennedy, a correspondent of Frank Gallagher from Donegal, wrote to him in December 1946 bitterly prophesying a betrayal of the national ideal:

> The Land Commission has ceased to function except to collect Annuities and two Ministers (Lands and Agriculture) are proclaiming in best [Patrick] Hogan style that there are too many people on the land. When criticisms at the Party fair [sic] best, but the Cabinet through long office have lost their moorings.
>
> We'll have English Holiday Camps in Gormanstown etc. and beautiful international airports and as sure as your name is Frank Gallagher the Irish-Ireland programme in schools will be watered down before Fianna Fail quits office . . .

His instinct was correct. Fianna Fáil was a broad Church party, or, looking at it slightly differently, had many different types of heretics within its ranks. MacEntee, the Catholic heretic from Belfast, expressed the view in 1954 that the Control of Manufactures Acts should be repealed or certainly modified:

> At least modifying its provisions so as to allow freer entry to foreign capital. In view of the recent dearth of current savings an increase of foreign capital would lead to the more rapid development of our national resources and thus provide additional employment opportunities and help to reduce emigration. [There would be political resistance to repeal and] the need for them is a first article of faith with the Federation of Irish Manufacturers which has in

recent years unsuccessfully sought to have even tighter restrictions imposed on the entry of foreign capital into Irish industry.[36]

However, he felt that foreign capital might not come to the Republic even if the Acts were got rid of: 'Any investor looking at the state of our economy in 1951, for example, could only conclude that this was a country to keep well away from.'[37] The dream of providing full employment and abolishing emigration did, however, haunt many an official mind; the hostility to, and distrust of, people earning their living in unexpected, original or non-standard ways such as trading at night, on Sundays or employing only family labour was not universally held. In 1944, the Department of Finance commented on a British White Paper on the possibilities of providing full employment in the post-war world, in words that tacitly repudiated de Valera's ideas:

It might be remarked that a high or rising standard of living is sometimes regarded, in Ireland and elsewhere, as implying something hedonistic or basely materialistic ... The maintenance of a reasonably high standard of living is one of the most important objects of statecraft. It is sought not merely or mainly for the sake of physical enjoyment or comfort, though these are not altogether despicable aims, but because it is a condition of culture and health and of social peace and contentment. In a free society, if the general standard of living is low, the standard among the poorer classes will be miserable. A low standard of living can be a danger.[38]

Lemass, going into opposition in 1948 and destined not to become Taoiseach until 1959, agreed with this view, and his frustration at being reduced to the opposition benches of the Dáil was reportedly obvious even in his body language.[39] By the mid-1950s, the view had finally become a settled one in the minds of many policy-makers and influential figures. Something would have to be done. However, the view that any Irish great leap forward would have to be led by agriculture was still held by many, although the voices of those who advocated industrialisation became more audible and were not confined to the small group of businessmen, academics and civil servants around Lemass. In fact, in the mid-1950s, Lemass was displaying some tendency to backslide in favour of agriculture, perhaps as a political tactic in a party where the farming interest was very powerful and in which local and small-town pressure groups were well organised. Meanwhile, the two wings of the labour movement were reuniting and were, in a few years, to flex their considerable muscle in the boom years of the 1960s.

Following on MacBride's 1956 memorandum on the economy, Whitaker began his own study. Entitled 'Has Ireland a Future?'—after a cartoon on the cover of *Dublin Opinion*, the national humorous magazine, portraying a worried and very feminine young Ireland ordering a fortune teller urgently, 'Get to Work! They're Saying I've No Future!'—Whitaker's work was presented to the Fianna Fáil Minister for Finance in December 1957.[40]

## HAD SHE A FUTURE?

One paradoxical sign of hope in 1956–57 was the evident hopelessness of traditional policies, and the resultant lack of resistance to their being replaced by a new departure. Whitaker was later to express his pleasure and surprise at the readiness of a Fianna Fáil government to perform a volte-face on economic policy, abandon protection, embrace free trade and move toward a developmentalist policy at the instigation of Lemass.[41] The story has often been told. Whitaker's *Economic Development* was delivered to government in May 1958, and a White Paper derived from it was published under the title *Programme for Economic Expansion* in November of that year. Whitaker's study became known in the civil service and academia as the 'Grey Book', much to the amusement of its author. It was published some days after its presentation to government and had its author's name attached to it, in a move which was unprecedented in Irish civil service history.[42] The White Paper was less of a clear departure from traditional Fianna Fáil lines; some rowing-back to traditional postures was visible in comparison with the 'Grey Book'. Whitaker, like Dillon earlier, had argued for commercial production of cattle and tacitly against tillage farming, whereas the White Paper backtracked from that position to some extent. Again, as John Horgan puts it, 'Another Fianna Fail policy, the radical decentralisation of industry, ensured the omission of Whitaker's proposal for establishing new industries at or near large towns, despite Lemass's own doubts about his party's policy. Whitaker had [also] proposed abandoning some agricultural price supports; the White Paper was not so specific.'[43] However, the White Paper nailed its colours to the mast, projecting a 2 per cent annual increase in GNP over the following five years. The committee behind the White Paper had excluded MacEntee, but included James Ryan (Finance), Paddy Smith (agriculture) and Erskine Childers (Lands), a go-between between the committee and de Valera.[44]

These new policies actually worked. Whereas the volume of GNP in 1958 was 2.5 per cent below the level of 1955 and was only 6.5 per cent above the level of seven years earlier, the economy began to turn around after 1958.[45] From 1960 to 1967, the economy actually expanded at a rate of 4 per cent per annum, a truly staggering acceleration by the admittedly dreary standards of Irish past performance. To an extent, this performance has to be put in the international context of the period, but so does the dim performance of 1945–60. Some years earlier, Lemass had been talking of expanding the economy by one-fifth or 20 per cent over seven years, or about something less than 3 per cent per year, an aspiration regarded by many as visionary. Kennedy *et al.* point out very fairly:

The favourable experience of the economy from 1958 to 1973 was not due solely to domestic policies. The period was one of faster and steadier growth in the world economy generally, with nothing quite so disruptive as the Korean War and the Suez crisis in the preceding period. Ireland's terms of trade improved considerably and in 1973 were 39 per cent above the 1957 level. There was a great increase world-wide in direct investment abroad by multinational companies, which made it easier to attract some to Ireland.[46]

Kennedy *et al.* go on, however, to say that internal, local influences were important and that Ireland was not merely echoing international trends in the 1960s, any more than it had been echoing them in the 1945–59 period by lagging behind its Western European neighbours. There was a consistently expansionary fiscal policy, 'led by an increasing Capital Goods Programme'. Even 'social' investment did not dry up. A general acceptance of developmentalism had evolved: an almost revolutionary consensus had developed, which gave legitimacy to the new departure of 1958. Garret FitzGerald, writing in the spring of 1957, commented rather presciently, echoing Desmond Williams, 'A notable feature of Irish life in the last few years has been the growth of public interest in the nation's economic welfare.' The recession of 1952 and the political and economic arguments that had followed had 'aroused a hitherto dormant interest in economic affairs; and the events [of 1956] . . . have turned this interest into a deepening concern at the weakness and instability of the Irish economy after a generation of self-government.'[47]

This new interest was quite widespread among the emergent educated middle class of the time. Sean Lemass, as usual, was one of the quickest of the senior men to spot this sudden psychological shift in public mood. In fact, one could almost describe it as a cultural shift as much as anything else. In the Dáil on 11 December 1959, Lemass growled, ' . . . the most encouraging feature in the national situation at the present time is the disappearance of the clouds of despondency which hung so heavy over the country only a couple of short years ago.' He went on to report that a real industrial take-off was happening and was quite dramatic, but that agricultural income was static. The much touted agrarian motor of Irish economic development turned out to be, in racing parlance, a stumer or dud, and the much dismissed or even maligned industrial and services sectors started to bring home the goods.[48] As Table 2 indicates, something indeed was changing in Ireland. The apparent, but rather illusory, dynamism of Northern Ireland, sometimes secretly admired, resented and envied down south, was to be emulated by the Republic in the 1960s almost for the first time since independence. One might even argue that the scandal, ideologically speaking, of British Ireland's doing better than Irish Ireland provoked the latter into embracing developmentalism.

To put it a different way, a 32-county independent Ireland might still have the living standards of 1945, or at least have taken far longer to wake up from the complacencies of the 1940s and break out of the constraints of conservative and obscurantist veto groups; after all, Northern Ireland also had such groups. One can quite easily imagine an all-Ireland commonwealth where Catholic and Protestant obscurantists conspired together to prevent social, cultural and economic change. The existence of the two parts of Ireland as separate political entities tended to generate a politics of mutual recrimination, but also, more healthily, a politics of competition and, however stealthily and partially, a politics of co-operation. Partition had certain advantages; it possibly prevented Olsonian sclerosis from becoming total in a right little, tight little all-island republic. Success on one side of the border tended to goad leaders on the other side to at least consider new approaches and policies. In this instance, the apparent relative success of Northern Ireland was particularly irritating in the minds of political leaders and ideologues who publicly denounced the real and alleged misdeeds of the northern unionist leadership. Northern economic success, very visible to southern eyes in the 1950s and 1960s, was quite as much an ideological embarrassment as were the doings of the IRA.

**Table 2  Average Annual Growth Rates, Independent Ireland and Northern Ireland, 1926–1973** [49]

| Period | Independent Ireland | Northern Ireland |
|---|---|---|
| 1926–38 | 1.3% | 0.7% |
| 1938–50 | 1.1% | 4.0% |
| 1950–60 | 1.7% | 2.6% |
| 1960–73 | 4.4% | 3.7% |

Belatedly, independent Ireland was joining the European and American club, but it had paid a large price for its delay in so doing, including the emigration of hundreds of thousands of young people and the denial of education to many over a long period. The sluggishness of the Irish economy resulted in part from a corresponding political sluggishness, caused in turn by weak and divided government paralysed by a stand-off between powerful veto groups. Gary Murphy has documented how a younger generation of civil servants and politicians broke this log-jam by astute political manoeuvring; Irish government was rein-vented as a neo-corporate entity in partnership with the leaders of the farming community, the Federation of Irish Industry and the trade unions. Interestingly, Irish industry's leaders of the time were apparently more in favour of than hostile to the dismantling of tariffs and the European departure; it merely needed the initiative of government.

An anecdote illustrates the way in which developmentalist decision-makers had to manoeuvre in a polity blocked by entrenched interest groups. Lemass and his long-time civil-servant adviser, John Leydon, concluded that the Control of Manufacturers Acts would have to be repealed. However, many local manufacturers, some of them personal friends of Lemass, would have reflexively opposed such a move. In 1958, Lemass therefore rescinded only the Acts for industries that exported the bulk of their produce. He changed the title of the new Act from a 'Repeal of the Control of Manufactures Act' to an Act for the encouragement of exports.[50] People selling on a small scale to the local market were not concerned and remained quiescent; as so often in Irish politics, words were more important than substance and horses were not to be scared.

## IRELAND AFTER FRUGALITY

The events of the 1950s preceded an economic transformation which, by Irish standards, was revolutionary and which, in its way, matched or even surpassed the extraordinary breakthrough of the 1990s. It must be remembered that independent Ireland, despite its modest economic performance in the mid-twentieth century, has always been among the top thirty or so independent states in income per head, the universe being the 50 to 200 independent or quasi-independent political entities in the world, depending on the historical era. In this section, I would like to offer an assessment of

Ireland's relative progress in the post-Lemass era, or the thirty years after the accession of Fianna Fáil to power under de Valera's last government in 1957.[51] The usual, even rather overworked, summary statistic offered by comparativists is, of course, gross national product (GNP), usually divided by the population and offered as a per capita number. A statistic of this kind can easily hide many kinds of discrepancies and anomalies. A country which collectively elects to have large families will, by that decision alone, generate a lower GNP per head statistic than a country with small families; Ireland before 1980 and Germany since 1945 offer examples of each pattern, respectively. Again, a healthy, well-fed and rich population will live longer, have more old people around and thereby shrink the GNPPC number. Ireland's per head statistic has been artificially deflated by both these effects historically.

GNP itself is a pretty tricky concept to operationalise. International GNP comparisons in US dollars, or in any other common currency, will be misleading to the extent that exchange rates do not reflect the internal purchasing power of currencies; the main effect seems to be that absolute income disparities are overstated. In the case of Ireland 1957–87, it seems that the GNP was somewhat understated in terms of internal purchasing power. Another problem is, of course, the existence of 'black economies', which in many cases may amount to a considerable proportion of GNP. Finally, in the case of very poor countries, where much economic activity is at subsistence level and remains untraded, there can be serious measurement problems, but this is not a serious difficulty in the present argument.

Bearing these caveats in mind, GNP is used as a tentative yardstick in an exercise in comparison. The universe is the twenty-four richest non-communist economies in the world, 1957–87, excluding oil economies and countries with fewer than 1,000,000 people, as ranked by the World Bank in 1985.[52] Table 3 (p. 155) gives, for the years 1957, 1976 and 1985, the GNPPCs for the twenty-four countries. By 1987, Ireland, although her performance had improved considerably, was actually relatively *poorer* than in 1957. The country was the twentieth richest in the world and income per head was about 54 per cent of the mean statistic for the twenty-four countries. Ireland was slightly richer than Spain and less than one-third as rich as the proverbially opulent United States. Ireland was about as rich as Israel and twice as rich as Portugal but noticeably poorer than Italy and New Zealand. Table 3 also indicates that the picture had not changed greatly in the thirty years under examination. Between 1976 and 1987, Ireland's relative standing improved slightly, possibly a harbinger of the extraordinary burst of growth to come in the 1990s. This was a period of sluggish growth generally in the developed world's economies compared with the economic *belle époque* of the 1945–73 era. Ireland's relative shift down the scale was indeed a result of the extraordinary post-war explosion of growth in the defeated countries of the Second World War, behaving, as they did, in impeccably Olsonian fashion. Japan in particular shifted during the period from a position of abject poverty and physical ruin to one of great economic strength and extraordinary productive capacity; before the Japanese recession of the 1990s, there was much loose talk of Japan's possible emergence as a superpower capable of challenging the United States. The tragic decline of New Zealand, cut off from its traditional United Kingdom market by the emergence of the European Union, is also documented. Table 3 also gives us the percentages by which national GNPPC at current prices changed between 1957 and 1985. Inflation, of course, expands these figures to near meaninglessness, but the rankings are significant. Japan heads the list with a spectacular increase in face-value GNPPC at current prices. In real terms, Japan's wealth per head probably quadrupled, admittedly from a very low starting point; in 1957, Japan was far poorer than even Ireland. Spain did well during the period, as did the less well-known cases of Finland, Austria and Trinidad. Interestingly, Finland and Austria did relatively better than the well-known cases of West Germany and Italy. Ireland's figure of 882 per cent probably represents a doubling of income per head, not a despicable performance and one that gave the country a ranking of fourteen out of twenty-four in progress made since 1957, just above Portugal and well ahead of the mature economies of the United States, Belgium, the United Kingdom, New Zealand and (a typological anomaly) Israel. Ireland did not have a spectacular economic breakthrough in the post-Lemass generation, but the country certainly rejoined the Western group of capitalist economies, for better or for worse.

Omitting Luxembourg, Ireland fared quite well in comparison with the ten other members of the European Community, which the country had joined in 1973. It is somewhat startling to note that in 1957 the United Kingdom was the richest of these countries and that Spain and Portugal were far poorer than Greece. Ireland ranked seventh in 1957 and eighth in 1985. The Irish rate of growth was the eighth highest of the eleven, ahead of Portugal, the United Kingdom and Belgium, but far behind Spain and Italy, the leaders of the Mediterranean tier, and countries recovering from a history of poverty and warfare. Again, Ireland's economic revolution was a slow burner and the country took a generation to shake off the legacy of the de Valera era.

Between 1987 and 2001, the Republic of Ireland went through a half-generation of quite unprecedented growth, with GNP growth rates routinely exceeding 7 per cent and occasionally touching 10 per cent. It has commonly racked up the highest growth rate of any OECD country. No similar period of growth has ever been experienced in Ireland in modern historical times; presumably the same goes for earlier periods also. The medium- to long-term political and cultural consequences of this extraordinary shift are yet to be understood.[53]

Significantly, in the current literature, despite the spectacular growth of the 1990s, an underlying disquiet seems to resurface from time to time, as though these good times could not last. It appears to be felt that the Republic must return to a time of exaggerated pessimism, as in the 1950s and the 1980s, after the respites of the exaggerated optimism of the 1960s and the 1990s. Because of the perceived collective experience of the country since the Second World War, a 'seven lean years and seven fat years' folk theory of Irish economic development seems to have taken hold, even in the woodier parts of the groves of academe. A variation on the theme is the often expressed, mainly left-wing view that since the high-technology investment is mainly foreign and chiefly American, the capital is footloose and gives no particular loyalty to Ireland. As soon as cheaper skilled labour appears elsewhere, the foreign companies will emigrate and leave Ireland back where she started.

To this writer, such thinking appears magical. The long-term curve of Irish developmental growth since the 1930s is upward and presumably will follow the classic S-curve known for generations by developmental economists. When the curve will flatten is, of course, known only to God. However, the investment in cultural capital since 1967 seems to promise another generation or so of skilled young workers coming into the domestic economy and a continuing developmental shift accompanied by a further cultural shift. Younger Irish people were, to a greater extent, being taught how to earn their living in non-traditional ways. Their ranks were now being augmented by returned Irish emigrants in large numbers, bringing foreign experience and points of view with them. Non-Irish immigrants were enriching the hitherto rather monist composition of Irish social culture. Furthermore, whatever about the mobility of international capital, the experience of having worked for one multinational presumably helps equip you to work for another one, or even teaches you how to set up on your own. Multinationals also supplied cultural capital in the form of work and technical experience.

The cultural revolution or, depending on one's point of view, cultural collapse, of the 1960s is looked at in Chapter 4. However, it does seem that it takes a sometimes scary economic downturn to force economically rational decisions injurious to the interests of political elites through the Irish governmental decision-making system. Such a pattern of decision-making was certainly evident in the late 1950s and again in the late 1980s; veto groups were forced to remove their vetoes when it was put to them that a general collapse of some sort might occur. Both late conversions to new policy lines coincided with a time of electoral instability, the rise of minor radical and conservative parties and absence from government of the Fianna Fáil party with its legendary capacity to mobilise popular consent even for rather unattractive and unpopular economic policies. Another often underrated factor involved in these policy shifts has been foreign intervention and

**Table 3 Ranking in Growth Rate and Gross National Product Per Capita, Twenty-Four Countries, 1957–1985, in Current US Dollars**

| Growth Rank | GNPPC 1957 | Rank | GNPPC 1976 | Rank | GNPPC 1987 | Rank | GNPPC 1985 as % 1957 |
|---|---|---|---|---|---|---|---|
| Portugal (15) | 224 | 24 | 1690 | 23 | 1970 | 24 | 880 |
| Malaysia (23) | 356 | 20 | 860 | 24 | 2000 | 23 | 562 |
| Greece (12) | 340 | 21 | 2590 | 20 | 3550 | 22 | 1044 |
| Israel (21) | 726 | 15 | 3920 | 17 | 4990 | 19 | 687 |
| Trinidad (3) | 429 | 19 | 2240 | 22 | 6020 | 18 | 1423 |
| Spain (2) | 293 | 23 | 2920 | 19 | 4290 | 21 | 1464 |
| Ireland (14) | 550 | 17 | 2560 | 21 | 4850 | 20 | 882 |
| Italy (7) | 516 | 18 | 3050 | 18 | 6520 | 17 | 1264 |
| NZ (24) | 1310 | 6 | 4250 | 15 | 7010 | 16 | 535 |
| Belgium (20) | 1196 | 7 | 6780 | 6 | 8280 | 15 | 692 |
| UK (19) | 1189 | 8 | 4020 | 16 | 8460 | 14 | 712 |
| Austria (5) | 870 | 16 | 5330 | 13 | 9120 | 13 | 1361 |
| Netherlands (10) | 836 | 13 | 6200 | 10 | 9290 | 12 | 1111 |
| France (13) | 943 | 11 | 6550 | 9 | 9540 | 11 | 1012 |
| Australia (17) | 1316 | 5 | 6100 | 11 | 10830 | 10 | 823 |
| Finland (4) | 794 | 14 | 5620 | 12 | 10890 | 9 | 1372 |
| Germany (8) | 927 | 12 | 7380 | 7 | 10940 | 8 | 1180 |
| Denmark (11) | 1057 | 10 | 7450 | 5 | 11200 | 7 | 1060 |
| Japan (1) | 306 | 22 | 4910 | 14 | 11300 | 6 | 3693 |
| Sweden (16) | 1380 | 4 | 8670 | 2 | 11890 | 5 | 862 |
| Canada (18) | 1947 | 2 | 7510 | 4 | 13680 | 4 | 703 |
| Norway (6) | 1130 | 9 | 7420 | 6 | 14370 | 3 | 1272 |
| Switzerland (9) | 1428 | 3 | 8880 | 1 | 16370 | 2 | 1146 |
| US (22) | 2577 | 1 | 7890 | 3 | 16690 | 1 | 648 |
| Mean | 935 | | 5200 | | 6919 | | |
| Ireland as % of mean | 58.8 | | 49.2 | | 54.4 | | |

*Malaysia excludes Singapore; Israel excludes territories occupied in 1967.*

comment. American aid and economic criticism in the 1950s undoubtedly hurried the Irish decision-making process, even if it did not quite amount to forcing Irish government's hand. Again, throughout the following decades, successive Irish governments used American business consultants to advise them and to endorse one preferred line of policy at the expense of alternatives favoured by other factions and groups. In recent decades, professional economists have become far more prominent in the decision-making process than was the case in the 1950s, when economics tended to be the preserve of the central civil service rather than academia. This reflects the far greater development of academic skills in Irish universities in recent decades than was the case in the 1950s, when social science departments were smaller, commonly controlled by clerics and certainly less well established in the international world of scholarship.

The real danger in the near future is not the possibility of capital flight, but rather a decision by Irish youth to avoid technical and scientific education as being too 'hard' or 'boring'. It is not clear that the old innocence about scientific views of the world has faded and been replaced by a wide and active appreciation of scientific modes of thought and an equally active engagement with science and technology on a popular level outside the level of computer usage. The old short-term empiricism still persists, combined with distrust for scientific ways of looking at the world. English empiricism of the 'muddle-through' variety and Catholic disregard for science cast long cultural shadows in Ireland.

However, the lesson of the 1945–66 period was basically learned; education was to be yearned for, not feared. John FitzGerald of the Economic and Social Research Institute was able to say in 1997 that 'in terms of domestic policy' the failure to develop the education system in the first half century of independence 'was probably the new nation's most glaring mistake'. He went on to argue that the investment in education during the following quarter century had been a major success, not least because it fed into economic development. FitzGerald also pointed to the important role returning emigrants played in Ireland's cultural revolution.[54] In the 1950s, one of the many debilitating effects of the relentless drain of emigration was an absence of energy or even cultural variety. FitzGerald puts it well:

> For a society which is exceptionally homogeneous in terms of race, religion and culture the returning emigrants have played an important role in introducing new experience, new ways of doing business, new expectations and a new vitality. In the 1950s when the traffic was all one way Ireland was a rather claustrophobic insular society. This was symbolised by the rather heavy censorship which was still exercised on literary works but it went much deeper than that. This is reflected in the literature of the time and the representations in the cinema of the period.[55]

By educating to a high level even those expected to emigrate, Ireland produced people capable of going abroad and earning a living in a skilled avocation, and also gave herself an eventual flow of *Irish immigrants* who typically became part of a new generation of innovators. The old, mean-minded custom of filling emigrant boats with unskilled men and women destined for low-paid jobs in England and America had actually been self-defeating. This studied neglect of the education of young people destined for the emigrant ship had actually cost the Irish who stayed at home dearly, partly because no later return immigration was possible, and partly because the diaspora, quite understandably, did not view the native regime back at home with any great fondness. Some of them sympathised more with the IRA than with the democratic Irish government.

# 04 | CHERISH THE CHILDREN

## EDUCATE THAT YOU MAY BE FREE

Education in newly independent Ireland was by and large controlled by religious organisations, effectively meaning that the vast majority of children, in so far as they got educated at all, got the education the Catholic Church thought they should get. In rural areas, education beyond the age of puberty was quite commonly resisted by farm families who saw it as an unnecessary expense and also saw little connection between the practicalities of life and education beyond an elementary level. Others saw education and training as essentially a ticket out of farm society to a wider world of towns and cities, whether in urban Ireland, Britain or America. Those who opposed emigration sometimes covertly saw such education and training as a danger to the pious and static rural society which they valued so much. The Catholic Church effectively controlled education and decided what that education should consist of, subject to modification by concessions to the new, hungry and ambitious Catholic middle class. Serious concessions also had to be made to the powerful neo-Gaelic lobby and also to the Protestant middle class, the latter declining in power and social influence, but still quietly self-assertive within its own fenced-off areas of finance, business, health and education. An apparently minor but eventually crucial non-denominational exception to the general pattern of ecclesiastical control was the underdeveloped but emergent vocational education sector. This politically disadvantaged sector was to become a very hot political potato. Much of third-level education also remained in secular hands, as did a small, but rather visible, number of secular secondary schools. Orphanages and 'industrial schools' were controlled by the Church, some of them being administered in a very brutal and commonly illegal manner.

The cultural and social importance of the Catholic Church was immense; in many ways the incremental victories of the ideological successors of the Sinn Féin movement in 1922 and 1932 amounted to a confirmation and an augmentation of the cultural, economic, social and political power of the Catholic Church. Since 1795, this power had been conceded by the British government in Ireland as a means of domesticating the Catholic Church within the British two-island state. Frank Hugh O'Donnell, writing in 1902 long before Irish independence, had famously referred to the Catholic Church as the 'Phanariot Church' in Ireland. He saw the Church as holding power within the island with the consent of London, much as the Orthodox Church in Turkish-controlled Greece had co-operated with the Porte to keep the subservient Greeks politically passive and loyal to the Christian faith.[1]

A brief look at the historical development of the Catholic Church in Ireland is appropriate. The social history of the Church in Ireland is tolerably well known. Here it is necessary only to sketch the main outlines of the rise to power of a national and popular Catholic Church in the island of Ireland and amongst the Irish Catholic diaspora in Britain, the United States, Australia and elsewhere. Prior to the Famine the leaders of the Church tended to be city men, commonly of 'Old English' (*Sean-Ghall*) descent, and the organisation was historically Anglophone. After the Famine, as the island became more English-speaking, the Church came to be led by men of Gaelic descent and became more ruralised as the western and more remote dioceses were organised. By the twentieth century, in a quiet internal revolution, most bishops were men who had been born in completely rural places. The Irish Catholic ecclesiastical establishment lost its older urban character and became dominated by the sons of farmers; this development paralleled a general ruralisation of Irish politics that occurred as democratisation took hold. Contrary to stereotype, then, this popular ecclesiastical movement, led by priests and other clergy, is quite modern, dating from the immediate post-Famine period. Under the leadership of the legendary Archbishop, later Cardinal, Paul Cullen, it rapidly gained an extraordinary social and cultural influence in the late nineteenth century in Ireland and elsewhere, a power that was often resented and even feared by the non-Catholic Christian and secularist forces that ruled the English-speaking world. In its structure, the Church was actually rather provincial, even localist and very decentralised. Each bishop tended to be a little monarch in his own diocese. Religious orders had autonomy from the Irish episcopate, holding their authority from their centres in Rome or elsewhere. Rivalries between regular clergy and diocesan clergy were sometimes intense.

As John Whyte and many other authors have observed, a feature of this extraordinary religious movement was the intense and persistent loyalty it was able to attract: the loyalty of a pious and literally believing people. Almost regardless of social class, most Irish people lived, until quite recently, in a world where the here-after was very close and as real as the landscape around them. Irish religious fervour was probably very old; the island had a tradition of monastic piety well over a thousand years old, and modern Irish popular religious practice had clearly pagan or superstitious, as well as Christian, roots. The poetry of William Butler Yeats, the writings of James Stephens, the stained glass of Harry Clarke, the painting of Jack Yeats and the art of many others were all heavily influenced by this vibrant, almost medieval, popular culture.

At the end of the nineteenth century, the Catholic Church, having been a major agent of the linguistic anglicisation of Ireland for two centuries, perpetrated an apparent volte-face. While continuing to ensure that its flock had a command of the English language, elements within the Church suddenly proceeded to back the nationalist project of reviving the almost moribund Irish Gaelic language as the common tongue of the new Ireland that was imagined as emerging in the twentieth century. Many clerics denounced the British for what was described as the terrible crime of eradicating the Irish language through the school system, a crass distortion of historical fact. In reality, the Church had itself clearly been a major anglicising influence in the country and had commonly ensured that the language of political and social power was transmitted to the younger generation, usually at the expense of eradicating the older language. The sudden support for the Irish language was driven in part by an opportunistic and Machiavellian wish to appropriate a cultural property which was evidently a source of political power, given the rise of popular nationalism in late nineteenth-century Ireland. The alliance of priests and patriots that was being forged required some clerical tergiversation.

Another motivation for this cultural turnabout was to preserve and celebrate the rural and traditionalist character of Irish society so as to protect the Catholic faith of the ordinary people. This entailed a blotting out of cultural cues emanating from sources other than the Church and elements sympathetic to the Church. As Joyce put it almost piteously in *Stephen Hero*, 'Do you not see, said Stephen, that they encourage the study of Irish that their flocks may be more safely protected from the wolves of disbelief . . .?' The Irish language was seen by Stephen Daedalus, Joyce's protagonist and alter ego, as an opportunity to 'withdraw the people into a past of literal, implicit faith. . . .'[2] The linguistic revivalist cause also came to be energetically championed by many in the Irish Republican Brotherhood, who saw in it a means of getting the idealistic young of Ireland on their side against the British government. Linguistic nationalism and religious fervour were to be ideological allies: an alliance of Faith and Fatherland that was to be of momentous importance in the new century.

At the beginning of the twentieth century, Ireland was inter- nationally famous for its devotionalism, being seen virtually as an Atlantic Tibet. Louis Paul-Dubois, a French writer who published a well-known book on the country in the first decade of the twentieth century, saw the Irish as an almost Asiatic people in their devotion to their religion. He commented on the extraordinary strength of popular religion in the country:

No one can visit Ireland without being impressed by the intensity of Catholic belief there, and by the fervour of its outward manifestations. Watch the enormous crowds of people who fill the churches in the towns, the men as numerous as the women; see them all kneeling on the flagstones, without a sound or gesture, as though petrified in prayer! Go to early mass on Sundays in Dublin and watch three or four priests simultaneously giving the Sacrament to throngs of communicants too great for the size of the churches.[3]

As John Whyte has pointed out, sixty years later, the same devotionalism, the same interest in religious topics, the same fascination with religious argument and the same involvement with Catholic charities, social movements, pilgrimages and books persisted in the Ireland of the secularising modern world of the late 1960s.[4] The doings of bishops and priests commonly attracted more attention, argument, humour and occasional resentment than those of politicians or film stars. Churches were jammed with worshippers on Sundays and holy days, and evening devotions were popular. Pious practices such as pilgrimages, those wonderfully termed things called 'pious ejaculations', rosary recitations, wearing of pioneer (total abstention from alcohol) emblems and member-ship of sodalities and confraternities were commonplace. People often wore 'bad language' badges (tiny white stars of David) and scapulars (pieces of brown woollen cloth symbolic of a monk's robe and worn next to the skin) which guaranteed salvation to the wearer were worn by a significant proportion of the total population. Serial rituals such as novenas were endemic. Pilgrimages to such holy places as Croagh Patrick, Knock, St Patrick's Purgatory and Lourdes were oversubscribed. Well-known priests appeared on television to expound various religious, social and political opinions, and these performances were occasionally national events on the same scale as an election or a football final. Sometimes these opinions were curious and eccentric and were listened to with a characteristic mixture of deference and amusement. Redemptorist sermonisers, the Catholic equivalent of hot gospellers, promised hellfire for similarly half-intimidated and half-entertained congregations. Issues such as Darwinian evolution, the creation story in the Old Testament, whether or not eating meat on a Friday was a mortal sin incurring eternal punishment or whether 'company keeping' (dating) was contrary to the will of God were matters for half-serious, half-humorous, pub or domestic debate.

During the period 1938–60, some kind of a peak was achieved in the intensity of this marriage between the post-Cullen Catholic Church and Irish society. The gradual, later precipitate, decline in Catholic power in the Republic of Ireland was just about visible in the mid-1960s and was to become very obvious in the following decades. Priests were just beginning to become ordinary or even comic figures rather than being seen as revered teachers, men to be feared or even beloved gurus. In 1966, for example, a bishop denounced a married woman for saying on television that she had worn only perfume on her wedding night, and was promptly drowned out in a national wave of collective laughter, the latter being a fact that rarely got into the history books. Thirty years later, priests came to be sometimes demonised as paedophiles and rapists.

However, back in 1945, Catholic cultural dominance was still complete in independent Ireland. A huge amount of human effort had gone into the construction of this ecclesiastical empire. As early as 1900, the apparatus was more or less complete, but in the twentieth century the Church concentrated on following its flock into the cities of Ireland, Britain and America. The Church put its considerable energies into building great churches, hospitals and a vast network of parish clergy, parish organisations and schools run by secular and regular clergy, newspapers, charities and, of course, missionary organisations. The Church, as we have seen, also had intellectual claims, claims that were increasingly challenged not only by outsiders, but, interestingly, by some priests as well. However, episcopal insistence on the Church's right to dictate policy in a broad range of social, cultural, intellectual and marital areas was maintained and successfully enforced among Irish Catholics until well into the late twentieth century. Archbishops and cardinals did not wait on Irish prime ministers; the leaders of the democratic Irish state waited like feudal barons on the princes of the Church in their palaces. In particular, the Church insisted on having a monopolistic control of the education of young people in a Church-owned and state-financed school system. Much ecclesiastically owned property in Ireland was actually purchased with taxpayers' money.

An early and influential 'insider' critique of Irish Catholic clerical political and cultural claims was made at the beginning of the twentieth century by none other than Fr Walter McDonald, a professor of philosophy at St Patrick's College, Maynooth, and its postgraduate extension, the Dunboyne Establishment. McDonald, whom we met briefly in Chapter 1, was most active as a teacher and writer in the historically crucial period of the last decades of the nineteenth century and the first two of the twentieth. Since its inception in 1795, Maynooth had been financed by the contributions of the rising Catholic middle class, but it had also needed British government tolerance and donations to exist at its inception; at that time, education of a Catholic kind was not quite illegal but was not encouraged. Thereafter, British government money financed Maynooth regularly, the purpose being to use Catholic priests to ensure that Irish young men and women were shielded from the anti-Catholic and insurrectionist politics of the French Revolution. A curious loveless alliance existed, in effect, between the Protestant British state in Ireland and the newly reorganised English-speaking Irish Catholic Church. London and Maynooth were united by a common terror of revolution, if by little else. It was this relationship that O'Donnell characterised as 'Phanariot'. It involved close co-operation with London, the spreading of clerical influence and the concomitant gradual eradication of the Irish language in favour of English as the language of a higher civilisation and, more importantly, as the language of polite society and of the superpowers of the age.

The emergent revolutionary associations after 1847 deeply resented this grip the clergy had on the popular mind. However, the would-be rebels were eventually forced to make their peace with the Catholic Church, partly by means of the priests and patriots alliance first invented by Geoffrey Keating and recreated in democratic form by Daniel O'Connell. This peace between rebel and priest was copperfastened by the mediation between revolutionaries, agrarians and priests engineered by Charles Stewart Parnell and his successors after the Land War of 1879–81. In the late nineteenth century, then, the Church forged a series of understandings with the leaders of an ever-stronger Irish nationalist popular movement, which by the beginning of the new century was starting to think seriously of taking Ireland into independence, and of doing so by force if necessary. The Irish language was only one of a number of cultural devices that were used to forge this strange alliance.

The increasing involvement of the Church in secular politics and in nationalism made McDonald uneasy. He was known as an independent-minded man in a Church that did not particularly value such independence. In fact, open dissent or even loyal intellectual opposition was feared and discouraged. His position was somewhat like that of George Tyrell, an Irish-born priest who publicly dissented on the international stage in 1908 against papal condemnations of 'modernism'. McDonald wrote a lot, and in 1906 founded the *Irish Theological Quarterly*. Much of his philosophical work came under interdict of the official Church authorities. Most of his books remained unpublished, or published in editions of one copy, which amounted to the same thing. He was a conspicuous victim of the general Victorian Catholic fear of free publication and general debate; in the early part of the nineteenth century, priests were actually forbidden to publish their writings. McDonald's book, *Motion: Its Origins and Conservation*, published in 1898, was ordered to be destroyed, and all its copies burned—a decision that perhaps seems extraordinary by modern standards, but which seems to have been routine by the standards of the times. In an extraordinary episode of public humiliation, Fr McDonald found himself going around the bookshops of Dublin, buying up copies of his own book and burning them. Copies have, however, survived. It seems that his theory of motion relegated the Deity to far too subordinate a position in the order of nature. The ecclesiastical censors of his time regarded his philosophical views as perhaps brilliant, but possibly theologically unsound and certainly politically dangerous, given the conservative and antimodernist panic phase the international Catholic Church was going through at that time. McDonald was regarded by his peers with some unease. Among other things, he had the unfortunate habit of pointing out that priest academics often contradicted each other, despite their ascribed character of near infallibility, as derived from papal claims. He was never deprived of his chair, although, in despair, he occasionally considered giving it up.

The events of 1916–19 and the formation of a new alliance between the Catholic Church and the advanced nationalist Sinn Féin party finally provoked him into something like open rebellion. He saw the Catholic Church as withdrawing its allegiance to the British state in Ireland and throwing in its lot with Sinn Féin and the project of Irish republican independence in an exercise of massive philosophical dishonesty. He published *Some Ethical Questions of Peace and War* in 1919 and his *Reminiscences of a Maynooth Professor* was published posthumously in 1925, edited by Denis Gwynn. In the latter work, he wrote angrily:

> I saw, with disgust, Irish Bishops, both here and in the United States and elsewhere, use claptrap phrases—about self-determination, rights of nations, government by consent, and other such catchwords—good enough for President Wilson or Mr. Lloyd George, but unworthy of men who were supposed to have mastered the science of ethics as taught in our schools. In the use of these phrases, only too often in a sense which is false, our Bishops were competing for popular favour with political leaders; becoming, in effect, demagogues, while they should remain Bishops.[5]

These two books reflected a long-delayed, last-ditch and reluctant rebellion by a worried and seriously ill man who loved his church and who had loyally obeyed an ecclesiastical system of thought control all his life because of his fidelity to his religion and his ecclesiastical and intellectual vocation. The books, published at a crucial historical juncture, represent an attempt at friendly and loyal criticism of an institution that he believed was endangering itself because of its hostility to freedom of thought, free speech and intellectual inquiry. It was also extending itself into the secular sphere in a way that would eventually endanger its core purposes. His ultimate objection was to its implicit political theory, one of obedience to authority rather than to equality of opinions in the Greek or modern senses. Historically his books formed a warning to a church on the verge of acquiring very considerable political power over an entire nation. It was a warning that was eventually to be proved valid, but only after two generations of extensive clerical cultural and political power in nationalist Ireland.

## GUILTLESS CROMWELLS

From the inception of the British-financed national school system in the 1830s, the churches had insisted on their right to educate the children of their own denomination so as to ensure that souls would remain in each of the true faiths and be denied to each of the false ones. The British and Irish taxpayers jointly financed this generally satisfactory arrangement—that is, satisfactory at least in the eyes of each of the true Irish faiths. Secondary and even tertiary education eventually became subject to the same denominational claims. By the time independence came, virtually the entire educational system on the island was controlled by clerics. The only third-level education available to many obedient Catholics was the underfunded and tiny Catholic university college run by the Jesuits in Dublin. The underground Dáil government of 1919 had no ministry of education; it seems that such a ministry, or to use the Irish term, department, was seen as superfluous or even impertinent. The idea that priests should control education appeared natural, inevitable and desirable. Furthermore, the idea that mass secondary and tertiary education of a type extended to the entire population was desirable and even required to build a modern economy scarcely existed other than in the minds of a few visionary reformers in the Sinn Féin movement.

Industrial schools commonly regarded their orphaned and indigent pupils as inferior beings, suitable only for menial employment and ineducable. They were therefore commonly left illiterate. Ireland was rural and its economy was agrarian, it was argued; practical wisdom and the 'Three R's' (at most) were all that were needed for most people. Higher learning was the province of the favoured and privileged few, many of them clerics. The Catholic Church went along with the neo-Gaelic campaign with some evident scepticism and unease, but insisted on the position of Latin, Greek and religious knowledge, even at the expense of science, modern foreign languages, geography, history and the social sciences.

It also seems to have been thought that as the Irish were to be farmers by and large, education for the modern world was unnecessary and even dangerous. This was argued in the face of the well-known contemporary example of Denmark, a nation with an advanced small-farm agricultural economy allied to an extensive and advanced educational system emphasising systematic approaches to farming at high scientific levels. On the plus side, the extraordinary Irish literary tradition owes something to this lopsided emphasis on grammar training in the educational system. In many ways, this point of view echoed the general thrust of Irish educational policy under British rule, which was to produce rather highly literate subalterns for a subordinate role in running a great empire. As an ironic by-product, Ireland got Joyce, O'Donovan/ O'Connor, Whelan/O'Faolain, O'Duffy, Ó Nualláin/Flann O'Brien/ Myles na Gopaleen, McGahern, Plunkett and a cloud of other novelists, playwrights and short-story writers of Catholic provenance, many of them eloquent liberals and anti-clericals.

As Minister for Industry and Commerce in the mid-1920s, Patrick McGilligan wrote privately in support of this modest and developmentally unambitious point of view. He argued that since agriculture was Ireland's basic industry, and industrialisation, as proposed by the radicals, could never aspire to more than satisfying the modest requirements of the home market, education of an advanced kind was superfluous for most people. If given to many laypeople outside clerical control, higher education would merely produce troublemakers, political cranks and fanatics. He seemed to think that young people, overeducated in relation to the employment capabilities of the Irish economy, had instigated the revolution of 1912–23. The political opinions of the revolutionary enthusiasts had been essentially crankish and unrealistic, he argued with some justification. Ireland should be ruled by level-headed men, loyal to their religion and free of the intellectual daftness that is often associated with higher education. McGilligan wrote:

It is a matter of opinion how far political instability may have its
roots in a failure to adjust economic opportunity to native intelligence, imagination and sensibility. But if a nation is to depend on
agriculture it must produce mainly a population of farmers: men
of patience, endurance, thrift and modest intellectual aspirations.
If it produces other types it must export them at an early age if it
is not to risk the continual inner ferment of disappointed and
distorted minds denied by circumstances their adequate exercise.[6]

To the mind of people like McGilligan, reacting to the excesses
of the revolution and the Irish Civil War, education was a political
danger rather than a process of investing in human capital;
educated people often had ideas above their station, ideas that
should not be transmitted through the educational system. The
'Troubles' of 1912–23 could apparently be in part blamed on the
access to education young people were getting for the first time in
the last decades of the union with Britain. It was strange that
many of these heirs to the Irish revolution, products of a newly
expanding educational system under British rule, should have
deeply conservative, even reactionary, perspectives on education
themselves. People such as Michael Tierney, later President of
University College Dublin, and John Marcus O'Sullivan, Minister
for Education 1926–32—both men with enlightened and relatively
secularist views—tended to be overshadowed by the others. Rural
tranquillity and 'modest intellectual aspirations' were safer, and
also made sense economically. This view of Irish society was
eventually reinforced by an extreme censorship of books and
films, reinforced ably by unofficial local censorships which
commonly prevented public libraries from stocking books that
would disturb the mind of the most conservative person in the
parish. University students were potentially dangerous young
people and were going to have to be kept under close surveillance;
it was common practice in the colleges of the National University
of Ireland to discourage the reading of books that appeared to be
pro-communist or anti-Catholic. Paul Blanshard's *The Irish and
Catholic Power* (1954), an anti-Catholic, well-informed and
extremely non-pornographic analysis of Irish politics, was under

lock and key in the library of University College Dublin as late as the mid-1960s and available to students only by special permission, a permission routinely given by amused and mildly baffled academics. Students were subjected to a systematic supervision by clerics, sometimes masquerading as chaplains or academics. Communism was regularly denounced, thereby mightily enhancing its attractions in the minds of a naturally rebellious youth.

An appropriately popular poem of the 1920s period was Gray's 'Elegy Written in a Country Churchyard', written in the early eighteenth century when the English revolutionary violence of the previous century was still fresh in English people's minds, much as the recent Irish violence was in Irish people's minds after 1923. In the country graveyard of the poem, the 'rude forefathers of the hamlet sleep'. Because of their parochial horizons and rural simplicity, they had lived blameless lives—the lives that God meant men to live, in the phrase of Eamon de Valera.

> But Knowledge to their eyes her ample page
> Rich with the spoils of time did ne'er unroll;
> Chill Penury repressed their nobler rage,
> And froze the genial current of the soul.
>
> Full many a gem of purest ray serene
> The dark unfathomed caves of ocean bear:
> Full many a flower is born to blush unseen
> And waste its sweetness on the desert air.
>
> Some village Hampden that with dauntless breast
> The little tyrant of his fields withstood;
> Some mute inglorious Milton here may rest,
> Some Cromwell guiltless of his country's blood.

A bucolic quietus was to be the solution to Ireland's incoherent yearnings toward individual freedom, self-realisation, equality, individualism and authenticity as dramatically expressed in the writings and deeds of the revolutionaries and the poets. There were to be no more rebellious people like Yeats, Joyce, Pearse or

Connolly, or, if such people were to appear, Ireland would be well able to do without them. Knocknagow was to be at peace, and the dream of Thomas Davis, epitomised by his aphorism 'educate that you may be free', was to be qualified almost out of existence.

> Far from the madding crowd's ignoble strife
> Their sober wishes never learned to stray;
> Along the cool sequestered vale of life
> They kept the noiseless tenor of their way.[7]

McGilligan, despite his attitude to higher education, was in many ways a developmentalist. For example, he was one of the most important driving forces behind the Shannon Scheme in the 1920s. However, his conservative and quietist attitude to education appears to have been widely shared. Certainly, de Valera seems to have acquiesced in some such perception of Ireland's educational system being essentially a static system for a static society. In fairness, in this he reflected the views of not only his priest friends, but also the culture in general. The Church's anti-modernist ideology chimed well with a general distrust of intellect, dislike of free speech and an occasionally shrewd and anti-intellectual sense of some higher education being pretentious and of little real use outside the purlieu of a small social and intellectual elite. On the question of increasing access to education beyond primary level, once de Valera's government had implemented the beefing up of the Irish-language instruction programme, it envisaged little real further change; in this the Fianna Fáil party echoed the views of the Catholic Church. In the Department of Education estimate speech for 1940, de Valera remarked with apparent satisfaction that 'for nine out of ten of our people, the primary school is their only educational experience.'

Michael Hayes, an old opponent who knew de Valera very well, reminisced years later in 1959–60 about Dev's 'remoteness from mundane affairs'. Despite this, in the little world of Irish politics he was the master; 'he understands it as does no other living man'. However, as he was a 'parochial', Irish politics was 'all he knows'. Hayes saw de Valera as a very provincial man of limited imagination.

He felt that he was also a highly intelligent man who knew his own limitations but refused to accept them. 'His dissatisfaction has developed into an inferiority complex which finds its expression in the rejection of everything with which he is not familiar from his [rural] youth up.' An interdepartmental committee concluded in 1936 that there was no need to raise the school-leaving age from fourteen to sixteen as had been suggested by modernisers. It argued that it would cause hardship in rural areas and would not solve the problem of dead-end jobs or improve the young people's employment prospects as adults. Poor families would lose a wage-earner, and the state would have to supply 'maintenance allowances' at a 'prohibitive' £500,000 per annum. The committee conceded that the large number of unemployed juveniles in the Free State would indeed benefit from more compulsory schooling, but only if the age were raised to sixteen, the normal age for starting employment. The basic articulated objection to extending secondary education was cost, in a country that already spent far less, proportionately, on education than England, Scotland or Northern Ireland.[8] The uncontrollability of educated laymen must also have been a consideration, particularly in the minds of clerics.

Seamus Ó Buachalla cogently argues that the general acceptance of a static situation was derived in part from personal ideological or temperamental conviction. However, this acquiescence existed also because of the Catholic bishops' second thoughts about the secular vocational educational system, a system which the churches had accepted in 1930 from the Cumann na nGaedheal government. A decade of apparently unexpected growth and reasonable success for the vocational sector seems to have convinced the bishops that 'a major mistake had been made by them in 1930 in accepting the ministerial assurances on the act.' If they could not contrive to have the act repealed and the system abolished, the bishops felt that they could at least ensure that religious instruction was included on the curriculum. James Murphy writes, in general agreement with Ó Buachalla, that the increasing popularity of the vocational courses led to 'much concern among Church authorities'. This concern eventually resulted in 'a number of limitations and changes being imposed on the vocational system which affected both the image and development of that system.' His research demonstrates that this pro-clerical concern was shared by key senior officers in the state's Department of Education; effectively, the Church had spies in the camp, partly by means of its network in the Knights of Saint Columbanus. Some of these people would certainly have been in breach of their legally binding promise to obey the Official Secrets Act had they been sharing policy matters with senior clerical figures. Some evidently were doing so. Murphy comments bluntly:

Since its introduction in 1930 the vocational education system had provided a potential threat to the Church's control of education. From the outset the vocational schools were limited to a two year continuation course and were not allowed to enter students for either the Intermediate or Leaving Certificates. The fact that in the 1930s the V[ocational] E[ducational] C[ommittees] were providing continuing education to an ever increasing number of students also presented the Church with cause for concern which had eventually led to the introduction of Memorandum V. 40. Had the recommendations of this committee [of the Department of Education in 1942] been accepted, it would have meant the removal of continuing education from VEC control to the Church. The Church had always been concerned about the non-denominational influence of the vocational schools.

In effect, what had been looked upon as an ancillary attachment of minor importance to the educational system began to look important, useful and popular, and therefore dangerous, because modernisation was occurring anyway and off-farm economic activity was increasing. The Church, according to T.J. McElligott, 'chose to ignore those pupils who attended vocational schools until such time as instruction in Religious Education was paid for by the Vocational Education Committees.' Sean O'Connor, a veteran civil servant and an innovative senior figure in the Department of Education in the late 1960s, remarked that the VECs, with the encouragement of the Department of Education, embarked on a fairly ambitious programme of expansion, and a high level of attainment was achieved. However, this 'high repute' did not impress sufficient numbers of parents because the limitations imposed by the Act on the duration and content of the courses put many people off and many parents, presumably rightly, 'saw larger horizons for their children in secondary schools.'

John Charles McQuaid, as Archbishop of the largest city in the country, was particularly exercised in the early 1940s by vocational and continuation education and its potential for non-Catholic or even anti-Catholic thought. The Dublin VEC was the only one in the country that had no clerical representation (County Cork had the most). At one stage he considered trying to block a senior appointment in the Department of Education's Technical Branch of a man suspected of German sympathies, but felt he might leave himself open to a civil action and held his hand. More importantly, perhaps, he ran into high-level internal resistance to his interference. In a memorandum of early 1942, in reaction to *Memorandum V. 40*, he set out the problem from his point of view. The Vocational Education Act of 1930 did not mention religious instruction, but he felt that technical schools were obliged by law to supply such instruction. McQuaid wrote:

> Consequently, it is largely a question of expediency whether the Vocational Education Act should be amended. As long as the mass of the people and of our public men are Catholic, we can get where we wish with the existing facilities; if the people or our public representatives cease to be Catholic, then even legal protection for Church rights will avail little. The only danger is that the Act—the first educational law passed by a native parliament—may be taken as the norm for future legislation. The return of the Six Counties, with a strong anti-Catholic representation in parliament, must also be reckoned with in the not too distant future. Specific mention of religious instruction in the Act might mean giving the same facilities to non-Catholic bodies, though on the other hand the Constitution recognises the special position of the Catholic Church as against ordinary recognition of other religious bodies.

According to McQuaid, the real problem was that there was 'no Church control over the teachers'. He went on to note that the ordinary teachers in technical colleges were appointed by the local VECs while Chief Executive Officers (CEOs) of the colleges were selected by the (apparently fiercely independent) Local Appointments Commission.

Theoretically, it is a serious matter in a Catholic country that the C.E.O.'s and teachers of general subjects in an important branch of education can be appointed without any reference to the bishop of the area. Canon 1381 would seem to demand the right of veto in such appointments. Witness the effort we have made to control the teachers in primary schools—by retaining ownership of the schools, having our own training Colleges, etc., and also the control we have over secondary teachers. Here again, reform is largely a question of expediency. As long as the people and public representatives are Catholic, it is to be presumed that we can secure that no unworthy man will be appointed as teacher or C.E.O.—through our influence on public men and with the people. If this matter were raised now, at this stage of the working of the Act, it might lead to misunderstandings, to an outcry about clerical interference: it would have to be discussed and agreed upon beforehand with the existing vocational teachers.

In a bizarre gesture, de Valera reportedly offered control of the vocational system to an unnamed religious order in the early 1940s, but the offer was turned down. After 1940, the vocational system was effectively starved of finance by a wartime Fianna Fáil government desperate for cash, reaching a nadir in 1946–47.[9] The departmental committee of 1942, referred to above, essentially reviewed the work of the continuation education programme and produced the major document mentioned above, *Memorandum V. 40*, which was designed to assuage Church concerns and to bind the vocational system to the purposes of language revival as well as religious instruction. This key committee was chaired by a senior civil servant from the Technical Instruction Branch of the Department of Education, J. P. Hackett, who had unusually direct access to John

Charles McQuaid. According to O'Connor, '*Memorandum V. 40* served de Valera's political purposes admirably in deflecting church criticism at least for a few years.' Furthermore, he argued, it had the effect of getting the vocational schools into the linguistic revival push at a time when the primary and secondary schools 'were tiring of the effort'. I argue below that de Valera's apparent dislike of vocational education was connected with his wish to slow down the process of social change in Ireland, a process which necessarily involved migration from smaller to larger communities; the dissemination of vocational skills merely encouraged and accelerated such migration.

O'Connor essentially agrees with Murphy and other commentators that episcopal objections and general conservatism prevented the expansion, as originally intended, of the vocational system into a fully-fledged parallel system to the secondary school system, with equal access to an emerging third-level system, as was normal in many European countries. This veto persisted despite a personal sympathy which Derrig entertained for the idea of extending vocational education. O'Connor comments on this political blockage that 'It was a state of affairs that could not have continued indefinitely.' The reason was that there had been a huge expansion of educational contact with mainland Europe (and, though interestingly he does not say so, those well-known English-speaking countries—the United States, England, Wales, Scotland and Northern Ireland). 'The ferment in education being experienced there [in mainland Europe] would surely create some stir in the placid—some would say stagnant—pool of Irish education.' On top of all this, as James Murphy argues, Fianna Fáil's harnessing of the system to linguistic revival probably damaged the meritocratic recruitment system for instructors. Murphy further suggests that de Valera's general scepticism about the value of vocational training or what might have been his indifference to it was seriously damaging.

If a more active role for politicians had been encouraged by de Valera [in the 1930s] it could have led to a great deal of public support for the vocational system. A possible explanation could be the fact that many of the top politicians were products of the secondary system and felt obliged to publicly endorse anything that would affect the position of secondary education in society. This might antagonise the Church which in turn could possibly place their position as public representatives in jeopardy.[10]

Another, and closely related, reason for the neglect of technical schooling was certainly snobbery and a habit of regarding technical work and manual labour as essentially low class and menial. In this, the Irish were echoing similar English attitudes of the time. Again, in a more practical and hard-headed vein, de Valera and many others genuinely saw vocational training as simply education for migration or even emigration: migration from the country to Irish towns and cities, emigration to English or American big cities. Clerics feared for the morals of these young people, while nationalists saw emigration as the draining away of the lifeblood of the nation. Others quietly saw the education of young would-be emigrants as a waste of taxpayers' money, and appear to have cared little about sending the surplus youth of Ireland into the outside world half-educated and unequipped to deal with it. As we have seen, a somewhat inchoate sense existed among many intelligent and conscientious policy-makers that all was not well with the educational system. At the same time, the elites, both ecclesiastical and lay, were very badly divided on the way forward, partly because their attitudes toward the problem were conditioned by Olsonian vested interests. This was a set of divisions that was to cost the country dearly.

A rather admirable, but scarcely appropriate, attitude toward the dangers of human knowledge seems to have informed the mind of a later, Inter-Party, Minister for Education, General Richard Mulcahy. Mulcahy launched the new Council of Education in 1950, whose remit consisted of a review and critique of the primary and secondary school curricula. Echoing Catholic teaching of the time, he remarked:

It is more than appropriate because of the occasion itself and of the times in which we live that I should record that in its relation with the individual, the family, and religion, the State approach to education in the Irish Republic is one which unreservedly accepts the supernatural conception of man's nature and destiny. It accepts that the proper subject of education is man whole and entire, soul united to body in unity of nature, with all his faculties, natural and supernatural, such as right reason and revelation show him to be. It accepts that the foundation and crown of youth's entire training is religion.[11]

Mulcahy continued by declaring that the inculcation of patriotism and an informed love of one's country's history and culture was a second great goal of education, and then remarked somewhat ominously, 'In the world of today advance of knowledge has led to endless destruction and misery.'[12] This attitude to knowledge may indeed be a wise one, but comes oddly from the mouth of a Minister of Education unaffiliated to the Afghan Taliban. The Council's 1954 recommendations reflected an almost wholly static and conservative, even complacent, outlook, as we have seen. Its first report was on the primary school curriculum and it recommended the formal recognition of the almost totally denominational nature of the system. This was to be implemented legally in 1965, just as the actual denominational character of the system was commencing to erode. As Sean Farren has suggested, this amounted to a ritualistic and triumphant end to the campaign against secular education which had been waged by the Catholic Church since the 1830s.[13] It was to be a very hollow victory. The recommendation implicitly ignored parental rights to choose, since 'if all national schools were to be regarded as "denominational", the possibility of establishing schools whose patrons might not wish to uphold particular denominational principles or any at all was rejected, at least implicitly.'[14] Farren points out that the entire report was based on a traditional Catholic idea of childhood; children were born in a state of sin and must be trained to virtue by the rigid enforcement of a moral code. 'Any sense that education might play a creative role in shaping the future of society was summarily dismissed.'[15] The sometimes extravagant use of corporal punishment by teachers and ecclesiastics on small children was commonly justified by cognate arguments.

Suggestions that the age of leaving school might be extended from fourteen to fifteen or even sixteen, as recommended as far back as the early 1920s by Michael Tierney, Eoin MacNeill and John Marcus O'Sullivan and reiterated by people associated with Archbishop John Charles McQuaid in the mid-1940s, were scouted as unrealistic and 'utopian'. In particular, it was argued by the Council of Education, 'there would be the difficult and invidious task of enforcement, finally by legal powers. Apart from the question of parental rights, it was most doubtful whether the strain, both economic and social which would be imposed on the public would result in a compensating educational benefit.'[16] Obstructiveness hid itself behind the usual alibi of expense. The idea that an expanding economy and a rapidly changing society might carry such 'strain' fairly easily, as was the case ten years later, seemed to be beyond the members of the Council, some of whom were older, celibate, childless and of rural background. Furthermore, the demonstrable fact that many parents, even in the 1950s, were increasingly willing to finance further education out of their own pockets did not impinge on their minds. A silent but very general groundswell of increasing discontent with the existing system was occurring, and younger Irish politicians, ears close to the ground as usual, commenced to take heed. After all, parents had more votes than priests or Gaelic League activists. Also, unlike most priests, lay parents commonly had children who were to be the voters of the following decade. The fact that Irish politics is intensely voter directed could have revolutionary as well as reactionary consequences.

## PRIESTS VERSUS PATRIOTS

Significantly, by 1954, the public, or at least what were later to be termed the chattering classes, were not to be fobbed off by this extraordinarily conservative and culturally patriotic set of recommendations for the status quo. Relatively well-off people were also voting with their feet or wallets and financing the education of their children privately wherever they could.

Increasing numbers of young people advanced to the Intermediate and Leaving Certificate examinations, with relatively little state finance or encouragement. The Catholic Church's system of secondary and higher education was commonly quite understandably exploited by ambitious young men looking for a free education at the Church's expense. Indirectly, they were, of course, getting this education at taxpayers' expense and at the expense of pious contributors to the Church's educational system. Occasionally a vocation to the priesthood was simulated to get special and privileged educational opportunities; once the coveted BA or doctorate was attained, the young men jumped over the wall. The voluntary labour of priests, brothers and nuns meant that education was supplied very cheaply in Ireland, a fact that the emergent Catholic middle class naturally took full advantage of. Ironically, this meant that the already highly elitist and sociologically middle-class near-monopoly of further education was being intensified by state and Church inaction and obstructiveness, as well as by the self-sacrifice of priests, brothers and nuns.

In a piece in the *Irish Press*, Patrick Cannon, President of the Federation of Catholic Lay Secondary Schools and a bugbear of clerical educationalists because of his liberal views claimed openly and eloquently in January 1959 that the now generally recognised economic underdevelopment of Ireland was directly caused by the educational system. It must be recalled that the *Irish Press* was the semi-official newspaper of the Fianna Fáil party. Fianna Fáil was securely in power at the time and about to be taken over by Sean Lemass. The recent White Paper on economic development had called for the expenditure of £50,000,000, Cannon wrote, and 'it was unbelievable that this document should have ignored education, and secondary education in particular.' Cannon pointed out that the economic development plan proposed a permanent committee of the secretaries of the relevant departments. 'That the Department of Education is not included certainly makes it evident that there is no realisation of the productive function and economic importance of education amongst those at the top responsible for the future development of our economic life.' Actually there was such a realisation, but people who shared this view were being

actively resisted and shut out of the decision-making process. Nor
was it a new realisation; nearly half a century later this omission
still beggars belief.

Finally, a very different approach to assessment of the educational
system was put in place, apparently by direct personal intervention of
the new Taoiseach, Sean Lemass, in 1959. Lemass bluntly announced,
cutting a Gordian knot, that the school-leaving age was to be raised to
fifteen as soon as possible and that the secondary school curriculum
was to be reviewed, reformed and extended also with all due speed.
He had hit the ground running following Dev's departure from
government in 1959 to go to the Phoenix Park as President of the
country. A policy change recommended by many Sinn Féin idealists
in the 1920s was finally implemented forty years later in a rather
moderate, even cautious, form; this was regarded by many as revolutionary. Patrick Hillery, Minister for Education, joined Lemass in
burying the Council for Education's reports by sounding a very
different note. Hillery announced in a tone that was quietly explosive:

> . . . if we are to overcome the degree of underdevelopment at
> which we find ourselves we must have more and more
> education. A large part of the State's responsibility was to foster
> the country's economic interests and the first essential in this
> regard was that the system of education should, as far as pos-
> sible, fit the students to face the modern world by, for example,
> promoting the teaching of science.[17]

As Sean Farren argues, social change and, just as important, the
acceptance of, and general wish for, such change forced the hand
of a newly willing government under Lemass and a generation of
political leaders just about to take control. These were men who,
other than Lemass himself, did not remember the revolutionary
period or the ideological enthusiasms of the 1900–22 era. Rather,
they had grown up in the depressed and defeated atmosphere of
the 1930–50 years; to them, independence was a dead fact and
needed no cultural or symbolic props such as a national language
or religious self-assertion. They also listened with sympathy and
recognition to the quiet argument of O'Faolain, Kelleher and so

many others in public and in private that the idea of a Catholic and Gaelicised Ireland as dreamed of by the revolutionaries and the teachers in the Christian Brothers schools was actually threatening to strangle the real English-speaking and urban Ireland that was emerging around them.[18] I have argued elsewhere that the period between 1944 and 1960 witnessed a gradual disintegration of the political alliance between 'priests and patriots' which had dominated the separatist movement before 1922 and which had, in effect, governed the emergent Irish state since independence. The dream Ireland of Faith and Fatherland that had filled the minds of so many political leaders was quietly abandoned, partly because of the eloquent public proddings of pundits like Cannon, Sheehy-Skeffington and O'Faolain.

The related idea that all desirable social and cultural change could be effected by direct state action rather than by impersonal social forces, the market and the efforts of many private individuals took far longer to fade from the minds of political decision-makers. The semi-state bodies that Lemass and others had set up in the 1930s and afterwards have only recently begun to come under intellectual and political siege. However, in the 1950s, the two sides of the nationalist establishment had already ceased to see eye to eye and the alliance had begun to decay. The nationalist and developmentalist component of the alliance increasingly came into open conflict with the puritan, culturally defensive and quietist component, and this conflict was becoming open by the late 1950s. The weakening of the integralist Catholic wing was accelerated in the early 1960s by Vatican II, a general council of the Catholic Church that set out to liberalise the official teaching of the Church. Vatican II also proceeded to modernise the liturgy by adopting vernacular languages and made friendly overtures to the other Christian churches and to non-Christian faiths as well. In effect, Vatican II declared the Counter-Reformation to be over after four hundred years of cultural and religious conflict. However, many would argue, cogently in my view, that it also attempted to liberalise the unliberalisable.

This ecclesiastical upheaval coincided with the political New Departure in Ireland and the economic shift of the 1960s. The patriots had come reluctantly or otherwise to the conclusion that economic and cultural protectionism would have to be abandoned in favour of free trade, and that multinational capital would have to be used to supplement local capital. It was also concluded that cultural protectionism in the form of book and film censorship was stultifying and that, in particular, education designed to produce pious patriots and nationalist priests would have to be replaced by education and training for economic growth. Young people were going to be shown how to earn their living in a changing, and often bewildering, world. If this meant less of a curriculum intended to promote an historicist and nostalgic mentality and an emphasis on classical studies in preparation for the priesthood, so be it. Essentially this is what duly happened, and happened very rapidly. However, there is still resistance to engineering and science training in Irish schools and colleges a generation later, much of it coming from the students themselves; profound cultural change takes time to work its way through a population. Another reason may be the rather esoteric and advanced teaching of mathematics and its detachment from concrete scientific and social issues. A further ironic reason is the general shying away from 'hard' subjects characteristic of the children of rich societies.

The nationalists, children as they were of Arthur Griffith's Sinn Féin, wanted to create a strong and modern nation with industries, cities, a growing population and a place among the nations of the earth, as the old slogan had vainly promised an earlier generation. Spreading what little wealth there was around equally in a stagnant rural and small-town economy protected against the big bad world by tariff barriers and cultural walls just didn't work, and everybody knew it after the crash of 1956. In effect, Ireland had to stop playing house on its own, over there on the western fringe of Europe. Educating young men and women for the priesthood and the convent, while signalling that the lay life was a distinctly inferior vocation, if it could even be termed such, was a recipe for cultural stagnation and sterility. It was a situation that had to be rebelled against by quiet withdrawal from the community in the form of silence, 'internal emigration' or even real emigration to countries where trying to earn one's living was an activity that earned admiration and respect rather than resentment, sneering and obstruction.

Furthermore, ideas and frank exchange of opinion were desperately needed in the prevailing atmosphere of intellectual and material bankruptcy; old-fashioned baiting of the intellectuals just didn't work. In the eyes of many of the newly educated young of the time, the country was washed up, and these were the people the new generation of nationalist leaders in Fianna Fáil and Fine Gael needed for support. Puritan patriots and priests had gamely tried to preserve and reproduce a certain social type, pious, familial, loyal to the native acres, culturally ingrown and obedient to clerical guidance in matters moral and intellectual. Education had been classical, grammar school in style and mathematical rather than applied. Beyond a fairly restrictive level, it was to be for the privileged few who were seen as the future ecclesiastical and political leaders of a Catholic Irish state. By implication or by direct administrative provision, everything else was somehow secondary or even inferior. By the 1950s, this entire project, although by no means intellectually contemptible, was seen as a threat to the nationalist one, and seen as such even by many of the younger priests.

An undercurrent of doubt about the social and cultural policies espoused by the clerical and lay leaders had always existed in the nationalist tradition, many-stranded as it always had been under the outward surface of apparent conformity. This undercurrent went back to Griffith's own doubts about the rural and conformist arcadias beloved of so many young Sinn Féiners and Gaelic Leaguers before 1912. These were young people reared on the novels of Charles Kickham and Canon Sheehan, novels which glorified rural Irish society of Victorian times, particularly the yeoman farmer culture of late nineteenth-century Munster. As early as 1903, Griffith had written of the 'cocky disparagement of the work of modern thinkers' which was characteristic of the 'shoddy side' of the nationalist cultural and political movements in Ireland. Young men praised an imaginary medieval Ireland and then wondered why the real country was decaying all around them, Griffith felt. While the world outside had intellectual vitality and economic growth, Ireland clung enthusiastically to her pictur-esque ignorance. 'Ireland's clever young men, while knowing better in private, announced in public that Ireland's innocence was more sacred than "the wisdom of an infidel world" and Ireland emigrates.' More than anything, Griffith argued, Ireland needed freedom of thought; much as Karl Marx was no Marxist, the founder of Sinn Féin was no Sinn Féiner.

Even then, at the beginning of the twentieth century, Griffith's ideas were being countered by prominent clerics. In 1903, Canon Sheehan was preaching for a clerical intellectual dominance of the new Ireland for a further half-century; his predictions were accurate. Educated laymen, he proclaimed, were not to be trusted with cultural leadership. Anticipating McGilligan, he argued that these young men would be the overeducated unemployed of the future and would be a menace. Griffith and those who thought like him were virtually snookered by the quietists for half a century.[19] Many writers and artists, in particular perhaps the writers of *The Bell* group centred on O'Faolain, echoed this plea for mental free-dom in the generation after independence. Modernisers who had made explicit connections between mental freedom, innovation and economic and cultural progress had always existed in the broader nationalist community. These had, in effect, been shunted aside in the 1930s by those who essentially opted for a pious stasis and who got their way because of electoral politics, the Great Depression and the isolation caused by the Second World War. This was partly the result of anti-modernism on the part of clerical thinkers, but also the result of a blocked political system, in which many issues of medium- to long-term national impor-tance became sidelined because of stalemates between sets of political, educational and ecclesiastical elites.

However, at bottom, the basic obstructiveness was clearly clerically driven. A covert and incoherent anti-clericalism existed, particu-larly among many of those who combined in themselves a relatively high level of educational achievement and subordination to clerical authority: the schoolmasters. These schoolteachers, commonly highly intelligent and products of an authoritarian but often intellectually lively teacher-training system, were themselves encysted in an ecclesiastically controlled educational apparatus. This system inculcated the same mixture of anti-modernist Catholicism and neo-Gaelic nationalism at senior levels as had long informed more junior levels of the system. Their reactive anti-clericalism therefore often took the form of a romantic and exaggerated republican nationalism combined with linguistic revivalism, sometimes of a markedly aggressive type. Commonly, a confusion of Catholic martyrology and the parallel marty- rologies of Tone, Emmet, Pearse, Connolly and the rest occurred, to the unease of better-informed or more clear-thinking Catholic priests; the Easter Rising occasionally seemed to be confused with the Resurrection of Christ.

Sometimes the anti-clericalism simply took the form of a quiet, withdrawn and unspoken agnosticism or atheism and helpless cynicism; certainly, many highly educated people of that period were simply internal emigrants who kept their counsel in what seemed to be a hopeless situation. However, concern about the situation was also expressed, more loudly and without fear, by sympathetic outsiders whose views seem to have influenced establishment opinion more effectively than those of internal commentators. The latter's criticisms were easily dismissed by the Irish weapon of ridicule and often seen as being treason in the ranks. In 1954, an Irish-American priest, Fr John A. O'Brien, edited a much discussed collection of essays entitled, rather alarmingly, *The Vanishing Irish*.[20] The title alone was enough to get a public reaction in an Ireland reeling from the economic and ideological shocks of the 1950s and with a strong folk memory of 'race death' ideologies in previous generations. The contributors collectively launched what amounted to a sustained attack on the intellectual assumptions of the Irish political and ecclesiastical establishment of the time. In 1955, Michael Sheehy published *Divided We Stand*, in which, for a newly attentive younger generation, he offered a calm and coherent critique of the official Irish government position on partition, a critique that looks quite advanced even now. The book was well timed, coming out as it did at the beginning of a new IRA campaign waged in the name of the principles touted by Irish governments. The doublethink of a noisy official anti-partitionism, combined with the imprisonment of IRA men who were obeying something suspiciously close to the official line, was made evident to many.[21]

In 1957, J.V. Kelleher, a well-known and respected Irish-American academic, published a more measured and detached analysis in an article published in the influential American quarterly, *Foreign Affairs*. Kelleher argued that a lack of intellectualism among Irish leaders, combined with an emigration-generated apathy among the general population, was almost literally killing the country. The evident official and ecclesiastical hatred of intellectual and psychological freedom was finally coming to be seen as a real threat to the entire nationalist project. Kelleher, rather like Charles Carter, sketched a little country living on the memory of real and imagined past wrongs, continually making excuses for itself, while the solutions for her ills were in her own hands. The Irish scarcely regarded their democratic government as being in charge of the country, he asserted; the country was actually run by the Catholic Church and powerful businessmen, civil servants and other public figures organised into a Catholic freemasonry, the Knights of Columbanus, he reported. 'Ireland has no right to be sick,' Kelleher wrote. 'If we compare its resources to other European countries . . . one can hardly avoid deciding that Irish ills are largely psychosomatic.' In a famous and much-quoted aside, he commented on Irish history that the real problem was that the Irish had had 'an almost fatally easy time of it' in the twentieth century.

Every cantankerous critic has the duty to hazard at least one positive suggestion. Since I have given so one-sided a picture, omitting all that makes Ireland pleasant and attractive—which it is—my duty is the stronger. I would, then, suggest that Ireland accept emigration as a major and, for the moment, insoluble native problem. They should cease to regard it as a historical accident. Accepting it, they should at the same time accept the responsibility for seeing that those who do emigrate go out into the world well enough trained and educated to make an advantageous start in their new countries. In the nineteenth century an Irishman with a sixth grade education was at no special disadvantage in England or America. Today, three out of four Irish children still do not go beyond the sixth grade; and the education they receive is half-ruined by concentration on a language they will never speak again, anywhere.

I am inclined to believe that if an educational system adequate for this task were created in Ireland—and its creation would necessarily involve real vigor, daring and imagination, as well as searching reappraisal of old 'principles' and actual conditions—the effects of the effort would soon manifest themselves in every aspect of life. Everything would be changed; and not impossibly, so much for the better that the young might decide to stay at home and make a go of the country after all. There is, to be sure, the danger that they might make a go of it in ways the present fatherly rulers could only regard with horror; but it is the ultimate function of fathers to be horrified, and the function of the young to insure it happens to them. Anyway, that prospect, for all its uncertainty, is a better one to face up to than the likelihood of things going on as they are. I cannot imagine the sudden sweeping outbreak of anti-clerical rage which some of my Irish friends so gloomily but confidently predict. I can, however, imagine that Ireland may do what no other nation has ever tried, and perish by sudden implosion upon a central vacuity.

Interestingly, the article struck a nerve and infuriated McQuaid in particular. He commented privately that it was 'pitiable' as a work of scholarship and was 'gravely wrong' on three unnamed issues and that it was pessimistic. 'Blanshard was not quite so hurtful.'[22] He seems to have been bewildered by such hostile criticism, thereby perhaps revealing how shielded he was from outside opinion by the authoritarianism of the system in which he was ensconced. Even teachers themselves raised their voices. Patrick Cannon had run into what seems to have been sustained clerical and episcopal resistance when he attempted to set up a lay secondary school for Catholics in Dublin which would not be controlled by Catholic clergy (Sandymount High). Cannon, as president of the 'Federation of Lay Catholic Secondary Schools', complained bitterly in 1961 that his organisation's views had been disregarded, that it had been excluded from the Council of

Education and from the Commission on Higher Education. Its
ideas about reform had been ignored:

> for many years our Federation experienced a strange reluctance
> on the part of the Department of Education to recognise this
> Federation as an educational body. We are glad to be able to
> inform you that when the reasons given by previous Ministers
> for Education for their failure to recognise this body fully were
> fully explained to the late Minister for Education, Mr. Sean
> Lynch, recognition was arranged without delay.

Evidently, he had been excluded by clerical and bureaucratic
manoeuvring. Happily, Jack ('Sean') Lynch, as Minister for
Education, had remedied that in the late 1950s in a quiet act of
what amounted to considerable political courage and creativity.[23]
In a penetrating series of articles in *The Irish Times* in 1961, duly
clipped by civil servants for the Taoiseach's file, T.J. McElligott,
another lively minded teacher of extensive experience, pointed out
that Northern Ireland, with half the population of the Republic,
managed to spend double the Republic's total on education, *in
absolute terms*. In other words, the North's spend per head was
approximately *four times* that of the south. Even the cheap clerical
labour could not compensate for this huge discrepancy. The
Republic's system was elitist and discriminated against the poor.
McElligott wrote angrily:

> . . . as long as Ministers of State and leaders of Church are insulated
> from the withering effects of an education that ends at fourteen,
> they will never feel that driving discontent with existing conditions
> that might move them to consider and effect change.[24]

Parents were reluctant to criticise the secondary school system
for fear of being seen as being out of step, McElligott claimed.
'Such is the range of clerical control and such the fear, or at best
apathy of the people they show little concern where their children
are taught, and less concern for what they are taught.'[25] A nascent
Irish movement of liberal opinion, *Tuairim* (Opinion), also put its

oar in, significantly through its London branch rather than through branches within Ireland. The Irish did not generally admit publicly what they knew to be the case, *Tuairim* commented, and that was that the Irish educational system was backward. This was the result not of a defensive patriotism, but of a simple fear of the clergy. This fear extended, ironically enough, to many of the priests themselves. In a rather scary thumbnail analysis of this zero-sum cultural and political climate, *Tuairim* reported, 'Churchmen have been reluctant to make constructive proposals lest they appear too dictatorial, politicians loath to change a system which appeared to be working reasonably well. Friction has been avoided at a heavy price: stagnation in the schools.'[26]

The numbers of children in industrial schools (borstals) were too high and, the writers added delicately, the children emerged from these institutions fit only for unskilled unemployment. Parenthetically, we now know that some of these schools were close to being brutal slave camps for children from underprivileged backgrounds. It is also clear that many of the young people were incarcerated for trivial offences or even for no offence at all. It seems that some clerical administrators actively canvassed for notionally delinquent children or children of 'unsuitable' parents to keep their capitation rates up. This 'unsuitability' was to be determined by the clerics, who thereby usurped the power of the courts and also went against the prevailing ideology of familism. The courts and the police were commonly complaisant. It is also now established, and it was fairly well known at the time through personal experience and grapevine rumour, that physical abuse and sexual assault frequently occurred in the school system generally, and such abuse and assaults were apparently particularly common and particularly uninhibited in the industrial schools and orphanages. Children were sometimes, in effect, legally or otherwise stolen from their parents by clerics. Pregnant girls, or girls who had been raped and were brave enough to talk about it in public, were effectively imprisoned in 'Magdalene Laundries' run in a fantastically authoritarian fashion. This imprisonment was also illegal, but police and judicial authorities were either afraid to intervene or were themselves complicit. Furthermore, there seemed to be no mechanism by which the running of these institutions could be regulated and the children protected. Officials who tried to put such mechanisms in place seem to have been sidetracked by bureaucratic manoeuvrings.

While he made no public comment on these murkier reaches of the clerical 'educational' empire in Ireland, McElligott excoriated Irish educational practice. There was little expressed public opinion on education, and the teaching of Irish interfered with the purpose of primary schools, he asserted. 'Parents tend to regard the clergy as the guardians of their interest in education and have shown no interest in founding parent-teacher organisations or complaining publicly of faults they notice in schools.' Lynch commented in May 1957 on the general demoralisation of the population, and felt that it had something to do with education and the public's passive attitude towards education, or even disregard for it:

> I cannot help feeling that if we were to take a greater interest in our system of education the teachers would feel less isolated in their battle for the mind of the country's youth, would feel more at one with the community generally and that far-reaching effects might be achieved which are evidently not being achieved at present.[27]

At last, internal opinion-formers were finding their voices and were being reacted to sympathetically by new men in power. Significantly, American Catholic sources had long been attacking, in particular, the orphanages and industrial schools in Ireland, which were controlled by the Church and the Departments of Justice and Education. Fr Edward O'Flanagan of Boys' Town fame, a well-known Irish-American priest, had visited Ireland in 1946–47 and roundly denounced the treatment of children in these institutions. For this he was attacked by Gerald Boland, the Minister for Justice, and by officials. James Dillon of Fine Gael joined robustly in this attack. In 1947, O'Flanagan wrote to Walter Mahon Smith in Dublin:

> It seems that in all of these discussions that we have had through the Irish Press since July [1946], we have been going around in a

vicious circle, getting nowhere, while some people over there [in Ireland] are doing everything to attack my main objectives, i.e.— unjust incarceration, unequal distribution of physical punishment both inside and outside the prisons and jails, and the institutionalisation of little children in great big factory-like places, where individuality has been, and is being, snuffed out with no development of the personality of the individual, and where little children become a great army of child slavery in workshops, making money for the institutions which give to them a little food, a little clothing, very little recreation and a doubtful education.

Boland, he claimed, had simply maligned his character in the Dáil chamber. O'Flanagan privately compared the Irish ecclesiastical and lay authorities to Nazis and fascists and questioned their ability to defend their stewardship of children in the eyes of God. The conditions in the industrial schools were, then, common knowledge, but little would happen until the Irish public took up the cudgels—something that did start to happen in the late 1950s.

All of this sudden, open articulation of complaints of a kind that had long been expressed covertly preceded, and possibly partly prompted, Hillery's setting up in October 1962 of a 'Survey Team', consisting of academics and civil servants and quite deliberately non-representative of the existing educational establishment. In a pattern that had by this time become familiar, outside authority was enlisted on the side of reformist purposes within the country. The research group was partly financed by the Organisation for Economic Co-operation and Development (OECD). It was to report in 1965, and that occasion was to constitute an historic event. Its *Investment in Education Report* affords an extraordinary and stark contrast to the Council of Education's reports of a decade earlier.[28] Using the tools of economics in particular, an attempt was made at a social scientific analysis of the educational system: a truly groundbreaking event at that time. The concept of education as a means by which society invested in the next generation informed the entire report, and its assessment of Irish education was devastating. It found that the Irish system was grossly neglectful of the children of the poorer classes in society, and that over half (53 per cent) of children left school at or before the age of thirteen. This was a stunning finding which made national newspaper headlines; these children had left 'no trace' behind them in the administrative apparatus.[29] The report concluded with the dry comment, 'Although this figure [of 53 per cent] is undoubtedly exaggerated, the annual emergence of such a large number of young people who apparently have not reached what is commonly considered a minimum level of education, can hardly be viewed with equanimity.'[30]

The evidence suggested that the general level of educational achievement among Irish emigrants to Britain was extremely low. 'In short, unemployment and emigration appear to be predominantly associated with lack of skills or other professional qualifications, while at the same time it is apparently necessary to import highly skilled people.' Little seemed to have changed since British times, when a large proportion of young people left school at age twelve, in effect functionally illiterate.[31] Restrictive practices, commonly enforced by the trade unions, abounded in Irish employment. The banks restricted hiring to below age 21, thereby in effect excluding graduates. The device of age restrictions on admission to apprenticeship was common—'. . . the age of entry (15 or 16) to apprenticeship effectively precludes the gaining of senior cycle education—in practice one cannot be a skilled tradesman and have a [high school] leaving certificate.'[32]

Language teaching bulked large in secondary schools—English, Irish, Latin and even classical Greek being the main languages taught. Among modern continental languages, only French got a look in, and it lagged far behind Latin.[33] French was taught mainly in fee-paying, middle-class institutions. Furthermore, French often seems to have been looked upon less as a cultural or business asset and more as a social decoration for young middle-class ladies and gentlemen. German was almost unknown, and occasionally seen as the language of a defeated and irrelevant culture. In effect, *no one* learned Spanish, Italian, Chinese, Japanese, Russian or Arabic. Irish education reflected the concerns of local, clerical, revivalist and middle-class forces, to the detriment or even total exclusion of the children of poor parents, whether urban or rural.

*Investment in Education* was, however, an extremely innovative document, and effectively legitimised a revolution in Irish education which, by the standards of developmentalists, was decades overdue. It was also long overdue by the standards of those of a previous generation who had hoped, in vain, that independent Ireland would be an enlightened, highly educated and essentially post-agricultural nation.

As we have seen, for many years vocational education was both a particular bone of contention between Church and state and scandalously underfinanced. It was, in effect, a neglected poor sister of the secondary and third-level branches of an extra-ordinarily underfunded 'middle class' post-primary educational system, surviving mainly by the virtually unpaid labour of clerics subject to a religious rather than an economic or intellectual discipline. Vocational education was a serious political problem, precisely because of its enormous potential popularity; it was useful, appealed to ordinary farming and working people and was innately secular; its teachers were predominantly lay. It was widely valued despite being rather looked down upon by some parents and priests. Neo-Gaelic ideologues and ruralists disliked it because it prepared young people for a world of work that was essentially non-agrarian. Again, as documented earlier, it was a political problem from the beginning. As early as the beginning of the 1940s, the professor of Education at Maynooth, Fr Martin Brenan, was complaining eloquently in the *Irish Ecclesiastical Record* that the vocational schools were expensive. Essentially he was comparing them with the Church-controlled secondary schools, with their clerical, low-paid labour; he seemed to think that people who were paid for their labour were somehow morally inferior and, perhaps, socially inferior to those who gave their labour voluntarily out of religious enthusiasm and conviction. Furthermore, the vocational schools did not give religious instruction. He also claimed that the Catholic secondary schools were actually better at teaching vocational subjects than were the vocational schools. This claim possibly had some validity, as there tended to be a brain drain away from the vocational system in favour of the more prestigious secondary school system. Brenan suggested that the vocational schools be taken over by the national schools, which were under the direct control of the local parish priest.

However, the Catholic Church, contrary to stereotype, was no monolith. Several clergy working in the educational system wrote in to the *Irish Ecclesiastical Record* to defend the vocational education system as it stood, and did so in very vigorous terms.[34] As we have seen, Brenan was involved with John Charles McQuaid some years later to take over the vocational sector completely. A closely related and even deeper worry in the minds of many clerics and cultural revivalists was the decline in farm population. They regarded with unease the growth of towns and the weakening of the appeal of rural life to young people attracted by the bright lights, the cinema, dancehalls and the freedoms of town life. Urban populations were inherently less controllable by priests than were rural communities because of size and relative anonymity; McQuaid's gargantuan attempt to control Dublin as though he were the parish priest of a huge Cootehill was doomed to failure, although it worked, after a fashion, for a generation.

Gaelic revivalists also had their demands on the educational system. Rural science and nature study, which (just) might have stimulated young people's interest in agricultural science, was made optional in 1934 to make room for more Irish. 'As a result of this regulation, there was a catastrophic fall in the number of schools teaching rural science or nature study.'[35] Brian Girvin argues, convincingly, that the insistence of the neo-Gaels and the Catholic Church on having a large say in educational policy encouraged, intentionally or otherwise, a sluggish approach to educational policy. In particular, if everything had to be run past the bishops, many things would simply never be attempted. Bishops were known to be defensive and often aggressively so in their political reactions. A culture of extreme conservatism, combined with an atmosphere of obstructive authoritarianism that sometimes verged on a very Irish kind of genial terrorism, informed educational policy. Girvin writes:

The end of the Second World War confirmed the triumph of social conservatism in Ireland. Nowhere was this more obvious than in the case of education where relatively few plans for educational reconstruction were devised even when the Department of Education was pressurised by de Valera to do so.

The social conservatism that had triumphed in de Valera's Ireland had the tacit, or even active, assent of most of Irish society. There was even an element of what Girvin terms pretty tellingly a 'smugness' in Irish cultural and social consciousness, when comparisons were made with war-torn post-Christian societies elsewhere. The idea that this condition could be continued indefinitely and merited defence and conservation was widely accepted. My assessment of the politics of education echoes Girvin's. The vocational schools were seen as a fly in the ointment because they were not controlled by the clerics, even though clerical presence on the Vocational Education Committees of the local councils was strong outside Dublin and some other towns. Girvin describes the vocational system as giving the impression that it was actually 'under siege'.[36] Certainly, some lecturers in the VEC system were indeed associated with what were seen as liberal, anti-clerical, extreme nationalist or otherwise radical views by the standards of the time. During the 1950s, despite a growing awareness of the importance of technical and vocational education, relatively little was done until the general crisis of the mid-1950s was resolved in the mid-1960s, fundamentally because of a chronic stand-off between the forces of Church and state. Quite apart from clerical qualms, many people seemed to have an impoverished and snobbish view of the role of vocational education. As we have seen, Sean Moylan was the honourable exception, and built 160 new vocational schools in the early 1950s but could not follow through because of electoral defeat in 1954. Moylan was an extraordinarily popular Minister among the teachers of the period, and was often regarded as the lost leader of Irish educational reform. De Valera evidently thought highly of his capacities, as he resorted to the desperate expedient of making him a senator in 1957 to enable him to become Minister for Agriculture (Moylan had lost his Dáil seat in that year). Moylan died shortly afterwards. Again, electoral instability and death seem to have stymied reformists in perhaps unexpected places. However, Jack Lynch was made Minister for Education in 1957 and turned out to be the first of a series of reformist Ministers.

Again, it was not until the 1960s that government spokesmen and academics began to speak of a new subject, the economics of education. As John Logan has cogently put it, two of the central propositions of this new academic area were firstly, that non-meritocratic education wasted the natural talents of less privileged children, quite apart from ethical considerations; education was not just about the inculcation of an ethical humanism, but also about earning one's living, which was itself an ethical consideration. The second and very practical proposition was that there was a demonstrable connection between the provision of mass education, particularly in applied and technical fields, and rapid economic growth in post-war Europe. 'In all of this the question of educational equality—the extension of schooling and an individual's access to it as a civil and social right—was for the time being conceptualised as a secondary concern.'[37] However, it took twenty years after the end of the Second World War for this apparently fairly elementary insight to become accepted in Irish political discourse. The year 1965 seems to have been a cusp one. Eileen Connolly of Dublin City University has, through content analysis of Dáil debates, designated this year as that in which legislators ceased to discuss decisions as choices in favour of or against change, but rather viewed them as choices of different ways of managing a process of change which was unavoidable and, perhaps, even to be welcomed. Academic chairs in Education at Irish universities commonly lay vacant for years, reflecting the general sense that education was mainly a religious or clerical activity and no business of academia. The UCD chair was vacant between 1950 and 1966, the chair in UCC was unoccupied from 1962 to 1969 and that in Maynooth was empty from 1956 to 1966.[38] The chairs were, it should be emphasised, finally filled in the late 1960s. It is no cliché: the 1960s were indeed a time when everything changed in Ireland, for better or worse.

## BREAKTHROUGH

Patrick Hillery, George Colley and Donough O'Malley were the
key ministers for education in the mid-1960s. Lemass, according
to his biographer, John Horgan, had 'sensed' a general wish for
reform in education; the verb is interesting. Hillery, frustrated by
the Department of Finance in his attempts to reform aspects of
the system, went directly to Lemass; a memorandum to the
Taoiseach from the Department of Education was sent by him in
January 1963.[39] Hillery envisaged a complete new nationwide post-
primary system, but kept his ultimate aim hidden. Interestingly, he
saw his way blocked by the usual sets of vested interests and
resolved to start by setting up schools in areas deprived of such
services. With a devastating if Aesopian sideswipe at the ecclesiastical establishment, Hillery wrote, 'Certain vested interests in
education would be annoyed at the introduction of such a school
on a national basis but in this particular [remote] area the
interests have not provided for the children and cannot therefore
object to state action.' He saw this pilot plan, designed for areas
which had essentially been neglected by Church and state (at the
Church's behest), as the thin end of the state's wedge, and a
general extension of the new schools to the entire country would
follow in due course. A shrewd perception of the political weak
points of his clerical opponents was pretty evident.[40] In a back-
handed way, however, Hillery's comments also give a sense of the
deadening power of clerical authority at even that late date.
Significantly, unlike Mulcahy some years earlier, Hillery clearly
resented that deadening.

Lemass as Taoiseach, James Ryan as Minister for Finance and
Hillery in the Department of Education seem to have been the key
figures at that juncture, with T.K. Whitaker, Sean O'Connor and
other key civil servants in the background as general advisers and,
apparently, as instigators at times. The pilot comprehensive
schools were built and formed the basis for the later community
schools, a device designed to co-opt ecclesiastical authority and
persuade the bishops to acquiesce in a general expansion of post-
primary education in the following decades. In any case, the
bishops would be unable to stand against such an evidently

popular project, even if they wanted to. Hillery and his successors had forced their hand.

*Investment in Education* followed in 1965, giving Colley an argument in favour of a policy of amalgamating undersized rural schools, a policy which he duly trundled past the Irish National Teachers' Organisation and the Catholic Church. However, all of this was overshadowed by O'Malley's sudden announcement in 1966 of 'free post-primary education'. On 10 September 1966, at Dún Laoghaire, Mr O'Malley addressed an audience of journalists, bluntly remarking that Irish independence had created as many problems as it had solved because it had led to a crisis of stability and a civil war. These disasters had been followed, he observed, by depression and by the Second World War. Unemployment and emigration had been chronic problems but great shifts were now occurring, and under the superficial calm of Irish society, profound cultural change was happening. Education was never more necessary, but many families could not afford to pay for the education of their children. Every year, some 17,000 children dropped out after finishing primary school. He finished off with a bombshell: free education to Leaving Certificate at age eighteen was to be provided immediately by government action. In 1967, in the Senate, O'Malley proudly announced that 99.9 per cent of letters from the public supported him, often in glowing terms. He intended vocational schools to be made on a par with secondary schools, offering a range of non-technical educational subjects as well, leading to a common Leaving Certificate examination. The Minister then went further, coming clean about the efforts of unnamed, but clearly identifiable, vested interests to block him:

No one is going to stop me introducing my scheme next September. I know I am up against opposition and serious organised opposition but they are not going to defeat me on this. I shall tell you further that I shall expose them and I shall expose their tactics on every available occasion whoever they are. I see my responsibilities to the Irish people and the Irish children. No vested interest or group, whoever they may be, at whatever level, will sabotage what every reasonable-minded man considers to be a just scheme. We may differ as has been said and we are all agreed on the conception of an approach to free education because this is all it is, even though I am catering for 75 per cent of the secondary school children.

As time goes on the fees and costs I suppose will increase at least and so must the assistance from the government. I had a deputation recently and a reverend gentleman as he went out the door, when I said to him 'Perhaps a £25 maximum now and maybe in a few years £35', he said jocosely but there was malice in his joke: 'You will never catch us. We will always be ahead of you.'

It was our Divine Lord who said 'Suffer little children to come unto me'.

There will be a lot of suffering if that is the mentality which prevails in Ireland. I am surprised and I am disillusioned because no Minister for Education came into this Department with more goodwill than I did and I was very surprised.

Maybe some day I shall tell the tale and there is no better man to tell it.

Christian charity how are you![41]

He never got to tell his tale. O'Malley was a slightly larger-than-life figure, a member of a well-known Limerick political family. Trained as an engineer, he was quite the boulevardier, dressed stylishly and acted in a genial and free-spending manner that brought instant public attention and popularity. He had a similarly extroverted and outspoken way of working and had a track record of rather noisy undergraduate radicalism in University College Galway. As an undergraduate, he already evinced a keen interest in education. He had a clearly expressed contempt for the use of religious organisations such as the Knights of Columbanus for personal advancement and financial gain. His unauthorised public announcement in 1966 caused private dismay and anger in political, official and academic circles. He had bypassed government, the Department of Finance and the ordinary policy-making process and appealed directly to the public. The bishops were completely bypassed and, essentially, snookered. Whitaker was taken aback, by all accounts, and wrote afterwards about the irrationalities that the decision was introducing into the educational system. It seems that Lemass was also taken by surprise, contrary to rumour and journalists' (particularly John Healy's of *The Irish Times*) stereotypes of the Taoiseach as someone who was covertly egging O'Malley on. O'Malley got away with it, but it has been cogently argued by Whitaker and others that the implementation of the scheme was badly planned as a result and unnecessarily costly. Furthermore, it had the unintended, inegalitarian and unfortunate side effect of sidelining vocational education yet again in favour of mainline senior-cycle secondary school education as the only real route to the high school Leaving Certificate. However, as O'Malley possibly would have said himself, it might have been the only way of breaking through what was, at the time, widely seen as a logjam of vested interests and conservatism. The Irish educational egg had to be broken to make the Irish educational omelette. O'Malley died suddenly following a heart attack in 1968, but he had very clearly made his mark.

'Free Education' certainly broke an ideological and psychological taboo, whatever the waste and inefficiency that accompanied its establishment. In rural areas, children were, for the first time, to be transported to school in little yellow buses. 'Free Education' was rapidly followed by the expansion of vocational and technical education; the real revolution here was the establishment of the Regional Technical Colleges (RTCs) in the late 1960s and their gradual elevation to high second-level and third-level institutions. Effectively, the old 'traditional equation of university education with higher education' became untenable and further education and training started to become a mass phenomenon.[42] The new colleges built substantially on the work and track record of the old vocational schools, much disregarded and feared for their potential by traditionalists in previous decades. An unfortunate by-product of the O'Malley coup was a tendency of vocational education institutes to attempt to upgrade themselves into third-level institutes at the expense of their second-level functions, thereby perpetuating the historical undersupply of second-level technical training. This meant that many working-class young people were still being short-changed by the system.

These crucial developments went back to a series of decisions made by Hillery in early 1963. Again, much of the inspiration came from outside: the investigating team from the OECD, operating as an authoritative source of opinion, analysis and recommendation, was literally non-Irish and therefore not trapped in the local elite consensus or sclerosis that had held so much back for so long.[43] The RTCs were accompanied by two new technically oriented third-level colleges ('National Institutes for Higher Education' or NIHEs), later to become the University of Limerick and Dublin City University. Within seven years, an entire elite consensus had evaporated so totally it looked as though it had never existed. To illustrate the magnitude of the change, John Logan presents data that point to an expansion of traditional university numbers from 9,000 to over 20,000 between 1961 and 1971 (more than a doubling). However, *third-level* students at technical schools and the new Regional Technical Colleges expanded from a little over 1,000 higher education (i.e. third level) students per year to about 4,000 in 1971 in the same period (essentially a quadrupling): an extraordinary jump, certainly reflecting a pent-up demand that had been lurking in society for a long time. Between 1964/5 and 1993/4, total numbers in third-level education went from 18,000 to nearly 93,000. Technical places went from under one-twelfth of the total to nearly one-half in that period.

Clearly, the dead hand of the Catholic Church's obsessions with religious education, ideological control and patronage, the obsession with linguistic revivalism combined with political timidity and ruralist disregard for further education had caused a quiet and almost indescribable, because negative, havoc in the form of thousands of school places that never were. To paraphrase an Irish journalist of the period (again, John Healy of *The Irish Times*), for many years nobody had shouted, *Start*.

By 1991, the gains of the 1960s had clearly been consolidated and built on; by then, the equivalent numbers of technical students amounted to nearly 30,000 students in a total state population that had increased by about a fifth. Technical and applied scientific education had finally arrived, having increased perhaps by an extraordinary twentyfold in terms of student places between 1961 and 1991. In fact, the rates of expansion of students going into further education accelerated after 1980: even in the bad years of the early 1980s, policy-makers and educationalists kept their nerve and the expansion continued. Paul Sweeney, in his *The Celtic Tiger*, has commented that this spectacular turnaround in education had been achieved 'in spite of gross neglect' of education during the years after the war. This neglect occurred despite the fact that other Western countries were pumping money into education and despite a traditional underfunding of education in Ireland, much of it instigated by ecclesiastics in alliance with businessmen and voters hostile to extra taxation to pay for state financing of education. Sweeney convincingly argues that the crucial event was the educational coup of O'Malley in 1966, and the gradual collapse between 1945 and 1965 of clerical and popular resistance to the idea of a generally educated and secular society.[44] Perhaps it would be more accurate and perhaps less kind to describe it as a process by which the idea of an educated society ceased to be something to be feared and despised *à la* McGilligan. Ireland paid dearly for its foregone opportunities between 1945 and 1960. Many people also sensed this at the time; the authentic popular cults of such very different perceived mould-breakers as Noel Browne, Kenneth Whitaker and Sean Lemass suggest as much.

## END OF AN ERA

Free mass second- and third-level education, together with the influence of television, foreign travel and higher standards of living, transformed Irish society, a transformation that was foreseen with nervousness, anger and foreboding by some of the older generation of leaders and, very obviously, by many traditionalists. Information became more freely available, and older forms of social control withered. Losses also occurred; the 1960s witnessed the destruction of the classical curriculum and the virtual cessation of teaching of the classical languages. The Catholic Church co-operated, as these languages were no longer needed by the Church of Vatican II. This piece of possibly understandable cultural Maoism was not noticeably accompanied by any spectacular growth in the study of modern languages. With the new freedoms came sexual openness and the end of the fear of powerful people. The arrival of the contraceptive pill in the mid-1960s offered an immediate and comic challenge to the blanket ban on contraceptive devices imposed by the law. Irish women were solemnly declared by their doctors to have the most irregular cycles in the world, and the 'Pill' was sold as a cycle regulator but not as a contraceptive. Words were, and are, very important in Ireland.

Manners changed; the traditional policy of excluding women from bar premises in public houses died, and as well as equality of opportunity, women achieved equality of manners. In 1973, the notorious 'marriage bar', which had forced women to leave public-service jobs on getting married, was abolished by a Fine Gael-led government. The motor car became ubiquitous, partly because of the extraordinary inadequacy of state transport services and, in particular, the strike-ridden character of the state-owned national bus company. Also with these changes came increasing levels of crime, including theft and violent crime. Drunkenness increased as incomes rose, and gradually became common to both sexes. Murder rates increased considerably, and an old innocence seemed to be dying. The sleeping giant of Irish politics, Northern Ireland, was also clearly stirring. In 1961, at the inaugural broadcast of the first Irish television station, de Valera had famously expressed his unease at the potential effects of television on the Irish people. He welcomed the new development in broadcasting which, on the one hand, could build up the character of the whole people but which could, if misused, lead to demoralisation, decadence and cultural collapse. In 1962, Lemass, in a long interview with a well-known Irish journalist, Desmond Fisher, accepted quite readily that Irish neutrality would have to go when European unity occurred, the latter being an event he had long foreseen and very clearly looked forward to. Fisher recalled:

> He predicted great changes in Ireland before the end of the century—contraception and divorce being legalised and materialism becoming widespread because of growing prosperity. Back in 1962, these predictions seemed, at least to me, to be a bit daring. Up to a point, he welcomed changed social mores, but I felt that he was a bit pessimistic about a future in which some of the good qualities of the Irish people would be lost or diminished.[45]

Even Lemass, then, had moments of unease about the long-term cultural consequences of his own new departure. Other old men looked with frank resentment at the new mohair-suited young tycoons who were taking over their party under the aegis of Lemass. The envy of the old for the young was very evident. Lemass, an old man in a young man's hurry if ever there was one, apparently wanted the entire Fianna Fáil gerontocracy to fall on its collective sword and get out of his way so that he could let the young men have their way. Patrick Smith, an old IRA veteran from the border county of Cavan, looking at Charles Haughey and the other mohair-suited Young Turks in the late 1950s, growled, 'There are worse ways of entering politics than with a rope around your neck.'[46] A few years later, in 1963, he and his pro-farmer stance were ditched suddenly by Lemass in favour of Haughey and the entente with the trade unions. Sean MacEntee resisted retirement, being quite eloquently unapologetic about his old age. Gerald Boland, one of the most rugged of the old men, actively despised the younger people. In March 1965, he wrote, 'Some of the young set make me actually sick and disgusted. And I feel inclined to kick myself for having helped to build up an organisation to be taken over by these chancers . . .' Sean T. O'Kelly wrote to MacEntee in a similarly uneasy vein at the same time: 'I hope the bold as brass young fellows will do as well for the country as the [boys of the] old brigade.'

Their psychology seems to have been that of the peasant farmer of that dying era who hung on to his farm as long as he possibly could before relinquishing control to an already ageing son; anthropologically, their behaviour was appropriate enough, as was their resentment of the passage of time. Enough of the older men stayed around to sustain Jack Lynch through the Arms Crisis of 1970 and help prevent all of Ireland descending into civil war in the 1970s, their understanding of the horrors of civil war being far more vivid than that of the younger men.[47] However, the Ireland they had dreamed of was dead around them, and they knew it. Oddly enough, many seem to have been secretly glad; a curious but quite strong vein of radical anti-clericalism and genuine attachment to an egalitarian style of liberal democracy ran through Fianna Fáil, often hidden under republican nationalist and Catholic rhetoric. In a way, they were being liberated from a collective hypocrisy enforced by communal psychology. 'Mind You, I've Said Nothing' was ceasing to be the unofficial national motto.

By 1970, it was possible for a young Irish academic, Joseph Lee, to give a slightly over-the-top but essentially on-target assessment of the results of Irish political sclerosis. In Lee's view, the Irish educational system had not only gifted the country with guiltless Cromwells, but had prevented underprivileged young people of high ability from getting anywhere in their own country. The result was an instantly recognisable conflict between mediocrity and occasional brilliance where the former commonly won out.

An obese [sic] educational system, where minimal entry require-ments guaranteed education to anyone, however stupid, who could afford it, and where absence of scholarships denied it to anyone, however gifted, who could not, produced a flow of educated hacks incapable of grappling with the country's problems and paralysing an economy particularly dependent on the quality of its human resources to compensate for the lack of natural resources.

The educational system achieved the intellectual isolation of Ireland much more effectively than Protection achieved economic isolation, and an alarmingly wide gap between best and average practice has afflicted politics, administration and scholarship no less than business. Not only managers, but researchers, had to be imported in droves in the early 1960s to raise the level of socio-economic analysis.

Lee was swimming in the wake of many ideological heavy-weights. In 1967, J.J. McElligott, the *éminence grise* of the Department of Finance, a man who had been with Pearse in the General Post Office during the Easter Rising fifty years previously, was brave again in his old age. He pointed publicly to the disproportionate number of pass degrees issued by universities. This, he argued, indicated a self-confessed mediocre human product and a generally third-rate level of student ability. He bluntly said that Irish could not be revived and that the ideologically driven emphasis on the language was lowering educational standards generally. Irish revival attempts over the previous forty years had got nowhere and had, he thought, been responsible 'for more than one educational setback'. Compulsory Irish had crowded out modern languages, science and business studies. The *Irish Press*, in a leader published in 1966, excoriated Irish national interest in science as being minimal and far inferior to such things in Northern Ireland.[48]

Lemass, in retirement in early 1969 and vividly conscious of his own mortality, essentially offered an analysis that agreed with Lee's. He reminisced about the utter lack of technical knowledge that he and his colleagues had suffered from in the 1930s. There was, he remarked, 'no industrial tradition' in independent Ireland and no body of 'trained industrial managers' to be put to work. He also reminisced to the effect that the 'constant propaganda from Fine Gael' to the effect that any attempt to industrialise Ireland was doomed to failure and was a waste of energy and money was no help.

When we look back on the enormous economic and social developments in the country in the last fifty years it has to be admitted that there have been great improvements in that time. I suppose young people today do not appreciate this. They do not understand what it was like fifty years ago when the British were still in occupation of the country, there was little or no industry, social conditions were appalling, and unemployment at the end of the first world war was acute. We were the first small nation to achieve independence in this century, and we had to do everything for ourselves without any help from the experience of other countries and without any of the international organisations which are now available to assist newly independent countries. Granted, we made a lot of mistakes but I think we achieved a great deal also. If we had available to us in the 1920s and 1930s the type of assistance that is available to new states today we would have been able to do a great deal more. Even without it we might have achieved more. Looking back now, it is possible to see that opportunities themselves were missed, but nevertheless we did a great deal.[49]

The Fianna Fáil developmentalists of the 1930s and after had, in effect, no real role models, he claimed, and he gave unstinting praise to the American aid agencies that gave Irish economic planners and leaders advice on development strategies after 1945. He also burst out with an emotional fervour evidently born of an intensely remembered sense of political and psychological isolation, 'After the war, when international agencies were set up, it was almost inconceivable to us that high quality American personnel could be made available free to advise us on our resources and development plans.'[50] With great emphasis, he remembered not being able to believe his luck and was enthused retrospectively by the extraordinary open-handedness of the Americans and the OECD. Coming from an experience of Irish impoverishment and concomitant mean-mindedness combined with British superciliousness, he was stunned by the generosity, practicality and egalitarianism of the Americans.

Rather diplomatically, Lemass avoided blaming anyone for the sluggishness of development in the area of education, instead laying the responsibility on the population in general; there had been no real demand for education up to the mid-1950s, he asserted, perhaps with less than total truth. He was not in the blame game, particularly as the Catholic Church and many of his own colleagues might have been easy targets; prior to his own time in power, leadership in this particular area had been spasmodic and weak, when not positively perverse. In effect, he blamed 'the people' retrospectively for the near-hostility to further education that was so prevalent in Ireland at the time. As I have suggested, this popular near-hostility did exist, but was allied with an equally popular and almost ruthless short-sighted utilitarianism, where skills had to be learned, often without the slightest regard for, or even awareness of, the philosophical bases behind them. Education was actually highly valued, but the unorthodox opinions which education inevitably encouraged were not; whatever about exile, Joyce's famous prescriptions of silence and cunning were needed if one were heterodox.

Lemass offered another prophecy, couched in the language of political economy:

Progress once it is properly started must accelerate all the time you see; this is the law of life. Just as invention, scientific invention, is always accelerating because it is working from a basis of established knowledge and that basis is always increasing. The same is true of national progress. As the national economic base widens the scope for progress widens also. You remember there was this fellow who wrote about the various phases of economic development, and talked about the 'take-off' stage. Well, we passed that take-off stage somewhere in the early sixties and now it is certain that our progress will continue. We ceased running down the taxi-way and got into the take-off during that period. And that's why I would say that progress must continue.

Unless there is another international slump of a major kind or some disastrous situation affecting the economy here progress will continue at probably a steadily accelerating pace during the next decade.[51]

Lemass died in 1971, two years later. His prophecy was to be fulfilled, if not immediately. He knew that the process of change that he had encouraged had, in turn, created a situation that was irreversible. Almost uniquely among so many Irish political leaders and ideologues in power in the twentieth century, this extraordinary politician was almost completely successful in what he eventually set out to do towards the end of a long political life. In a way, he was a wrecker of an old ideological construct, but a wrecker only so that he could create a new country, while having occasional private misgivings about what it was he was up to. After all, in the minds of some, he was selling out all the communal, egalitarian and ruralist ideals that had been fought for over a generation previously, and the cult of betrayal was rather deeply encysted in Irish political culture's republican tradition.

It should also be recalled that the attitudes toward technical, applied and mass education in post-independence Ireland, attitudes people like Lemass had to struggle against instinctively, mirrored those prevalent in England at the time. Ireland was, in a sense, suffering from a version of the English Disease, or a disdain, institutionalised since the time of Cardinal Newman and Arnold of Rugby, for non-humanist, 'applied', technical education in engineering, physics, chemistry and the skilled trades. Lemass and his allies could see this, and eventually decided to do something about it.[52] Certainly, they would very probably have looked with disfavour and bored frustration on the recorded opinions of the notional founding father of University College Dublin (UCD), nowadays the largest university in the Republic of Ireland. In 1852, around the time he was actively involved in the founding of UCD's ancestral college, Cardinal Newman wrote:

> You see then, Gentlemen, here are two methods of education; the one aspires to be philosophical, the other mechanical; the one rises towards ideas, the other is exhausted upon what is particular and external. Let me not be thought to deny the necessity, or to decry the benefit, of such attention to what is particular and practical, of the useful or mechanical arts; life could not go on without them; we owe our daily welfare to them; their exercise is the duty of the many, and we owe to the many the debt of gratitude for fulfilling it. I only say that Knowledge, in proportion as it tends more and more to be particular, ceases to be Knowledge . . .[53]

The dichotomy is a false one, and demonstrably such; there may be 'two cultures', as in C.P. Snow's famous phrase, but the division is not intellectually based, but derived from sociological considerations such as those of status, class and political power. Science, technology and engineering are not 'different' intellectually from philosophy, literary studies, history, economics or the appreciation of art; in principle, an educated person should be as informed about astronomy, architecture, engineering and physics as about classical literature, foreign languages, philosophy or social history. Irish partition had been applied to the world of the intellect as well as to the religious communities, the classes, the sexes and the island itself. The notion that there were 'high ideas' which had little or no connection with the 'mechanical arts' is Platonic and aristocratic. Plato apparently believed that no one who had actually worked for a living was fit to rule the state, as such a person was inevitably banausic, that is, associated with a manual trade, low-class and ignoble.

Here we have the real root of the fatal innocence about science and the link between scientific theory and practical application—a link necessary to both—that ran through so much of Irish as well as English intellectual culture. This was the innocence which actually shocked the OECD team in the early 1960s. This innocence or, more accurately, a socially structured ignorance reproduced through the school system, was regarded by experts from outside these islands initially with incomprehension, and subsequently with a growing dismay.[54]

In an eerie way, the OECD comments echoed the remarks of George Fletcher, Assistant Secretary in charge of Technical Instruction from 1904 to 1927 in the old Department of Agriculture and Technical Instruction, writing in 1915, one year before the Easter Rising and a generation and a half before the OECD assessment. Fletcher's diagnosis was to go essentially ignored for fifty years afterwards. He wrote:

It is not yet realised that profound change was brought about by the industrial revolution, by the introduction of machinery and steam power, by the essential change in the nature of apprenticeship and the conditions of manufacture, and by the never-ending application of science to industry, had rendered the technical school essential to industrial progress. Yet it is true to say that the vast majority of our youths never receive any school education after the age of thirteen or fourteen—they never enter a continuation school or a technical school—hence they receive little direct education for their business in life, such a state of things constitutes a grave national danger and calls for immediate remedy.[55]

Because of Olsonian processes, or processes very similar to such, it took fifty years for an independent democratic Ireland to actually act on a diagnosis similar to Fletcher's. Even a generation later, despite great advances, the culture has not fully recovered the ground lost between 1915 and 1965 because of the outcome of the Irish revolution.

## MAN OF MYSTERY

The man who was at the centre of this extraordinary cultural revolution in Irish establishment thinking was something of a mystery to some of his contemporaries and old comrades in Fianna Fáil and the Old IRA. Lemass has become a kind of mythical figure in Irish popular culture, although of a very different type from those other mythicised figures, Eamon de Valera and Michael Collins. Todd Andrews, a senior executive close to the Fianna Fáil establishment, thought only Thomas Wentworth ('Thorough'), a famous English administrator in early seventeenth-century Ireland, compared with him. Andrews was also struck by his lack of interest in ideas for their own sake. Lemass was fond of golf, card-playing and the horses. When asked about his reading habits, he used to grin and say, 'Wild West'. Andrews also remembered his unusual concern with his clothes and appearance, even when on IRA active service or in a prisoner-of-war camp; Lemass explained his fastidiousness by claiming it to be a morale booster. Certainly, all his life Lemass was a very stylish dresser in the Humphrey Bogart tradition; in his earlier years, his dark, Italianate features made him a striking, even handsome, man. Rather like de Valera, he did not look stereotypically *Irish*.[56] A fascinating letter survives in the Andrews papers in University College Dublin from Edward Mac Aonraoi, a veteran Sinn Féiner, civil servant and pro-Treatyite who afterwards supported Fianna Fáil on the grounds that it had the right ideas about protectionism, development and economic separatism. Mac Aonraoi seems to have known Lemass well, but repeatedly referred to his old boss in a letter to his old friend Andrews in 1980 as 'that enigmatic man'.

> I assume you [i.e. Andrews] think of him as a perfect and ruthless administrator. I agree entirely; he would have made a perfect [British] Indian civil servant. But as a statesman? As a pragmatist he was an outstanding politician. Immensely clever but not intellectual. As I go on I am more and more baffled. I remember how he used to fill pages of a file on Rank Limerick flour-mill and whether their quota should be 10,000 or 15,000 barrels of flour. Waste of his time, when history was being made,

by him and a few others. But I am sure he never thought of himself as a history-maker. But then I call him an enigma. I mean it because he must have had charisma to be the leader he was but it was of a strange type. To get a historical parallel I can only think of another, equally far-fetched: Parnell, the same inscrutability, without close friends and few acquaintances. I don't think he knew a civil servant in his Department except [John] Leydon. The story went that he refused to know about any appointment lest he be accused of jobbery. Very like Parnell I imagine there were TDs in Fianna Fail that he never heard of and very few he would even know in the street.

As for his achievements, I wonder. The industrial development policy was really forced on him by the economic war, but he certainly engineered it well, like the Rank case from day to day. But when it came to high economic and financial policy he left it all to Brennan and McElligott with a complacent [recte complaisant?] Finance Minister . . .[57]

The famous conciliatory visit, in 1965, to Terence O'Neill, Prime Minister of Northern Ireland, came to naught in the light of subsequent events, Mac Aonraoi felt. However, Lemass would have stood no nonsense from the British, unlike Lynch, whom Mac Aonraoi, like so many of the veteran Sinn Féiners, seems to have considered as post-republican. Lemass, he felt, knew nothing about Ireland outside Dublin; he spoke no Irish and felt revivalism was not his strong suit and so left that side of things to others. Incidentally, de Valera had often urged Lemass to learn the language, and the younger man had, rather like the nation, engaged in what amounted to passive, if respectful, resistance. His wife wrote excellent Irish.

Mac Aonraoi was not alone in being mystified by Lemass because he was so unlike the Gaelic League veterans who constituted so many of his colleagues and their civil servants. The standard biography by John Horgan is, after all, entitled *Sean Lemass: The Enigmatic Patriot*.[58] Andrews, however, seems to have thought in his saturnine way that there was less to it than met the eye. His own view was that Lemass was old and tired and came to the job too late. However, that did not prevent Andrews from echoing many of Mac Aonraoi's opinions in his own published reminiscences. James Dillon offers a different, and rather shrewd, explanation for the Fianna Fáil leader's mysteriousness: he didn't particularly like being Taoiseach.

> I once heard Lemass say, at a public meeting in the King's Inns, that he had never known a day's happiness since he became Taoiseach, that his mission in public life was Industry and Commerce. While he was there he was happy, because he was doing useful work; from the time he became Taoiseach, he felt himself a supernumerary.[59]

His lack of enthusiasm for the top job was perhaps his greatest strength; he could leave it with a sigh of relief. Shortly after becoming Taoiseach, he wrote to de Valera, '[s]ince I took over as Taoiseach, I have not ceased to wonder how you carried the burden for so long without showing the strain. You are a wonderful man and surely tough as teak.'[60] For an apparently reluctant Taoiseach who felt himself a supernumerary, he made rather an impact on Irish politics and society. McQuaid apparently disapproved of him, remarking in 1956 about him in a letter to the Papal Nuncio that, as Minister for Industry and Commerce, Lemass had been 'chiefly responsible for the very noteworthy socialisation of our country.'[61] He seems to have seen Lemass coming, but misread his potential.

# 05 | DEVELOPMENTALISTS

## INDUSTRIAL DEVELOPMENT AUTHORITY

The years after 1945 saw a gradual and often reluctant acceptance of the proposition that Irish underdevelopment was neither inevitable nor desirable. It was further gradually accepted that Irish cultural pessimism was self-fulfilling, and therefore both futile and harmful. Furthermore, an agrarian, static Ireland, or even a Griffithian Ireland with an idealised 'balance' between agriculture and light industries scattered around the country, looked less and less attractive. The ageing elites of an ageing little country slowly came around to accepting the view that Irish education, as supplied by the churches, was increasingly unsuited to the demands of the modern world, but it took more than a decade for this crucial change of mind to be acted upon in any wide-reaching way. Eventually educational policy was changed and took concrete executive form in the mid-1960s in the shape of a rebellion by democratic government against episcopal veto. The original touchstone was the apparently unstoppable flow of emigrants from the Ireland of de Valera, going, after 1945, mainly to England rather than to the traditional destination of North America. While the Irish elites wrangled and sometimes pretended that everything was fine, hundreds of thousands of young people voted with their feet. In the 1950s, this flood grew even greater and seemed reminiscent of the great flight from the stricken island after Black Forty-Seven.

As we have seen, elites and the population were hopelessly divided on the means to be used to develop the country, and even on whether the country should ever be developed at all. Some secretly wished it to remain underdeveloped, or at least tradition-ally agrarian as it always had been. It was therefore fatally easy for a well-organised group to kill a developmentalist initiative while still in its embryo form. In an insecure and inexperienced culture, the Irish favoured weapon of ridicule could easily be used to silence or isolate proponents of change. Intimidation of dissidents was easy—so easy that it rarely needed to be resorted to; people kept their mouths shut for fear of angering powerful people and damaging their chances of a career. For example, it was impossible to suggest in public that one of the central reasons for Irish under-development and poverty was the Catholic practice, imposed by the clergy on women in the absence of contraception, of having large families regardless of the prospects of rearing children in any kind of real prosperity. This was commonly believed, but rarely said in public. Occasionally there were murmurings as to how it was that middle-class, relatively well-off people seemed to have relatively small families. They seemed to know something that the rest of us didn't.

Furthermore, opinion rather than knowledge seems to have dominated much of the discussion; Irish elites, inexperienced in managing an economy, were unsure how best to go forward. After all, many leaders were far more concerned with preserving what were seen as benign aspects of existing society, rather than with eliminating inequality and poverty; stasis had its proponents. The isolation and stasis generated by neutrality during the war years, combined with a huge out-migration to England, strengthened reactionary and nostalgic forces in Irish society and politics, sometimes to bizarre proportions.

However, in 1949, an initiative was taken that was to have extremely significant consequences for Irish economic develop-ment and social change during subsequent decades. The Inter-Party government decided to set up a stand-alone economic develop-ment agency, the Industrial Development Authority (IDA). The new agency was originally seen as having a strong research function, thereby reflecting elites' awareness of the inadequacy of their own understanding of developmental problems. The proposed agency echoed earlier Industry and Commerce proposals, and also reflected an increasing awareness of Czechoslovak and other foreign experiments with such agencies during the pre-war years. It also seems to echo a proposed economic 'Co-ordinating and Executive Board' of experts proposed by Arnold Marsh in 1945. The final initiative was inspired by Alexis FitzGerald, a young Fine Gael intellectual of the period. The new Fine Gael minister for Industry and Commerce, Daniel Morrissey, replacing Lemass as chairman of his empire, introduced a bill in early 1950 to legalise the infant organisation retrospectively. Morrissey bluntly declared the country to be 'underdeveloped industrially'. Much Irish capital was invested abroad, he pointed out.[1]

The purpose of the new agency was to 'advise and assist the Government in the intensification of industrial development on the best possible lines.' The four directors would not be civil servants, but they would preside over staff transferred from the Trade and Industry branch of the Department of Industry and Commerce.[2] By the Irish standards of the time, the IDA would have an unusually large remit for an organisation that was awarded a good deal of autonomy. Lemass, now in opposition, was openly furious at what he apparently saw as an asset-stripping exercise being performed by Fine Gael on his old stamping ground of Industry and Commerce. He saw the new agency as a time-waster of a kind with which he felt he had long been too familiar, and this time-waster was being set up at a time when economic development decisions had to be taken immediately. He argued that the IDA would simply do academic studies and hold up decisions that needed to be taken urgently. Presumably he had in mind the coming of the Cold War and the imminence of war in Asia. 'It is a typical product of the Fine Gael mind . . . [of Fine Gael's] negative approach to national problems.' He claimed as usual that Fine Gael was, and had always been, hostile to economic development. Fine Gael was a party that implicitly believed that agriculture was the natural industry of the country and industrial development was not feasible or desirable. Lemass further asserted that, in fact, industrialisation was inevitable and necessary. The IDA was merely a tarted-up version of the old Cumann na nGaedheal Tariffs Commission of the 1920s, with its conservative and cautious remit, he believed. Actually voices had been raised within the Inter-Party government to this effect, and it had also been privately argued that the new agency would merely reduplicate the efforts of Industry and Commerce, Agriculture and, of course, Finance. John Leydon, Lemass's long-time civil-servant adviser, discreetly scotched these perhaps self-serving objections as absurdities. Furthermore, he did so very decisively 'within the lodge' of the civil service, an institution one might expect to be sceptical of such initiatives.[3] Behind this gut hostility to the fledgling new agency, it is difficult not to detect something of Lemass's contempt for the more theoretically minded of intellectuals and more garrulous of academics. There is also a clear echo of 'Treaty politics' and the tariff issues of the 1922–38 period, Cumann na nGaedheal having been a pro-agriculture low-tariff party, whereas the young Fianna Fáil had made a pro-industry high tariff one of its foundation stones after 1927. Lemass declaimed:

We have the prospect that the whole economic situation here may deteriorate drastically after 1952. That is our zero hour. If we are going to do anything to strengthen the national economy, to repair the gaps in our industrial organisation, to get into a position in which we can balance our international trade, we have to do it, if we can, before 1952.[4]

Lemass's view in 1950 was apparently that there was no time to be lost in doing studies and that sort of thing; he was to soften his opinions later, under the influence of intellectuals such as Alexis FitzGerald and Patrick Lynch. Presumably Leydon had something to do with this change of heart as well. By late 1957, Lemass was reconciled to a revamped, much-expanded and far more powerful IDA. However, back in 1950, the Inter-Party government stuck to its guns in the face of his anger. Morrissey, although a Fine Gael minister, was not an aboriginal pro-Treatyite die-hard; his early political background was actually Labour Party, he was a well-known Tipperary businessman and trade unionist and, in 1931, in support of a hard line on IRA activity, had joined what became Fine Gael. Because of this relatively 'neutral' political background, with no republican blood on his hands, he was therefore more acceptable to people of anti-Treatyite traditions than were hardcore Fine Gael people of the Civil War leadership cohort. Unlike Dillon or possibly McGilligan, he was also firmly in favour of industrialisation, like most of the Labour people. Introducing the bill in the Senate in December of that year, Dr T.F. O'Higgins, standing in for Morrissey, painted a vivid and dismaying picture of official ignorance of the actual structure and potential of the Irish economy, an ignorance which it would be the IDA's job to remedy.

The primary function of the authority is that of planning new industries. As part of this work, the authority has been examining the steps necessary to undertake a survey of industrial resources and possibilities, so as to obtain as clear a picture as possible of what has been done and what still remains to be done and what resources and facilities are available or can be made available. This survey will be carried out by the staff of the authority under its direction and supervision, and thereafter will be maintained up to date on a continuing basis for the use and information of the Government, of industries already established and yet to come into being, and for the use of the authority itself.

The survey will show for the first time in comprehensive form the structure of existing industrial enterprise and will be a valuable indication of industrial possibilities. By this means, supplemented by information obtainable from the Central Statistics Office and other Government agencies, there will be available for each important manufacturing activity information on many aspects about which little is known at present, except in so far as an individual concern is aware of its own background. We do not know at present, for example, how much capital is invested in industry or how it is represented by buildings, by plant and machinery, by stocks of raw materials or of partly or finished goods, by debtors and by other assets. Neither do we know how these vary from year to year and from one industry to another.

We do not know how industry is financed, for example the extent to which the capital is provided by shareholders, debenture holders, bankers, creditors and reserves. We do not know how many shareholders have provided the capital nor have we any information as to the dividends they receive, which is in itself an indication of whether times are good or bad. Much more information can be obtained than is now available in respect of each industrial product, as to the extent and type of employment given, as to wages and earnings, labour turnover, welfare schemes, unemployment experience, etc. So also can information be obtained bearing on the manner in which the distribution of industrial products is organised. Generally, the survey will show how and where the country is industrialised, the yearly progress in the case of each important activity, and the extent and location of the human and natural resources which allow of further development.[5]

Already, the Minister went on, preliminary research had led to the discovery of many potential gaps in the market that corresponded to potential production capacity. The authority's general approach was to establish whether or not a product not produced in Ireland could be produced here at competitive cost and for an available market. Availability of capital, labour, raw materials, power, fuel, plant, etc. was to be examined. Possible entrepreneurs were to be approached and put in contact with each other if necessary. A central, and apparently revolutionary, theme running through the Minister's speech was the theme of *information*. Parenthetically, secrecy seems to have been so ingrained in Irish social culture as to ensure that one hand did not know what the other was doing, to the detriment of the efforts of both. Industrialists, like everybody else, behaved secretively, even when it might have been in their interest to share and exchange information. In effect, government policy-makers and private entrepreneurs alike were blinded by a dearth of elementary information, and action was necessarily badly informed. The disregard for the idea that diagnosis should wait upon investigation was part of a general syndrome of unintellectual or even anti-intellectual thinking. The facts were presumed (often quite wrongly) to be known; all that was really needed was the resolve to do something about them. Courage, determination and a 'can-do' mentality were superior to criticism. Empirical research was no substitute for 'common sense' and a common reaction to academic commentary was 'sure we knew all that anyway.' The sad fact was that they actually didn't. Myles na gCopaleen remarked once, cleverly and unfairly, that ten years of de Valera's Institute for Advanced Studies had resulted in two great discoveries: that there was no God, but that there had been two St Patricks. There was something very Catholic about this disregard for research, a disregard that infected Irish universities as well. In retrospect it seems extraordinary that Irish government could, more or less voluntarily, know so little about the economic affairs of the country it was supposed to be governing. O'Higgins continued:

> Of equal importance is the function of bringing about an expansion of existing industrial enterprises. Indeed, it is in this field that results can often be achieved most rapidly. In its examination of applications for tariffs, for quotas and for duty-free import licences, the constant aim of the authority is to bring about as wide as possible an expansion of existing industrial activity. Again, an instance of which I am aware will illustrate what is and what can be done in this respect. In the examination of a tariff application the authority undertook a survey of an industry in which so many competitive firms operated that a comprehensive picture of output did not exist. The goodwill of the manufacturers concerned towards the authority enabled confidential figures of output to be assembled by the authority, which, in conjunction with its statistical research showed for the first time a substantial scope for increased output and employment in a particular direction. This direction hitherto had been obscured by the complexities of the industry. In the examination of other tariff applications similar results emerged through co-ordinating the aim of expansion of output with that of affording protection.[6]

A general theme that ran through the debates in both the Dáil and Senate was the very old one of the alleged desirability of decentralising manufacturing activities from Dublin to the rural areas so as to stabilise rural and small-town society. One IRA veteran, farmer Martin Corry of east Cork and Fianna Fáil, actually wanted to *force* industrialists to locate away from Dublin. This theme of the monster-as-Dublin ran through much of Irish popular culture from the time of Parnell on; after all, radical Dublin had supported the Uncrowned King when the country had deserted him under the leadership of the priests. It should be recalled that this alleged Great Wen of Dublin had slightly more than 600,000 citizens in 1950. This refers to the County Borough, Dún Laoghaire and County Dublin, much of the area being quite rural at that time: scarcely a dramatic urbanisation, but enough to cause a sociological unease in the mainly rural society of the time. After all, the entire population of the state was scarcely three million. The Minister openly admitted his own inability to determine the location of new industries. Typically the investors wished to locate in Dublin or Cork, being, among other things, eager to remain close to a pool of relatively trained labour of a sort that small towns, let alone completely rural areas, could not possibly have supplied without extensive in-house training provided by the investors themselves. Lurking behind his remarks was a perhaps subconscious awareness of the ill-trained and ill-educated character of much of small-town and rural Ireland, whose education had been provided or denied by forces discussed in Chapter 4. These forces, strong in Dublin, were utterly irresistible in rural and small-town Ireland.

George O'Brien, a professor of economics at UCD and a university senator, put his finger on a parallel sensitive point during the Senate debate on the IDA bill. Civil servants, he pointed out, dominated Industry and Commerce and could easily come to predominate in the new IDA as well. These officials were commonly recruited at Leaving Certificate level (high school diploma-level examination taken at age seventeen–eighteen) or even at age sixteen (Intermediate Certificate Examination). The IDA needed a twin-track recruitment system so as to escape civil service restrictions on hiring graduates, O'Brien argued. He noted that US industry employed far more graduate labour than did its British equivalent, and pleaded for consideration by the new IDA for graduate manpower. O'Brien said:

> The suggestion is very definitely made by these [Anglo-American] productivity inquiries that the employment of graduates has had good results. One of the reasons always put forward for reducing or limiting the financial subventions to the Irish universities is that so many of our graduates have to emigrate to seek employment. I believe that the difficulty could be surmounted to some extent if the [industrial development] authority could find employment for specialised research workers from the ranks of university graduates.[7]

The general theme of Irish economic development needing people of far better general educational level than was then current was harped upon by increasing numbers of political leaders in the 1950s. Conspicuous among these leaders was Todd Andrews.[8] Andrews was close to the Fianna Fáil leadership and had been an energetic and innovative promoter of semi-state enterprise in the peat exploitation board (Bord na Móna) and in Córas Iompair Éireann (CIE), the semi-state national public transportation company. Andrews was an advocate of education in general and of applied and technical education particularly. As an old UCD Commerce student, he seems to have had a low regard for Arts-style humanist education, seeing it as rather pointless. In 1957, he quite bravely commented on the poor education and training of the generality of Irish farmers and their unnecessary sociological inferiority complex.[9] Again, in 1958, in an address to Cumann na nInnealtóirí, the Institute of Engineers, he made the devastating comment that of a total of under 2,000 engineers employed in the Republic, 1,500 were employed by the state and the local authorities, while fewer than a hundred were employed by the private sector. Parenthetically, by way of comparison, there were more than 8,000 engineers working in the Republic of Ireland in 1996, with a population 25 per cent larger: more than a 400 per cent increase in the absolute number of engineers. On another occasion, in 1957, he pointed out that only one new hotel had been built since the state was founded, recommended the licensing of casinos, the encouraging of foreign investment and the abolition of taxes on business profits. He also recommended the abolition of income tax as being a brake on economic initiative and a British device unsuited to Irish circumstances.[10] He was a defender of semi-state enterprises on the grounds that it was in these organisations that a native Irish managerial cadre had emerged for the first time outside the rather narrow range of the old, mainly Protestant-owned, firms such as Guinness (brewing) and Jacobs (biscuits). In 1959, in a speech on the modernisation of CIE, he said:

Not the least of the achievements of the semi-state companies has been the production in Ireland of managers. The pattern of the Irish economy is largely dominated by family businesses and in the nature of the case, family-owned businesses do not as a rule provide the scope and opportunity for energetic, intelligent men to allow them to achieve their reasonable ambitions. These semi-state organisations do provide such opportunities and as such provide a cadre of leadership which in the almost violently changing economic conditions which are about to come to pass, will be one of our greatest strengths. The experience and know-how which they have gained in large-scale and scientific management will be available when the large units of organisation in the private sector of the economy, which must inevitably come with the Common Market, have to be created and managed.[11]

At the beginning of the 1960s boom, he again sounded a note of warning about the dearth of trained people in the workforce. In 1962, speaking at a Dublin technical college, he praised 'wise' government initiatives such as the setting up of the National Apprenticeship Board in 1960 and the ongoing official study, under OECD auspices, of Irish education. He evidently felt that all of this was really too little too late and went on to predict, quite rightly, that the new Irish boom of the 1960s was liable to be undermined by an absence of trained personnel. The retardation of education over the previous two decades was going to result in a crippling of Lemass's new departure.

It is not improbable that one of the factors that will retard the rapid rate of industrial expansion, which we must have if we are to keep pace with the highly developed countries of Europe, will be an inadequate supply of skilled craftsmen.[12]

Lemass had made a similar point as early as 1948 at a UCD Fianna Fáil cumann public meeting when attacking the cancellation of the transatlantic air service by the Inter-Party government. The new government was throwing away an opportunity of building know-how, he suggested rather sadly. Aviation was going to be a key industry in the future post-war world, and Ireland was depriving itself of important expertise. He wished to build up cadres of skilled workers and managers who would be able to compete internationally in what was the hot new technology of the time. The *Irish Press* reported:

Asked about the ban on the trans-Atlantic air service, Mr. Lemass said that he thought the service had considerable possibilities. Part of the capital invested in the giving of skill to our own people had been lost. The government decision was deplorable, because the one thing needed here [in Ireland] was to increase occupations which involved a high degree of technical knowledge and training.[13]

Fianna Fáil certainly had a developmentalist theory which ascribed a relatively central role to state enterprise. In the view of men like Andrews and Lemass, these enterprises were there partly for cultural reasons: to build up a cadre of experienced managers. In this the party was unlike Fine Gael, whose approach as represented by the early IDA was one of a little governmental help for our private enterprise friends in the form of information concerning possible products, possible markets, possible alliances and the gathering of information about the structure and level of economic activity in the country. Even the collection of GNP statistics was at that time an innovation and regarded by many as a rather mysterious and perhaps questionable activity. In fact, it was common to denounce the very concept of GNP as philosophically doubtful and indicative of pseudo-science. It was also voguish to pronounce that economics was merely the science of greed, of fumbling in the greasy till, and an intellectual pursuit unworthy of a 'spiritual' people, etc. Later, common sense prevailed, and the approaches of both Morrissey and Lemass came to be seen as complementary rather than as necessarily antagonistic and incompatible.

However, it is also clear that, in Fianna Fáil eyes, part of the purpose or at least the rationale of the public-sector enterprises was investment in Irish human capital. This is a point which, whatever its validity, seems to have passed many economic commentators by. In effect, the semi-state bodies were intended not only to fulfil their formal mandate, but also to build up among younger people a culture of work discipline, hands-on capacity, entrepreneurship and management. The state was to provide on-the-job training, experience and education of a kind that, up to the fairly recent past, had not been given to large numbers of young men and (latterly) women, typically of Catholic and modest backgrounds. Aer Lingus, Bord na Móna, CIE and the rest were to be educational bodies and experimental institutes as much as anything else. A certain element of ideological evasion may have lurked behind this viewpoint, as the church-run national educational system, heavily biased towards the humanities as it was until the mid-1960s, was not amenable to the reforms envisaged by such people as Andrews or Lemass. The state seems to have felt that it could not really take the Catholic Church on as far as education was concerned, and perhaps even felt that it did not really need to. In effect, 'on the job' training was envisaged as a *substitute* for formal full-time secondary and tertiary education and training of an applied kind. This was so because the ecclesiastically dominated secondary system and the impoverished vocational system, impoverished partly because it was disliked by powerful priests, did not produce the needed personnel beyond a certain fairly low, albeit quite competent, level. To an extent, there was also some hostility to 'academic', unapplied 'Arts' degree education on the usual grounds that it was airy-fairy, useless or pretentious. Occasionally the hostility was anti-clerical; it was believed by some that the humanities courses really were only meant to produce priests. Sometimes it was class-derived—humanities seemed to be a luxury interest of upper-middle-class students.

Furthermore, this idea of the semi-state bodies as being in part educational or quasi-experimental organisations constituted a view that was genuinely held, and it is also true that many of Ireland's modern managers, academics, journalists and business-people emanated from the tradition of the civil service and the semi-state bodies. I am not aware of any sociological study which demonstrates this proposition, but casual empiricism suggests its general validity. State service, whether in the army, police, civil service, teaching or the semi-states, was the commonest way by which a young man, and, latterly, a young woman, of ability and energy but no capital or social connection could make their way into some sort of white-collar modernity in the little world of Ireland. Furthermore, the civil service's central departments clearly saw themselves as a reservoir of brainpower which existed nowhere else in Irish society outside academia and which was therefore in itself a national asset. A strong sense of institutional pride characterised government departments such as Finance, Local Government, Industry and Commerce, and Health, and semi-state bodies such as the ESB, Aer Lingus, the IDA, Córas Tráchtála (trade institute) and Bord na Móna. The educational semi-states such as Foras Talúntais (agricultural institute), the Institute of Public Administration, the Economic Research Institute (later to be the Economic and Social Research Institute) and Foras Forbartha (development institute) possessed this ethos in an even more pronounced form.

**THE NEW ISLAND**
The overwhelmingly dominant power in the world of post-war Western Europe was, of course, the United States. In the eyes of the Irish, America, the New Island (*An tOileán Úr*) of Gaelic legend and Yeatsian imagery, was the most obvious role model for mod-ernisation. Because of traditional ties and historically influenced affinities, the United States was psychologically more acceptable to the Irish as a mentor than was the old enemy to the east. This was so despite trade union, isolationist and communist-inspired unease about America's military ambitions for Europe. Irish eyes often saw the United States as an almost mythological country of

unimaginable wealth, power and capability. However, understanding of American business methods, management techniques
or even of American history, politics and culture was often very
limited; there was no chair of American studies in any Irish
university. The obvious importance of the United States was made
even more evident by what was termed at the time (1947 onwards)
the 'Dollar Crisis', or the scarcity in Ireland of that vital currency
needed to import into Ireland many goods unavailable anywhere
in Europe. In many cases, America was the only supplier of
advanced machinery, many chemicals, foodstuffs and building
materials because the US was the only major economy undamaged
by war, and that economy constituted in itself over 50 per cent of
world industrial production. These goods would have to be
purchased with dollars, the effective buying currency of both of
the American continents. It followed that Ireland, like everyone
else in Europe at the time, would have to try, in rather unpro-
pitious circumstances, to sell into the markets of the western
hemisphere to earn the precious greenbacks.

American importance was also symbolised more immediately
by what was generally termed the Marshall Plan, or the European
Recovery Program (ERP). The ERP consisted of a massive
infusion of dollars into allied, neutral and ex-enemy countries on
the ruined continent in the form of grants and soft loans with a
view to rebuilding the European economies. Ancillary purposes of
ERP were to combat the quite considerable appeal of Soviet
communism to European workers and ensure a friendly Europe
for American investment. The latter considerations made some
neutralists look askance at the package. In fact, Sean O'Faolain felt
impelled to run a symposium on Irish anti-Americanism in *The
Bell*. However, the Department of External Affairs commended the
Program to the new Inter-Party government in April 1948, partly
on the interesting grounds that it was the first step along a
presumed road toward European economic co-operation, and also
that it involved no entanglement with the countries of the British
Commonwealth.[14] MacBride, the new Minister, seems also to have
circulated to government copies of an editorial in the *Donegal
Vindicator* of 24 April 1948, announcing in an almost apocalyptic

tone that Marshall Aid was the greatest opportunity Ireland had
had in decades to develop herself as a modern country.

> The Universities, the business world, the agricultural committees,
> the Church, should all be raided for the economists, sociologists
> and technicians to form that Committee of State Planners that
> we have all been dreaming and talking about.
> For this is IT.[15]

Marshall Aid funds, MacBride told his colleagues excitedly,
should be used to 'lift ourselves out of our present rut'. The money
earmarked for Ireland under ERP looked like being about stg£30
million per year for four years. This was an enormous amount of
money by the standards of the time, approximating in size, for
example, to the sum total value of Irish imports for 1944. In purchasing power, it equates possibly with €10 billion in the values of
2003.

> Should this sum, or anything approaching it, become available
> for development, we should be able to transform our country;
> it would provide an opportunity such as never offered itself
> before of building our economy on really constructive lines.[16]

However, when MacBride realised shortly afterwards that the
money might be in the form of a repayable loan rather than an
outright grant, he changed his tune quite rapidly, contemplating
equally excitedly Ireland's foregoing Marshall Aid rather than
incurring a debt which the country could repay only by bank-
rupting itself.[17]

The combined circumstances of partially repayable 'soft' loans
from America, the dollar 'famine' that afflicted Europe, a traditional nationalist aspiration to make the country less dependent on
the equally traditional British trade and European Cooperation
Administration (ECA) urgings all together prompted the Irish to
look first at the American markets. Paul Hoffman of the ECA
suggested in 1949 that the Irish should be doing more about
selling whiskey and tourism to the Americans. He also suggested

a full-scale duty-free area at Shannon Airport to relieve Americans of their surplus cash as they entered or exited the gateway of Europe (a modest duty-free shop had started in 1947). The IDA approached an unnamed Czech national who had had experience in the pre-war Czechoslovakian export agency, an organisation which had become very successful and was a much imitated model in post-war Europe. On similar lines, a friendly Irish-American businessman, John A. Hamill, suggested an Irish agency in the United States to sell Irish manufactures in that huge but unfamiliar market. The IDA proposed in October 1949 that an Irish trade agency be set up, preferably by Irish manufacturers themselves, to organise and develop an export trade in industrial products, set up branch offices abroad, handle credit risks, assist with export procedures and research foreign markets. Finance, in the person of McElligott, was very sceptical about this idea, asking why it was incumbent upon the Irish government to do for Irish manufacturers something which they should be doing for themselves. However, the Department also did admit:

> Our manufacturers as a whole have a very limited knowledge or experience of export trade and apart from their reluctance to enter into an unknown and highly competitive field, the share of any particular manufacturer in export trade would be relatively so small that it could not bear the expense of an adequately staffed and operated export department.[18]

It seems that the Department of Finance was mounting as objections to the IDA's ideas a diagnosis of the problem that was actually rather similar to that of the IDA. In fact, the objections, if looked at from a slightly different angle, amounted to a strong argument *in favour* of some kind of government-backed trade agency, as Irish industry was so small scale, underdeveloped and fragmented as to be collectively incapable of joint action in its own collective interests. The objections constituted, quite extra-ordinarily, a statement of the problem for which the IDA's proposed export board constituted a possible solution. In any event, the export board finally materialised in December 1951 in the form of Córas Tráchtála. This was one of the last such national export boards to be constituted in the OEEC countries and one of only two not to have export guarantee schemes and credit incentives in place, because of a Department of Finance veto. However, these schemes and incentives were to follow in due course.

Irish-American and Marshall Plan contacts expressed frustration at reported Irish foot-dragging on the issue of dollar earnings. As early as December 1949, an American representative of the European Cooperation Administration complained:

> As I have discussed the matter with Government officials, I find everyone most friendly and receptive to suggestions, but little action seems to follow. I have been impressed in some instances by the lightness of concern about it, in other instances by the expressed hopelessness as to Ireland's ability to do anything substantial about it, and in still other instances by the apparent feeling that it is not Ireland's problem but that it must be solved by action entirely outside of Ireland. Some appear to feel that something is going to happen to take care of it.
>
> I have reluctantly come to the conclusion that Ireland is not facing up to this problem.[19]

The commentator was picking up a general Irish cultural pessimism or chronic defeatism about the prospects of the country that was to be noticed again two years later by the American business consultants of the 'Stacy May Report' of 1952. This latter very professional and well-organised examination of the Irish economy commented extensively on the risk-averse nature of Irish farming, the cultural pessimism of policy-makers and a general lack of self-assurance that was self-defeating and fundamentally unjustified. This was combined, the American analysts concluded, with an *étatiste* authoritarian fondness for top-down controls that stultified initiative:

> ... our study has shown that in Ireland, despite a general assumption of opposition to the socialist credo, the state has assumed a far larger role in the channeling of investment funds than in England

under a Labor Government. The heavy hand of Government
controls has extended widely over all business operations in a
manner that has tended to stifle private initiative. Price controls,
exercised not as an emergency measure but as a continuing
instrument, have tended to become profit controls, justified not as
a means of controlling inflation, but on the ground that profits
beyond a certain minimum are an evil that should be penalized
regardless of whether they result from monopoly or from superior
efficiency of operation in a fully competitive situation.[20]

A memorandum to government from the Department of
External Affairs in May 1950 relayed similar harsh American
comments on Irish temperamental passivity from the Marshall
Aid sources, anticipating the Stacy May strictures of 1952:

As indicated to the government by the Minister for External
Affairs, severe criticism of our lack of action to increase dollar
earnings, especially in respect of the tourism industry, has been
voiced by Mr. Hoffman, Mr. Harriman, Colonel Posey, Mr.
Clements and Mr. Carrigan to the Minister . . .[21]

The External Affairs memorandum went on to express concern
that American perceptions of a chronic Irish governmental reluctance to get the country's own house in order might endanger
prospects of further Marshall Aid largesse:

Apart from the urgent necessity for earning more dollars the
Minister for External Affairs considers, on the basis of reports
received by him in conversations which he had with various high
ranking E[uropean] C[ooperation] A[dministration] officials, that
what is considered to be our lack of interest and lack of action
concerning dollar earnings may adversely affect the amount of
ECA grant aid which may be available to Ireland in the year July
1950– June 1951. It will be recalled that, originally, the allocation of
any ECA grant to Ireland was strongly opposed. As a result of close
contact and cooperation with the ECA coupled with diplomatic
action, it was possible in the current year, to obtain an ECA grant
of $3 millions. Steps have been taken by the Minister for External

Affairs to obtain a much higher ratio of grant in the coming year. It has even been suggested that the total allocation to Ireland this year should be by way of grant; it is understood that ECA are likely to press for at least a grant of 50% of the total allocation of aid to Ireland.[22]

Marshall Aid was suspended abruptly in May 1951, partly because of the Korean War, and was terminated in 1953 with the coming to presidential power of the more isolationist Republicans under Dwight D. Eisenhower.[23] It could be, and was, argued that one undesirable aspect of the American money was its tendency to habituate normally hyper-thrifty Irish government departments to relatively spendthrift practices; the presence of American money meant that departments were able, to some extent at least, to avoid the necessary discipline normally imposed upon them by the Department of Finance. The fiscal crisis of 1956 was partly caused by a government spending pattern that proved very difficult to change; departments and ministers got the financial bit between the teeth more easily than hitherto. In 1955–56, a fiscal crisis of the state developed, party because of this propensity. In September 1956, T.K. Whitaker wrote an extremely worried letter to Gerard Sweetman, Minister for Finance in the second Inter-Party government:

> You are the only Minister who fully understands how narrowly we have avoided failure in recent months . . . The plain fact is that, largely as a result of Marshall Aid, our capital expenditure is mounted on a scale far above the erratic level of our savings and when these decline—as they have done over the last year or so—our difficulties become acute.[24]

Somewhat earlier, Whitaker had bluntly pointed out that Ireland's assets had been accumulated during the two world wars and were, in effect, being spent. He went on to make a devastating comment on Irish economic development since the war: 'we have been living on capital since 1947.' During the 1956 crisis, something like panic set in even among clerical circles. Reverend Michael

O'Carroll announced in *Hibernia* (The Knights of Columbanus magazine at that time) that the massive flow of emigrants was a national 'challenge' and that Ireland's very 'national existence was at stake'. The attractions of booming England were obvious when contrasted with the dismal state of affairs at home, he wrote. Irish society was unattractive and oppressive, and people wished, very naturally, to escape from it. In England, Irish emigrants

> . . . are well paid, they enjoy amenities they cannot have at home, they have larger opportunities for self-improvement and self-advancement. They are not hopelessly held back by barriers thrown up around certain classes and groups.[25]

Parenthetically, during both wars, Irish agriculture made huge profits because Britain, with a population thirteen times greater than that of the twenty-six counties, was transformed temporarily into an enormous captive market for Irish foodstuffs. The crisis of 1956 was overcome, but was to set a pattern of recurrent instability in government spending in future decades, essentially driven by 'windfall' gains in the form of bursts of unexpected GNP growth seen as somewhat similar to the 'windfalls' of 1914–18 and 1939–45. This tendency was intensified by the propensity of Irish governments to spend in reaction to the electoral cycle rather than in an economically rational response pattern to the business cycle. Politics and economics tended to stultify each other. However, as Bernadette Whelan argues, the real long-term effect of Marshall Aid was to expose Irish decision-makers and much of the broader Irish public to an American business culture. This was a culture that valued competitiveness, hard work, efficiency and ambition rather than mere local status, market restrictions in favour of certain firms and general rent-seeking. The Americans do seem to have succeeded in waking some of the Irish up. The trade union movement, at first critical of what nowadays would be called 'Fordism', eventually began to listen receptively to American labour representatives speaking of capital-intensive production processes. The Americans argued that although these processes did indeed destroy traditional work procedures and therefore traditional jobs, they also did eventually generate a better-paid and better-trained workforce in the medium to long run.[26] Union interest in these arguments was strong despite, or perhaps because of, the fact that Irish groups going on early fact-finding missions to the United States rarely included union representatives. Union leaders were, however, uneasy at the high profile of women in American industry, one official commenting in rather typical Irish zero-sum fashion:

> In Ireland we do not encourage the employment of women in heavy industries, and apart from the social aspect, women's presence in industry would prejudice any hopes of continuity of employment for adult male workers.
>
> Family life as we know it needs a woman in the home, and therefore to cite a typical example of a mother of four children in America working eight hours a day, drawing the same remuneration as her husband, the same consideration could not be afforded the children in the upbringing, as would be afforded to the same size family in Ireland. It is true to say that we saw sincere family life in some of the workers' homes we visited whilst in Pontiac, but, taking the long view, women cannot shed any of the responsibilities of womanhood if the great Republic of the West is to exist on a Democratic basis.[27]

Whelan convincingly argues that orthodoxies of this kind, shared by employers, politicians, ecclesiastics, opinion-formers and union leaders alike, ensured that 'emigration, unemployment and falling industrial output characterised much of the 1950s' and also that 'the symbols of American prosperity remained illusive for most workers though still sought after.'[28] Old-fashioned attitudes, anti-intellectualism and an ideological cast of mind that saw economic development as bringing in its train great evils such as marital breakdown, materialism, secular education, secular mentality and 'anglicisation' played an important role in keeping Ireland underdeveloped throughout the 1950s and even afterward. The irrationalities in Irish industry, education and public service went beyond the simply old-fashioned; they seem to have been defended energetically in myriad ways. Demarcation lines in industry, an increasingly archaic and clericalised educational system, a deep divide between the classes in society and a Victorian central and local governmental system scarcely changed since 1900, despite some streamlining, were predicated on the assumption that Irish society was static and unchanging. This organisational glacis provided massive and passive resistance to innovation and much-needed change.

The increasingly gerontocratic and localist style of Irish politics did not help. The unpublished version of the ECA's *Ireland: A Country Study* of 1949 commented worriedly on the fact that the political leadership of the Republic was abnormally old; at that time, the Republic had the oldest political leadership in democratic Europe. Actually, the Irish leaders were not all that terribly old. Fianna Fáil in 1947 noisily denounced 'stupid talk' about the government consisting of old and tired men. The actual average age of the Fianna Fáil government in 1947 was 56, de Valera being the oldest at 65, and Lemass and Patrick Smith being both the youngest at 48 years of age—hardly a group of Methuselahs.[29] The writers of the ECA report would have worried more had they known that these leaders were to still be in power in the early 1960s, ten years older and only very possibly ten years wiser. The real problem in the late 1940s was not the average age of the government, but the fact that there were virtually no young cadet members in the group getting ready to take power. The generation born after 1905 had very few representatives in the Fianna Fáil leadership; the most conspicuous among this small group was Erskine Childers, and even he was 43 in 1948—no spring chicken. Only in the mid-1950s did the new men, born in the 1920s and later, begin to materialise as potential leaders in Fianna Fáil and Fine Gael. It is significant that an age gap of thirty years or even more separated them from the previous leadership group. The generational gap was exacerbated by the channelling of young men and women into the republican cul-de-sac of Clann na Poblachta; Sean MacBride was 45 in 1948, Jack McQuillan was only 27, Noel Browne was 33.

Irish democratic parliamentary representatives were famously described by Basil Chubb, writing in the early 1960s and quoting a remark made by Michael Hayes more than a decade earlier, as 'going about persecuting civil servants'.[30] In other words, Dáil deputies saw themselves not so much as legislators or policy-makers but rather as agents of their constituents. As such, they were defenders of particularistic, individual and local interests. Local pressures were very powerful, and have had, it has often been argued over the decades, the effect of spreading govern-mental largesse around the country, often in 'penny packets'. At the very beginning of the IDA's career, the Underdeveloped Areas Act, 1952 introduced special financial incentives for industries setting up in western and midland regions of the country. Even a future head of the IDA, Padraic White, vigorously defended this tendency of Irish politics, evidenced when he was interviewed to join the IDA in 1970:

> I later found out that they gave me a job in the new Regional Planning Team even though it wasn't the job I had applied for. Why? Because, it seems, I was so carried away, at that first inter-view, with my opposition to the *Buchanan Report* published in 1968, which favoured concentration of industry in growth centres. As a Leitrim man, I felt strongly about the need to bring industry to the smaller towns and communities as well.[31]

For better or worse, gerontocracy and localism were beginning to be central characteristics of the Irish polity at mid-century. The former was probably the more dangerous of the two, although the more easily eradicated. As we have seen, Lemass had to overcome great resistance on the part of the older men to his rather brutally enforced generational shift in the early 1960s. Even as early as 1948, exhaustion of political ideas and a hankering after a vanishing era made the Irish leadership respond sluggishly to new challenges, even when these challenges were clearly seen and understood. The world of 1948 was utterly unlike the world of the 1930s, and light years away from the Victorian world of their youth; after all, most of them had been born in the ten years centring on 1895, in a country which, even by the standards of that era, was pretty old-fashioned and rural. Also, even though innovative men with great capacity existed in all of the major parties, it was generally only Fianna Fáil, with its greater weight, internal unity and discipline, popularity and grip on public opinion which could really deliver major and far-reaching policy changes. Furthermore, the party's leaders were quite capable of denigrating policy changes brought in by other parties' leaders, even when they secretly agreed with them and perceived their necessity. Automatic oppositionism as a political style aggravated the already noticeable sluggishness of the policy process. There was also a touch of the English disease: a propensity to tear down the policy edifices that the other side had been trying to build up.

## OUT FROM UNDER

The early IDA was neither fish nor flesh, and calculatedly created so as to be neither. Finance had muttered about its being liable to be controlled by 'a gang of crackpot socialist planners' and feared, rather bizarrely, that it might 'crowd out' private business. Its directors were not civil servants, although its rank and file were. As Padraic White wrote decades later, 'The new Authority occupied a slightly ambiguous position, being neither fully within nor wholly outside departmental structures.'[32] The new organisation showed a distinct propensity to proliferate organisationally. In 1952, it was split into the IDA proper to promote new investment and a new industry board (An Foras Tionscal) which assessed projects and made decisions on development grants.[33] The IDA's mandate was later extended geographically, and in 1956 the Export Profits Tax Relief Act gave 50 per cent tax relief on export profits, upped to 100 per cent two years later by a Fianna Fáil government.[34] These developments were followed by the modifications to the Control of Manufactures Acts, Whitaker's 'Grey Book' of 1958, and the First Programme for Economic Expansion of 1959–63.

An interesting feature of the evolution of the IDA was a drift away from scatter-shot patterns of grant-aided welcome for any industry in favour of a tendency to 'make bets' on certain types of industry. This reflected in part a process of learning by experience that eventually made the IDA an internationally envied repository of experience, wisdom, long-range thinking and simple cunning in the area of developmental economics and politics. Early, and very much on target, 'guesstimates' used by the IDA in such targeting exercises were electronics ('cybernetics') and pharmaceuticals. An eventually successful slow-burner was food processing. Occasionally there was a spectacular failure; an ill-fated attempt by the French company Potez to build light aircraft near Dublin came to nothing. However, in general, Irish economic take-off in the 1960s was substantially accelerated by the efforts of the IDA and its ancillary organisations. American, German and British investment, much of it attracted by the IDA, poured into Ireland. Eventually the civil service link came to be seen as an encumbrance, and in 1970, the IDA became an independent organisation with its own recruitment system and direct relationship to government.[35]

The revolutionary initiative of the 1920s which created the Shannon Scheme, a massive hydroelectric power station on the River Shannon, was the often unacknowledged prototype of later highly successful governmental initiatives such as the creation of the IDA and the Shannon Free Airport Development Company (SFADCo). The Shannon Scheme, a brilliantly conceived world-beater at the time, was looked at sceptically by Joseph Brennan of the Department of Finance as being too ambitious for a fledgling little country still recovering in 1924 from a destructive civil war. Private enterprise was canvassed on the idea and appeared incapable of taking it on. Eventually, Siemens, a German company eager to break into the English-speaking world, made a very attractive offer to build the complex. Patrick McGilligan and Ernest Blythe overrode the objections of the Department and of the proponents of rival schemes. The Scheme was one of the models looked to by an admiring Franklin Roosevelt in the late 1920s when he was considering the massive initiative which resulted in the Tennessee Valley Authority (TVA). Roosevelt openly cited the Irish scheme as the prototype for TVA. TVA was itself cited in turn by Brendan O'Regan as one of his models for the Shannon Free Airport Development Company (SFADCo); ironically, the true intellectual ancestor of both TVA and SFADCo was a few miles up the river in the very visible form of the Germanic architecture of the Ardnacrusha power station.[36] The Shannon Scheme, a brainchild of the first Irish government and a project which was so inspirational at the time, almost got written out of history while being secretly admired. The Scheme could never be forgiven for having been the brainchild of Cumann na nGaedheal rather than of the emergent Fianna Fáil. This happened perhaps on the analogy of the airbrushing of Michael Collins out of official history books, and why it happened is a question for the analyst of political culture, and particularly the political subculture of the Fianna Fáil party. Again, Irish cultural pessimism, 'begrudgery' and cultural inferiority complex failed to even recognise a native Irish success when it saw one in front of it, and preferred to think of an American precedent. Many years later, Lemass was twitted by a journalist about an article he had written for *An Phoblacht* in 1925 denigrating the Scheme on the grounds that it would be vulnerable to enemy air attack in a future war. His good-humoured response was to the effect that he had been a very young man in 1925. Presumably he later looked back in a similar mood at his early hostility to the IDA.

## THE FRENCH ARE ON THE SEA

America was one opening in the new world of post-British Ireland. Europe was to be very much the second, as Lemass had clearly foreseen back in 1929. Gary Murphy has pointed out that Ireland's refusal to join either the General Agreement on Tariffs and Trade (GATT) in 1948 or the North Atlantic Treaty Organisation (NATO) in 1949 has been used to argue for a studied isolationist Irish foreign policy stance. This alleged isolationism has, he argues convincingly, been overstated and even misunderstood.[37] As we have seen, as far back as the early years of the Free State, Irish political leaders and governments were aware of the long-term potential of a Europe that seemed forever out of reach, given the circumstances of depression, empire and warfare. Admittedly, the Irish joined the Organisation for European Economic Co-operation (OEEC) rather reluctantly, and mainly because getting Marshall Aid was conditional on membership.[38] The continuing obsession with partition, particularly in the mind of MacBride, fuelled Irish reluctance to become involved in NATO. Partition continued to be used as an explanation for, and even excuse for, independent Ireland's admitted underdeveloped condition. However, Ireland signed up promptly enough for the Council of Europe in 1949. Again, the Council was used as a stage for publicising the evils of partition, things which looked rather trivial when measured against the ruin of Europe, the dismemberment of Germany, the imposition of communist tyrannies on millions of Europeans, the murder, displacement and persecution of tens of millions of people and the possibility of a new European war, this time with a real possibility of nuclear weapons being used.[39] As late as 1951–54, Fianna Fáil still apparently thought of trade with Britain as the only short-term way forward. Marshall Aid and the OEEC link were sometimes taken by the party as merely being a device for burdening the Irish with extra debt. Lemass, however, was thinking otherwise, consistent with his pre-war perspective on the long-term potential of Europe, both economic and political. By election time in early 1957, Lemass was back to public boosterism in the form of an aggressive modernising rhetoric. He asserted that it was the very 'survival of the nation that is involved now' after ten years of unstable and incompetent Inter-Party government.

> The assertion that this country can get out of its difficulties is based on the belief that Irish workers, given the same tools and leadership as workers elsewhere, can achieve equivalent productivity, that Irish farmers, given access to credit and expert advice, can achieve in time the same output per acre as farmers elsewhere, that the country can produce men trained for leadership in commerce, industry and finance, as competent as any elsewhere and that it can give itself a government which understands what the situation calls for and which can get the required effort started.[40]

An awareness of the impending importance of Europe also existed among diplomatic circles, and this grew stronger as the 1950s wore on. Interestingly, the Europe commonly imagined was a union of the northern European countries (Britain, France,

Germany, Benelux and the Scandinavian countries); Italy, Spain and Portugal were regarded as underdeveloped and therefore not capable of withstanding the competition from the more modernised northern nations. The latter two were also politically unacceptable because of their authoritarian regimes and past associations with European fascism. In fact, it occurred to many that the label of underdeveloped country could possibly be applied to Ireland also, a northern country only in geographical terms. However, in 1954, the Irish government was already seriously discussing the possibilities of the economic unification of Europe and Ireland's role in the process.[41] The gradual emergence of Garret FitzGerald, a lively young economist with a pronouncedly Europhile outlook, presaged Ireland's future growing awareness of the importance of a new European trading bloc which would supplement that of the United States and decisively displace the old exclusionary trading systems of the great European empires of Britain, France, Belgium, Holland and Portugal. Murphy writes:

> While the Irish realised that powerful trading blocs would change the economic landscape of Western Europe, it would be fair to say that the prospect of a European free trade area embracing the member countries of the OEEC was not initially viewed by Irish policymakers with any great enthusiasm, given that the dismantling of protection was seen as a serious threat to Irish industry. Furthermore, the removal of barriers to imports into Britain would eliminate Ireland's preferential position in that market *vis-à-vis* other OEEC countries. Yet the weakness and instability of the Irish economy after a generation of self-government, and the evident failure of traditional protectionist economic policies to achieve their declared objective, led many to question the validity of these policies and to seek effective alternatives. As Garret FitzGerald pointed out at the time [in 1957]: 'The emergence of the Free Trade Area plan, and its presentation to the Irish public, could scarcely have been more opportune . . . and the interest, even excitement which this proposal has aroused throughout the country provides remarkable evidence of the existence of this new and receptive climate of opinion.'[42]

However, for some time, Irish opinion remained nervous of open competition. Despite these reservations, the Irish reacted with hostility and indignation in 1961 to a well-intentioned suggestion by a French negotiator (Jean Deniau) that the Republic should be given underdeveloped status and refused admission in favour of associated state status. Coming from a still-developing France, a country still recovering from the political follies of the Fourth Republic, this looked to the Irish to be a bit rich. It is fair to admit, however, that for certain purposes, the Irish opportunistically claimed to be under-developed, while for other purposes they proudly asserted their notionally developed condition.[43] The Irish left, insurrectionist republicans, anti-militarists and Catholic isolationists came to form a broad, incongruous, noisy and usually ineffective opposition to Ireland's increasing involvement in Europe after 1956. Half a century later, the same minority coalition endures, similarly ineffective but echoing traditional and fundamentally reactionary attitudes of the kind we have encountered earlier in this narrative.

## CONTEMPORARY PERCEPTIONS

The Republic of Ireland has been transformed in the past fifty years—a social and cultural transformation masked by an apparent constitutional and party-political conservatism. Life expectancy has increased considerably, standards of education have rocketed, particularly since the 1960s, women's participation in the workforce has increased enormously, farming has become far less central to Irish society and economy and non-marital births have gone from an almost negligible proportion of the total to about one quarter of the total. Economic output per head in 2000 was over five times what it had been in 1950, in a population and workforce 25 per cent greater. The Republic has gone from being Britain's ranch to being a serious smaller developed economy. It is useful to recall from contemporary official and foreign journalistic sources what the country looked like at that time to educated observers with a developmentalist perspective in mind. A Swedish observer, writing in 1954 and clipped by Industry and Commerce for the Taoiseach, saw the Irish customs service as highhanded and 'troublesome':

The difficulties for foreign manufacturers to gain a footing on the Irish market are increased by a system of customs suspensions, which are, as a rule prolonged only six months at a time.[44]

The lack of capital was immediately evident, the writer continued, and the government had a positive dislike of foreign capital, although this was now changing because of the influence of Lemass. However, he reported incredulously, there was a prohibitive 50 per cent tax on company profits. It is evident that even a Swedish writer, coming from a highly statist country, thought that the Irish had a perverse and self-defeating attitude toward economic activity, again echoing the Americans of the ERP and the Stacy May Report.[45] An American observer, James M. Mead, writing for the *Washington Post* of 14 March 1954, had a more sympathetic, hopeful and flattering perception of a country in an admittedly pretty grim condition.[46] He was evidently of Irish-American extraction.

After about seven hundred years of awful travail, Ireland got its own destiny in its own hands in 1922. It had to learn from scratch to stand on its own feet in a fiercely competitive and often hostile world. The magnitude of this Irish 'Operation Bootstrap' will compare with the progress of any nation . . .

Despite a veritable 'industrial revolution' of recent years, Ireland's economic core remained the agricultural sector, he wrote. With American advice and funds, Irish agriculture was improving very rapidly, and land rehabilitation had, the writer asserted, been pushed forward 'ahead two generations'. The writer assured his readers that the growth of industry was an enormous achievement given the historical background of 'a nation which for centuries was mostly a vast, run-down farm.'[47] There seem to be some echoes in Mead's report of a conversation with Lemass, or some official close to Lemass.

A very different type of observer, the English writer Evelyn Waugh, spent several years looking for a big house or castle in Ireland where he could act out his fantasies of being Lord of the Manor, but gave up eventually. He wrote in his diary in 1952:

Among the countless blessings I thank God for, my failure to find a house in Ireland comes first. Unless one is mad for fox hunting, there is nothing to draw one ... the houses, except for half a dozen ... are very shoddy ... the peasants are malevolent. All their smiles are false as hell. Their priests are very suitable for them, but not for foreigners. No coal at all, awful incompetence everywhere. No native capable of doing the simplest job properly.

Waugh was trying to escape high British taxation as exacted by the Labour government of Clement Attlee. Englishmen like him were referred to collectively in Ireland, with quiet humour, as the Retreat from Moscow. Nancy Mitford wrote to him in her characteristic tone of extended irony after his return to England. She told him that she was mystified as to why he hadn't finally settled in Ireland, on the grounds that the country was so much made for him. After all, Ireland had 'lower orders aplenty', who were possessed of a 'terrible politeness'. The poor Irish are impoverished, she noted. In fact, they were:

so miserable that they long for any sort of menial task at £1 a week, the emptiness, the uncompromising Roman Catholicism, the pretty houses of the date you like best, the agricultural country for Laura, the neighbours all low-brow and ... all 100 miles away, the cold wetness, the low income tax, really I could go on for ever.

An American journalist, James Winchester, interviewing de Valera on his return to power for the last time, remarked in passing while questioning the Taoiseach that he felt that there was much talk of the youth of Ireland 'deserting a sinking ship' and that younger people could see 'no hope' for a future for themselves in Ireland. Dev naturally enough scouted this idea.

In 1956, in the midst of the fiscal crisis, Industry and Commerce drafted, at the request of the Portuguese government, a general summary of the Irish economic situation and Irish governmental policy. The Department memorandum asserted that, in general, the Irish government preferred private enterprise to public enterprise, except in cases where private capital would be unlikely to do the job, as in the case of electricity generation or peat bog exploitation. Ireland's relative backwardness was clearly seen as resulting from a studied neglect allied with mischievous policies during the long period of British rule. The memorandum continued:

Due to historical causes, industrial development in Ireland had been neglected during a long period. When other countries were making great strides in industrial progress. Consequently, when the new state was set up in 1922 special measures were necessary to foster and encourage the growth of industry. In particular, it was essential to adopt a vigorous policy of protection to enable new industries to become established in the face of competition from abroad. Other measures of importance included the provision of financial assistance to new industries requiring capital and unable to raise it through normal commercial channels; assistance to industrial enterprises was given in approved cases by means of State guarantees of interest and principal in respect of loans raised by them; in addition Industrial Credit Company was specially established and financed out of state funds to underwrite capital issues and to provide other financial accommodation in suitable cases.[48]

In 1940, a Board to investigate the possibilities of minerals exploration was set up. In 1946, the memorandum stated proudly, the government had set up an Institute for Industrial Research and Standards. Other such state agencies dealing with tourism, harbours, aviation and marine transportation were also listed, in a clear attempt to portray the Republic to the Portuguese as a go-ahead, enterprising little country. The aspiration to be such a country clearly existed, whatever about the reality. State responses to foreign inquiry reflected an underlying official unease and wish to present things as being rather better than they actually were, or were feared to be. The old tendency, derived from nationalist propaganda traditions, to blame 'history' or 'the British' lurked behind even the clinical blandness of official prose, but there was an underlying awareness that, whatever about the past wrongs of Ireland, now the real responsibility lay in the hands of the Irish themselves, and it wasn't immediately obvious that they were making a very good fist of it. ECA and Stacy May had had the necessary effect. It took the crisis of 1956 to finally unblock residual resistance to wide-reaching policy shifts.

## POLITICS OF FEAR

One seldom-admitted explanation for the political and ideological volte-face of the mid-1950s was a simple fear of social unrest, political instability and a general crisis of the state. Whitaker actually used the word *failure* in his 1956 note to Sweetman, and the rhetoric of the Republic as a failed state was quite noticeable at the time, as we have seen. It seems extremely unlikely that political instability derived from final economic collapse would have led to some kind of classic coup involving a takeover either by the Army or by the IRA. What is more visualisable in hindsight is a gradual post-de Valera 'Peronisation' of the polity, with an anti-intellectual populist politics dismissing the ordinary wisdom of economic science in favour of an emotional redistributivism combined with a new explosion of Anglophobe irredentist nationalism. A vicious circle of populist irrationalism in political life might have driven the economy into free fall—the Republic of Ireland as a Latin American country, Europe's answer to Uruguay. None of this actually happened in other than fragmented and relatively minor ways. However, it can be safely said that another ten years of the gerontocracy and of the traditional protectionist and beggar-my-neighbour politics would have indeed led to a moribund polity with little capacity for self-reinvention and renewal. Things did not get that far simply because such an eventuality was anticipated and feared. Also, by 1970, the survivors of the revolutionary generation were in their seventies and were forced to watch their juniors by forty years easily wielding the power their elders had striven so passionately to win half a century earlier. It has been pointed out by many Irish historians that the 1950s saw the end of a phase of a style of nationalist politics that was effectively *anti-economic*.[49]

The new departure of the latter part of the decade was cross-party and also shared by politicians from both sides of the political fence, civil servants and leading academics in the area of economics and economic policy. In their different ways, Lemass, Costello, Sweetman, Ryan, Whitaker, Patrick Lynch, Charles Murray, MacBride, McGilligan and MacEntee at least broadly agreed on the necessity for fairly drastic change. Murray in particular was an intellectual *éminence grise* during this period, attacking protectionism and its destructive effects on the economy as early as March 1957.[50] Even prominent ecclesiastics such as Bishop William Philbin added their support to the general consensus. In a nutshell, the new departure involved less social investment and more investment in productive forms of capital such as advance factories, subsidies to industry, technical education and education in general and infrastructure. Infrastructure, oddly enough, was still not conceived as including roads. Presumably roads, like telephones, were still considered to be a convenience rather than a necessity. Ireland's long love affair with the motor car had already started, but was accompanied by a studied hostility to road-building. Again, veto groups in the form of the local authorities and the railway interest prevented road-building and local shopkeepers prevented the bypassing of towns; in this at least there was no new departure.

As Ronan Fanning has observed, the policy shift symbolised by the 'Grey Book' and *Economic Development* had an important psychological dimension, and it also marked the beginnings of the generational change in Irish politics which I have sketched in Chapter 4. Fanning writes:

Consensus was critical because the larger historical significance of the publication and reception of *Economic Development* was ultimately psychological. Indeed one of its most quoted passages opens with the assertion that there was 'a sound psychological reason for having an integrated development ... After thirty-five years of native government people are asking whether we can achieve an acceptable degree of economic progress'. At this level the extraordinary success of *Economic Development* occurred because so many badly wanted it to succeed. People craved the beat of a different drum and if the tunes to which they now began marching were still patriotic—albeit from a new hymnal of economic patriotism—then so much the better.[51]

All this also suggests that Ireland was in some ways going through a somewhat old-fashioned exercise, similar in spirit to Franklin Roosevelt's New Deal ('We have nothing to fear except fear itself') and, very much more distantly, the Soviet and Nazi Four- and Five-Year plans of the 1930s, all of which partook partly of economic programming or 'planning', and all of which had embedded in them, in very different ways, an important 'psychological' element of patriotic moral rearmament. The Irish new departure also coincided with communist China's collective leap into economic irrationality under Mao's Great Leap Forward, which must have caused the occasional tremor of unease. In the Irish case, the memory of the 'Emergency' period was still very much alive in the minds of the younger middle-aged, and a call to national solidarity of the kind that Lemass and Whitaker appeared to be making rang a familiar and welcome emotional bell in the minds of many trade unionists, managers, public servants, businesspeople, journalists and ordinary citizens. After all, many had volunteered for military service during 1939–45, in a context of no conscription—a context which was highly unusual in the Europe of that time, to put it mildly; 'Step Together' was, in a way, the unofficial national anthem of the generation born around 1920. A kind of collective patriotism and wish to participate in state- and church-run voluntary organisations still affected people's minds in a way that is probably not imaginable in the more individualised, relatively impersonal and urban Ireland of a generation later. Lemass was able to remark as early as December 1959 that his version of moral rearmament had actually worked. In the Dáil he observed, '. . . the most encouraging feature in the national situation at the present time is the disappearance of the clouds of despondency which hung so heavily over the country only a couple of short years ago.' James Ryan bluntly admitted in 1960 in a letter to Lemass that the abandoning of old formulae and old ideological mainstays had actually been forced upon them by circumstances that simply stared them in the face and would not go away.

. . . As regards emigration, we have all been forced [emphasis added] to the conclusion that the only effective answer is industrialisation, accompanied by intensification and improvement of agricultural production, tourism, afforestation and fishing.

In the 1950s, the generation born in the 1920s and 1930s was about to take over power from the revolutionary generation born in the 1880s and 1890s, and both knew that this was happening.[52] As was characteristic of post-Famine Ireland, generations were abnormally long, age gaps of forty or fifty years between fathers and sons being quite common. People tended to postpone marriage until economic circumstances permitted, and this applied not only to farm society, but also to much of the emergent working and middle classes as well. This situation is generally taken to have derived from the owner-occupier family farm society that was established in Ireland after the Great Famine and the Land Acts of 1879–1903 which effectively handed the land of Ireland over to the tenantry of a peacefully dispossessed landlord class.[53] The delaying of the occasion of inevitable succession to power, property and adulthood made the impulse to reject the values of the previous generation, always present in younger people, much stronger and more aggressive and even destructive than was normal. The contrast between the historical experiences of the generation born after 1885 and that born after 1935 strengthened a psychological difference between young and old. The younger people had forgotten British rule, or rather had never experienced it. To them, England was rather the progressive welfare state, generous, tolerant and free in a way that independent Ireland was not. This feeling of generational conflict was exacerbated by the sudden refusal of younger people to emigrate in the large numbers that had been traditional. This again was matched by an equally stubborn propensity among some older people to attempt to force on the young their values and perspectives on the world. This particular generational transition seems to have been the last involving a 'long generation', as generational change in Ireland now resembles that of other Western cultures, father–son age gaps being about thirty years.

# 06 | SECULARISM AND CULTURAL SHIFT

**CULTURAL SHIFT**

The late 1950s very belated Irish dash for growth—driven in part by an intellectual despair, a belated sense of perhaps being left irretrievably behind and in large part by the growing impatience of a younger generation of political leaders—actually worked. Outside capital started to come in and Irish governmental agencies, led by the IDA, trained themselves to accommodate foreign businessmen rather than trying to put obstacles in their way, which had sometimes appeared to be the traditional approach. British, French, German and American firms set up branch factories in Ireland, attracted by a relatively low-wage economy and an English-speaking and reasonably well-educated workforce, although its technical training left much to be desired. Representatives of Liebherr Cranes, one of the early arrivals, found that they had to persuade the company's Kerry workforce to work a five-day week regardless of the seasons, the weather, feast days or football matches and further found that they had to teach the workers the metric system. To their dismay, they occasionally discovered that the Irish workers sometimes did not know the foot–inch system very well either.

Economic production, which had been almost static in the first forty years of independence, expanded, as we have seen, at a rate close to the OECD average in the twenty-five years from 1960. By Irish standards, this was epoch-making, but by OECD international standards of the time, it was scarcely spectacular.

Reckoning Irish economic progress from 1922 rather than 1960 would evidently present an even less flattering picture. After nearly forty years of independence, Ireland in 1960 was a very poor country, even by the standards of some communist countries of the time. The proportion of the workforce in agricultural production had been nearly 60 per cent at the time of independence, and was still over one-third in 1961. The industrial workforce, less than one-tenth of the workforce in 1922, was only about 15 per cent in 1961. By 1980, it was to be 30 per cent. To put this development in other words, by 2000, the numbers employed in agriculture, in a traditionally and ideologically 'agrarian' island state, totalled about one-tenth of the workforce. In the 1970s, the economy became clearly non-agrarian for the first time and a political system founded on, and designed for, a mainly rural and small-town nation was called upon to face up to the task of governing an increasingly urban country. 'Modern' Ireland had clearly arrived. Popular culture was revolutionised. In common with other Western countries, that aboriginally American creature, the teenager, arrived in the 1940s and 1950s, first in the cities and later everywhere. The growth of a stratum of relatively moneyed and leisured youth in society shifted the relationships between generations and led to a new, if temporary, cultural gap between parents and children.[1] The old abrupt transition from childhood to adulthood at around age fifteen was replaced by an extended 'third age' of youth, extending from about fifteen to the mid-twenties. Irish popular music ceased to be derived from Irish or British music halls and became increasingly modelled on American originals, in so far as it was not simply overwhelmed by Elvis Presley, Buddy Holly and Eddie Cochran. Even the revival of folk music in both English and Irish, which occurred in the 1960s, was inspired as much by the fashions of New York as by the efforts of Ciarán Mac Mathúna and Seán Ó Riada.

Elites were well aware that economic change was going to lead to cultural change and that education and the mass media promised, or threatened, to do the same. The most perceptive observers of changes in Irish popular *mentalité* were probably the Catholic priests, who had a ready-made system of surveillance in the form of the diocesan clergy networks. In the early 1960s, an

American Jesuit, Fr B.F. Biever, carried out the first sociological survey of political opinion ever carried out in the Republic. The sample was of Dublin City and County Catholics; tragically, it appears that the original data set is lost.[2] Surveys of Irish political and religious attitudes prior to the 1970s are not only scarce, they are methodologically rather primitive, few of them inquiring elaborately into political beliefs. However, Biever's survey was quite sophisticated, while dealing mainly with attitudes toward religion and clerical authority.[3] It did, however, deal in passing with political matters and contained a fairly elaborate battery of questions by the standards of the period.

The portrait of Dublin Catholic culture revealed by this 1962 survey is quite startling. Attitudes to the Catholic Church varied little by class or region of birth. For example, almost 90 per cent of the sample agreed that the Church was the greatest force for good in Ireland. Over two-thirds of the sample endorsed the proposition that if one followed a priest's advice, one could not go wrong. Priests were seen as the natural social, economic and political leaders of the country, and their status was so high that the politicians of Leinster House (the home of the Irish Parliament) were utterly overshadowed. Cynicism about politicians, lay leadership and an accompanying extreme and crippling suspicion about lay attempts at social leadership were widespread and had deep cultural and historical roots. One respondent conceded that the clergy 'might make mistakes' occasionally, but believed that they were not out for themselves and he would rather be wrong with his priests than 'right with those damn crooks in Dublin'. Another remarked, 'You can't trust anyone in this country except the priest; he *has* to be honest!' Again, a respondent commented, 'People gripe about the censorship in the press and say that the priests are too powerful. No priest can be too powerful. If we had followed what the priests have been telling us for years, we would be content now with what we have, and not be getting all excited about being like the rest of Europe.' One was openly scornful about secularising the educational system: 'You know, there are some people who think the government should run education. Imagine that!' The Catholic Church had done a 'good job', he felt.

Having listened to 'them fools' in the Dáil shouting, insulting each other and 'doing nothing', he thought that Catholic Church influence should actually be increased. Another said bluntly that priests were better educated and that it would be stupid not to accept their leadership. When asked what side they would take in the event of a clash between Church and state, 87 per cent said that they would back their church.[4]

Biever described the democratically elected politicians of the Republic of Ireland as being quite helpless in the face of such a cultural climate; by a simple, popularly imposed iron political necessity, most important legislation was routinely cleared with the clerical authorities in advance.[5] The Irish democratic political process was heavily tinged with theocracy, for the overwhelming reason that the majority wished it to be that way. However, it should also be remembered that because of Church control of the educational system, the clerics ensured that the majority continued to think that way. The virtues and near-infallibility of the Catholic ecclesiastical machine and the goodness and wisdom of its priests, nuns and brothers were extolled in classes on religious knowledge and Church history in schools, in the press, from the pulpit and elsewhere. Furthermore, given the extremely inadequate nature of the Irish welfare state of that time, the Catholic Church was looked to gratefully for sustenance by an impoverished and half-educated electorate, and was rewarded with the poor man's payment: political and even electoral support. As Biever put it, the Irish were indeed 'priest-ridden', but they liked it that way.

Again, the clergy liked to wield their power; Catholic political leaders were forbidden to attend the funeral services of their non-Catholic colleagues, friends and constituents, and they generally abided by this prohibition. Public figures genuflected and kissed the ring of a bishop when encountering one in public. It should be borne in mind that the Church did not provide education, and often an excellent education supplied by dedicated and sometimes brilliant teachers, merely out of the goodness of its collective heart. It supplied education because it wished to recruit faithful servants, 'soldiers of Christ', missionaries to the English-speaking world and Catholic leaders of a Catholic people: priests and middle-class professionals and businessmen. Some Catholic orders, the Christian Brothers in particular, imparted a potent mixture of muscular Christianity, an often rabid patriotism and an authoritarian and puritan lifestyle. A particular political style combining a bullying style of argument with holier-than-thou postures characterised some of the products of their schools. Lay Catholic organisations, most conspicuously the Knights of Columbanus, controlled official and unofficial censorship systems, acted as what might best be termed as para-clerics for the bishops and, in their spare time, reportedly scratched each others' backs in business. Many unbelievers in public life kept their opinions strictly to themselves and even joined the Knights and similar organisations for safety's sake. Sending a child to a non-Catholic school was punishable by excommunication, entailing an imagined eternal damnation if one were to die before reconciliation with the Church was effected. The same rule applied in the Dublin Archdiocese to Catholics wishing to go to Trinity College Dublin rather than University College Dublin, the latter being referred to by Fr Biever as 'obviously second best'. It must be remembered that Irish religious culture was one of literal belief in God, Christ, the Virgin birth, miracles, saints, heaven, hell, purgatory, limbo and all the rest of it—a belief system partly pre-Christian in origin and certainly non-Christian in psychological texture. Catholic schoolchildren were conscripts in a compulsory system driven by spiritual threats backed up by a politically powerful church, as were their parents. A version of what the English historian E.P. Thompson has termed spiritual terrorism kept Catholic Ireland in line for an entire century.

However, hindsight wisdom tells us that the public belief system that Biever was documenting at the beginning of the 1960s was already becoming the past rather than the future. Even in 1962, incipient change was visible and more change was seen as inevitable. Those few who had completed secondary education were far more willing to question clerical prerogatives and formed an important but isolated and clearly alienated group, not so much, perhaps, from the priests as yet as from the popular culture which endorsed the power of priests. Irish democracy was hierophile, and the newly educated Catholic middle class was denied political leadership or political power by the mass of their fellows and many of the clergy. Whereas an extraordinary 88 per cent of the sample endorsed the proposition that the Catholic Church was the greatest force for good in the country, an equally striking 83 per cent of that small minority which had been educated to Leaving Certificate (taken at age seventeen or eighteen) or beyond disagreed with it. Biever writes:

> Consistently throughout our study of the motivational role of the Catholic church in Ireland we have been called upon to advert to an articulate though pronounced minority of Irish Catholics who in key areas have manifested unqualified disagreement with the majority attitudes ... They are young; they are educated; they are laymen. We have indicated our own hypothesis that the power struggle (if it can be glorified by such a title) in Irish Catholicism is not found between clergy and laity, but between clergy and laity against the intellectual 'new breed'. In our considered opinion they represent the greatest challenge which Irish Catholicism will have to face in the next decade. The points which they attack are basic ones; the attitudes which they manifest are uncompromising. They are skeptical and coldly objective as they point to the failures of the clergy in their role of national leadership. They resent clerical dogmatism and authoritarian motivation which, in their opinion, becomes vulnerable in areas in which the church has no special competence. They openly question undue church influence in areas of social concern, and articulately call into question the advisability of church monopoly in education.
>
> Most of all, however, they are thus far frustrated men. Helplessly they face the overwhelming majority complacency and the staggering lack of educational potential which the church-oriented school system has produced. They speak and they write, but thus far their audience has been severely circumscribed to members of their own conviction; they have in effect been talking only to themselves.

They were determined not to emigrate, the classic solution for Irish dissidents, and 'the angry young men of Ireland' of the new

Catholic and post-Catholic middle class were a profound future challenge to the traditional power structure of the country.[6] The split between the more- and less-educated segments of the population was quite dramatic; while the rank and file of the population loyally looked to the priests for political, social and intellectual leadership, there was, according to Biever, 'a solid core of what we may call the intellectual elite who flatly deny the contention [that clerical leadership was desirable]'. He concluded that there was a 'ferment of disillusionment among the intellectuals [sic] as to the efficacy of the church in the performance of her social functions.' One of this section of the sample expressed himself thus:

> No, I don't think the Church is the greatest force for good, and you know why? She doesn't let us speak here ... The clergy make all the decisions, and all we have to do is obey ... I am sick and tired at being looked upon with suspicion simply because I have an education. Priests aren't the only ones with brains, you know, although you couldn't tell it to hear them speak or see them act ... The Church censors the press, it censors the magazines, it censors the television ... what doesn't it censor? Is this the greatest force for good? Not to me, it isn't! It seems to me that the Church is more interested in keeping a strangle-hold on the people than in making us better as a nation, and that I don't buy ...

Biever juxtaposes this opinion quite neatly with a defence of the Church by some members of the clergy. The Church, one cleric said, was the 'only force [for good] left'. Some of 'your smart intellectuals' had forgotten, he claimed, that the priests never deserted the people in times of want and suffering. Another remarked, 'we have more education, thank God, and with that education comes the responsibility to lead. I think we are [leading].' Some had some doubts, and one said thoughtfully, 'The politicians are new to the game; we have few economists, our professional people leave. Who stays? We do.' One apparently average man remarked 'We are simple people, sir ... child-like, maybe childish, in many ways. We can't behave ourselves without help; no one can. That's what I like about the Church; if you are wrong, by God you'll hear about it!'[7]

In the early 1960s, then, an undercurrent of nascent anti-clericalism, certainly feeding on older radical traditions, but also derived from the generally non-Catholic English-speaking universe in which the Irish found themselves historically and culturally, ran through the newly educated upper stratum of a relatively modestly educated culture. Historical evidence strongly suggests that the middle-class resentment of Church power dated back much further, and certainly was strengthened by the Dignan affair of 1944 and the Mother and Child incident of 1951. It has been argued here that specific incidents of clerical bossiness generated a permanent minority annoyance that derived from earlier and analogous incidents. The minority was, however, a key one: the new middle class and the future rulers of the country. A parallel subterranean resentment of political clericalism also ran through the republican tradition because of the Church's opposition to the (unpopular) IRA rebellion against the Second Dáil in 1922 and the Church's condemnation of IRA activities during the resultant Civil War of 1922–23. Anti-clericalism among otherwise pious Catholics was also rooted in the Fenian tradition and sections of the trade union movement. A small, but conspicuous, number of Protestant and secular intellectuals such as Hubert Butler and Owen Sheehy-Skeffington and Catholic opinion-formers such as Sean O'Faolain and Michael Sheehy also bore witness to an independent liberal secularist tradition, a tradition that was commonly covertly admired and vaguely feared. An early symptom of an underlying ideological tension between Church and state was afforded by the Pike Theatre affair of 1957–58, involving the illegal police persecution of a tiny avant-garde theatre and its owners by a bullying Irish government. The police ordered the owners to close down *The Rose Tattoo*, a play which, even by the standards of 1957, was quite innocent. The officer who ordered the closure had not even seen the play himself, thereby providing another fine example of Irish cultural research. The Minister for Justice was possibly trying to prove that the Fianna Fáil government was as censorious as the Knights of Columbanus in its bid to take back the Government Board of Censorship of Publications from them. The Minister also seems to have been reacting to backbench opinion in the party.

The affair caused widespread fury among normally staid Catholic middle-class people. The government was dumbfounded by the fact that the owners, Alan Simpson, an Irish Protestant army officer, and Carolyn Swift, a Jewish Englishwoman, simply refused point blank to close the show down on the grounds that they were doing nothing illegal. They behaved just as good individualistic liberals should behave, and saw the government off in court, at the cost of their own financial ruin and the wrecking of their marriage. Interestingly, the Irish Army backed up Simpson against the government and a rather shamefaced Garda Síochána. Off-duty soldiers provided Simpson with an unofficial bodyguard. The police force knew well that it had been pushed into a false position by its political masters. It is significant also that, for once, the Archbishop had nothing to do with this disgraceful incident, but a simple fear of his possible opinions seems to have driven the Minister for Justice of the time, Oscar Traynor, hero of the War of Independence and anti-clerical Dublin soccer fan. After all, Traynor had defied the specific instructions of McQuaid in 1954 by going to the Ireland–Yugoslavia soccer match in Dublin that year. The point here is that the brave ex-guerrillas of Fianna Fáil were themselves terrified of episcopal power: the bullies were also cowards. The Irish Army had a mind of its own: comrades of Simpson, men of the Second Field Artillery unit, had helped build the theatre, and the word 'Traynor' became a code word for a drill order which was to be ignored in Irish Army basic training. Another force behind the assault on the Pike seems to have been Peter Berry, secretary of the Department of Justice and an anti-Semite.

As we have seen, a massive anti-clerical reaction in the next generation was predicted by James Meenan as early as 1944. This was in the context of McQuaid's fantastically heavy-handed 'invasion' of UCD during the war years and his engineering of an intellectual takeover of the social sciences. It could be argued that the Irish Catholic Church, by sweeping aside the nascent 'Christian Democrat' tendency in Irish lay society in 1951, irretrievably damaged the prospects for a lay political Catholicism. In effect, it handed over a younger generation to liberal or socialist anti-clericals, people who did not, and do not, represent any broad swathe of Irish public opinion. Over the past half-century, Irish journalism has become increasingly liberal, leftist, often anti-clerical and sometimes anti-American, and is far more radical, albeit in a rather abstract and often extremely self-indulgent fashion, than the general population. The clinging to power by the Catholic Church after popular goodwill had waned seems to be partly at the root of this situation.

Certainly, back in 1962, many of this younger generation clearly bitterly resented the Church's popular power. The anti-clerical reaction which Meenan had foreseen in 1944 was quietly occurring. Biever worriedly commented that the Irish priest was caught in a dilemma. Essentially he was confronted by a slowly emerging educated stratum which required more sophisticated and educated solutions to contemporary problems than what Biever termed the 'platitudes' which had satisfied an older gener-ation. He might have added that this new stratum resented clerical power and wished a slice of that power for itself; it was eventually to get it. However, back in 1962, the Irish priest was confronted by his real constituency of support, the Plain People of Ireland, and by the 'suspicious gaze' of the many 'simple people . . . who were hostile to change of any kind'.

This situation was to change, but opinion change was to occur at a glacial pace. As late as 1971, an opinion poll in *This Week* reported that only 22 per cent of the adult population favoured legalisation of divorce in the Republic. Even young people opposed it, although by smaller majorities; of people under 25 years of age, 39 per cent of men and 28 per cent of women supported such a move—scarcely a revolt of flaming youth. Older people feared a consequent worsening in the quality of family life if contraception were legalised, while younger people rejected this evidently Church-inspired view: a large majority of young men and a large minority of young women supported the legalisation of contra-ceptives. In reality, the law on contraception had become a bad joke. The age cut-off point for liberal views was at around the early thirties. Almost certainly, much of this shift was caused by the Pope's veto on contraception in 1968, which provoked a quiet and very general rebellion among women, who had hitherto been noticeably more quiescent and pious than the men. The magazine commented on the clear signs of mobility of public opinion on issues on which the Catholic Church had taken an uncompromising stand. However, it admitted rather airily, 'Neither can it be said that a large majority of the Irish people is chafing under the imposed legal restraints of a Catholic Theocracy.' Ireland was a 'typical pluralist society with a vast divergence in views' between the generations, younger people being evidently more liberal. There was a large generation gap in the country, the magazine opined, and younger and richer people were more generally liberal in their outlooks than older or poorer people. Contraception was an immediate and urgent issue, and the politicians would have to face up to it quickly. The younger age group was now 'politically in the ascendant' and was divided sharply on the issue of contraception. 'The significance of these age groups on the future moral, social and cultural development cannot be underestimated.' Actually the issue was already a dead one as far as the under-thirty generation was concerned. However, Catholic Ireland was alive and well in 1971, although showing its age somewhat.[8]

Back in 1962, Biever had concluded that the Church's leaders had tried to solve the problem simply by brooking no rivals. They had 'progressively estranged the intellectual class as our data conclusively indicated' and 'deprived Ireland of that vitality both so desperately need by almost forcing the talented intellectual to seek his fortunes in another country.' Alexander Humphreys, in *New Dubliners*, a sociological study of the city, published in 1966 but derived from fieldwork done in 1949, came to a somewhat similar conclusion, noticing an incipient anti-clericalism in the new Catholic upper middle class as early as mid-century, perhaps picking up an echo of the Dignan affair or the already incipient Mother and Child crisis. Using his own considerable literary and historical insights rather than the intellectual apparatus of sociology, Sean O'Faolain came to an interestingly similar conclusion in his well-known book-length essay *The Irish* (1947), as revised in 1969. He prophesied, or, perhaps, warned, that Catholic authoritarianism ('Rule by Command'), so deeply entrenched in clerical culture, would wreck the Church in Ireland eventually. He foresaw the

Irish of the future evolving in a 'French' fashion, ignoring Church instruction in the conduct of their daily lives and availing of the ceremony and institutional charisma of the Church on the great occasions of birth, marriage and death.

> One might . . . conclude that Irish Catholics—and indeed Irish people of every Christian denomination—might be trusted to act as their French counterparts do. However, the old habit of Rule by Command is so deeply rooted here that it is likely to persist for a long time to come. On the other hand the younger generation deeply resents it, is far more outspoken in its resentment than it ever was before, and—as has been happening for many generations in Italy—is likely soon to reduce the word Catholic (as distinct from 'practising Catholic') to a merely nominal value unless their Church learns quickly that these younger people, probably the best part of modern Irish life, are the scattered beginnings of an intellectual elite that with skill it could still hitch to its star.

Loyal 'in-house' journals such as *The Furrow* from time to time carried similar pieces of rather worried advice. Individual liberal priests made rather frantic attempts to repair the alienation that was occurring in a quiet, underground and even polite way between the educated laity and the clerical apparatus. Sometimes they found themselves silenced by their own superiors. J.P. O'Carroll, in an article published in 1991 in *Irish Political Studies*, offered an interesting explanation for the Church's almost pathological inability to pay much attention to such apparently reasonable, friendly and even prudent warnings from laypeople and priests alike. Irish ecclesiastics and their flock could not, he argued, think in such incremental and bargaining styles. Traditional Irish Catholic political and social thought was absolutist in style, he argued, and there was only one way of looking at the world: the right way. O'Carroll was writing mainly about the abortion issue, but he proposed that traditional Catholics saw abortion as part of a general anti-traditional 'package' which included divorce, contraception and sexual permissiveness. This package presaged a generally uncontrollable 'permissive' society which could be avoided only by imposing on everybody, Catholic and non-Catholic alike, ground rules enforced by lay and ecclesiastical authorities, which could be trusted to brook no open opposition or even debate. Cultural *and legal* supremacy was the only solution which many of the traditionalists could even contemplate as being in any way acceptable.[9]

In 1979, Pope John Paul II visited Ireland in what was a truly mythic event. The entire population of the Republic turned out to welcome the pontiff at huge mass meetings in Dublin, Galway and other venues. This hugely popular and charismatic man besought the Irish to hold on firm to the faith of their ancestors and assured the nation that it was a beacon of holiness and loyalty in a faithless world. The Irish accepted this valuation of themselves. Attendance at religious services increased, temporarily altering the tendency toward a gradual decline, which had become visible in the 1970s. Nine months later, thousands of children were born and christened John Paul or Jane Pauline; contraception seems to have been abandoned for a time. Then the birth rate plunged rapidly toward the European average. The Irish had tried the traditional religious life one last time, and found they didn't really like it. The papal visit may actually have had the effect of destabilising an already fragile public-belief system.

O'Faolain was to live long enough to see himself gradually turning into an Irish Cassandra. As we have seen, a paralysed Church failed to hitch the young men and women to its star, to use O'Faolain's phrase; it was probably incapable of doing so, for political and intellectual reasons. More importantly, it was stymied by very deep-seated cultural forces as well. All of this ties in well with the Lemass revolution; an exasperation with the clerical and educational establishments seems to have informed even pious Catholic leaders, and led to new departures in government policy which would have appeared impossible *as well as undesirable* ten years earlier. Irish popular Catholicism was not visibly damaged in any immediate way by this slow-moving confrontation, and remained vital and effective for quite some time afterward. In the 1980s, Catholic forces in the form of the priests, bishops and Knights fought aggressive, successful and often unscrupulous battles on the issues of divorce and abortion. These were Pyrrhic victories which possibly merely rendered the emergent liberal consensus far more angry and even implacably anti-Catholic than it ever need have been. In effect, a pattern of confrontation had been set up which most clerical leaders, and many secularisers, found impossible to break out of, although many on both sides heartily wished that they could have disengaged from it. Most Irish Catholics still loved their church. Arguably, the overconfidence engendered by this simple, but falsely reassuring, fact led to a disaster decades later.

Fr Feichin O'Doherty, Professor of Logic and Psychology in University College Dublin, was born in the United States and was also a scion of a well-known Derry republican family. He published a much cited, and rather prophetic, article in the Jesuit periodical, *Studies,* in mid-1963.[10] Ostensibly this essay was a general discussion of the utility of the science of social psychology to an understanding of human social development, but it was actually an extended meditation on the future of Irish society. This meditation was evidently prompted by Vatican II, which had opened on 11 October 1962, and also the recent economic changes that had followed the publication of *Economic Development* and the implementation of its proposals. O'Doherty argued that Irish society was changing in a seismic fashion, and that there was a danger that its leaders might simply behave like so many King Canutes in trying to hold back change rather than going with the flow, so to speak. Incidentally, literally going with the flow was the original purpose of the real King Canute, who, very sensibly, ordered the incoming tide to go out to demonstrate to his courtiers his own powerlessness. O'Doherty, who saw himself as a moderniser and more 'advanced' than many of his clerical colleagues in academia and the hierarchy, warned against any clinging to a dying past, often imagined as having been far better than it actually had been. 'Even those,' O'Doherty wrote, 'who are most keen on the impossible, the pickling of a culture, which can only result in its death, have themselves changed without recognizing the fact.'

Our society is in a highly mobile phase at present. In fact we are going through a deep and far-reaching cultural revolution. We shall expect to find the sort of ideas I have been concerned with verified in our midst now or in the very near future. Perhaps what we need most at present is to examine the social institutions, beliefs, practices, and taboos in our midst, with a view to seeing which of them are merely man-made, and which are changeable, which could be altered without undue loss, and which are not changeable. There is no way known to man whereby a culture can be preserved intact, while at the same time remaining a living thing ... if there is one thing known with certainty by the social psychologist, it is simply this: that a culture is something lived, not pickled; and life means change ... I mean far-reaching changes in the self-image of our people, the transition from a horizontally unstratified society to a highly stratified one, from a lived christianity to a post-christian society, the switch from national to international interest, from conditions of no leisure in one generation, to holidays abroad in the next, from acceptance of traditional values and beliefs to their total rejection as with Joyce, from subsistence farming to the affluent society, from a peasant-structured and institutionalized society (as in Arensberg) to a middle class way of life, and all this in one or two generations.[11]

This 'fear of change' which he perceived included a fear of loss of identity in the context of a Europe that was already being seen as integrating. He declared this fear to correspond in society to the fear of loss of identity on the part of the schizophrenic individual. Resistance to change had its merits, but could lead to an 'unhealthy conservatism'. It commonly had emotional and non-rational roots, O'Doherty felt. 'We do not like the source from which the suggestion of change comes' or do not fully understand the change. Possibly, he speculated, 'we are simply afraid of the unknown in a primitive childish way'. Change might also be resisted for short-term selfish reasons because of an incapacity to see the possible gains for others and for future generations. 'Good and desirable changes, such as increased automation in industry' must be planned for and introduced systematically, rather than

reluctantly allowed to happen. 'On the whole, lack of understanding, bad communications, and suspicion, prejudice or hatred
would be a fair summary of the reasons why resistance to change
is so widespread.'[12]

O'Doherty saw himself as a moderniser and he assumed that in
the new pluralist Ireland that was going to emerge, there would be
plenty of room for social and political leadership by the clergy.
However, among many clerics, resistance to change rather than
creative management of an increasingly dynamic society was to
characterise much of Catholic social and political practice and
even Catholic thought in the Republic of Ireland in the following
generation. To be fair, much of this resistance, particularly in the
later period of the 1980s and 1990s, was driven not so much by
Irish clerical leaders as by the Vatican, ever more completely and
damagingly out of touch with Irish cultural and political realities
as time went by. Resistance also came from lay Catholic leaders
often acting without the wholehearted co-operation of the clergy.
Lay leaders were commonly more intransigent and uncompromising than the priests, partly because they were commonly
less educated and certainly less sensitive to the nuances that lay in
much of Catholic doctrine. As the clergy grew older and their
ranks thinned, lay Catholic leaders became more powerful and
self-assertive. The weaker the Irish Church became, paradoxically
the more intransigent its public postures became. Back in 1963,
Fr O'Doherty was being quite prophetic, but he was also, like
O'Faolain, being somewhat of a Cassandra in that he was fated
not to be believed, or, even if believed, to be disregarded. This
resistance led to a growing division between political leaders,
economists, sociologists, journalists and others who, like O'Doherty,
saw change in society as something inevitable and desirable to be
managed or channelled rather than resisted, on the one hand, and
many Catholic leaders and social thinkers on the other, who
instinctively resisted such change point blank. The ideas of a
dynamic and changing society versus a static and virtuous one
faced each other: Aristotle versus Plato. The Church found itself
simply retreating to a position of defence of its territory that was
commonly opportunistic rather than principled: a turf war.

Alternatively, like McQuaid or O'Doherty, it imagined a modern future in which its power and prerogatives remained intact despite rapid technological and economic shifts. The result was an eventual total loss of intellectual leadership by the ecclesiastics and their replacement by politicians, academics, civil servants, technical experts and journalists. Possibly such a secularising development was inevitable, but it is also true that the liberal wing of the Church, which for the first time in a century found a small voice in the wake of Vatican II, found itself in a minority. Certainly it was resented, disregarded, set aside and sometimes persecuted by the traditionalist ecclesiastical establishment in Ireland. Independently minded priests sometimes found themselves sent to the ecclesiastical equivalent of Siberia. Clerical intellectuals were commonly sidelined or even silenced, *à la* McDonald. Catholicism in Ireland was the site of an intellectual tragedy, or, perhaps more accurately, an unintellectual tragedy.

Secularisation, it has often been observed, is a general cultural characteristic of modern societies. Certainly, over the past one hundred years European societies have witnessed a great ebbing of the tide of traditional religion; the ocean of faith is smaller than it once was. The contrast with North America is quite striking, and the counterexample of the United States, a very religious country, indicates that the death of faith has nothing in particular to do with modernisation or economic development, but everything to do with politics. In particular, faith in the modern world seems to be liable to be poisoned by an overly intimate relationship between Church and state and, more generally, by an intimate relationship between ecclesiastical organisations and political power. Such a relationship eventually tends to be seen as illegitimate, particularly in a modernising society which has become highly educated. Jesus, when faced with an intellectual trap in the form of a coin, did, after all, say, 'render unto Caesar the things that are Caesar's and unto God the things that are God's', a remark that looks very much like a statement of the doctrine of separation of Church and state. The American extreme version of this doctrine has, ironically, saved American Christianity from this particular fate.

Ireland was long held to be an exception to the general tendency toward secularisation, and certainly it is the case that religious faith and possibly values usually associated with such faith appear to have survived relatively intact in both parts of Ireland and in the United States among Western countries. In this, at least, the Republic of Ireland and Northern Ireland appear to have behaved more as American than as European provinces. Loss of deference to priests and the Church's official teachings has gone much farther in Ireland than has a loss of faith. Many people who ignore the Church's instructions, who rarely go to mass on Sundays and who never go to confession still see themselves as good believing Catholics. In other words, Ireland is not so much becoming secularised in the sense of possessing a culture of unbelief or atheism, although there are many unbelievers and atheists. Rather, it is that Ireland is becoming *declericalised*; the laws and rules of behaviour laid down by priests for laypeople to conform to came to be defied and afterwards simply increasingly ignored, which, from the Church's point of view, was worse. In fact, the process may be over, and only cultural relicts such as parts of the IRA insurrectionist subculture, parts of Fianna Fáil and the very rural and the very old have any real organic connection with parts of the clerical *apparat*. Interestingly, surveys indicate that secularisation has occurred at about the same slow level in both the Republic of Ireland and Northern Ireland. This is so despite the very different social structures and political systems in the two Irish states.[13]

As late as the mid-1980s, the Republic was still showing an unusually heavy reliance on religious faith as a general governor of one's personal ethical thinking, according to survey evidence of the time. However, a clear age divide was visible, those under age 45 not stressing it as much.[14] In other words, those born after about 1940 and coming to adulthood after 1960 or thereabouts were clearly thinking in more secular terms about personal and social ethics, rather than taking guidance from a perceived transcendent and divinely inspired morality. Furthermore, these people were nearly always the product of Catholic schools, where a strong emphasis was laid on religious formation and the blending of ordinary instruction with the imparting of a religious outlook. It seems that even such education had a clearly secularising effect, as it opened minds to a world of argument and relativism and weaned one away from authoritarian and dogmatic styles of thought and disputation. The Second Vatican Council seems to have come at the crucial moment, but the real motor of change seems to have been the synergy between education and economic development. Education was apparently encouraging a greater psychic individualism and a decreasing willingness to adhere to rules and moral standards set from above without some prior argument. Increasing wealth or *embourgeoisement* led to increasing psychic independence and decreasing ability by elites to control opinion or behaviour. In a phrase, people became more free. Lemass's intuitive foreboding about the cultural consequences of the policy changes that he had wrought almost by force was justified.

Ireland was participating, with some delay, in a general process of cultural change associated with higher levels of education, relative affluence and urbanisation everywhere in Western Europe and North America. It should be recalled that, even forty years on, and despite dramatic cultural change, secularisation has not occurred in Ireland to anything like the extent to which it has in those veteran unbeliever nations, England and France. It took the clerical scandals of the 1990s, a series of self-inflicted wounds on the Catholic Church, to wreak serious and probably irreversible damage to the Church's previously central position in Irish society and culture. These scandals themselves only became conceivable in a context in which secularisation was actually affecting the minds of the priests themselves, so that traditional religious beliefs, clerical self-discipline and sexual puritanism had seriously weakened among them. Priests and nuns were far more likely to have sexual partners than of old. Commonly they lost their 'vocations' because of the contradiction between the celibate discipline demanded of them by the Church on the one hand and the belief of general society on the other that an active and routine adult sexual life was natural, fulfilling and good for you. The stigma of illegitimacy disappeared, as we have seen, and the taboo on homosexuality also faded, partly because of prompting from

Brussels. On the other hand, the moral basis of Irish society has not changed beyond recognition, and Catholic-derived moral imperatives, particularly with regard to abortion, still have a considerable power over people's minds.[15]

Ireland prior to the 1970s was commonly regarded by political scientists as being in many ways a closed society—that is, a society which shut out unwelcome ideas coming in from outside and did so with considerable success. It was also a secretive society, in that some ideas and viewpoints were held privately and not expressed in public for fear of opprobrium or even damage to reputation or career prospects. Irish political culture may have indeed been, as Basil Chubb famously argued back in the late 1960s, post-British, nationalist, just about post-peasant, Catholic, loyal and anti-intellectual. It was also, however, authoritarian and secretive. Power-holders were commonly control freaks, to use modern terminology. Public unbelievers found it difficult to get jobs as schoolteachers or lecturers, for example. However, Irish Catholicism was itself wide open to one source of outside ideas: the international Catholic Church. The collapse of political Catholicism in the Republic of Ireland was caused by an internal crisis within international and Irish Catholicism as much as by any internal change in Irish society's economy. Many priests ceased, for perfectly valid conscientious reasons, to believe in the necessity for clerical social leadership in the old integralist fashion. Despite urbanisation and the fading of peasant society, most people seemed, until quite recently, to be content enough with the social leadership offered by, or imposed by, the Catholic priests. What really happened was the decay of the idea in people's minds that vocation to the priesthood or convent was desirable or, latterly, even all that virtuous. Paedophiles penetrated the Church's organisation in order to have access to children. Child rape by clerics became an open scandal in the Irish and international Catholic Church in the 1990s. Homosexuality, formally regarded by the Church as a disorder, became fairly common in the ranks of the male clergy. In the United States, the possible bankruptcy of some Catholic dioceses has been discussed quite seriously. Furthermore, the idea that the words of priests amounted to law also faded. Jeremiah Newman had been quite right back in the early 1960s—once people stopped working on the farm, went to towns and cities and started to read, they would cease to want to be clerics, and the old admiration for the priest as hero would evaporate. Education offered a correlated threat, although Newman did not point this out. He was afraid that his world, a world in which he was an important person, would die, and it duly did. However, some priests, nuns and brothers themselves gradually ceased to believe in the theory of vocation traditionally offered to them, partly because of the sense of betrayal experienced by them in witnessing the behaviour of some highly placed clerics.

At the same time, it is quite clear that social position and level of education achieved were slowly bringing about the situation that Jeremiah Newman had feared. It was also a situation that he and many other policy-makers had wished to avoid, but which increasingly became an inevitable consequence of the policy decisions of the 1960s. Furthermore, it seems quite clear that the beginning of the cultural shift had already occurred in the 1950s. Survey evidence demonstrates this proposition quite firmly, and indicates that the shift was generational, although social circumstance had the effect of slowing or accelerating the intergenerational change in attitudes. There is an intriguing contrast between the slow and almost calm Irish transition to a relatively secularised society between 1957 and 1997 and the Quebecois abrupt transition from a Catholic confessional society to a post-Catholic society after the fall of the Duplessis government in 1960. In the case of Quebec, ecclesiastical public entanglement in what were seen as the rather extrovertly corrupt machine politics of the Duplessis administration accelerated the fall from power of the Catholic clergy in the province. It could also be that since Quebec had its own national language (French), it needed the ideological 'glue' of Catholicism rather less than did the English-speaking Irish, whose Catholicism had actually evolved into an ethnic-marker in the seventeenth century. Oddly or otherwise, in the case of the Irish Catholic Church, it seems that the Church was seen as untainted by the sometimes corrupt activities of senior Irish politicians; it was regarded as being above such things, quite inaccurately. Eventually it had to do its own self-tainting, as it did to spectacular effect in the 1990s. The Church often treated with Irish business at one remove, through the Knights of Columbanus and similar organisations. Disgraced Irish politician Ray Burke, entangled in financial scandals in the late 1990s, was, in his youth, a Knight. However, no one blames the priests for Burke's long and dishonest political career, or those of his colleagues in the Fianna Fáil party, Charles Haughey and Liam Lawlor, or their Fine Gael opposite number, Michael Lowry. Perhaps they should be looked at afresh as being choice products of a clerical educational system that emphasised a very narrow version of social morality and had little of an ethics of economics to teach.

Table 1 reports religious attitudes by age, social position and levels of educational achievement twenty years after the Lemass revolution.[16]

### Table 1  Percentage Believing (1981): 'There Is Only One True Religion'

| a. By Age | | | | | | |
|---|---|---|---|---|---|---|
| 18–24 | 25–34 | 35–44 | 45–54 | 55–64 | 65–74 | 75+ |
| 31% | 36% | 44% | 54% | 55% | 67% | 70% |

| b. By Age of Completion of Education | | | | | |
|---|---|---|---|---|---|
| Up to 15 | 15 | 16 | 17–18 | 19–20 | 21+ |
| 54% | 52% | 48% | 41% | 31% | 28% |

| c. By Occupation | | | | | | |
|---|---|---|---|---|---|---|
| Farmers | Unskilled | Skilled | Non-man | Profess'al etc. | Student | Unempl'd |
| 46% | 47% | 43% | 31% | 27% | 27% | 42% |

Biever and Newman were quite right, Biever by relatively detached American social scientific insight and Newman by that and by politically informed Irish instinct: educate them and lose your control. The picture in Table 1 clearly demonstrates that a huge divide existed between the increasingly educated young and the still devout and unquestioning culture of the older people of the de Valera era. By age, a clear division was visible between those born before and after about 1940, and thereby coming of age respectively in the pre- or post-Lemass eras. Again, the Leaving Certificate (seventeen–eighteen years) divide is quite stark; it should be remembered that simply having managed to stay in school long enough to sit this examination was a marker of high social status as well as of educational achievement. Furthermore, everything cross-correlates with occupation, farmers and workers being more traditional and white-collar workers and professionals being more 'modern'. Other evidence indicates that large farmers were far less traditional in their outlook than were small farmers. Interestingly, those born during the era of British rule were even more traditionalist in their religious attitudes than the 'de Valera generation'. An entire world of belief and cultural power was disintegrating.

## THE REVENGE OF THE PAST

The recession of the traditional culture of literal belief in the general population and within the body of the clergy affected the Catholic Church internally in many profound ways that have yet to be fully studied. It is strange, little more than a decade later, to read even John Fulton's brilliant and saddening study of Irish Catholicism, *The Tragedy of Belief* (1991), or the first edition of Tom Inglis's magisterial study of the Catholic Church in Ireland, *Moral Monopoly* (1987), in the light of the cultural earthquakes of the 1990s. Both of these important books describe an Ireland and a Catholicism that no longer exist.[17] Again, both describe a powerful Catholic Church whose cultural and political grip on Irish society seemed quite intact, pervasive and impervious to change. Partly because of his own awareness of the fact that so much had changed in the 1990s, Inglis rewrote *Moral Monopoly* and republished it in 1998. This second edition reads almost like a different book about a different country.

The Republic of Ireland was unusual for many years in combining a genuinely functioning liberal democracy with most, if not all, of the standard individual rights associated with such a system on the one hand and, on the other, a popular, 'top-down' religious hierarchy which claimed a monopoly of the truth on matters of morality and many areas of public policy. As late as 1988, Blanshard's *The Irish and Catholic Power* of 1954 remained to quite an extent a valid description of the Church's powerful, if always contested, grip on Irish culture and society. An unavoidable contradiction existed in the system in that the values of free discussion and the right to question official Catholic truths had to coexist with a Church whose theory of truth was not evidential but oracular, to use the terminology of Tom Inglis. The source of truth was divine and transmitted to the faithful through the Pope, the bishops and the lower clergy. Once this system was challenged by simple open discussion or even by public information about the private activities of clerics, it tended to lose its magical power over people's minds. Inglis argues that the chief vehicle of such information and discussion has been the mass media, particularly television. Since the early 1960s, religious matters were freely debated on Irish television, particularly on the programmes of Gay Byrne, easily the most important broadcaster of his generation. In the first decades of television, it was quite revolutionary to see bishops, priests and politicians trying, often ineptly, to defend their opinions and policies in front of increasingly emboldened lay audiences. However, the 1990s saw a quantum leap: Irish television and newspapers started to report clerical misdemeanours, as did the readily available news features programmes of Northern Irish and British television stations. Inglis writes:

The type of stories being told about the Church [in *The Irish Times*] in 1996 was quite different. What would have been considered unbelievable stories in 1987, had by then become commonplace. There were stories about: (*a*) a Donegal priest charged with child sex abuse; (*b*) victims complaining about a sexually abusive priest in Co. Wexford; (*c*) the jailing of a paedophile priest in Kilkenny; (*d*) the resignation of Bishop Wright in Scotland; (*e*) a file on sex abuse by Dublin priests being sent to the Director of Public Prosecutions; (*f*) a Brother walking free after child sex abuse charges were dropped; (*g*) two cases of Wexford priests charged with sexually assaulting young males and (*h*) a Dublin man telling of his abuse as a child by a priest.[18]

Inglis comments that although the absolute numbers of sex scandals involving priests or brothers was not so large, the stories had the cumulative cultural effect of 'rupturing' the popularly perceived uniform and perfect commitment of the clergy to the teachings of the Church. These scandals had the further effect of activating the collective memory, often covertly retained by many non-powerful people, of previous decades of abuse by empowered clergy. Suddenly, hundreds of cases of sexual abuse, physical assault, effective imprisonment of young women and enslavement of children came to be researched and reported in the media. Television documentaries and cinema film documented and re-enacted various episodes in the experiences of orphans, unmarried mothers and young delinquents who were ill treated in clerically run and owned institutions. The most damning fact to emerge was not the nature of the abuses and assaults, but the undeniable proposition that senior clerics, up to and including archbishops, had actually shielded the wrongdoers and protected them from investigation by the secular legal authorities. This was typically done by moving the delinquent clerics on to a different parish or to a new job where, in many cases, they could reoffend until exposed. They were then permitted to move on again, with the connivance of clerical authority. A conspiracy of silence which had protected the Church in the twentieth century came to a sudden and dramatic end. Dozens of elderly clerics were jailed for offences committed twenty or thirty years previously in a pattern of state intervention in ecclesiastical affairs that would have been utterly unimaginable a short ten years earlier. A Church that had behaved almost as a government without parliamentary supervision, with power and without real responsibility was quite suddenly shorn of that power. The past wreaked a terrible revenge.

**END OF AN EXPERIMENT**
Secularisation in Ireland, together with the concomitant collective humiliation of the Irish clergy, marked the end of an ambitious social and political experiment on the part of the Catholic Church, one which was prefigured by Cardinal Cullen's modernisation of the Irish Catholic Church in the late nineteenth century and

which was first put forward after independence. This was the project of building a Catholic society that fully realised Catholic social and moral values within the framework of an independent democratic country. Tridentine social and ethical values were to be reconciled with the institutions and practices of Anglo-American liberal democracy, the latter ceding power in areas where the former claimed primacy. Ireland was also to be a guinea pig for ideas of reorganising society along what were commonly described as vocational lines. Vocationalism was very much a fashionable idea during the years after the First World War, and attracted thinkers on the left and right of society. The central idea was that electoral territorial democracy was incomplete on its own, but needed to be supplemented by, or even supplanted by, economic representation. As man was a creature who realised himself through labour of hand and mind, a polity which did not represent him through his work was not truly democratic or truly representative, it was argued by Catholic ideologues of the 1920–60 period. Typically, vocationalists proposed the adding of a vocational chamber to the parliament to supplement the territorially elected lower house, this chamber being elected, selected or appointed by economic 'chambers' into which the great branches of human industry were to be organised. Heavy industry, light industry, education, cultural workers, people working on the land, clergy, professional people and the various skilled trades were envisaged as electing representatives to this chamber. Fascist countries often set up just such systems of organisation. Experiments of this kind were imposed by fascist or quasi-fascist regimes in Italy, Spain and Portugal, sometimes complete with uniforms that were colour coded by profession, trade or 'vocation'. The Catholic Church in Ireland, inspired by such ideas promulgated in papal encyclicals, was attracted to these schemes.

Another related ideological thread which encouraged interest in vocationalism was a prevailing ideology of the previous generation which is sometimes termed *distributivism*. Distributivism stemmed from a common view of the capitalist world held by many thinkers at the end of the nineteenth century. Hilaire Belloc, an English Catholic writer of French extraction, was influential, and impressed both the young men of the Irish Republican Brotherhood ('Fenians') and the Catholic priests of the time.[19] The central idea of these writers was the wish to find a 'middle way' between what were seen as the two great threats of the modern world—unbridled finance capitalism on the one hand and tyrannical state socialism on the other. These were seen as threats that were sometimes regarded as inherent in the logic of the development of industrial society. Ernest Blythe, writing in 1913 in the pages of the IRB paper, *Irish Freedom*, proposed a 'co-operative commonwealth'. 'Anarchic' free enterprise would not be permitted, and as agriculture was the mother of all industry, no stable or sane economic order could endure that was not based on agriculture. No great industrial trusts or big universal trade unions would be permitted. Instead, property rights to small parcels of property, combined with voting control over the organisation of the economy, would be spread as widely as possible among the population.[20] This would break down the adversarial relationship between labour and capital, and a harmonious democratised political economy would soften this distinction by combining in the person of each citizen both of the principles of labour and ownership. Some of these ideas were clearly reminiscent of Chartist ideas of two generations previously: the artisan cottage with roses growing around the door.

Clerical writers also joined in. Fr P. Coffey of Maynooth, writing in 1920 in the extreme nationalist, anti-Semitic and sectarian integralist *Catholic Bulletin*, offered an elaborate critique of James Connolly's ideas on the evils of capitalism. In a well-written and closely argued set of articles, Coffey accepted that capitalism was evil, but for reasons other than those offered by Connolly. Capitalism's real evil was not its exploitative nature, but its tendency to make property rights impossible for the vast bulk of mankind. Capitalism had the effect of splitting society into a small group of owners and a vast mass of propertyless people, the latter being essentially proletarians. Like Blythe, Coffey suggested the spreading of ownership among the workers and the bending of financial institutions to the needs of the co-operative commonwealth.[21] These ideas remained current in ecclesiastical and political circles right up to the 1960s, and seem to continue to inform much of the practice of Irish economic policy and collective pay negotiation in a residual fashion even in the twenty-first century. Irish home ownership policy, which has resulted in the Republic having one of the highest home ownership rates in the world, is partly derived from these ideas; economists sometimes argue that the social stability achieved by this policy has denied capital to enterprise in preference for bricks and mortar. These distributivist ideas were in part echoes of the Catholic social thought of the period, but they were also echoes of the authentic success in the late nineteenth century, in Munster in particular, but also in north-western Ireland, of dairy co-operatives and creameries. The ideology also harmonised with the historical fact that Irish farmers were now outright owner-occupiers of small to medium-sized farms following on the peaceful revolution symbolised by the Land Acts. Irish smallholders commonly evolved co-operative or *meitheal* systems centring on work-sharing, machine hire and barter at local level. An archaic local solidarity also promoted a 'stick together' ethos in local small-farm communities. Syndicalist socialists saw some things which seemed sympathetic to their ideology in vocationalism, and mainline Irish trade unionists found them of interest also. In a more remote fashion, these ideas dovetailed with a communalist anti-individualism of Irish political culture which I have discussed elsewhere.[22]

Fear of big business and big labour united the large centre in Irish society, based as it mostly was at that time on the small owner-occupier farm and the small business or trade. Both of these half-imaginary bugbears were, after all, easily seen as English inventions. In some ways, this ideological tradition, promoted most insistently by Catholics, resembled fascism in being a centrist ideology in the terms offered by Seymour Martin Lipset, but it did not, by and large, possess the extremism of means or the romanticism of style characteristic of true fascism.[23] Amid considerable pomp and circumstance, de Valera's government appointed a commission in January 1939 to look into the possibilities of reorganising the state along vocational lines; it is fairly evident that many people secretly hoped that this departure would bury the entire matter.[24] This followed the sop de Valera had given to the vocationalists in the Constitution of 1937, in the form of a formally vocationally organised Seanad Éireann. This upper house had little real power and the actual vocational content in its representative system was notional rather than real; like Dáil Éireann, the Seanad was overwhelmingly a party chamber. Like so many of de Valera's constitutional devices, Seanad Éireann was an ideological red herring, and clearly intended to be so.[25]

The Commission on Vocational Organisation reported in 1943. It proposed an elaborate system of vocational boards elected by the main sections of the economy: agriculture, professions, commerce, transport, finance and industry. It was heavily weighted in favour of agriculture, and to some extent toward industry. 'Experts' to the tune of twenty could be co-opted to form a body of 120 members in all. The proposals, printed in an enormous volume, dropped stillborn from the presses, and a certain governmental hostility to them was evident in the Dignan–MacEntee exchanges over the proposed vocationalisation of the health system in 1944, as recounted in Chapter 2. The contempt shown by the vocationalists for civil servants was quite evident. Joseph Lee and Dermot Keogh have, rightly, put their collective finger on Bishop Michael Browne's exaggerated respect for the professions and patronising attitude toward public officials. Susannah Riordan has further argued convincingly that Dignan's advocacy of his health scheme was aggressive, clerical and populist. Brian Ó Nualláin (Myles na gCopaleen/Gopaleen in his civil servant role) described the scheme and the Commission on Vocational Organisation's proposals as advocating 'what one might call a neo-fascism. Both assail the fitness of the government to carry out several of its most material duties.' Furthermore, he pointed out, the proposals demanded that these functions be transferred to bodies not answerable to parliament. Fundamentally they displayed a disregard for electoral democracy, a contempt for politicians and public servants and a subconscious arrogance derived from the bishops' belief that they were the rightful rulers of the country. Tom Barrington of the Department of Local Government carried out a costing of the Dignan scheme which suggested that it would be about twice as expensive as suggested by its advocates. Riordan writes:

While the lack of popular enthusiasm for vocationalism is evident with hindsight, Myles na gCopaleen recognised that Dignan's combination of right-wing Catholic ideology with a broad popular appeal and an anti-State rhetoric was a potent one. The tendency of the vocational movement—whether or not it was inherently undemocratic—to foster a climate of contempt for the existing parliamentary forms should not be underestimated.[26]

It could be argued, as Riordan does, that there was a serious philosophical battle involved here, and even that that event, rather than the Church–state clash of 1948–51, marked the real beginning of the long, slow demise of clerical power in independent Ireland. It was, after all, the first time a bishop had been seen off publicly by a minister, and also the first time civil servants more or less publicly demolished his pronouncements by putting forward the better intellectual argument. Further, it witnessed the energetic, if mildly incongruous, defence of democratic institutions by lay bureaucrats, backed up by tough ex-guerrilla politicians, fending off authoritarian power-seeking senior clerics.

In the years after the Second World War, collective bargaining of wage rounds became traditional, and it is still used to maintain industrial peace. Various vocational bodies representing farming, labour, employers and government have come and gone and have been used to smooth the pace of economic and social change. However, the dream of reorganising Irish democracy completely along such lines came to be seen as old-fashioned, a return to the guild system or even neo-medieval. Above all, it came to be seen as naive and unrealistic. From the point of view of this book's argument, vocationalism seems to have envisaged a static society, mainly agrarian, with vested interests being protected by official structures. In effect, the proposals of the Commission looked like intensifying the kind of corporate structure which small polities are prone to develop in any case, as argued in Olsonian fashion in the Introduction. Ireland's politics were zero-sum enough, it could be argued, without actually engineering an intensification of that stultifying characteristic. The anti-individualism and authoritarianism of the thinking of the vocationalists is also evident, as was their disregard, if not actual contempt, for the processes of electoral representative democracy. A de facto separation of powers operated between Church and state, the economy and foreign affairs remaining by and large out of the reach of the clergy. The area of foreign policy did occasionally become contested, perhaps most conspicuously in 1957, when a spat occurred between the Department of External Affairs and Cardinal John Spellman, an American. The issue was Irish support for a United Nations motion which proposed the discussion of the possible seating of communist China in the international organisation. Spellman came off worst. Catholic control of the heights of civil society remained formally confined to education and to aspects of the health-care system, and the Church retreated somewhat in other areas of civil society. As we have seen, that retreat has now become a rout half a century later.

## COMPARATIVE PERSPECTIVES
Independent Ireland tended to compare itself to its neighbour and erstwhile master, Great Britain, and also, naturally, to Northern Ireland. To be fair, many senior leaders were less parochial and looked to other small states such as Denmark, New Zealand or Finland. Others again looked at Nazi Germany or the Soviet Union. Another very important and culturally inevitable index of comparison was the United States, sometimes seen in an almost mythical fashion as the land of fabled plenty beyond the western ocean. More immediately, the United States was seen as the source of a significant adjunct to Irish national income in the form of emigrants' remittances, or dollars sent back to the Old Country to help out relatives in Ireland. Most of these comparisons were economic and simply consisted of comparing GNP figures, standards of living and availability of career opportunities. Ireland rarely came out of such comparisons well, and an entire tradition has grown up, as we have seen, of exaggeratedly bewailing any lagging behind and equally of exaggeratedly praising any perceived outstripping of her neighbours.

However, it may be that other, perhaps as useful, comparisons can be made in non-economic matters. In particular, in the generation after independence, Ireland was the only stable democracy in the world whose citizens were nearly all devout and believing members of the Catholic Church. This fact itself has made the country appear worthy of closer examination by many writers over the decades. A study which I have used extensively earlier, Blanshard's well-known book of 1954, *The Irish and Catholic Power*, was a sustained examination of how Catholic and democratic principles of authority overlapped in Irish political culture. The purpose of the book was avowedly comparative, as it was intended as a grim warning to Americans of what might happen to democracy in their country were the Catholic Church ever to attain the allegiance of a believing majority of citizens. Blanshard's Ireland was a model of what a Catholic United States might look like in some future era. Predictably, a Catholic America was foreseen by him as being less free than the actual mainly Protestant America, restrictions on free speech, certain types of education, sexual mores and divorce being certainties. The Ireland of 1953 was seen by Blanshard as a scary pilot version of a possible American future.[27] Certainly, many Catholics in both Europe and America thought in terms of takeover by biology; Catholics were more fertile than non-Catholics, and in the pre-war era, Pius XII actually welcomed the Hitlerite expansion of the German Reich into the south and east because it entailed the incorporation of more Catholics into the hitherto Protestant-dominated Bismarckian *Kleindeutschland* Reich. He loved Germany and yearned for a Catholic Germany, not a Nazi Germany. It seems that he imagined with a fantastic innocence that the latter could, somehow or other, get him the former. Similarly, Catholicism was demographically dynamic in the United States, and similar hopes of a Catholic America were entertained. In Ireland, some hoped rather similarly for a demographic takeover of Northern Ireland by Catholics.

Blanshard's fear of Tridentine Catholicism was quite understandable during that era. Since 1848, the Catholic Church had shown at best an ambivalent attitude toward electoral democracy and quite often a clear preference for right-wing, anti-communist and anti-democratic government in both Europe and Latin America. In part, this reflected the upper-class and aristocratic social origins of many leading clerical leaders in the Church. It also echoed the anti-clericalism of much of the French Revolution, and, more immediately, Pius IX's turning against the idea of an Italian democracy after 1848–51. It was not until after the defeat of European fascism in 1945 that the Church finally came to terms more or less unreservedly with international Christian democracy. Some would suggest unkindly that it had little choice. However, Irish Catholicism has always differed from continental or Latin American Catholicism in its attitudes to democracy. A democracy whose citizens listened to, and sometimes obeyed, the instructions of their priests was both evidently attainable and to be welcomed from the Church's point of view. This reflects the relatively humble middle-class and farm origins of most leading clergy in Ireland in the past two centuries and their close relations with the ordinary people. In part, this relative openness to political democracy characteristic of the Irish Church parallels other differences between the English-speaking democracies as a group of countries and continental European countries of Catholic tradition as another such group of countries. Freemasonry, for example, is a milder creature in the former group of countries than it has been historically in the latter. Also, the extreme anti-clericalism which was historically so conspicuous in Western Europe has no real parallel in the English-speaking world; instead, there has typically been a straight stand-off between Catholic and Protestant varieties of Christianity, the latter being traditionally dominant pretty well everywhere except in Ireland. Thus, Irish Catholicism had to ally itself with a powerful Irish national democratic culture in the form of the O'Connellite tradition, personified by later leaders such as Isaac Butt, Charles Stewart Parnell, John Redmond, William T. Cosgrave and Eamon de Valera. Contrary to the assertions of some commentators, Irish democracy has always had a clearly liberal strand to it, often temporarily buried by Catholic triumphalism, but never killed off.

Catholicism was therefore forced into a relationship with the democratic Irish state that approximated to the relationships historically enjoyed by *Protestant* churches in countries such as Sweden, Norway, Denmark or, for that matter, Great Britain.

Politically the Irish were hybrid: papal Calvinists.[28] In the Anglophone world, political Protestantism has tended to lose ground slowly before the forces of secularisation, indifference, unbelief and the claims to pluralism of other religions, whether Christian or non-Christian. In Ireland, the same process has been eating away at a powerfully organised neo-traditional Catholicism for over fifty years. In effect, the historic authoritarianism of Tridentine Catholicism was gradually worn down by the intense populist democratic aspect of Irish political culture, the insistence on free speech and the demand for information about the decisions of powerful people. The bizarre papal decision in 1968 to outlaw contraception merely pushed an already ailing patient over some kind of cliff. Liberalism, that much feared enemy of the Tridentine tradition, has had a victory in Ireland. However, in this, Catholic Ireland is not an island. The scandals of Irish Catholicism, particularly those involving sexual misconduct and financial irregularities, have been replicated throughout the English-speaking world and, to an extent, elsewhere in the Catholic world as well. American Catholics are now in open rebellion against a hierarchy seen by many pious and believing Catholics as corrupt and even evil.

Writing in 1981, John Whyte detected a general tendency towards secularisation or, rather, declericalisation, in both continental political Catholicism and in the Catholicism of the English-speaking countries. He wrote of a general move away from the 'closed' or top-down authoritarian 'ghetto' Catholicism of Vatican I Catholicism and towards a more 'open' and non-authoritarian Catholicism of a post-Vatican II world. In his classic *Catholics in Western Democracies*, Whyte argued:

> ... by the beginning of the nineteen-eighties, the wheel is coming full circle. Catholics in continental Europe and those in the Anglo-American world are closer together in their political behaviour than they have been at any time since the eighteen-forties. Both are moving nearer the open end of the spectrum. In both groups of countries, Catholic parties and social organisations are declining, de-confessionalising themselves, or both. Episcopal guidance to

the electorate is less frequent and more cautiously phrased than it used to be. There is a greater diversity of opinion. Instead of being clustered disproportionately towards either the centre-right (as in continental Europe) or the centre-left (as in the Anglo-American world), Catholics seem more evenly spread across the left-wing voting in Anglo-America at the very time when left-wing views have become increasingly fashionable among some Catholics in continental Europe.[29]

In fact, with hindsight wisdom, what was seen twenty years ago as a liberalisation of traditional Tridentine Catholicism and the dawn of a new era can now be seen as a major collapse of traditional clerical and episcopal authority. It can also be seen as a major chapter, perhaps, in the story of the declericalisation of Western Christianity. Some would be inclined to go further and regard it as a late, if dramatic, chapter in a huge macrohistorical process best termed the dechristianisation of the West.

The Irish experience demonstrates that even an apparently all-powerful and historically beloved Church ensconced in power by a liberal democracy can be far more fragile than it appears to be. Like any political party or democratic government, it cannot, in the medium to long term, drift too far away from the concerns of the electorate, or show itself to be operating in a way that is seen as being contrary to the long-term interests of the population or the nation. Most importantly of all, it cannot permit itself to be seen as breaking trust. Furthermore, when such an organisation develops a habit of deriving its power from fear or self-interest as much as from faith or love, it courts real catastrophe when the fear and the self-interest evaporate. Ireland came to be seen by the Church as a nation created for the purposes of the Church, a nation whose own secular interests and collective purposes would have to be pushed aside so as to make way for the purposes of organised international Catholicism. After 1945, the Church gradually came to be seen as operating in ways that were undemocratic, cruel, contrary to the interests of the broader nation and, in particular, the interests of future generations. Eventually, political elites rebelled against this situation, and, crucially, their rebellion was ratified by the electorate. As this book has argued, that much derided decade of the 1950s was the period in which the irreconcilability of the interests of Church and nation was first vaguely sensed by large numbers of ordinary people as well as by political leaders, the clerical monopoly of education being the touchstone. Irish voters did not vote for clerical politics, but for the politics of economic development and the pork barrel. Democratic politics was the true agent of declericalisation in Ireland and elsewhere in the West.

There is an historical irony in this. For many minds, the true founding event of modern independent Ireland's democracy was the fall of Charles Stewart Parnell in 1891 and the subsequent split in the pan-nationalist Irish Party between Parnellite and anti-Parnellite wings. Parnell's fall resulted from a sexual misde-meanour that made his party's alliance with the British Liberal Party no longer viable under his leadership. The Catholic Church relentlessly hounded him from power, to the lasting embitterment of many Catholics; the fall of the Uncrowned King of Ireland is a political leitmotif of the greatest Irish *Bildungsroman* of the twentieth century, James Joyce's *A Portrait of the Artist as a Young Man*.[30] The collapse of clerical power in Ireland a century later was directly related to the obsessional nature of the Catholic clergy's attitudes toward people's sexual life, its attempts to regulate it in all kinds of rather strange and often heartless ways and the gradual exposure of the seamy and even criminal side of many clerics' own sexual practices. Maybe we have witnessed Parnell's revenge.

Other Irish interest groups have had their travails as well, but have weathered the storms of modernisation rather better than the Church. Irish trade unions, to be seen as rather backward-looking, reactionary and occasionally archaic institutions during the immediate post-war period, have lost their once very large memberships and much of their bargaining power. Furthermore, many foreign investors have refused to run union shops and have made that refusal stick in a society with traditionally very strong unions. Unions in Western countries are generally less important and less politically powerful than they were in the first post-war decades, and Ireland is no exception to this generalisation. Irish unions' attitudes to development, innovation and the European Union have sometimes been reactionary and self-regarding. Business is still politically powerful, but the wave of scandals that overran the Church has been echoed in a parallel huge wave of scandals involving large-scale corruption, bribery and illegal practice by well-known business firms, many of them closely connected to powerful figures in the Fianna Fáil party. Again, these stories would never have surfaced twenty years previously and would have remained at the level of uncorroborated journalists' gossip and pub talk. Irish political parties are similarly far less secretive and authoritarian in their political styles than they used to be; the original top-down, secretive and oracular template of the Catholic Church's organisation has ceased to be the model even in the case of Fianna Fáil. De Valera as Fianna Fáil's lay archbishop, mysterious and remote in demeanour, was replaced by men of a distinctly non-charismatic stripe, managerial in style rather than romantic or pseudo-heroic. Furthermore, there is clear survey evidence to the effect that the traditional automatic party loyalties of old are in full decay; the 'rational choice' floating voter has clearly got the upper hand over the 'socialised loyalties' voter of yesteryear. Only Fianna Fáil can still count on the automatic support of the Fianna Fáil family 'houses', and there are far fewer such houses than there were. Obvious reasons are disillusionment with the leaders over the past thirty years because of public awareness of corruption, the decay of traditional nationalism, the recession of the seas of both political and religious faith and increased public education. The general decay of traditional political-party organisations in advanced Western societies has been shared by the Irish. The information revolution in Ireland, generated by the demand for information of an increasingly educated and sceptical public, has hurt the powerful in the secular world as well.

One key to the Catholic Church's success in Irish politics and social culture was its air of being *essential*, that somehow the Irish would never be able to cope with civic life without the good priests and nuns to lead them, advise them (well or idiotically) and provide for them. This was in part an echo of a traditional

English scepticism about the ability of the Irish to rule themselves without the help of the English or of an Anglo-Irish aristocracy. Catholic priests tended to see themselves as a kind of alternative aristocracy, with a God-given right to rule over a people not really capable of self-rule. In the nineteenth century, after all, Irish electoral politics commonly was reducible to a struggle between two feudal lordships for the vote of the Irish peasant—the lordship of the land and the lordship of the spirit.[31] A feudalism of the spirit survived the fall of Irish terrestrial landlordism by a century. As we have seen, an abundant contempt for independent lay political and social leadership, a contempt originally derived from clerical arrogance, existed in the popular mind as late as 1960. Parenthetically, the IRA's contempt for the Irish experiment with democracy has similar Catholic and clerical roots. The apparently necessary centrality of the Church to Irish society may have been the greatest illusion of all in the Irish House of Illusions.

Another key to the success of the Church in keeping a grip on the minds of Irish men and women until late in the century was the absence of a large, highly educated stratum of men and women in Irish Catholic society until the twentieth century was well under way. Wisdom of hindsight informs this writer that, consciously or unconsciously, Catholic clerics feared the emergence of such a stratum for the obvious and sufficient reason that it would be uncontrollable by them in the medium to long term. Such a fear is prefigured in Canon Sheehan's pronouncements of the 1900s. An awareness of this uncontrollability certainly lay behind McQuaid's and other bishops' determination to superintend students of philosophy and the social sciences in the universities from 1943 on, a suzerainty which did not die in Dublin until McQuaid's forced retirement in 1972 at the hands of the Vatican. It may be that the true revolution of the 1960s was not the economic upturn of that decade, but rather the breakneck expansion of the second- and third-level education systems that was forced through by Hillery and O'Malley in the middle of the decade.

In 1966, the American political scientist, Harry Eckstein, offered a well-known argument concerning the tendency toward congruence in social institutions in democratic and non-democratic polities. Fundamentally, Eckstein's central idea was that authoritarian top-down institutions can coexist with overall non-authoritarian democratic institutions, but that the existence of an important authoritarian institution such as a church which has the loyalty of most of the population will tend to coexist most happily with a democracy which has rather authoritarian tendencies itself, or with a non-democratic regime. In other words, the authoritarian organisation 'infects' the non-authoritarian polity.[32] Writing as he was in the mid-1960s, he saw the Roman Catholic Church as being the most obvious authoritarian organisation which commonly cohabited with Western democracy. Historically, the Church had often been hostile to democracy. Another authoritarian tradition was that represented by the series of mass and genuinely popular communist parties which at that time similarly appeared to offer a serious threat to democratic values. Arguing in the political contest of the 1960s, Eckstein wrote:

Catholicism, by subjecting its adherents to a highly authoritarian relationship, and one which involves extremely powerful psychological sanctions, certainly does nothing itself to reinforce democracy. Potentially it always threatens to introduce an incongruity into a democratic society, so that in any democracy there exists a fair probability that Catholicism will have dysfunctional consequences. But no more than a fair probability. If a democracy is sufficiently hedged about with authoritarian elements, the incongruity between government and church need not be very great. Moreover, if the church does not play a very important role in the associational life of a society, or if between church and government there exists a multiplicity of less authoritarian institutions, even associations with a religious tinge, the incongruities will be diminished, in the sense of being mediated and reconciled. Whether or not Catholicism will inhibit or undermine democracy depends, therefore, not only on the inherent characteristics of Catholicism, but also on the nature of the governmental pattern and the vigor (and particular characteristics) of associational life in a society.[33]

The Irish experience actually confirms this general insight, but also offers another one, one that this writer believes to be rather important and to have some intellectual significance in the field of comparative politics. That is, the Irish case supports, if it does not decisively confirm, the proposition that the infection can go the other way. In effect, the liberal-democratic, individualist and even populist characteristics inherent in an authentic constitutional and free social order can eventually break down the top-down, secretive and closed characteristics of any authoritarian organisation. The key word here is, of course, 'eventually', but in the lifetime of nations two generations need not seem too long. Furthermore, the existence of such a free order will, *in the long run*, have its way with the authoritarian apparatus, essentially regardless of its historical grip on collective *mentalité* or the institutions of a democratic state. Keynes famously remarked that in the long run we are all dead, but the present generation lives in Keynes's long run. Irish democracy has exerted a persistent pressure on authoritarian institutions, whether they be the Catholic clerical apparatus or the secretive and authoritarian traditions of Irish republicanism and Irish communism.

The most spectacular example of just such a rot is offered by the demise of Soviet communism in Russia and Eastern Europe between 1948 and 1989. George F. Kennan, writing in the late 1940s, foresaw such a rot lasting for more than a generation. Precisely such an analogous breakdown is what has been happening to Irish Catholicism in the past forty years, and this general effect has been extended to the public institutions of state as well. The once-secretive institutions of the post-British state and of the educational system have gradually come under increasing pressure to divulge their secrets and to explain the reasoning behind their policy decisions. Occasionally they are also forced to defend themselves in the courts. Not only is the old Faith and Fatherland alliance dying, but the historically authoritarian, commonly extra-legal and secretive Irish political style of governance is increasingly being challenged by ever stronger and more insistent pressures to move towards more inclusive, open and publicly assessable ways of working. This is perhaps the true silent revolution in Irish political culture, and it is one that has very old roots in Irish political history. It was, after all, back in 1906 that Michael Davitt, the famous Irish agrarian radical, speaking in the context of Catholicity and liberal democracy in the English-speaking world, notoriously remarked, 'Make no mistake about it, my Lord Bishop of Limerick, Democracy is going to rule in these countries.'[34]

## IRELAND IS NOT AN ISLAND

Ireland's opening up to America and Europe after 1957 did far more than enhance the country's trade performance or open up world perspectives to minds that had long been accustomed to rather narrow horizons. It certainly did do these things, but also in the medium term this emergence from relative isolation led to a profound rearrangement of the power relationships inside the country itself. In effect, the Madison problem cited in the Introduction, in which small countries are seen as vulnerable to takeover by interest groups with interests unsympathetic to the general national interest, ceased to apply. Local veto groups increasingly came to be seen as anti-national and as targets—fair game for denunciation as being in restraint of trade or other cultural activity and therefore acting against the collective interest of the nation. Trade unions are forced into corporate styles of bargaining and cease to be seen as representatives of the working people in general; in Ireland, where there had been an historically highly unionised polity with unionisation rates of well over 50 per cent of the workforce, the rate had sunk to about 30 per cent of the workforce by 2001. The older idea of building up the country behind tariff barriers and cultural barriers came to be seen as stultifying and self-defeating. As suggested in particular by Peter Katzenstein, small states in world markets are forced to compete internationally as 'Austria Inc.', Sweden Inc.', etc. The nation-state itself, as much as, or even rather than, the individual firm, does the competing. This kind of international competition is typically carried on by means of quasi-corporatist structures which encourage the building of centrist consensus and close liaison between business leaders, trade unions, foreign investors and national government. Also pulled into this net are the leaders of the knowledge industry in the universities, research institutes and the research sections of manufacturing firms. International organisations such as the OECD and the EU also have an important role to play. Ireland is no longer an island as far as developmental thinking is concerned, but very much resembles the small trading states discussed by Katzenstein. These trading states resemble the 'market-state' proposed by Philip Bobbitt as being the future form which today's nation-states are fated to take.[35]

In the market-state, direct pressure from international sources becomes more difficult for internal interest groups to resist. As we have seen, the impact of Marshall Aid programmes and the administrators of the ECA on Irish political and administrative leaders was very considerable. Similarly, the European Union has had enormous direct and indirect impact on Irish society and culture. In an analogous way and in a very different cultural arena, the impact of events in international Catholicism on the affairs of the Irish Catholic Church was seismic.[36] The interaction of local reformers with trends in international education forced on Irish education a series of great changes. The general sense of being 'left behind' sparked Ireland's attempt at a breakout from under-development in the 1950s. Internal individuals and groups hostile to the status quo had the increasingly ready backing, moral support, advice, publicity and manpower of internationally organised networks. The same, of course, applied to those groups supportive of the status quo. A conspicuous example of this was the well-organised international campaign in support of Catholic groups in Ireland which strove to retain legal and constitutional prohibitions on contraception, divorce, family law and abortion. Because of the end of Ireland's status as a cultural island, Irish ideological and cultural debates have lost something of their local peculiarity and have come to resemble and directly echo such debates elsewhere.

The Irish experience also warns political scientists, particularly those trained in the American behavioural or rational choice traditions, never to play down or ignore the semi-independent role of ideas in political action. Ideas often come from traditions, long extant in the collective culture and forming part of a repertoire of courses of action deemed at some times to be undesirable or unsuitable, and later on deemed by key actors to have seen their day finally come. Alternatively, new ideas are imported into the culture, or old ideas repackaged in more prestigious garb as American, Marxist, scientific or Catholic sets of ideas coming in from outside. Robert C. Lieberman has called recently, in the perhaps unlikely forum of the *American Political Science Review*, for American political scientists to 'bring ideas back in'.[37] He complains that many 'institutionalists', by which he means legal, structural and behavioural theorists all lumped together, have slipped into the almost Marxist habit of regarding ideas as essentially epiphenomenal entities. An example he cites is the habit of voting behaviour specialists of collapsing political disputes 'typically to a single dimension'.[38]

Ideas in politics, by contrast, are often complex and multi-dimensional. Ideational accounts of politics also challenge the tendency of institutional theories to take the interests and aims of political actors as given, whether they are determined by individual rationality, group affiliation or cultural patterns. Rather, actors' understanding of their own interests is apt to evolve as the ideological setting of politics changes. More generally, ideational theories seem to challenge the institutional emphasis on structure, aggregate organisational or behavioural regularities, as the principle guiding force behind political behaviour. A focus on ideas suggests, rather, the possibility that human agency can defy the constraints of political and social structures and create new political possibilities.[39]

In practice, Edelman proposes a blend of institutional and ideational approaches and uses the US civil rights campaigns of the 1960s as a concrete example of how to do it. The Irish post-war confrontation with the challenge of the modern world in the form of possibilities of economic development together with the linked possibility of profound cultural change offers another good example of how institutional systems and systems of ideas interact in a complex way in political life. In this, as in so much else, Ireland has joined the world.

# NOTES

**Abbreviations**

AD UCD    Archives Department, University College Dublin
DDA       Dublin Diocesan Archives (Catholic)
DIC        Department of Industry and Commerce
NA         National Archives, Dublin
NLI        National Library of Ireland

**Preface** (PAGES vii–ix)

1. See my *1922: The Birth of Irish Democracy*, Dublin: Gill & Macmillan, 1996. Many of the ideas in the early part of this book received an early airing in University College Cork, May 1992 and at the Daniel O'Connell Workshop, Caherdaniel, County Kerry, October 1992. See my 'Political Power and Economic Development in Ireland: A Comparative Perspective', in *People Power: Proceedings of the Third Annual Daniel O'Connell Workshop*, Dublin: Institute of Public Administration, 1993, 32–6.

2. Strangely, censorship did not apply to theatre, and Dublin and provincial theatre generally remained subject only to extra-legal objection and protest, commonly emanating from ecclesiastical and republican elements. An incident involving an experimental theatre (the Pike Theatre) in Dublin in 1957 was the only major exception to this generalisation, and it appears the Pike affair was partly a by-product of a power struggle between the Department of Justice and the Catholic secret society, the Knights of Saint Columbanus. Irish theatre was one of the few cultural success stories of the period, the Abbey Theatre becoming the first state-sponsored theatre in the English-speaking world. Many have argued that this largesse was a poisoned gift. After 1945, a remarkable amateur theatre movement grew up in Dublin and the provinces, partly because of the leadership offered by the Dublin, Cork and Galway theatres, almost as if to show what could be done in Ireland were the stifling effects of a censorious authority ever to be removed.

**Introduction** (PAGES 1–24)

1. AD UCD/P7/a/197, Mulcahy Papers, 6 December 1922, *The Times*, same date.
2. AD UCD/P7/D/I/1, 8.
3. AD UCD/P7/D/58, 9.

# NOTES

295

4. Tom Garvin, *1922: The Birth of Irish Democracy*, Dublin: Gill & Macmillan, 1996.

5. Irish-language terminology can be confusing for many, including many Irish people. Taoiseach means 'leader' and was the word proposed, but not used, in 1922 for 'General of the Army' by Hugh Kennedy of Cumann na nGaedheal. From 1937 on it has been the official title of the Irish prime minister; the title before 1937 under the Constitution of the Irish Free State was President of the Executive Council, a title which reflects a desperate attempt by the pro-Treatyites of 1922–23 to look 'republican'. The Free State was disestablished in 1937 (not 1949, as is commonly believed). A distant analogy with Führer and Duce was suggested by de Valera's adaptation of the term 'Taoiseach', but the analogy is a creatively false one, like so many of de Valera's ideological devices. Dáil means 'assembly' and a member of the Dáil is a TD or *Teachta Dála* (Dáil deputy). Fianna Fáil means 'Soldiers of Destiny', the destiny in question being that of the Isle of Destiny, *Inis Fáil* ('Innisfallen') or Ireland. The pattern of renaming everything official, political and bureaucratic in poetic Irish phrases echoes the romantic Gaelic League tradition that so heavily informed the founders of the Irish State. To put it mildly, these institutions named so romantically have been less than totally romantic in practice.

6. On non-decisions, see Peter Bachrach, *The Theory of Democratic Elitism*, Boston: Little Brown, 1967. On the mentality of the new elites, see in particular AD UCD P53/377, Michael Hayes Papers.

7. Paul Bew and Henry Patterson, *Sean Lemass and the Making of the New Ireland*, Dublin: Gill & Macmillan, 1982; Brian Girvin, *Between Two Worlds: Politics and Economy in Independent Ireland*, Dublin: Gill & Macmillan, 1989; John Kurt Jacobsen, *Chasing Progress in the Irish Republic: Ideology, Democracy and Dependent Development*, Cambridge: Cambridge University Press, 1994. On a more macro scale, see Denis O'Hearn, *The Atlantic Economy: Britain, the US and Ireland*, Manchester: University Press, 2001. A pioneering economists' general study of the Irish transition is Kieran Kennedy and Brendan Dowling, *Economic Growth in Ireland: The Experience since 1947*, Dublin: Gill & Macmillan, 1975.

8. Girvin, 200–201.

9. On Irish cultural change in general, the standard work is Terence Brown, *Ireland: A Social and Cultural History, 1922–85*, London: Fontana, 1985. On the secularisation of both Catholic and Protestant education resultant on economic development, see Brown, 'Two Schools of Thought about Thought in Schools', *Sunday Tribune*, 22 May 1994. On the shift in public political culture between 1950 and 1980, see my 'Change and the Political System', *Administration*, XXX (1982), 21–43. Cf. E.B. Titley,

*Church, State and the Control of Schooling in Ireland, 1900–1944*, Kingston and Montreal: McGill-Queen's University Press, 1983.

10. Kennedy and Dowling, *Economic Growth in Ireland, passim.*

11. Ibid. xvi.

12. AD UCD/P53/304 (225) Michael Hayes Papers.

13. Brendan Walsh, 'Interpreting Modern Ireland: Time for a New View?', *Studies*, vol. 80, no. 350 (Winter 1991), 400–407 at 405–406.

14. Mancur Olson, *The Rise and Decline of Nations*, New Haven, CT: Yale, 1982; Olson, *The Logic of Collective Action*, Cambridge: Harvard University Press, 1967.

15. Olson, *The Logic of Collective Action, passim.*

16. On ideology by proxy, see Angus Campbell *et al.*, *The American Voter: An Abridgement*, New York: Wiley, 1964, 126–7.

17. It is possibly significant that the term 'boycott' is of Irish provenance, referring to the agrarian strike that was carried out against an unfortunate Captain Boycott of Achill Island, County Mayo in the West of Ireland during the Irish Land War of 1879–81.

18. James Madison, *Federalist Paper Number Ten*, as in Clinton Rossiter (ed.), *The Federalist Papers*, New York: Mentor, 1961, 77–84.

19. Olson quote, *Rise and Decline*, 40. Dahl as quoted by veteran Irish political journalist Stephen Collins, *Sunday Tribune*, 3 November 2002; some things never change, apparently.

20. On pluralist democracy the classic discussions are in Robert Dahl's *Polyarchy: Participation and Opposition*, New Haven, CT and London: Yale University Press, 1971, and his *Democracy and its Critics*, New Haven, CT and London: Yale University Press, 1989. Carroll quote, D.S.A. Carroll, 'Foreword', in Ivor Kenny, *Government and Enterprise in Ireland*, Dublin: Gill & Macmillan, 1984, 1–9. Monopolies in Ireland are described for two very different generations in Arnold Marsh, *Full Employment in Ireland*, Dublin: Browne and Nolan, 1945, 220–23 and Cathal Guiomar, *The Irish Disease*, Dublin: Oak Tree Press, 1995, 33–48. Superficially, little seems to have changed, but at least the second book is angry about the deadening effects of monopoly on economic and social progress. Back in 1945, Marsh thought that, in a small country, monopolies were inevitable but that their behaviour could be controlled by a patriotic and responsible government. This view is now considered naïve. An argument related to this is contained in Joseph Lee's magisterial *Ireland 1912-1985, Politics and Society*, Cambridge: Cambridge University Press, 1989.

21. On the 'alliance between the welfare-dependent and the politically powerful privileged', see Walter Dean Burnham's classic *Critical Elections and the Mainsprings of American Politics*, New York: Norton, 1970. For an example of the cyclical view of US political life, see Samuel P.

Huntington, *American Politics: The Promise of Disharmony*, Cambridge, MA: Harvard University Press, 1981. On the Irish case, see Richard Breen, Damien F. Hannan, David B. Rottman and Christopher T. Whelan, *Understanding Contemporary Ireland*, Dublin: Gill & Macmillan, 1990; the book is reviewed by Brendan Walsh in *Studies*, vol. 80, no. 320 (Winter 1991), 400–407; authors' response, ibid., 407–411.

## Chapter 1. Politics and Development in Ireland (PAGES 25–61)

1. The ex-Axis countries (Germany, Japan and Austria) had the highest growth rates, these being countries whose elites were eliminated or very much weakened by the defeat of 1945. France and Finland, suffering defeat in 1940 and 1945, respectively, also had high growth rates, although Finland's was less spectacular; in a sense, Finland's defeat in 1945 was less than total, and political and legal continuity was maintained. Neutral Ireland was a laggard, but so were neutral Sweden and Switzerland. Denmark and Norway, defeated in 1940, had different experiences afterward, Norway turning in a superior performance, having been given a harder time by the Nazis because of her brave attempts to resist invasion. In the case of Denmark, as in Finland, institutional continuity was maintained, the Germans treating 'Nordic' Denmark with kid gloves for racist reasons; Denmark was regarded, in the insane official view of the regime, as a genetic reservoir which was, if anything, more purely Germanic than the Reich itself. The Nazis even permitted the Aryan Danes to go ahead with a completely democratic general election in 1943, the Danes demonstrating their excellent genetic quality by ensuring that the local Nazi party did very badly. The greatest irony is that the triumphant victors in the war, the Anglo-Saxon powers, did relatively poorly afterwards in the economic contest.

2. David Horowitz, 'Patterns of Ethnic Separatism', *Comparative Studies in History and Society*, vol. 23 (1981), 196–216. On the Irish combination of slow growth and high political development, the seminal work is Frank Munger, *The Legitimacy of Opposition: The Change of Government in Ireland in 1932*, Beverly Hills, CA: Sage, 1975. For a critique of the ensuing debate on the Munger thesis in Irish political science, see Bill Kissane, *Explaining Irish Democracy*, Dublin: University College Dublin Press, 2002. Kissane emphasises the importance of civil society imposing its will on revolutionaries and radicals.

3. For Horowitz, the motor of secession is clearly driven by elite ambitions. Backward areas which have a cadre of relatively well-educated people, e.g. Ibo south-eastern Nigeria, later Biafra, 1959–66, are reluctant to secede and only finally do so under exceptional pressure such as extreme discrimination, denial of educational opportunity, physical threat or

undermining of their local power base. Educationally backward elites in backward *or* advanced regions secede early if they can get away with it. However, advanced elites in either backward or advanced regions are rarely attracted to secession because they see their future as being with the empire or other large state. This is the case unless there is active discrimination against them. The Ibo were content to be the backbone of the Nigerian civil service until their very success generated resentment among the Hausa and Yoruba peoples. After the anti-Ibo pogroms of 1966 the Ibo leaders seceded, formed the secessionist state of Biafra and touched off a horrific civil war.

4. On the clerical takeover of much of Irish political and civic life after 1922 and up to 1939, see Patrick Murray's quietly devastating and thorough analysis, *Oracles of God*, Dublin: University College Dublin Press, 2000. Also see Kissane, *Explaining Irish Democracy*. On Exit and Voice, see Albert O. Hirschman, *Exit, Voice and Loyalty*, Princeton, NJ: Princeton University Press, 1970; 'Exit, Voice and the State', *World Politics*, vol. XXXI, no. 1 (October 1978), 90–107; 'Exit, Voice and the Fate of the German Democratic Republic: An Essay in Conceptual History', *World Politics*, vol. XXXXVI, no. 2 (January 1993), 173–202. See also his *Shifting Involvements: Private Interest and Public Action*, Princeton, NJ: Princeton University Press, 1982.

5. For a partly dissenting view, see John Regan, *The Irish Counter-Revolution, 1921–1936*, Dublin: Gill & Macmillan, 1999; on the origins of Irish political parties, see Tom Garvin, *The Evolution of Irish Nationalist Politics*, Dublin: Gill & Macmillan, 1981. Also see Garvin, *Nationalist Revolutionaries in Ireland 1858–1927*, Oxford: Clarendon, 1987, and *1922: The Birth of Irish Democracy*, Dublin: Gill & Macmillan, 1996. On O'Connell, see Garvin, 'O'Connell and the Making of Irish Political Culture', in Maurice O'Connell, *Daniel O'Connell: Political Pioneer*, Dublin: Institute of Public Administration, 1991. Munger (op. cit. supra note 2) comments, as an American outside observer, on the apparently surprisingly mature character of Irish politics even ten years after a civil war.

6. In a sense, Patrick McGilligan, another northern Catholic, was another outside observer, but a quietist as much as a developmentalist.

7. John Horgan, *Sean Lemass: The Enigmatic Patriot*, Dublin: Gill & Macmillan, 1997. 'Jackeen' is an Irish slang term for a native Dubliner (cf. 'Cockney'). 'Culchie' is Dublin argot for a countryman.

8. See my 'Political Culture and Economic Development', 54.

9. On the economic irrationality of land redistribution in the 1930s and 1940s, civil service advice of Deegan as quoted is in NA/S6490; MacEntee quote, AD UCD/P67/108 (262–4). See the discussion in my *The Evolution of Irish Nationalist Politics*, Dublin: Gill & Macmillan, 1981, 201–203. On Irish agriculture in general, see Paul Rouse, *Ireland's Own Soil*, Dublin: Irish Farmers' Journal, 2000. The classic study of Irish civil service

involvement in policy-making is Ronan Fanning, *The Irish Department of Finance*, Dublin: Institute of Public Administration, 1978.

10. AD UCD/P67/108 (263).

11. Ibid. For a similar contemporary analysis of Irish agriculture, see Henry Kennedy, 'Our Agricultural Problem', in Frederick Charles King (ed.), *Public Administration in Ireland*, vol. II, Dublin: 1949, 44–58. See also R.C. Geary, 'Irish Economic Development since the Treaty', *Studies*, vol. XL, no. 160 (December 1951), 399–418, and Paul Rouse, *Ireland's Own Soil*, 1–35.

12. AD UCD/P67/271. On creditworthiness of farmers, *Memoranda and Minutes of Evidence: Commission of Inquiry into Banking, Currency and Credit*, Dublin: Stationery Office, n. d. (1938), 465.

13. AD UCD/P67/271. Some years later, as Minister for Lands, Erskine Childers expressed similar views on farmers to Archbishop McQuaid. See DDA AB8/XVIII Government Box 8, Department of Lands, 5 December 1958.

14. AD UCD/P67/125.

15. Ibid.

16. NA/S12884, 24 July 1942.

17. On Dillon, Maurice Manning, *James Dillon*, Dublin: Wolfhound Press, 2000, 316–17.

18. McGahern quote, *Cara*, vol. 35, no. 2 (March 2002), 'The Perfectionist', 42–6, quote at 42–4.

19. As quoted in Tom Garvin, 'The Destiny of the Soldiers: Tradition and Modernity in the Politics of De Valera's Ireland', *Political Studies*, vol. XXVI, no. 3 (September 1978), 328–47, at 346–7.

20. Jeremiah Newman, 'The Priests of Ireland: A Socio-religious Survey', *Irish Ecclesiastical Record*, Fifth Series, vol. XCVIII (1962), 1–27, 65–91. Newman failed the present writer for theological reasons in a post-graduate examination in Anthropology in 1965 in the Irish government training college at the Institute of Public Administration. Newman believed my soul to be in danger. The external examiner reversed this pessimistic verdict as far as this world was concerned. Newman was an ardent admirer of the political arrangements in modern Islamic countries. In later years, he felt that contraception would result in a depopulated western Europe being overrun militarily by the Russians. See Olivia O'Leary, 'Newman: The Mullah of Limerick', *Magill*, February 1985. The sobriquet was coined by Conor Cruise O'Brien.

21. Sean O'Faolain, 'Principles and Propaganda', *The Bell*, vol. 10, no. 3 (June 1945), 189–205, quote at 202–203.

22. Sean O'Faolain, 'Eamon de Valera', *The Bell*, vol. 10, no. 1 (April 1945), 1–18, quote at 7.

23. Ibid., 15. 'Gombeen-man' is an insulting Irish colloquialism for a usurer, or dishonest trader (from Irish *gaimbe*, interest). By extension, an intellectually dishonest academic, politician or journalist.

24. Ibid., 17–18.

25. 'Principles and Propaganda', 205.

26. AD UCD/P80/1364C, Desmond FitzGerald Papers. See also Tom Garvin, *Nationalist Revolutionaries in Ireland*, Oxford: Clarendon, 1987, 107–38.

27. AD UCD/P80/1219. On Francis Hackett's general view of Ireland, see his fascinating *Ireland: A Study in Nationalism*, New York: Huebsch, 1920 (first published 1918).

28. AD UCD/P80/622, 31 May 1940; 4 May 1941.

29. Max Weber, *The Protestant Ethic and the Spirit of Capitalism*, London: Unwin, 1930, first published in German 1904–1905; R.H. Tawney, *Religion and the Rise of Capitalism*, London: Murray, 1944, first published 1929. On the local Irish argument, see Horace Plunkett, *Ireland in the New Century*, London: John Murray, 1904. The Catholic defence and rebuttal of Plunkett is contained in Rev. M. O'Riordan, *Catholicity and Progress in Ireland*, London: Kegan Paul, Trench and Trubner, 1906.

30. Weber, 181.

31. Plunkett, 101.

32. Plunkett, 103.

33. Walter MacDonald, *Some Ethical Questions of Peace and War*, Dublin: UCD Press, 1998, 133–40, first published 1919.

34. Maurice Moynihan (ed.), *Speeches and Statements by Eamon de Valera 1917–1973*, Dublin: Gill & Macmillan, 1980, 402–403.

35. Brian Girvin, 'Political Culture, Political Independence and Economic Success in Ireland', *Irish Political Studies*, vol. 12 (1997), 48–77; on the 'possessor principle', Joseph Lee, *Ireland 1912–1985*, Cambridge: University Press, 1989. On the relationships, or lack thereof, between development and independence, cf. Richard Rose and Tom Garvin, 'The Public Policy Effects of Independence: Ireland as a Test Case', *European Journal of Political Research*, vol. XI, 1983, 377–98.

36. Here I may be putting words into Girvin's mouth, but it seems to be the general gist of a rich and complex argument. Anthony Burgess commented famously on the fiction of John McGahern, 'I know no one who has caught so well the peculiar hopelessness of contemporary Ireland.' Penny Perrick comments accurately that Burgess was 'confusing hopelessness with lack of expectation'. See *Sunday Times*, 6 January 2002.

37. AD UCD/P7b/210 (26), Mulcahy Papers; native speaker anecdote, *Leader*, 31 July 1909.

38. NLI MS/18,349, Frank Gallagher Papers, 27 April 1940.

39. NLI MS/18,339, Frank Gallagher Papers, 'S.F. Lemass, some time in 1929–30', memorandum, 1–2; I am indebted to John Horgan for drawing my attention to this extraordinary document.

40. Ibid., 2–4, my paraphrase and summary. Myles actually suggested that the solution to Ireland's partition problem was the creation of thirty-two county republics.

41. Ibid., 4–9, 22–3, my paraphrase and summary.

42. Ibid., 19–20.

43. Ibid., 20.

44. Ibid., 25–8, my paraphrase and summary.

45. Ibid., 32–3.

## Chapter 2. Crossroads (PAGES 62–111)

1. Brian Barry, conversations, 1970s. See Cormac Ó Gráda, 'From Frugal Comfort to Ten Thousand a Year: Trade and Growth in the Irish Economy', in Ray Ryan (ed.), *Writing in the Irish Republic*, London: Macmillan, 2000, 263–82. On Ireland and European unity initiatives, 1948–55, see D.J. Maher, *The Tortuous Path*, Dublin: Institute of Public Administration, 1986, 12–31. See also Ireland, *The European Recovery Programme: Basic Documents and Background Information*, Dublin: Stationery Office, P. no. 8792, n. d. (1948); Ireland, *The European Recovery Programme: Ireland's Long Term Programme (1949–1953)*, Dublin: Stationery Office, P. no. 9198, n. d. (1948) and Economic Cooperation Administration, Washington, DC, *Ireland: Country Study*, Washington, DC: United States Government Printing Office, 1949. Education is never mentioned other than in a passing way in these three contemporary documents.

2. AD UCD/LA/56 James Meenan Papers. Quotations from LA56/14 /1–96, 20 October 1940; 19 October 1941. An eyewitness, hostile, well-informed and very useful sketch of the Irish political climate in the early 1950s is given in Paul Blanshard, *The Irish and Catholic Power*, London: Derek Verschoyle, 1954. On McQuaid, the standard book is John Cooney, *John Charles McQuaid: Ruler of Catholic Ireland*, Dublin: O'Brien Press, 1999. Brian Inglis, *West Briton*, London: Faber and Faber, 1962, 73–4 describes wartime Ireland as being in a condition of cultural decline. On Brian Ó Nualláin's cultural despair, see *The Irish Times*, 29 March 2002, which documents his perceptions of the quasi-fascism of certain Irish-language revivalists. Myles na Gopaleen 'Binchy and Bergin and Best' quote, Kevin O'Nolan (ed.), *The Best of Myles*, London: Picador, 1977, 266.

3. Ibid., 18 February 1944. On Whyte episode, see Tom Garvin, 'The Strange Death of Clerical Politics in University College Dublin,' *Irish University Review*, vol. 28, no. 2 (Autumn–Winter 1998), 308–314, an account derived carefully from John Whyte's personal information to the writer. David Sheehy informs me that there is no information on this episode in McQuaid's files; there is irony in the fact that Whyte was actually

McQuaid's favoured historian. On Collis/Deeny episode, James Deeny, unpublished and untitled memoir in my possession, courtesy of James Deeny. On McGahern incident, *Irish Times Education and Living Supplement,* 21 May 2002.

4. Ibid., 18 February 1944; 3 December 1944.

5. On Horgan, AD UCD/LA/56/14/97–177, 27 October 1949; 11 June 1950; 16 January 1950.

6. Ibid., 14 October 1951; on the same melancholy topic of clerical meddling in civic and intellectual life, see John O'Meara, 'Guardians of Truth', *Irish University Review,* vol. 26, no. 1 (Spring–Summer 1996), 1–14; Tom Garvin, 'The Strange Death of Clerical Politics . . .'; also John Bowman, '"The Wolf in Sheep's Clothing": Richard Hayes's Proposal for a New National Library of Ireland, 1959–60', in Ronald Hill and Michael Marsh (eds.), *Modern Irish Democracy,* Dublin: Irish Academic Press, 1993, 44–61. A thoroughly sensible proposal to amalgamate the library resources of UCD, TCD and the National Library of Ireland was sabotaged in deference to McQuaid's weird sensitivities.

7. LA 56/14/1–96, 11 March 1943. On the often bizarre political phenomena termed the Gaelic League and the Irish Republican Brotherhood, see Tom Garvin, *Nationalist Revolutionaries in Ireland,* Oxford: Clarendon, 1987. On Williams, see Peter Somerville-Large, *Irish Voices: An Informal History 1916–1966,* 233.

8. LA 56/14/1–96, 12 March 1943; 27 March 1943.

9. Ibid., 2 November 1943.

10. Tim Pat Coogan, *Ireland Since the Rising,* London: Pall Mall Press, 1966, 90. Denis Johnston, *Nine Rivers From Jordan,* London: Verschoyle, 1953, 366–80. Much film censorship was indeed puritan and obscurantist, but it also was commonly informed by a very real and practical fear of public disturbances in cinemas; see Martin S. Quigley, *A U.S. Spy in Ireland,* Dublin: Marino, 1999, *passim,* a fascinating and sympathetic view of the country by the only American spy (and possibly the only real spy) never to have been rumbled by Colonel Dan Bryan's highly efficient security service.

11. James Deeny, *To Cure and to Care,* Dublin: Glendale, 1989, 63; Elizabeth Bowen, *Notes on Eire,* Millstreet: Aubane Historical Society, 1999, 14–15. See Brian Fallon, *An Age of Innocence,* Dublin: Gill & Macmillan, 2000, an already standard work. For an entertaining example of the often lively character of public debate, an example which demonstrates both the intellectual superiority of some public servants to some bishops and a generally high level of civic freedom, see Steven Curran, 'Could Paddy Leave off from Copying just for Five Minutes: Brian O'Nolan and Eire's Beveridge Plan', *Irish University Review,* vol. 31, no. 2 (Autumn–Winter 2001), 353–75.

12. Frank McCourt, *Angela's Ashes*, London: Harper Collins, 1996.
13. For an early version of an argument like this one, see Tim Pat Coogan, *Ireland Since the Rising*, London: Pall Mall Press, 1966, 94–115. One leader who clearly foresaw this post-war scenario as early as 1929–30 was, as we have seen, a young Sean Lemass. His nationalist and isolationist dirigisme was short term. Philosophically he was, back in 1929, in favour of an international European business civilisation, modelled substantially on the United States. Copy in NLI MS/18, 339, Frank Gallagher Papers. John Horgan was the first to make this important point in his *Sean Lemass: The Enigmatic Patriot*, Dublin: Gill & Macmillan, 1997, 351–2.
14. NA/S12884.
15. NA/S12900.
16. Ibid.
17. NA/13221A; *The Irish Times*, 3 July 1945.
18. NA/S13529.
19. NA/S13526.
20. NA/S13527.
21. Ibid., 11 June 1948.
22. NA/S11987B, October 1945; 2 July 1946. See also AD UCD/P150/2648, Eamon de Valera Papers, on wartime planning for the post-war period. Cf. Cormac Ó Gráda, op. cit. supra, on consensus between government and opposition concerning protectionism during these post-war years.
23. *The Irish Times*, 3 April 1944; NA/S21900.
24. *The Irish Times*, 17 August 1944.
25. NA/S15015A, 7 June 1954; Ireland, *Council of Education: Terms of Reference and General Regulations*, Dublin: Stationery Office, n. d. (1950), 1–12.
26. Deeny quote, NA/S13444B, 17 October 1945; Donal McCartney, 'Education and Language, 1938–51', in *Ireland in the War Years and After, 1939–51*, Dublin: Gill & Macmillan, 1969, 67–79.
27. AD UCD/P67/299, MacEntee Papers, 10 February 1948 for Childers quote; on Lemass in 1924, John Horgan, *Sean Lemass: The Enigmatic Patriot*, Dublin: Gill & Macmillan, 1997, 33; on education, John Sheehan, 'Education and Society in Ireland, 1945–70', in J.J. Lee, *Ireland 1945–70*, Dublin: Gill & Macmillan, 1979, 61–72, quote from 61–2. On the subsequent educational revolution in general, see Tony White, *Investing in People: Higher Education in Ireland from 1960 to 2000*, Dublin: Institute of Public Administration, 2001.
28. On prophylaxis and the Army, Francis Hackett, 'De Valera's Ireland', *American Mercury*, January 1945, 29–38, at 36. On McQuaid and VD, Richard Timoney, conversations, 1970s. On Dignan episode, John Whyte, *Church and State in Modern Ireland*, Dublin: Gill & Macmillan, 1971, 101–104 and 109–117; AD UCD/P67/257, MacEntee Papers, 8 March 1945,

15 March 1945, 22 March 1945, 23 November 1945 and quotation from memorandum, Department of Local Government and Public Health, 24 January 1945. Labour grass-root pro-Dignan reaction, 2 February 1945, 8 March 1945, 22 March 1945. Also see AD UCD/P67/170, 257, 258, 270.

29. John Horgan, *Noel Browne: Passionate Outsider*, Dublin: Gill & Macmillan, 2000, 20. See Noel Browne, *Against the Tide*, Dublin: Gill & Macmillan, *passim*. See also Tom Garvin, 'Tortured Soul' (review of Horgan), *The Irish Times*, 14 October 2000. For a critical contemporary view of Browne, see James Deeny, 'Towards Balancing a Distorted Record: An Assessment of *Against the Tide* by Noel Browne', *Irish Medical Journal*, vol. 80, no. 8 (August 1987), 222–5. On Pearl Dunlevy and Dorothy Stopford Price, *The Irish Times*, 15 June 2002.

30. Adrian Redmond (ed.), *That Was Then, This is Now*, Dublin: Central Statistics Office, 2000, 34. I have stolen the subtitle 'Life and Death' from Mary Heanue's excellent essay in this admirable collection, as I have taken so much else; I simply could not think of a better title for the theme.

31. Ibid., 34–5, 37.

32. Ruth Barrington, 'Introduction', in Tony Farmar (ed.), *The End of an Epidemic: Essays in Irish Public Health 1935–65 [by] James Deeny*, Dublin: A & A Farmar, 1995, 1–23 at 9–10.

33. Blanshard quote, *The Irish and Catholic Power*, London: Verschoyle, 1954, 63. On the 1938 outcry, DIC/ST1/TIZ 2168 (3A), 7 April 1993. On authoritarianism and Irish political culture, David Schmitt, *The Irony of Irish Democracy*, Lexington, MA: D.C. Heath, 1973.

34. Dáil Debates, 70 (2 February 1938), 62–3.

35. DIC/ST3/TIZ 6A, 25 January 1949.

36. DIC/ST3/TIZ 6A, 14 January 1948.

37. DIC/ST3/TIZ 6A, 18 and 19 April 1948.

38. DIC/ST3/TIZ 6A, 12 January 1949.

39. DIC/ST8/TIZ 6/81, 15 March 1961.

40. DIC/ST1/TIZ 2/68, January 1969.

41. DIC/ST1/TIZ 2/68, April 1969. See *The Irish Times*, 28 March 1997 on small-town shopkeepers' persistent attempts to wipe out casual street trading in the mistaken belief that such trade takes business away from the established shops. Smaller towns were the most hostile to such trade, thereby offering this writer an explanation for their deserved smallness.

42. Brendan M. Walsh, 'Economic Growth and Development, 1945–70', in J.J. Lee (ed.), *Ireland 1945–70*, Dublin: Gill & Macmillan, 1979, 27–37, quote from 27. On Ó Slattara, Paul Bew and Henry Patterson, *Sean Lemass and the Making of the New Ireland*, Dublin: Gill & Macmillan, 1982, 19–20.

43. Walsh, 28.

44. Ibid.

45. AD UCD/P35a/109, Patrick McGilligan Papers, 8 July 1950; *The Leader*, 28 January 1950.

46. AD UCD/P35a/109, 17 May 1950.

47. Ibid. On the genesis of this archaic road-maintenance system, see Tom Garvin, *1922: The Birth of Irish Democracy*, Dublin: Gill & Macmillan, 1996, 63–91.

48. AD UCD/P35b/149.

49. AD UCD/P35c/4, February 1949.

50. Donnchadh Ó Corráin (ed.), *James Hogan: Revolutionary, Historian and Political Scientist*, Dublin: Four Courts Press, 2001, *passim*. The key text is James Hogan, *Election and Representation*, Cork: Cork University Press, 1945. Perhaps significantly, the book was distributed not only through commercial publishers, but also through the Government Publications Office at a bargain price. His argument seems to have had friends in high places; de Valera did not like PR.

51. AD UCD/P67/278 (9), MacEntee Papers.

52. AD UCD/P67/278 (30, 32), MacEntee Papers.

53. Brian Inglis, *West Briton*, London: Faber & Faber, 1952, 109. Arnold Marsh, *Full Employment in Ireland*, Dublin: Browne & Nolan, 1945.

54. Inglis, 114. On corruption allegations, AD UCD/P150/2752, Eamon de Valera Papers, where the Department of the Taoiseach observes mordantly in 1947 that such allegations since 1932 have coincided with by-election contests.

55. León Ó Broin, *No Man's Man*, Dublin: Institute of Public Administration, 1982, 156.

56. *The Irish Times*, 29 April 2002.

57. NA/S14474A, *The Irish Times*, 10 March 1950, as clipped for the Taoiseach.

58. AD UCD P67/261, MacEntee Papers.

**Chapter 3. Agonising Reappraisal** (PAGES 112–157)

1. The standard account of this election and the resulting government is David McCullagh's already classic *A Makeshift Majority: The First Inter-Party Government, 1948–51*, Dublin: Institute of Public Administration, 1998. See also Kevin Rafter, *The Clann: The Story of Clann na Poblachta*, Cork: Mercier Press, 1996; John Horgan, *Noel Browne: Passionate Outsider*, Dublin: Gill & Macmillan, 2000; Michael Gallagher, *Political Parties in the Republic of Ireland*, Dublin: Gill & Macmillan, 1985; Peter Mair, *The Changing Irish Party System*, London: Pinter, 1987. For Lindsay anecdote, Patrick Lindsay, *Memories*, Dublin: Blackwater Press, 1992, 151–2. On the

persistence of 'Civil War Politics' into the 1970s, see interview with Jack Jones, pollster extraordinaire, *The Irish Times*, 21 December 2001.

2. McCullagh, 1–2.

3. Ibid., 32–3.

4. The classic formulation is Brian Farrell, *Chairman or Chief? The Role of Taoiseach in Irish Government*, Dublin: Gill & Macmillan, 1971.

5. McCullagh, 33; John Garvin, conversations, 1970s.

6. McCullagh, 33–4.

7. McCullagh, 34.

8. AD UCD/P35a/93, Patrick McGilligan Papers; John Garvin, conversations, 1970s.

9. McCullagh, 37.

10. Seamus Ó Buachalla, *Education Policy in Twentieth Century Ireland*, Dublin: Wolfhound Press, 1988, 67–8.

11. Ibid.

12. Ibid.

13. Ibid., 69.

14. Ibid., 274.

15. Ibid.

16. Ibid.

17. Ibid., 277–8.

18. NA/S14186, 16 November 1947; 8 December 1947; 11 November 1948. On this, see also AD UCD/P150/2752, Eamon de Valera Papers, 26 November 1947.

19. NA/S14186, D/Health to Taoiseach, 25 November 1947; Whitaker warning, AD UCD/P35c/4, February 1949. Williams as quoted in Ronan Fanning, 'Economists and Governments: Ireland 1922–52', in Antoin A. Murphy, *Economists and the Irish Economy from the Eighteenth Century to the Present Day*, Dublin: Irish Academic Press, 1984, 138–56, at 138.

20. AD UCD/P35c/95. On amoral familism, Edward Banfield, *The Moral Basis of a Backward Society*, New York: Free Press, 1958. On the transatlantic air-service saga, *Irish Press*, 19 May 1948; NA/S8835, S13820A, B, C, D. Also NA/S9565, S13941, S14209; Lemass reaction, AD UCD/P91/140, C.S. Andrews Papers. Turlough Lynch letter, *The Irish Times*, 9 January 2002; Frank Gallagher comment, NLI MS/18,380 (2), Frank Gallagher Papers.

21. For 'high marks or the boat . . .' see John McGahern, *The Dark*, London, Panther, 1967 (first published 1965), 91–8. On MacBride report, AD UCD/P35b/58, 17 November 1956. See Ronan Fanning, op. cit., *passim*, on the use of statistics in Irish economic analysis and the parallel resistance thereto in much of Irish academia.

22. MacBride report.

23. Ibid.

24. Ibid.

25. Kevin Rafter, *The Clann: The Story of Clann na Poblachta*, Cork: Mercier Press, 1996, 172–3.

26. NA/S16211, 19 March 1957; 1 April 1957. C.F. Carter, 'The Irish Economy Viewed from Without', *Studies*, no. 46 (1957), 137–49.

27. NA/S16211, 1 April 1957.

28. Ibid.

29. Ibid.

30. Ibid.

31. Ibid.

32. Ibid.

33. NA/S14463A, 'Ireland: Foreign Articles and Comments 1949–61'.

34. NA/S15359, 4 July 1958; international comparison figures for telephones, C.L. Taylor and David A. Jodice, *World Handbook of Political and Social Indicators*, 3rd ed., New Haven, CT: Yale University Press, 1983, 188–90.

35. AD UCD/P35c/180, 27 June 1927.

36. AD UCD/P67/223, 1954. Kennedy quote NLI MS 18, 336, Frank Gallagher Papers, 18 December 1946.

37. Ibid., 1954.

38. AD UCD/P67/264, 1944.

39. John Horgan, *Sean Lemass: The Enigmatic Patriot*, Dublin: Gill & Macmillan, 2000, 133.

40. Ibid., 176; NA/S16066A, as cited by Horgan. Cartoon, *Dublin Opinion*, September 1957.

41. Horgan, 176.

42. Ibid., 177.

43. Ibid.

44. Ibid. MacEntee has been inaccurately stereotyped as an ideological bureaucrat. In fact, he seems to have been a liberal democrat, opposed to inordinate claims on power and society by either prelates or civil servants; the latter he tended to discover to be his allies. He was also a doughty, clever and 'difficult' in-fighter. See Tom Feeney, 'The Road to Serfdom: Sean MacEntee, "Beveridgeism" and the Development of Irish Social Policy', *The History Review*, XII (2001), 63–72 (Department of History, University College Dublin).

45. Kieran Kennedy, Thomas Giblin and Deirdre McHugh, *The Economic Development of Ireland in the Twentieth Century*, London: Routledge, 1988, 62–3.

46. Ibid., 65–6.

47. Ibid., 65–6.

48. As cited in NA/S16673A (Dáil Debates, 11 December 1959, 1531–3).

49. Taken from Kennedy *et al.*, 118.

308 PREVENTING THE FUTURE

50. Dr Cyril White, University College Dublin, conversation, 22 May 2001. A possible prompt on which Lemass acted was supplied by Senator E.A. Maguire, a well-known businessman who, during the Senate debate on the Act, excoriated the tax system for making everyone poor: 'Let us have incentives and liberalisation and get away from controlling manufacturers.' Senate Debates, 21 May 1958, 513–17, quote at 517. A general account is given by Gary Murphy, 'Towards a Corporate State? Sean Lemass and the Realignment of Interest Groups in the Policy Process 1948–1964', Administration, vol. 47, no. 1 (Spring 1999), 86–102.

51. An early version of this exercise was published as Tom Garvin, 'Wealth, Poverty and Development: Reflections on Current Discontents', Studies, vol. 78, (Autumn 1989), 312–25.

52. Sources for Table 3: Bruce Russett et al. (eds), World Handbook of Political and Social Indicators, New Haven, CT: Yale University Press, 1961, 149–57; World Bank, World Development Report 1977, Washington: Oxford University Press, 1977, 184–5; World Development Report, 1987, 194–5.

53. Brian Nolan, Philip J. O'Connell and Christopher J. Whelan, Bust to Boom? The Irish Experience of Growth and Inequality, Dublin: IPA, 2000. Also see Kieran Allen, The Celtic Tiger: The Myth of Social Partnership in Ireland, Manchester: Manchester University Press, 2000.

54. John FitzGerald 'Through Irish Eyes: The Economic Experience of Independence in Europe', Dublin: Economic and Social Research Institute, Working Paper 89, 1997, 2. See also his 'Ireland's Failure—and Belated Convergence', Dublin: Economic and Social Research Institute, Working Paper 133, 2000.

55. FitzGerald, 'Through Irish Eyes', 5.

Chapter 4. Cherish the Children (PAGES 158–214)

1. Frank Hugh O'Donnell, The Ruin of Education in Ireland, London: David Nutt, 1902.

2. James Joyce, Stephen Hero, London: Four Square, 1966, 53; see the discussion in Tom Garvin, Nationalist Revolutionaries in Ireland, Oxford: Clarendon, 1987, 56–106. On the social origins of ecclesiastical leaders, data in private possession, mainly derived from Bernard J. Canning, Bishops of Ireland 1870–1987, Ballyshannon, Co. Donegal: Donegal Democrat, n. d. (1987). For an unaffected, unsentimental, hilarious and disturbing autobiographical account of rural childhood and primary education in pre-war Ireland, see Andrew D. Forrest, Worse Could Have Happened, Dublin: Poolbeg, 1999. An entertaining account of clerical bossiness in an Irish village is contained in Honor Tracy, Mind You I've Said Nothing, London: Methuen, 1953, 91–101. See also Roger Moran, The Wildfowler, Dundonald: Blackstaff, 1982. Mary Raftery and Eoin

O'Sullivan, *Suffer the Little Children*, Dublin: New Island, 1999 gives a horrific portrait of Ireland's clerical Gulag. A useful, and surprisingly little-used, preliminary sampling of Irish clerical nationalist outlooks for the period is provided by the *Capuchin Annual*, published by the order between 1931 and 1977.

3. L. Paul-Dubois, *Contemporary Ireland*, London; 1908, 492–3, as cited in John Whyte, *Church and State in Modern Ireland, 1923–1979*, Dublin: Gill & Macmillan, 1980, 4. An excellent study of the role of the Christian Brothers in forging the Irish alliance of 'Faith and Fatherland' is contained in Barry M. Coldrey, *Faith and Fatherland*, Dublin: Gill & Macmillan, 1988. On the schools and clerical control, E. Brian Titley, *Church, State and the Control of Schooling in Ireland 1900–1944*, Dublin: Gill & Macmillan, 1983.

4. Whyte, 5–6.

5. Walter McDonald, *Reminiscences of a Maynooth Professor*, London: Jonathan Cape, 1925, 396; to caution readers: other editions are commonly defective. McDonald, *Some Ethical Questions of Peace and War*, Dublin: University College Dublin Press, 1998 (first published 1919). On Tyrell, see George Tyrell, *Medievalism*, London: Burns & Oates, 1994 (first published 1908). *Motion* survived, and a copy has come into my possession *per viam occultam*.

6. AD UCD/P35b/10, McGilligan Papers. On the systematic campaign of cultural and political control waged by the Catholic Church which culminated in a secondary-level educational system dedicated to the needs of the Church and the new middle class and relatively little else, Tom A. O'Donoghue, *The Catholic Church and the Secondary Curriculum in Ireland 1922–1962*, New York: Peter Land, 1999. See also E. Brian Titley, *Church, State and the Control of Schooling in Ireland, 1900–1944*. On the Catholic Church's fear of the educated layman, see Tom Garvin, *Nationalist Revolutionaries in Ireland 1858–1928*, Oxford: Clarendon, 1987, 60–64; Canon P.A. Sheehan, *Under the Cedars and the Stars*, Dublin: Browne & Nolan, 1903. McGilligan's attitude to further education does not seem to have changed subsequently; as late as 1948 he suggested a reduction of university student numbers by raising the standard of matriculation so as to save the taxpayers money (AD UCD/P35d/52, 14 July 1948). Monsignor Michael Nolan has reminisced to me that Tom Derrig, Minister for Education 1932–48, privately expressed the view that education beyond the elementary level destroyed children's ancestral cultures.

7. Thomas Gray, 'Elegy Written in a Country Churchyard', as in Edward Leeson (ed.), *The New Treasury of English Verse*, London: Pan, 1980, 243–7. Censorship was commonly extended informally and extra-legally to books written in support of unpopular, unorthodox or heterodox opinion, and such books were commonly withdrawn from public library

shelves; Dermot Foley, conversations, 1970s. See 'The Hidden Hand', *The Irish Times*, 31 March 1938, for a report on such unofficial censorship systems. Official censors commonly banned paperback editions and exempted more expensive hardback editions of the same book. On the non-republican and non-radical temper of pre-independence UCD students, later to be the new elites of independent Ireland, Senia Paseta, *Before the Revolution*, Cork: Cork University Press, 1999, esp. 148–54.

8. De Valera quote, Seamus Ó Buachalla, *Educational Policy in Twentieth Century Ireland*, Dublin: Wolfhound Press, 1988, 268; Michael Hayes on de Valera, AD UCD/P53/377, Michael Hayes Papers. On 1936 Committee, Arthur Maltby and Brian McKenna, *Irish Official Publications*, Oxford: Pergamon Press, 1980, R58/1.

9. On this strange and almost incredible de Valera anecdote, Ó Buachalla, 269. Murphy citation, James Murphy, 'The Establishment and Development of Vocational Education in Ireland, With Particular Reference to Teacher Training Courses, 1930–1960', M. Ed. Thesis, 1993, Department of Education, University College Dublin, quote at 114, see 114–116. McElligott quote, T.J. McElligott, *This Teaching Life*, Dublin: Lilliput Press, 1986, 122. Sean O'Connor quote, Sean O'Connor, *A Troubled Sky*, Dublin: Educational Research Centre, St Patrick's College, 1986, 11. McQuaid quotes, DDA/AB8/B/XVIII/ Box 7, 'Continuation Education 1942'. Italicised words underlined in black ink in original typescript. There is no date, but early 1942.

10. Ó Buachalla, 269; O'Connor, 12; Murphy, 51, 88. On J.P. Hackett, Murphy 167; Marie Clarke, conversation, 23 November 2001. Hackett passed internal Departmental documents unofficially (and illegally) to McQuaid, including *Memorandum V. 40*. See DDA/AB8/B/XVIII/ Box 7, 25 March 1942. On Derrig, AD UCD/P150/2648, Eamon de Valera Papers, 7 February 1945.

11. Ireland, *Council of Education: Terms of Reference and General Regulations*, Dublin: Stationery Office, n. d. (1950), 12.

12. Ibid.

13. Sean Farren, *The Politics of Irish Education, 1920–65*, Belfast: Institute of Irish Studies, 1995, 228.

14. Ibid., 228–9.

15. Ibid., 229. On the connection between education and economic development, see summary of the literature in OECD, *The Well-being of Nations: The Role of Human and Social Capital*, Paris: OECD, 2001 (written by Tom Healy and Sylvain Côté), *passim*.

16. Ibid., 231–2. On McQuaid and the raising of the school-leaving age to sixteen, *Council of Education*, 12. Some old IRB leaders regarded education as something the state or Church should not provide; young

people should struggle for it, much as they had done themselves, in the School of Hard Knocks. See P. S. O'Hegarty's similarly muscular views in León Ó Broin, *Just Like Yesterday,: An Autobiography*, Dublin: Gill & Macmillan, n. d. (1985), 160–61. The underlying idea that the lower orders should not be educated is in Jonathan Swift; see George Orwell, 'Politics *vs.* Literature: An Examination of *Gulliver's Travels*', in his *Inside the Whale and Other Essays*, Harmondsworth: Penguin, 1966, 121–42.

17. As quoted in Farren, 237. Cannon quotation from *Irish Press*, 10 January 1959, as clipped in NA/S12891C. The obsession with religious formation and disregard for technical and scientific education was not peculiarly Irish or Catholic, but was apparently another 'intellectual' reach-me-down derived from English models, like so much of modern Irish social culture. See John Wilson Foster, *Recoveries*, Dublin: UCD Press, 2002 on Irish religious attitudes to Darwinism and science in general in the nineteenth century. For Britain's version of the same debilitating syndrome, see Corelli Barnett, *The Audit of War*, London: Pan, 1986. See NA/S15359, memorandum for government, 4 July 1958 from Department of Education, agreeing to the desirability of reinstituting nature study in primary schools and extending science teaching in secondary schools, abolished a generation earlier in favour of 'double Irish'. The Department stated in the same breath that the Minister for Education did not consider that it would be 'in the national interest to reduce the extent to which Irish is taught.' Increased staffing would be needed in primary schools. A fascinating *tour d'horizon* of the public debate on Irish education is contained in Andrée Sheehy Skeffington, *Skeff*, Dublin: Lilliput Press, 1991. See also Michael S. O'Neill, 'The Restructuring of Educational Provision in Ireland in the 1960s', *The History Review*, vol. XII (2001), 154–61. A courageous article by Fr Kevin O'Leary appeared in *Hibernia* in February 1959, pointing out that the normal relationship of one-third academic, two-thirds technical ratio in secondary education was actually reversed in Ireland. A similarly brave article by Professor John J. O'Meara of UCD appeared in *Hibernia* in April 1961, pointing to the crippled condition of vocational education and tracing this to clerical obstructiveness. This obstructiveness was, as is argued here, in turn derived from the limitations of clerical manpower and a concomitant unwillingness to permit the laity to encroach on the Church's empire.

18. Tom Garvin, 'A Quiet Revolution: The Remaking of Irish Political Culture', in Ray Ryan, *Writing in the Irish Republic*, London: Macmillan, 2000, 187–203. See also Tom Garvin, 'The Politics of Denial and Cultural Defence: The Referendums of 1983 and 1986 in Context', *Irish Review*, 3 (1988), 1–7; Garvin, *Nationalist Revolutionaries in Ireland*, Oxford: Clarendon, 1987, 56–77. See in particular Terence Brown, *Ireland: A*

*Social and Cultural History*, London: Fontana, 1981, and Paul Blanshard, *The Irish and Catholic Power,* London: Verschoyle, 1954. Raymond James Raymond puts the ideological crisis earlier, during the war years, in his 'Eamon de Valera: Diplomatic Failure, Economic Seer?' in Sidney Poger (ed.), *The 'De Val-Era' in Ireland*, Boston: Northeastern University, 1984, 43–62. See also his more developed argument in his 'De Valera, Sean Lemass and Irish Economic Development', in J.P. O'Carroll and John A. Murphy (eds.), *De Valera and His Times*, Cork: Cork University Press, 1986, 113–33.

19. *United Irishman*, 25 July 1903. On Sheehan, Garvin, *Nationalist Revolutionaries*, 62. For a Catholic critique of Irish clerical fear of education, Michael Sheehy, *Is Ireland Dying?* London: Catholic Book Club, 1968, 181–98. Internal evidence suggests the book was written in the early 1960s.

20. John A. O'Brien (ed.), *The Vanishing Irish*, London: Allen & Unwin, 1954.

21. Michael Sheehy, *Divided We Stand*, London: Faber, 1955.

22. J.V. Kelleher, 'Ireland . . . And Where Does She Stand?', *Foreign Affairs*, 1957, 485–95. Quote from 495. Secret societies, the Knights of Columbanus in particular, had great influence in policy-making and patronage. There is no satisfactory study of this much resented organisation. McQuaid quote, DDA AB8/XVIII/06, Box 522/2 10 April 1957.

23. NA/S12891D/1/61. On clerical exclusion of lay and parental opinion formers from educational policy, see O'Donoghue, 111–32.

24. Ibid. (*The Irish Times*, 26 and 27 October 1961).

25. Ibid.

26. NA/S16603/B.

27. Ibid. Lynch quote, *Irish Press*, 2 May 1957.

28. Ireland, *Investment in Education: Report of the Survey Team Appointed by the Minister of Education in 1962*, Dublin: Stationery Office, n. d. (1965). Flanagan citation, letter from Fr Val J. Peter, *The Irish Times*, 21 February 2002. Many Irish parents wrote to Flanagan confirming his general picture. I am grateful to the administration of Boys' Town Nebraska for supplying me with a file of copies of these letters, Dáil Debate and newspaper clippings, hereafter referred to as Boys' Town: Ireland. Physical abuse of children was not confined to Catholic schools, nor to Eire; Northern Ireland was castigated too. See also *The Irish Times*, 9 April 2002. I am also indebted to Anthony Keating, conversation, 6 December 2002.

29. *Investment in Education*, 140.

30. Ibid.

31. *Investment*, 178. On pre-1922 conditions, Brian Girvin, 'The State and Vocational Education, 1922–1960', in John Logan (ed.), *Teachers' Union*, Dublin: A & A Farmar, 1999, 62–92, at 68. I follow Girvin substantially

on Vocational Education, but see, in particular, Marie Clarke, *Vocational Education in a Local Context, 1930–1998*, Ph.D. Thesis, Department of Education, University College Dublin, 1999. I am grateful to Marie Clarke for sharing her vast fund of information on the history of Irish education.

32. *Investment*, 172. In 1967, McQuaid had his swansong; he objected to proposals for comprehensive education in Dublin on the usual grounds. The Secretary of the Department under Donough O'Malley replied in terms that suggested it was none of McQuaid's business. Memoranda were issued by the Department to the heads of universities to the effect that the demand for vocational education was overwhelming. In most countries, it was argued by the civil servants, secondary education broke down to one-third taking grammar school and two-thirds taking technical school. In Dublin, the ratio was 82 per cent grammar to 18 per cent technical, and this could not go on, the Archbishop was informed in distinctly hostile tones. See DDA/AB8/b/ XVIII/Box 7, 1 August 1967, 16 October 1967.

33. *Investment*, 277.

34. Rev. M. Brenan, 'The Vocational Schools', *Irish Ecclesiastical Record*, vol. 57, 1941, 113–27, 406–418; correspondence at 368–82. See Brenan to McQuaid, DDA/AB8/B/XVIII/Box 7, 16 May 1942, on 'Continuation Education'.

35. Rev. M. Brenan, 'Agriculture and Our School System', *Irish Ecclesiastical Record*, 1942, 193–208, quote at 207.

36. Girvin, 86; quote supra, Girvin, 81.

37. John Logan, '"All the Children": The Vocational School and Education Reform 1930–1990', in John Logan (ed.), *Teachers' Union*, 276–303, quote at 287. On Moylan, see James Murphy, 117.

38. Eileen Connolly, conversations, 1999. On education in academia, J.J. Lee, *Ireland 1912–1985*, Cambridge: Cambridge University Press, 586–7.

39. John Horgan, *Sean Lemass; The Enigmatic Patriot*, Dublin: Gill & Macmillan, 2000, 293.

40. Ibid., 293–4.

41. Ibid., 297. On O'Malley's 1966 speech, Sean O'Connor, *A Troubled Sky*, Dublin: Educational Research Centre, St Patrick's College, 1986. His 1967 speech, *Seanad Debates*, 9 February 1967, 1089–90; also quoted in Anthony Keating, *Secrets and Lies: An Exploration of the Role of Identity, Culture and Communication in the Policy Process Relating to the Provision of Protection and Care for Vulnerable Children in the Irish Free State and Republic 1923–1974*, Ph.D. Thesis, Department of Communication, Dublin City University, 2002, 223.

42. Michael McGinley and Frances Donoghue, 'The Modern Union: The Teachers' Union of Ireland 1973–1994', in Logan, op. cit., 235–75, at 263.

43. Logan, "'All the Children"', 293–5; Tony White, *Investing in People: Higher Education in Ireland from 1960 to 2000*, Dublin: Institute of Public Administration, 2001, 282–3.

44. Ibid., 294. See Paul Sweeney, *The Celtic Tiger*, Dublin: Oak Tree Press, 1998, 104–105; cf. John FitzGerald, *The Irish Times*, 19 April 2002. Organised religion commonly fears secular education. The connection between a lack of secular education and weak economic development with reference to Islam and the Arab world is powerfully argued by David Landes in his *The Wealth and Poverty of Nations*, London: Little Brown, 1998, 408–411. He also points to Catholicism and economic and intellectual failure in Spain, as epitomised by the four-century-long failure to exonerate Galileo. See the definitive study by Michael E. Porter, *The Competitive Advantage of Nations*, London: Macmillan, 1990.

45. As cited in Horgan, *Sean Lemass*, 225. De Valera as paraphrased in Dermot Keogh, *Twentieth-Century Ireland*, Dublin: Gill & Macmillan, 253.

46. John Garvin, conversations, 1960s.

47. On the generational rift in the Irish elite in the 1960s, see Al Cohan, *The Irish Political Elite*, Dublin: Gill & Macmillan, 1972; RTÉ Television broadcast on Desmond O'Malley, tape in private possession, 29 April 2001. Boland and O'Kelly quotes, AD UCD/P67/403, Sean MacEntee Papers. On the mentality of Fianna Fáil elites of the time, the indispensable and classic book is C.S. Andrews, *Man of No Property*, Dublin and Cork: Mercier Press, 1982. A useful summary of the educational shift since the 1950s is supplied in Annetta Stack, 'Relinquishing Educational Dominance: The Catholic Church and Irish Secondary Schools', *History Studies*, University of Limerick, vol. 2, 2000, 69–77.

48. Joseph Lee, review of James Meenan, *The Irish Economy Since 1922*, *Spectator*, 19 December 1970; McElligott, in Ireland, *Report of the Commission on Higher Education*, Dublin: Stationery Office, 1967, vol. II, 914–22, at 914 and 921–2; *Irish Press*, 22 September 1966.

49. Michael Mills, interview with Sean Lemass, *Irish Press*, 21 and 24 January 1969.

50. Ibid.

51. Mills, interview with Sean Lemass, *Irish Press*, 5 February 1969. The 'fellow' was evidently W.W. Rostow, a well-known and fashionable American developmental economist of the late 1950s and the 1960s. The key books are Rostow, *The Stages of Economic Growth*, Cambridge: Cambridge University Press 1960 and his *Politics and the Stages of Growth*, Cambridge: Cambridge University Press 1971. Lemass had evidently read the former work to advantage; it was a set text for first-year Economics undergraduates in University College Dublin in 1961. A

related, and still interesting, 'take-off' text in comparative politics written in that era was Cyril Black, *The Dynamics of Modernization*, New York: Harper & Row, 1966. The beginnings of a sea change in official attitudes to technical education is documented in Organisation for Economic Co-operation and Development, *The Training of Technicians in Ireland*, Paris: OECD, 1964. The international team noted that Irish elite incomprehension of the need for scientific education was vast, and a serious cultural handicap.

52. See Correlli Barnett, *The Audit of War*, London: Pan, 2001 for a devastating analysis of the consequences of the takeover of English higher education by romantic and neoclassical humanists, engineering and science being relegated to the province of sometimes brilliant genteel amateurs. Similar social types, sometimes labelled the 'practical men', i.e. untrained and uneducated men, ran, and often ruined, traditional English business.

53. Barnett, 213.

54. See OECD, *Training of Technicians in Ireland, passim*. For the definition of 'banausic', see Liddell and Scott, *Greek-English Lexicon*, Oxford: Clarendon Press, 1949, 126.

55. James Murphy, 'The Establishment and Development of Technical Education . . .', 20–21.

56. AD UCD/P91/156, C. S. Andrews Papers.

57. Ibid.

58. Mac Aonraoi, AD UCD/P91/156, C.S. Andrews Papers; John Horgan, *Sean Lemass: The Enigmatic Patriot*, Dublin: Gill & Macmillan, 1997; Brian Farrell, *Sean Lemass*, Dublin: Gill & Macmillan, 1991. Mac Aonraoi applied a version of an Irish proverb to the Lemass style of efficiency and his leaving linguistic revival to others: *Ní thig leis an nGobadán an dá traghadh do fhreastal* [lit. the pipit cannot attend to two ebb-tides at once]; do one thing at a time. I have used the Dineen version rather than the O'Rahilly version here. For a businessman's view of Lemass, see Alex Findlater, *Findlaters*, Dublin: A & A Farmar, 2001, *passim*.

59. James Dillon, unpublished memoir, 'The Memoirs', 1981, 72.

60. AD UCD/P150/3497, Eamon de Valera Papers, 16 July 1959.

61. DDA AB8/B/XVII/06, Box 522/2, 14 April 1956.

## Chapter 5. Developmentalists (PAGES 215–250)

1. Dáil Debates, 9 March 1950, 1584–5. See Arnold Marsh, *Full Employment in Ireland*, Dublin: Browne & Nolan, 1945, 173–7.

2. Ibid., 1586.

3. Lemass quote, Dáil Debates, 9 March 1950, 1596–7, 1600; Leydon anecdote, NA/S14474A, 11 November 1949, 26 January 1950.

4. Dáil Debates, 9 March 1950, 1603–1604.

5. Senate Debates, 6 December 1950, 5–6. On FitzGerald and Lynch and their influence on Lemass , see in particular Ronan Fanning, 'The Life and Times of Alexis FitzGerald', *Magill*, September 1985, 34–49.

6. Ibid., 6 December 1950, 7.

7. Ibid., 58; Corry quote, Dáil Debates, 9 March 1950, 1642–3.

8. See his autobiographies: C.S. Andrews, *Dublin Made Me*, Dublin and Cork: Mercier Press, 1979; *Man of No Property*, Dublin and Cork, Mercier Press, 1982.

9. AD UCD/P91/136, C.S. Andrews Papers.

10. AD UCD/P91/136.

11. Ibid. Todd Andrews was an avid reader, particularly of management theory. His writings are peppered with references to the work of American-based theorists such as James Burnham (*The Managerial Revolution*), Peter Drucker and William H. White (*The Organisation Man*). These authors were very much in vogue with Irish civil servants in the late 1950s, particularly the group associated with Tom Barrington, who founded the Institute of Public Administration, the Irish civil service training institute, at that time.

12. AD UCD/P91/136. Alfred Kuehn commented in 1962 that 'the majority of [Irish] industries report difficulty in obtaining skilled labour.' See his *Prospects of the Irish Economy in 1962*, Dublin: Economic Research Institute, 1962, 16. For a truly pioneering social scientific assessment of Irish inferiority complexes and deep-seated indifference, if not hostility, to technological prowess, see Bruce Biever, *Religion, Culture and Values*, New York: Arno Press, 1976, 402–405 (survey fieldwork carried out circa 1962).

13. *Irish Press*, 27 April 1948. The related issue of the Shannon Stop concealed a dislike of Dublin's potential dominance. As late as November 1953, the Fianna Fáil government felt that if Aer Lingus were allowed to fly directly into Dublin, it might become impossible to force foreign airlines to use Shannon; horror of horrors, they might all fly into Dublin. See NA/S13820 B/2, 6 November 1953.

14. NA/S14299, 20 April 1948. On minority ambivalent feelings about the American connection, see *The Bell*, vol. XVII, no. 2 (May 1951), 7–18 (Sean O'Faolain); *The Irish Times*, 20 January 1951 (Louie Bennett); also *The Bell*, vol. XVII, no. 3 (June 1951), pieces by Bennett, Hubert Butler, Brigid Lalor, D. Sevitt.

15. NA/S14474B, 4 May 1948.

16. NA/S14474B, 13 May 1948.

17. NA/S14474B, 19 May 1948, 2 June 1948. In a letter to McGilligan, Muriel Bowen opposed Marshall Aid on the grounds that it entailed 'servitude to the dollar' and was 'bad politics' (AD UCD/ P35/253, 28 September 1948).

18. AD UCD/P35b/51, 6 October 1949. The Department appears to have been reliant on traditional remote stimuli such as fiscal policy changes rather than close analysis and intervention by government in economic organisation and processes. See Till Geiger, 'The Enthusiastic Response of a Reluctant Supporter: Ireland and the Committee for European Economic Cooperation in 1947', in Michael Kennedy and Joseph Morrison Skelly, *Irish Foreign Policy 1919–1966*, Dublin: Four Courts Press, 2000, 222–47, at 247 n. 72.

19. On Córas Tráchtála, I obediently follow Bernadette Whelan, *Ireland and the Marshall Plan, 1947–1957*, Dublin: Four Courts Press, 2000, 343. Hoffman story, AD UCD/P35c/8, 26 August 1949, E. Rowe Dutton to McElligott. ECA official's quote, AD UCD/P35b/52, 7 December 1949.

20. IBEC Technical Services Corporation, *An Appraisal of Ireland's Industrial Potentials* ('Stacy May Report'), New York: 1952, 80.

21. AD UCD/P35b/52, 4 May 1950.

22. Ibid.

23. Bernadette Whelan, *Ireland and the Marshall Plan, 1947–1957*, Dublin: Four Courts Press, 2000, 400.

24. AD UCD/P35c/117, 14 September 1956.

25. AD UCD/P35c/117, 5 September 1956. O'Carroll quote, *Hibernia*, July–September 1956.

26. Whelan, 354–5.

27. As quoted in Whelan, 356–7 (*Report on the Visit of a Team from the Congress of Irish Unions to the USA in 1951*, Dublin: 1952, 18–19).

28. Whelan, 358.

29. AD UCD/P35b/149. Cf. Al Cohan, *The Irish Political Elite*, Dublin: Gill & Macmillan, 1972; AD UCD/P150/2756, Eamon de Valera Papers, 'Fianna Fail Achievements' (1947). According to Kevin Boland, despite the age gap between the two men, there was no ideological quarrel between Lemass and de Valera; see *Magill*, May 1986.

30. Basil Chubb, '"Going About Persecuting Civil Servants": The Role of the Irish Parliamentary Representative', *Political Studies*, vol. 11, no. 3, 272–86.

31. Ray MacSharry and Padraic White, *The Making of the Celtic Tiger*, Cork and Dublin: Mercier Press, 2000, 197.

32. White in MacSharry and White, 184.

33. Ibid., 186.

34. Ibid., 187.

35. Ibid., 191–2.

36. On SFADCO, ibid., 192–3. On the Shannon Scheme generally, Andy Bielenberg (ed.), *The Shannon Scheme and the Electrification of the Irish Free State*, Dublin: Lilliput Press, 2002; Maurice Manning and Moore

MacDowell, *Electricity Supply in Ireland: The History of the ESB*, Dublin: Gill & Macmillan, 1985, 17–53.

37. Gary Murphy, '"A Wider Perspective": Ireland's View of Western Europe in the 1950s', in Michael Kennedy and Joseph Morrison Skelly, *Irish Foreign Policy 1919–1966*, Dublin: Four Courts Press, 247–64 at 247.

38. Ibid., 248.

39. Ibid., 250–51.

40. Murphy, 251. Lemass quote, *Irish Press*, 18 January 1957.

41. See, for example, NA/S15747; S14106A-L; S14638A-K.

42. Murphy, 253.

43. NA/S16023C/61, 2 May 1961.

44. NA/S14463A, Hans Swedberg, 'The Industry and Foreign Trade of the Republic of Ireland'.

45. Ibid.

46. As clipped in NA/S1446A.

47. Ibid. For a re-emergent Germany's semi-official interest in the Irish market's future potential, Ernst Hickmann, *Irland: Ein Markt am Rande Europas*, Dusseldorf: Econ Verlag, 1953. The country was perceived to have a future; the introduction remarks, 'The aim of this work is to give those interested in trading with Ireland an overview of the structure and growth of this small but promising market (*zukunftsreichen Marktes*) [my translation].

48. Waugh and Mitford as cited in Peter Somerville-Large, *Irish Voices: An Informal History 1916–1966*, London: Pimlico, 2000, 250. For report for Portuguese government, see NA/DIC/E22/3/72A, 1956. On Winchester interview, AD UCD/P150/3093, Eamon de Valera Papers, 9 December 1957.

49. See in particular Ronan Fanning, 'The Genesis of Economic Development', in John F. McCarthy, *Planning Ireland's Future*, Dublin: Glendale, 1990, 74–111.

50. Ibid., 94–5.

51. Ibid., 104–105.

52. See Al Cohan, *The Irish Political Elite*, Dublin: Gill & Macmillan, 1972; Tom Garvin, *Nationalist Revolutionaries in Ireland, 1858–1928*, Oxford: Clarendon, 1987, 48–56. Lemass quote, Dáil Debates, 11 December 1959, as clipped in NA/S16673A. Ryan quote, NA/S16673A, 5 December 1960.

53. Conrad Arensberg and Solon T. Kimball, *Family and Community in Ireland*, Cambridge, MA: Harvard University Press, 1968, *passim*. On social snobbery as a barrier to early marriage, see John Casey, 'The Things I Didn't Understand', *Hibernia*, March 1959.

**Chapter 6. Secularism and Cultural Shift** (PAGES 251–293)

1. On cultural change in modern societies, see Ronald Inglehart, *Culture Shift in Advanced Industrial Society*, Princeton, NJ: Princeton University Press, 1990. See also Stephen Harding, David Phillips and Michael Fogarty, *Contrasting Values in Western Europe*, London: Macmillan, 1986; Peter Ester, Loek Halman and Ruud de Moor, *The Individualizing Society*, Tilburg: Tilburg University Press, 1994. On Ireland in particular for the period in question, B.F. Biever, *Religion, Culture and Values: A Cross-Cultural Analysis of Motivational Factors in Native Irish and American Irish Catholicism*, New York: Arno Press, 1976 (research carried out 1962); Michael Sheehy, *Is Ireland Dying?* London: Catholic Book Club, 1968; John Raven, C.T. Whelan, Paul A. Pfretzschner and Donald M. Borock with John Whyte, *Political Culture in Ireland: The Views of Two Generations*, Dublin: Institute of Public Administration, 1976; Michael Fogarty, Liam Ryan and Joseph Lee, *Irish Values and Attitudes*, Dublin: Dominican Publications, 1984. Liebherr anecdote, John Garvin, conversations, 1960s.

2. B.F. Biever, op. cit. The data set is lost (personal communication from author).

3. Biever, 270–71, 306.

4. Biever, 397.

5. Biever, 226–7.

6. On 'priest-ridden' Irish, Biever, 226–7. On TCD and UCD, 499. On the young men, quote 519–20, 522. An historically useful, if fictional and satirical, view of 'the Knights' and their less than ideal relationship with Irish business and the Catholic clergy of the time is contained in Mervyn Wall, *No Trophies Raise*, London: Methuen, 1956.

7. Quotations as in Biever, 226–31.

8. Biever, 278. *This Week*, 25 June 1971, 13–15, quote on 15. On the Pike affair, see Gerard Whelan with Carolyn Swift, *Spiked*, Dublin: New Island, 2002, a brilliant reconstruction of a much hushed-up incident. See also Lionel Pilkington, *Theatre and the State in Twentieth-Century Ireland*, London: Routledge, 2001, 151–7. McQuaid approved of the government's action, although he had nothing to do with it. The Knights of Columbanus had considerable local political clout of a kind that is not readily measurable. Some local councils of the Knights were used as resources in electoral politics. Oliver J. Flanagan, a senior Knight and well-known populist politician, reportedly used local Knights to damage the campaign of his electoral rival; see *Magill*, May 1983.

9. Biever quote, Biever 497, 503; Sean O'Faolain, *The Irish*, Harmondsworth: Penguin, 1969, revised edition of work first published 1947, 120–21; Alexander Humphreys, *New Dubliners*, London: Routledge and Kegan

Paul, 1966, 219; J.P. O'Carroll, 'Bishops, Knights—and Pawns? Traditional Thought and the Irish Abortion Referendum Debate of 1983', *Irish Political Studies*, vol. 6 (1991), 53–72. See also Sheehy, *Is Ireland Dying?* On the Knights in general, the pioneering work, based on partial information, is Evelyn Bolster, *The Knights of Saint Columbanus*, Dublin: Gill & Macmillan, 1979. The argument is mildly sympathetic to the organisation; such access to information as Sister Bolster acquired was at the insistence of Archbishop Dermot Ryan, McQuaid's successor, a man who was acutely aware of the damaging effect the Knights' secretive habits had on public opinion. See review of Bolster's book (Brian Trench) and corrective letter from Bolster, *Magill*, September 1979, October 1979. The reviewer notes that the Knights had gone into decline about 1970, and that by 1979 were at their lowest numerical strength ever, again confirming the argument that secularisation in Ireland is nothing particularly new.

10. E.F. O'Doherty, 'Society, Identity and Change', *Studies*, Summer, 1963, 125–35.

11. O'Doherty, 131. This article was originally cited to considerable purpose in Terence Brown, *Ireland: A Social and Cultural History 1922–1985*, London: Fontana, 1985 (first published 1981), 267. The Arensberg referred to is Conrad Arensberg, American anthropologist and co-author of a famous functionalist study of Irish rural life in the 1930s, Conrad M. Arensberg and Solon T. Kimball, *Family and Community in Ireland*, Cambridge, MA: Harvard University Press, 1968 (first published 1938).

12. O'Doherty, 133.

13. Inglehart, *Culture Shift*, 223; Stephen Harding, David Phillips and Michael Fogarty, *Contrasting Values in Western Europe*, London: Macmillan, 1986, 13. See also Inglehart, *Modernization and Postmodernization*, Princeton, NJ: Princeton University Press, 1997, 224–8.

14. Harding *et al.*, 19.

15. Rona Fitzgerald and Brian Girvin, 'Political Culture, Growth and the Conditions for Success in the Irish Economy', in Brian Nolan, Philip J. O'Connell and Christopher T. Whelan, *Bust to Boom? The Irish Experience of Growth and Inequality*, Dublin: Institute of Public Administration, 2000, 268–85.

16. Michael Fogarty, Liam Ryan and Joseph Lee, *Irish Values and Attitudes*, Dublin: Dominican Publications, 1984, *passim* and 123–34. On Quebec, 'Canada' in Stuart Mews, *Religion in Politics*, London: Longmans, 1989, 35–9; cf. also Katherine O'Sullivan, *First World Nationalisms*, Chicago and London: University of Chicago Press, 1986. As early as 1965, Augustine Martin of the Department of English at UCD felt that he could comment that the literary stereotype of Irish society as being

hostile to the creative writer was already obsolete. See his 'Inherited Dissent: The Dilemma of the Irish Writer', *Studies*, vol. LIV, no. 213 (Spring 1965), 1–20. On Chubb's original portrayal of Irish political culture as was, Basil Chubb, *The Government and Politics of Ireland*, Stanford, CA: Stanford University Press, 1970, 43–60.

17. Tom Inglis, *Moral Monopoly*, Dublin: Gill & Macmillan, 1987; John Fulton, *The Tragedy of Belief*, Oxford: Clarendon Press, 1991. See also Tom Inglis, *Moral Monopoly: The Rise and Fall of the Catholic Church in Ireland*, Dublin: University College Dublin Press, 1998, a heavily revised edition, hereafter cited as *Moral Monopoly II*. A recent study is Louise Fuller, *Irish Catholicism since 1950*, Dublin: Gill & Macmillan, 2002. For a sketch of Church–state relationships as they were in 1989, see Tom Garvin, 'Ireland', in Stuart Mews (ed.), *Religion in Politics: A World Guide*, London: Longman, 1989, 119–22.

18. *Moral Monopoly II*, 216.

19. Tom Garvin, *Nationalist Revolutionaries in Ireland 1858–1927*, Oxford: Clarendon, 1987, 121–2. Distributivist ideas also surfaced in the post-1923 IRA as well. See Brian Hanley, *The IRA 1926–1936*, Dublin: Four Courts Press, 2002, 182.

20. *Irish Freedom*, February, March 1913.

21. *Catholic Bulletin*, April, May, June, July 1920.

22. Tom Garvin, *1922: The Birth of Irish Democracy*, Dublin: Gill & Macmillan, 1996, 123–55.

23. Garvin, *Nationalist Revolutionaries*, 122–5.

24. Ireland, *Report of the Commission on Vocational Organisation*, Dublin: Stationery Office, 1943.

25. Tom Garvin, *The Irish Senate*, Dublin: Institute of Public Administration, 1969.

26. Dermot Keogh, *Twentieth-Century Ireland: Nation and State*, Dublin: Gill & Macmillan, 1994, 146–51. See in general Susannah Riordan, '"A Political Blackthorn": Sean MacEntee, the Dignan Plan and the Principle of Ministerial Responsibility', *Irish Economic and Social History*, XXVII (2000), 44–62, quotes at 49, 61. On Barrington, Keady and Garvin (civil service) views on Dignan, AD UCD P67/257(1) and (2), Sean MacEntee Papers. On the Irish experiment with vocationalism generally, Don O'Leary, *Vocationalism and Social Catholicism in Twentieth-Century Ireland*, Dublin: Irish Academic Press, 2000.

27. Paul Blanshard, *The Irish and Catholic Power*, London: Verschoyle, 1954.

28. I am indebted to Daniel Seiler for this idea. On Church and state relations in Western democracies, I am indebted to the ideas of Stein Rokkan and John Whyte.

29. John H. Whyte, *Catholics in Western Democracies*, Dublin: Gill & Macmillan, 1981, 116.

30. James Joyce, *A Portrait of the Artist as a Young Man*, London: The Egoist, 1917. See Conor Cruise O'Brien, *Parnell and His Party*, Oxford: Oxford University Press, 1956, and also F.S.L. Lyons, *Charles Stewart Parnell*, London: Collins, 1977.

31. Cf. the discussion in Roy Foster, *Modern Ireland, 1600–1972*, London: Allen Lane, 1988, 386–90.

32. Harry Eckstein, *Division and Cohesion in Democracy: A Study of Norway*, Princeton, NJ: Princeton University Press, 1966, 225–88. On authoritarianism and Irish democracy, see David E. Schmitt, *The Irony of Irish Democracy*, Toronto: Lexington, 1973. Also, see Rachel A. Cichowski, 'Sustaining Democracy: A Study of Authoritarianism and Personalism in Irish Political Culture,' Paper, Center for the Study of Democracy, Irvine, CA: University of California, 2000.

33. Eckstein, 272.

34. As quoted in Blanshard, op. cit., 318. This argument of mine is, I find, nothing new. Cardinal Mercier of Belgium, in his anti-Modernist Lenten pastoral of 1908, remarked on the 'unconscious assimilation of the constitution of the Catholic Church to the political organisations of our modern countries.' Döllinger was, he believed, trying to foist liberal representative democracy on the eternal Church. See George Tyrrell, *Medievalism*, Dublin: Burns & Oates, 1994 (first published 1908), 29. On Kennan, George F. Kennan, *At a Century's Ending: Reflections, 1982–1995*, New York: Norton, 1996.

35. Peter J. Katzenstein, *Small States in World Markets*, Ithaca and London: Cornell University Press, 1985; Philip Bobbitt, *The Shield of Achilles*, London: Allen Lane, 2002. For a new and refreshing comparative perspective on Irish political development, see Stephen Howe, *Ireland and Empire: Colonial Legacies in Irish History and Culture*, Oxford: Oxford University Press, 2000.

36. On the Catholic Church's international crisis of authority, see in general, John Cornwell, *Breaking Faith*, London: Penguin, 2001. On the Irish case, Fuller, op. cit., 237–68.

37. Robert C. Lieberman, 'Ideas, Institutions and Political Order: Explaining Political Change', *American Political Science Review*, vol. 96, no. 4 (December 2002), 697–712.

38. Ibid., 698.

39. Ibid., 698.

# INDEX

international, 270, 271–2, 282–6
Irish language and, 55, 56, 160–1,
   165
lay leaders, 255, 266
loyalty to, 160
Mother and Child Scheme, 117,
   126, 258, 261
nationalism and, 160–1, 164–5
Pope's visit, 263
reorganised, 31, 275–6
secularisation, 163, 259–75
society as a producer of priests,
   45–6
survey (Biever), 253–7
Vatican II, 182, 203, 264, 267, 269
as veto group, 7–8, 23
vocationalism and, 276
vocations, 46, 180, 270–1
censorship, 165, 169–70, 183, 255, 258–9
   wartime, 78, 79
charismatic leadership, 15
Chartism, 277
Chiang Kai-Shek, 117
child abuse, 95, 163, 190, 270, 274–5
child mortality, 93–4, 104
Childers, Erskine, 89, 147, 236
China, 117, 249, 281
Christian Brothers, 182, 255
Chubb, Basil, 236–7, 270
Churchill, Winston, 112
CIE (Coras Iompair Eireann), 12,
   100, 204, 223, 224, 226
citizenship, 9
civil rights, 66, 293
civil service, 2, 57
   appointments, 115
   as a career, 227
   conservatism, 26, 31
   IDA and, 222, 239
   institutional pride, 227
   marriage bar, 204
   vocationalism and, 279–80

Civil Service Commission, 115
Civil War, 1–2, 258
   effects of, 29, 32, 83, 113, 169
Clann na Poblachta, 108, 115, 118,
   119, 132, 236
Clann na Talmhan, 44, 109, 115, 118,
   132
Clarke, Arthur C., 142
Clarke, Harry, 160
Coffey, Fr P., 277
Cold War, 66–7, 117, 217, 241
collective action, 13–23
collective bargaining, 280
Colley, George, 198, 199
Collins, Michael, 3, 33, 212, 240
Collis, Dr Robert, 72
Commission on Higher Education,
   189
Commission on Vocational
   Organisation, 278–80
communism, 16, 56, 64, 170, 228, 241
   collapse of, 290
   fear of, 16, 64
   in trade unions, 29–30
community and comprehensive
   schools, 198
computers, 65
Congested Districts, 35
Connolly, Eileen, 197
Connolly, James, 56, 171, 186, 277
Constitution (1922), 3
Constitution (1937), 3, 71, 94, 120,
   279
consumerism, 101, 109, 204
contraception, 203–4, 216, 260–1, 284
   venereal disease and, 90
Control of Manufactures Acts, 143,
   144–5, 150, 238
Coogan, Tim Pat, 78
cooperatives, 278
Córas Tráchtála, 227, 231
Cork, 97–8, 222